Animation and
Scientific Visualization
Tools and Applications

Animation and Scientific Visualization
Tools and Applications

edited by

R.A. Earnshaw
University of Leeds, UK

and

D. Watson
IBM UK Scientific Centre,
Winchester, UK

ACADEMIC PRESS
Harcourt Brace & Company, Publishers
London   San Diego   New York   Boston
Sydney   Tokyo   Toronto

ACADEMIC PRESS LIMITED
24/28 Oval Road
LONDON NW1 7DX

United States Edition published by
ACADEMIC PRESS INC.
San Diego, CA 92101

A catalogue record for this book is available from the British Library

ISBN: 0-12-227745-7

Typeset by Photo·graphics, Honiton, Devon
Printed in Great Britain by The Bath Press, Bath, Avon

Contents

Color Plates are located between pp. 112 and 113.

Contributors

J.J. Barley
Scientific Software-Intercomp (UK) Ltd, 1st Floor, Gladstone House, Crabtree Office Village, Eversley Way, Egham, Surrey, TW20 8RY

K. Brodlie
School of Computer Studies, University of Leeds, Leeds LS2 9JT, UK

S. Bryson
Applied Research Branch, Numerical Aerodynamic Simulation Systems Division, NASA Ames Research Center, MS TO45-1, Moffett Field, CA 94035, USA

B.M. Collins
IBM UK Scientific Centre, Hursley Park, Winchester, SO21 2JN, UK

T. David
Department of Mechanical Engineering, University of Leeds, Leeds LS2 9JT, UK

J.L. Encarnacao
Fraunhofer Institute for Computer Graphics, Wilhelmminenstr. 7, D-6100 Darmstadt, Germany

G. Englert
Fraunhofer Institute for Computer Graphics, Wilhelmminenstr. 7, D-6100 Darmstadt, Germany

G. Fenini
ENEL-DSR-CRIS, via Ornato 90/14, 20162 Milan, Italy

K. Goodson
IBM UK Scientific Centre, Hursley Park, Winchester, SO21 2JN, UK

S. Haas
Fraunhofer Institute for Computer Graphics, Wilhelmminenstr. 7, D-6100 Darmstadt, Germany

D. Haumann
IBM Research, T.J. Watson Research Center, Yorktown Heights, New York 10598, USA

J. Haus
GHER, Sart-Tilman B5, University of Liège, B-4000 Liège, Belgium

M. Jern
VP Research, UNIRAS, 5429 LBJ Freeway, Suite 650, Dallas, TX 75240, USA

B. Kamgar-Parsi
Naval Research Laboratory Code 5585, Washington DC 20375, USA

E. Klement
Fraunhofer Institute for Computer Graphics, Wilhelmminenstr. 7, D-6100 Darmstadt, Germany

D. Krömker
Fraunhofer Institute for Computer Graphics, Wilhelmminenstr. 7, D-6100 Darmstadt, Germany

F. Loseries
Fraunhofer Institute for Computer Graphics, Wilhelmminenstr. 7, D-6100 Darmstadt, Germany

J.M. De Martino
Fraunhofer Institute for Computer Graphics, Wilhelmminenstr. 7, D-6100 Darmstadt, Germany

W. Müller
Fraunhofer Institute for Computer Graphics, Wilhelmminenstr. 7, D-6100 Darmstadt, Germany

R.R.V. Petermann
Fraunhofer Institute for Computer Graphics, Wilhelmminenstr. 7, D-6100 Darmstadt, Germany

L.J. Rosenblum
US Office of Naval Research, European Office, 223 Old Marylebone Road, London NW1 5TH, UK

G. Sakas
Fraunhofer Institute for Computer Graphics, Wilhelmminenstr. 7, D-6100 Darmstadt, Germany

J.J. Stephen
Tessella Support Services plc, 3 Vineyard Chambers, Abingdon OX14 3PX, UK

W.K. Stewart
Deep Submergence Laboratory, Woods Hole Oceanographic Institution, Woods Hole MA 02543, USA

L.A. Treinish
Visualization Systems Group, IBM T.J. Watson Research Center, PO Box 704, Yorktown Heights, NY 10598, USA

J. Walton
NAG Ltd, Wilkinson House, Jordan Hill Road, Oxford, UK

D. Watson
IBM UK Scientific Centre, Hursley Park, Winchester, SO21 2JN, UK

J. Wejchert
ESPRIT Basic Research, European Commission, BU29 6/74, B-1049 Brussels, Belgium

D.W. Williams
IBM UK Scientific Centre, Hursley Park, Winchester, SO21 2JN, UK

About the editors

Rae Earnshaw is Head of Computer Graphics at the University of Leeds. He has been a Visiting Professor at Illinois Institute of Technology, Chicago, USA, Northwestern Polytechnical University, China and George Washington University, Washington DC, USA. He was a Director of the NATO Advanced Study Institute on "Fundamental Algorithms for Computer Graphics" held in Italy in 1985, a Co-Chair of the BCS/ACM International Summer Institute on "State of the Art in Computer Graphics" held in Scotland in 1986 and a Director of the NATO Advanced Study Institute on "Theoretical Foundations of Computer Graphics and CAD" held in Italy in 1987. He is a member of ACM, IEEE, CGS, EG and a Fellow of the British Computer Society.

His interests are graphics algorithms, human–computer interface issues, scientific visualization, graphics standards, fifth generation graphics software, workstations and display technology, mathematics of computer graphics, CAD/CAM, graphics system building and education issues.

Dr Earnshaw has written and edited 17 books on graphics algorithms, computer graphics and associated topics, and published a number of papers in these areas.

Dr Earnshaw Chairs the Scientific Visualization Group at the University of Leeds, is a member of the Editorial Board of The Visual Computer, Vice-President of the Computer Graphics Society and Chair of the British Computer Society Computer Graphics and Displays Group.

David Watson is a member of the Visualization Group at the IBM United Kingdom Scientific Centre where he specializes in the application of advanced visualization tools and techniques to scientific and engineering problems. His interests cover a broad range from underlying techniques through implementation methods to new application areas.

He joined IBM in 1984 and worked in mainframe graphics before moving to the Scientific Centre in 1988 to join the Visualization Group. Here his work has ranged from architecting a visualization system to European Technical Consultancy on Visualization both within and outside IBM.

Dr Watson sits on the British Computer Society Computer Graphics and Displays Group Committee.

ADDRESSES OF EDITORS

Dr Rae A. Earnshaw
Head of Graphics
University of Leeds
Leeds LS2 9JT
United Kingdom
Email: R.A. Earnshaw@uk.ac.leeds

Dr David Watson
Visualization Group
IBM UK Scientific Centre
Hursley Park
Winchester
Hants SO21 2JN
United Kingdom
Email: dwatson@winvmd.vnet.ibm.com

Acknowledgements

Many people have supplied information on their uses and applications of scientific visualization. Many designers and implementors have supplied details of their software and its applications. We express our thanks and appreciation to all those who have contributed.

DISCLAIMER

The views expressed by the contributors of information on products is believed to be accurate and given in good faith. However, authors and publisher do not hold themselves responsible for the views expressed in this volume in connection with vendor products or public domain products. In addition, the authors and publisher do not hold themselves responsible for the accuracy or otherwise of data extracted from vendor specifications.

COPYRIGHT MATERIAL

Some slides are reproduced by permission of their originators and these are noted in the text. Some materials are reproduced by permission of other publishers and societies.

COVER IMAGE

The image of the cloudless earth on the cover appears courtesy of NASA Goddard Space Flight Centre. Visualization is by Lloyd Treinish, reproduced by permission of IBM Yorktown Heights. © IBM.

Foreword

On a winding road, a gleaming sports car performs flawlessly, even though it is yet to be built. A hurricane causes tremendous flooding, but no actual damage occurs. A new drug is synthesized and its properties analyzed, with no chemicals in sight. A new multi-thousand circuit chip is designed, inspected and tested, without being fabricated. Spectacular special effects for a new movie are created and tried out in seconds, without weeks of assembling elaborate physical models.

These scenes are but a few examples of visualization and interactive simulation already in use today, in leading laboratories today, and offer a glimpse into what will be the pervasive paradigm of scientific exploration and the creative process in many disciplines. Interactive simulation of complex problems is being discovered in laboratories around the world, due to the increasing affordability of interactive large-scale computing and the ability to depict results with vivid realism on high-resolution displays.

The cumulative effect of cost performance improvements, arising from the use of microprocessors and parallelism, will enable many classes of problems in diverse fields of human endeavour to be solved interactively. Presenting the results of a computation via image animation appeals to our intuition, engaging the human mind in intense, iterative problem-solving.

Perhaps the most important aspect of these revelations is that they ultimately deal with the human visual channel. The visual conduit has the highest bandwidth of any of our senses, and a surprisingly large proportion of the brain is devoted to vision and visual analysis. The brain's organizing power is so strong that it can discern the minutest detail in a sea of seemingly random patterns. Harnessing this power and channeling it more effectively in a virtual laboratory can accelerate the pace of invention, innovation, and discovery.

The tools of visualization and interactive simulation have the potential to enhance human capabilities, enabling man to better understand his natural world, through insights not possible before. Predicting what the human mind is capable of when amplified with the power of computation and visualization technologies is not possible, but I am convinced that it will be nothing short of spectacular. The papers in this volume present important scientific advances in achieving this revolutionary paradigm of interactive simulation and visualization.

Abraham Peled
Vice President, Systems and Software
IBM Research Division
Yorktown Heights, New York

Preface

This volume is based upon the presentations made at an international conference at IBM UK Laboratories on the subject of "Animation and Scientific Visualization". Its objective was to bring together some of the leading practitioners and exponents in the field and to explore some of the issues in animation and visualization and its associated hardware and software technology.

Based on this initial conference and subsequent exchanges between the editors and the authors, revised and updated papers were produced, and further international contributions have been added. These papers are contained in the present volume.

We thank all those who contributed to this effort by way of planning and organization, and also all those who helped in the production of this volume.

R.A. Earnshaw
D. Watson

Introduction

Computer graphics has attracted a vast following over the past 30 years. The lure of objects spinning on a screen, photo-realistic renderings of car bodies, and the fascination with incredible forms of computer art have all contributed to a growth of interest in the technology.

A shift in emphasis away from pure computer graphics has been observed over the last 10 years. The tools and techniques of advanced computer graphics have developed a new identity during this time: visualization. This is more than the collection of a set of algorithms for shading, lighting, and rapid spinning of objects. It is an attempt to embody the usefulness to which the tools and techniques can be put.

Numerous protagonists of the art and science of computer graphics now recognise that they have been "doing" visualization all along. This is a recurring feeling when a label is given to an embryonic discipline. Most of us, however, wish we had thought of the label ourselves!

In drawing together the chapters for this volume we have chosen material in order to cover a broad base of visualization topics. The emphasis is on practical examples and experience rather than generalization. The material is presented in four sections: Introduction and Overview, Techniques, Theory and Models, and Applications.

Within the Introduction and Overview some of the basic techniques used in visualization today are shown to have their origins not in computer graphics but in early cartographic and diagrammatic presentations. This is followed by an examination of the current move away from graphics programming interfaces and what may be described as turnkey systems into the flexible or visual programming paradigm of visualization toolkits.

Rather than reiterate the standard methods of visualization, e.g. isosurface, vector streamlines, color mapping etc. the papers of the techniques section serve to illustrate the powerful use of visualization. In order to examine complex phenomena in areas such as finite element analysis, and fluid dynamics requires insight into both techniques and the underlying science. The chapters discuss practical considerations in the use of visualization and animation for both scientific and aesthetic purposes.

Theory can often be said to follow practice in many areas of investigation, the intuitive method of scientific progress is both well tried and productive in nearly all fields of endeavor. Visualization can be said to be developing theory in an intuitive way. The Theory section of the volume discusses a number of important issues in scientific visualization and its theoretical basis. Statistical analysis gives the user some degree of confidence in the results of the test applied, what can be said of the "confidence" of a visualization? Much depends on the underlying structure of the data under examination and the models one uses in analysis of such data. These questions are raised and directions offered in the chapters by Brodlie and Treinish. Visualization software poses a particular challenge when attempting to characterize the relative performance of available commercial products. A scheme for measurement of relative performance is presented which goes further than the "spinning teapot syndrome".

In the Applications section we have drawn examples from a wide range of fields of interest. A broad spectrum was our deliberate intent in order to illustrate the application of animation and visualization techniques to real problems. This approach is useful in two ways: as an illustration of the utilization of tools and techniques, but also to provide a stimulus to readers from one discipline with examples from another. Utility of techniques is well shown in the chapters by Treinish and David who both employ a wide range of methods to examine individual problems. Haus also discusses the ways in which the choice of technique is important in gaining the maximum insight from data. For an example of insight gained into a large volume of time series data by the use of animation and scientific visualization the chapter by Barley and Williams should be examined.

The material for the book was gathered not only to cover a broad range of topics but to cover two further goals. Firstly, animation as an aid to the scientist in the presentation and explanation of their work; therefore an emphasis has been placed on the use of animations together with traditional screen shots. Secondly, scientific visualization in terms of the application of tools and techniques to real problems; here the inclusion of some background science has been encouraged in the papers to help set the scene for the purpose behind the work, rather than a concentration on "how it was done".

A general theme the material is to provide a mixture of science, tools, techniques, and applications to practical problems. Visualization is a broad term and new applications are emerging rapidly. Keeping pace with developments is an ever more difficult task. The chapters collected in this volume will not only bring you up to date but take you into the future!

Part I

Introduction and Overview

Chapter 1
Data visualization – has it all been seen before?

Brian M. Collins

1.1. INTRODUCTION

The SIGGRAPH panel report *Visualization in Scientific Computing* (McCormick *et al.*, 1987) is usually acknowledged as having initiated the explosion of workshops, conferences, books and specialized journals in this "new" field of data visualization.

However, the field did not suddenly start in 1987. In fact there have been two major periods when the trend has been to visualize numerical data separated by a period when nonvisual data representation has been the fashion. The first period, which lasted from around the middle of the 17th century to the beginning of the 20th century, saw techniques for visual data representation developed by some of Europe's greatest scientists, including Halley, Watt, Descartes, Lambert, Playfair and von Humboldt. The second period started in the early 1960s, soon after the introduction of the computer, when methods of data representation developed during the first period were used in chemical crystallography, biology and medicine. It is the author's opinion that the intervening period, which was characterized by the use of tables and statistical methods in analysing data, has masked the first period of data visualization from today's scientists.

Thus, this review is concerned with providing "evidence" which will support answers to the following two questions:

1. Have computers contributed to new techniques for the visual representation of numerical data?
2. Have computers made the visual representation of large amounts of numerical data tractable?

The subsequent sections contain a summary of definitions, a historical review of the varied visual methods for representing data and a detailed chronology of the early examples of each technique, both before and after the introduction of the computer. This is followed by a taxonomy of visual data representation techniques commonly used with computers, and the final section provides answers to the two questions, based on the "previous evidence".

ANIMATION AND SCIENTIFIC VISUALIZATION
ISBN 0-12-227745-7

1.2.   SOME DEFINITIONS

Some time ago (see Beniger and Robyn, 1978) the following predictions were made:

1978   James Beniger and Dorothy Robyn

In the future, innovations in statistical graphics are likely to follow developments in computer graphics hardware and software, and might be expected to include solutions to problems generated or made tractable by the computer and associated technologies.

Solutions might be expected to include innovative use of both graphical and non-graphical dimensions only recently rendered technologically accessible, including colour computer graphics, person machine interaction, computer animation, three-dimensional computer graphics and holography and mechanically controlled sound.

These predictions have largely come true during the intervening years. However, the benefits of the visual representation of numerical data had been recognized considerably earlier, for example:

1637   Rene Descartes

Imagination or visualization, and in particular the use of diagrams, has a crucial part to play in scientific investigation.

1811   Alexander von Humboldt

Whatever relates to extent and quantity may be represented by geometrical figures. Statistical projections which speak to the senses without fatiguing the mind, possess the advantage of fixing the attention on a great number of important facts.

More recently formal definitions have been proposed:

1987   McCormick, DeFanti and Brown, the authors of the SIGGRAPH panel report *Visualization in Scientific Computing*, proposed the following definitions:

Applying graphics and imaging techniques to computational science is a whole new area of endeavour, which Panel members termed *Visualization in Scientific Computing*.

The ability of scientists to visualize complex computations and situations is absolutely essential to ensure the integrity of analyses, to provoke insights and to communicate those insights to others.

This can be compared with a recent dictionary definition of the terms:

1990   *Oxford English Dictionary*

[Visualization is] ... forming a mental picture of something not visible or present, or of an abstract thing ... .

[Computer graphics is] The production of diagrams, patterns, etc, by means of a computer.

In other words, visualization is the *end* and computer graphics is the *means to that end*.

1.3. HISTORICAL PERSPECTIVE

1.3.1. Before computers

The following is not meant to be a definitive history of data visualization, it is more a "dip into the archives" which is intended to demonstrate that data visualization has a surprisingly long ancestry; for more details see the books by Tufte (1983, 1990).

Astronomy, meteorology and cartography

The earliest examples of data visualization, from astronomy, meteorology and cartography, were driven by the demands for accurate aids to assist sailors in navigating the oceans and for surveys of the land to assist the military.

Influenced by the mechanical astrolabes of the early Middle Ages, the Bavarian lawyer and amateur astronomer Johann Beyer published the first modern set of star charts, the *Uranometria*, in 1603. He plotted star positions based on the observations of the Danish astronomer Tycho Brahe, which were accurate to one minute of arc. Beyer was also the first to draw them on a grid of latitude and longitude lines using the ecliptic coordinate system.

The famous English astronomer Edmond Halley was the first modern scientist who had the ability to reduce large amounts of numerical data to a meaningful representation. He published the first meteorological chart in 1686: a map of the world showing the distribution of prevailing winds over the oceans by the use of arrow plots. In 1693 he published mortality tables for the city of Breslau, which were one of the earliest attempts to correlate one variable (mortality) with a second variable (age). He also commanded the first sea voyage undertaken for purely scientific purposes, to observe variations in magnetic compass readings in the South Atlantic. The results were published in 1701 as the first magnetic charts, which included curved lines (today called isolines) that indicated positions in the oceans having the same variation of the compass.

The use of contour lines on topographic maps to represent elevations above sea level, and on nautical charts to represent depths, came with the advent of accurate surveying techniques. These were first employed from the middle of the 18th Century, when France, England and Switzerland undertook elaborate national surveys to produce maps for military reasons. If a coastline – being the zero elevation – line can be considered a contour line, then contour lines first appeared around 1748 in the *Carte Geométrique de la France*. But the more usual, nonzero elevation contour lines were not in common use until after the British Ordnance Survey Act of 1841.

An isothermal chart (lines of equal temperature), prepared by Alexander von Humboldt in 1817 for low and middle latitudes of the Northern Hemisphere, was the first use of isoline methods to show the geographic distribution of a quantity other than elevation. This was followed by isochromatic lines (equal color) in 1829, isogeothermal lines (equal temperature below the surface of the earth) in 1832 and isobars (equal pressure) in 1864. The general term isopleth from 1877 (equal value of a property) is not commonly used today; the term isoline is used.

Geography and geology

It was not until towards the end of the last century that data visualization expanded to include techniques other than isolines and into other scientific disciplines. In geography, color was used in maps between contour lines and in the representation of different types of vegetation.This followed the use of gray-scale on contour maps of North Wales by Aaron Arrowsmith in 1818. In geology, color was used in maps to represent different rock types.

Medicine

The field of medicine was revolutionized by the discovery of X-rays by Wilhelm Röntgen in November 1895. This was followed extremely rapidly by the generation of the first stereo pair of X-ray photographs (of a mouse) in March 1896 by Elihu Thompson. This development was no doubt made possible by the passion at the time for parlour room amusements, thus the *Wheatstone Stereoscope* for traditional photographs had been in popular use since 1838. More importantly, James MacKenzie-Davidson developed measurement techniques in 1898 for the location of foreign bodies using stereo X-ray photographs. These were extensively used during the First World War to assist surgeons in locating bullets and shrapnel.

However, X-ray photographs have limitations because a three-dimensional volume of data has been flattened on to a two-dimensional image, losing much of the three-dimensional information. The resolution of this problem came with the emergence of transverse axial tomography in 1938, which allowed X-ray sections or slices to be generated. This was mostly the work of William Watson. An excellent historical review of X-rays in medicine can be found in Webb's (1990) book.

Chemical crystallography

X-rays also revolutionized the field of chemistry with the technique of X-ray diffraction, which allows the positions of the atoms in a crystal to be determined. It was pioneered by Laue in 1912 and refined by Bragg in 1921. An X-ray diffraction pattern is used to calculate the electron-density in a three-dimensional volume using Fourier synthesis. This data is represented as electron-density contour maps (for an early example see Robertson, 1953), and comprises a set of isolines at different electron-density values on a number of equally spaced two-dimensional slices within the three-dimensional volume.

In 1968 this culminated in the *Richards Box* (Richards, 1968). In this elegant device the electron-density contour maps were drawn on to transparent sheets, which were then stacked up with separators to reproduce the three-dimensional volume. A 45° half-silvered mirror was placed behind the stack of density maps such that they were reflected towards the viewer. A proposed three-dimensional physical model of the atoms in the crystal structure was then built and placed behind the 45° mirror (through which they could be directly seen by the viewer). Each atom in the model was moved until it appeared to coincide with appropriate elctron-density contours. This resulted in a best-fit three-dimensional model for the crystal structure.

Biology

Related techniques were used in biology, based on the serial sectioning of specimens. The reconstruction of the third dimension from serial electron micrographs by Bang and Bang (1957) was achieved by taking micron-thick slices from the specimen, in this case a nasal cell from a ferret. Each slice was photographed in an electron microscope and the images were traced on to transparent acetate sheets which were stacked up with separators. Different cell structures (mitochondria, nucleus, etc.) were traced in a different color.

Fluid dynamics

The field of experimental fluid dynamics has contributed many of the techniques which are used in the visualization of vector properties. Thus ribbons were fixed to the surfaces of aircraft and ships' hulls, in wind tunnels and tanks respectively, to observe the fluid flow and vorticity fields; they were the physical origin of the concept of streamlines. Smoke particles were released in wind tunnels and dyes injected into liquids to observe the motions of the fluid particles; they were the physical origin of the concept of particle advection.

1.3.2. Early use of computers

The earliest use of computer graphics was probably in the SAGE air defence system on which work was begun in 1949, with the first installation in 1958. It processed radar data and displayed aircraft movements on a cathode ray tube. Reviews of the early period, for example those by Benest (1979) and by Chasen (1981), are dominated by advances in computer graphics hardware and software and applications in computer-aided design (CAD). There are hardly any references in these reviews to the early use of computers for what today is termed data visualization. However, Hopgood (1991) presents some early examples from computational fluid dynamics (1962), terrain mapping (1963) and complex cartography (1964). The application areas of chemical crystallography, biology and medical imaging were in fact the first to use computers extensively for visualizing numerical data, some early examples of which follow.

Chemical crystallography

A computer program to compute contour maps of electron-density for X-ray crystallography was described by Dayhoff (1963). This consisted of an algorithm for detecting isolines in a two-dimensional array of data on a regular grid, a "marching squares" algorithm (to plagiarize the more recent "marching cubes" terminology). A program for isosurface generation in a three-dimensional volume of electron-density was reported by Wright (1972).

The information on atomic positions obtained from X-ray diffraction data is not a set of discrete points but an average position, caused by the fact that, above absolute zero, the atoms exhibit thermal motion. The work of Johnson (1965) on molecular dynamics resulted in ORTEP (the Oak Ridge Thermal Ellipsoid Program) which used an ellipsoid to represent the envelope within which the atomic center could be found based on its thermal motion (the first tensor glyph?).

Molecular modeling started in 1964, with a protein-folding system developed at the Massachusetts Institute of Technology (MIT) by Levinthal, but the goal proved too difficult to achieve. The article which described the requirements for molecular modeling, again by Levinthal (1966) contains many requirements which have only recently been satisfied in commercial systems.

Biology

Weinstein and Castelman (1971), used a microtome to obtain slices from a catfish retina specimen. Optical microscope images were scanned at 8 bits per pixel at a resolution of $1024 \times 1024(!)$ to produce digital gray-scale section images. These were registered, and an edge-detection algorithm applied to generate digital outline sections. Two methods were employed, one was a computer-generated image of the combined digital outlines as a stereo pair, and the second involved printing the digital gray-scale sections on to transparent sheets as stereo pairs and stacking up the sheets with separators.

Medical imaging

The work by Greenleaf *et al.* (1970) on the processing and display of medical data (isosurfaces of constant radioactivity for pulmonary blood vessels containing isotopically labeled microspheres) was really ahead of its time. This is particularly true of the data visualization techniques used (transparent, nested three-dimensional surfaces and stereo pairs) and the quality of the images.

There are many more examples from the 1970s and the major references are to be found in the following sections. For readers who would like more information on all the literature available, the present author's bibliography (Collins, 1991) contains references and a keyword index to over 500 publications in the field of data visualization.

1.4. CHRONOLOGY OF TECHNIQUES

The following contains a synopsis of the earliest examples of the techniques used for data representation of which the author is aware. For more details see the works by Robinson (1982), Funkhauser (1937), Tilling (1975) and Beniger and Robyn (1978).

1.4.1. Before computers

In the headings below, the letters S, V and MV refer to scalar, vector and multivariable data types respectively.

Coordinate systems

1137 Unknown Chinese – cartesian coordinates: map of the *Tracks of Yu the Great*. An accurate cartographic map showing the rivers, coastline and cities of part of China on a latitude/longitude grid. Nothing like it was produced in Europe until after about 1550 (Figure 1.1).

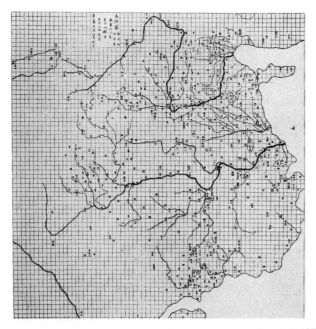

Figure 1.1. Cartesian cordinates – Map of the *Tracks of Yu the Great* (1137, unknown Chinese).

1603 Johann Beyer – spherical coordinates: *Uranometria* (see under astronomy, meteorology and cartography in Section 1.3).

1637 Rene Descartes reintroduced the cartesian coordinate system into mathematics.

Line charts(S)

10th century Illustration of the inclination of the planetary orbits as a function of time (Figure 1.2).

1663 Christopher Wren built a clockwork instrument to measure wind direction, rainfall and temperature. This was the first invention which resulted in the automatic production of a graph. Unfortunately none of the graphs survive.

1779 Johann Heinrich Lambert showed periodic variation in soil temperature in relation to the depth under the surface. The greater the depth, the greater the time-lag in temperature responsiveness.

Lambert also gave an example of a case in which graphic presentation could be used to detect a periodic variation and to determine its period, the mean annual magnetic variation over an interval of 200 years which has a period of 400 years.

1785 William Playfair, English political economist, published *The Commercial and Political Atlas* which contained 44 charts, most of which

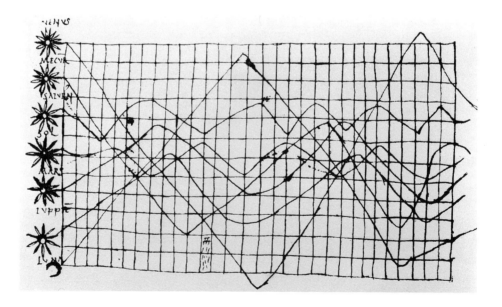

Figure 1.2. Line charts(S): illustration of the inclination of the planetary orbits as a function of time (10th Century).

were time lines. A chart of imports and exports of England to and from North America from the year 1770 to 1782 was particularly innovative. The value of imports and exports over time were shown on the same graph by differently colored lines and the area between the two lines was also colored, with trade deficit in red (Figure 1.3).

On inspecting any one of these charts attentively, a sufficiently distinct impression will be made to remain unimpaired for a considerable time, and the idea which does remain will be simple and complete, at once including the duration and amount.

Scatter plots(S)

1686 Edmund Halley measured the height of mercury in a barometer at different elevations above the earth's surface and derived a relationship between atmospheric pressure and altitude by plotting a graph.

1764 James Watt performed graphical analysis of empirical data when he plotted the temperature versus the pressure of steam from which a relationship between steam pressure and boiling point was deduced.

From these elements I laid down a curve in which the abscissae represented the temperatures and the ordinates the pressures, and thereby found the law by which they were governed, sufficiently near for my then purpose.

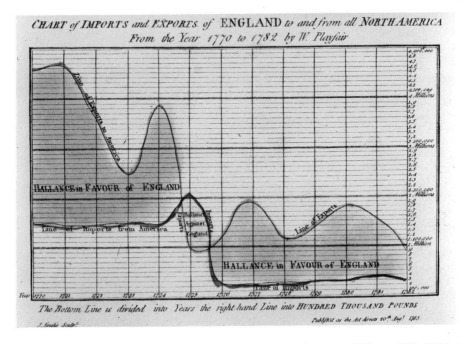

Figure 1.3. Line charts(S): chart of imports and exports from the year 1770 to 1782 (1785, William Playfair).

Contour maps(S)

1594   Pieter Bruinsz, Dutch surveyor, published a map of the river Spaarne with lines joining points of equal depth, now called isobaths (Figure 1.4).

1641   Athanasius Kircher described how to make an isoline map showing the distribution of magnetic declination over the earth. However, printing costs precluded publication.

1701   Edmund Halley published the first map employing and "popularizing" isolines as a means for showing the spatial variation of a phenomenon, in this case magnetic declination (Figure 1.5)

The Curve Lines which are drawn over the Seas in this chart, do show at one view all the places where the Variation of the Compass is the same.

1752   Phillipe Buache produced a map of the English Channel with isolines of depth (now called isobaths).

The use I have made of the soundings, and which no one has employed before me to convey the depths of the sea, seems to me very appropriate to make known in a sensible manner the gradient or slope of the coasts, and ... which shows us by degrees ... the bottoms of the basins of the sea.

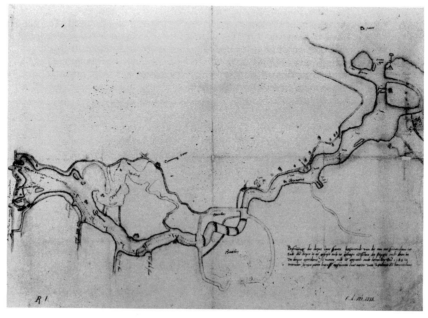

Figure 1.4. Contour maps(S): map of the river Spaarne with lines joining points of equal depth, now called isobaths (1594, Pieter Bruinsz).

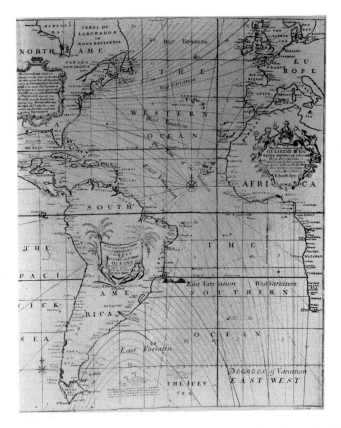

Figure 1.5. Contour maps(S): the first map "popularizing" isolines; in this case of magnetic declination (1701, Edmund Halley).

1782 Marcellin Du Carla published a map of an imaginary group of islands as a suggestion of how to show height on a map using isolines (Figure 1.6).

1791 J. L. Dupain-Triel produced the first real contour map, employing Du Carla's theoretical scheme, showing France.

1817 Alexander von Humboldt produced a small map with isothermal lines of average annual temperatures which showed the basic characteristic of zonal temperature distribution, namely, that the rate of decrease with increasing latitude differs on the eastern and western sides of continents. The technique had great impact in the scientific community (Figure 1.7).

1838 Heinrich Berghaus produced the first world map with isothermal lines.

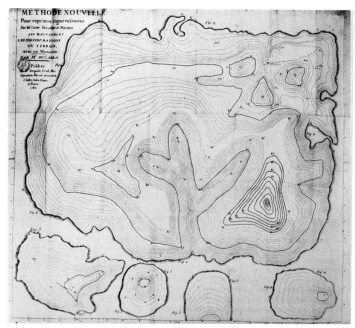

Figure 1.6. Contour maps(S): map of an imaginary group of islands suggesting how to show height using isolines (1782, Marcellin Du Carla).

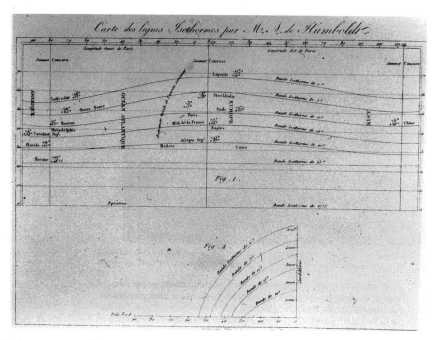

Figure 1.7. Contour maps(S): map with isothermal lines of average annual temperatures (1817, Alexander von Humboldt).

Contour maps(S) with hypsometric tinting

1746 Phillipe Buache produced the earliest geological maps, one of which shows the continuity of rock formations either side of the English Channel (Figure 1.8).

1798 J. L. Dupain-Triel produced a contour map of France with shading between contour lines.

1839 Oluf Nikolay Olsen produced the earliest map of annual precipitation (hyetographic map) which was a shaded map of parts of Europe and Africa. Shading highlights similar areas, such as the "Bande sans pluie" across North Africa.

1841 Heinrich Berghaus produced the first European hyetographic map with hypsometric tinting (Plate 1).

Figure 1.8. Contour maps(S) with hypsometric tinting: map showing rock formations across the English Channel (1746, Phillipe Buache).

1850   August Petermann produced the first world hyetographic map with hypsometric tinting.

This map represents, by different tints of shading, the comparitive amount of rain that falls in various localities of the globe. The deepest tints denoting the greatest quantity, and the blank spaces the rainless districts. The enormous diminution of the average quantity of rain from the equator to the poles will be observable at a single glance ... .

1857   Nils Ravn produced the first "isopleth" maps of population density (of Denmark) (Plate 2).

Colour maps(S)

1741   Gottfried Hensel produced maps which were hand colored according to language group. He published four maps, inspired by Leibniz, who proposed the use of maps on which language areas could be marked.

1775   Gottlob Glaser was the first to use color to distinguish the various mineralogical formations. He observed that it would have been easy to give a more detailed written account but that he kept it brief because the reader could extend it by reference to his map.

1810   Georges Cuvier and Alexandre Brogniart worked out the faunal sequence of the strata of the Paris Basin using fossil assemblages, which resulted in a geological map with a colored code of rock ages.

1843   Gustav Kombst made a systematic and logical illustration of color coded ethnic groups across Europe.

The three great varieties of Caucasian species have been pointed out, the Celtic by blue, the Teutonic by yellow and the Sclavonian by red. The subvarieties of the varieties have different shades of these fundamental colours. Wherever there has been a crossing of these varieties or subvarieties, it is indicated by a mixed colour, in such a manner that the colour predominant in the mixture points out the predominant national element. Thus green, in its different shades, points out a mixture of Celtic and Teutonic blood.

1846   Alexander Johnston produced a world map of the distribution of monkeys and lemurs. Indicated that South America could once have been directly connected to Africa, over 60 years before the theory of plate tectonics was proposed (Figure 1.9).

Height maps(S)

1879   Luigi Perozzo produced a colored relief drawing based on data from the Swedish censuses of 1750 to 1785. The drawing, given the name "stereogram" was widely reproduced in the literature. It plotted population as height with ordinate and abscissa as age group and census year respectively (Figure 1.10).

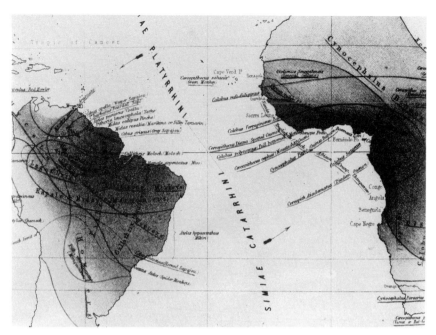

Figure 1.9. Color maps(S): world map of the distribution of monkeys and lemurs (1846, Alexander Johnston).

Volume rendering(S)

1896 Elihu Thompson generated the first pair of stereo X-ray photographs, of a mouse, only a few months after the invention of X-rays (Figure 1.11).

Streamlines(V), arrow plots(V) and particle traces(V)

1665 Athanasius Kircher produced the earliest maps of ocean currents using streamlines and included one world map in his *Mundus Subterraneus*. These show no sense of direction, such as by arrows, so that one would need to read the text to learn the nature of the circulations.

1685 Eberhard Happel showed Pacific ocean currents using streamlines with no indication of direction.

1686 Edmund Halley published a world map of ocean winds as an illustration to accompany a paper describing and attempting to account for the earth's wind systems. Since no traditional symbolism for showing wind direction and strength existed, Halley had to devise one. He appreciated the problem of trying to make clear the complex structure of the wind systems at the earth's surface and flatly stated that it could be done better by a map than by words (Figure 1.12).

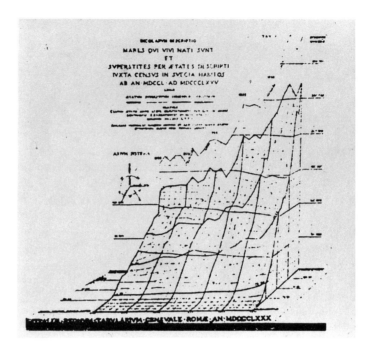

Figure 1.10. Height maps(S): colored relief drawing based on data from the Swedish censuses of 1750 to 1785 (1879, Luigi Perozzo).

... the sharp end of each little stroak pointing out that part of the Horizon, from whence the wind continually comes, and where there are Monsoons the rows of stroaks run alternately backwards and forwards, by which means they are denser than elsewhere.

To help the conception of the reader in a matter of so much difficulty I believe it necessary to adjoyn a Schema, shewing at one view all the various Tracts and Courses of these Winds; whereby 'tis possible the thing may be better understood, than by any verbal description.

1850   August Petermann published a thematic map of ocean currents for whole oceans and the world with ocean currents and temperatures concurrently.

1883   Osborne Reynolds conducted experiments to study the transition process from laminar to turbulent fluid flow in long glass tubes by injection of dye (Figure 1.13).

Icons(MV)

1782   August Crome used point symbols to show the geographical distribution in Europe of 56 commodities.

1851   An unknown cartographer produced a map showing the number of rainy days in year in Britain (Plate 3).

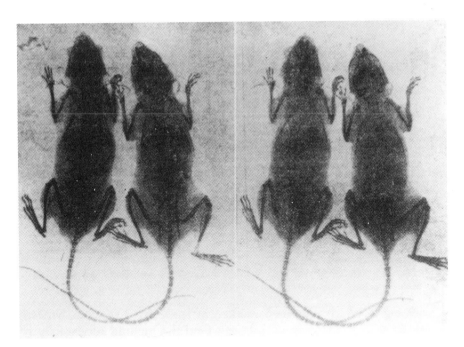

Figure 1.11. Volume rendering(S): the first pair of stereo X-ray photographs (of a mouse) (1896, Elihu Thompson).

The quantity of rain which falls in particular spots is indicated by the size of the blue circles, and not their number.

1857 Florence Nightingale used "Coxcombs", now called polar area charts, as part of her campaign to improve sanitary conditions for the army.

1957 Edgar Anderson used circular icons with rays to represent multivariate data.

1966 Pickett and White showed triangle side length and orientation for four variables.

1973 H. Chernoff plotted two variables in traditional two-dimensional scatterplot but used facial characteristics to represent the third, fourth, etc. variables.

1.4.2. Before computers and early use of computers – crystallography

Though data visualization is often considered to be a product of the 1980s, many of the techniques for data representation were first implemented in the 1960s in the application of computers to chemical crystallography.

1963 Dayhoff: Electron density maps using isolines (IBM program no. 62-825-486)

1965 Johnson: ORTEP (Oak Ridge Thermal Ellipsoid Program) – using tensor glyphs

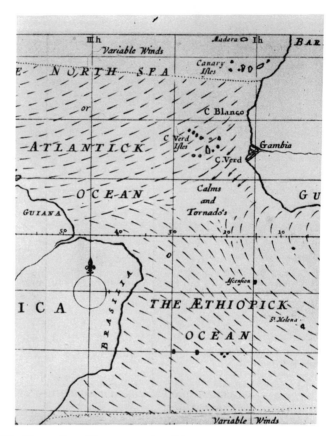

Figure 1.12. Streamlines(V), arrow plots(V): part of world map of ocean winds (1686, Edmund Halley).

1966   Cyrus Levinthal: Project MAC at MIT

1968   Richards: "Richards Box" – molecular model plus electron density maps (non-computer physical model)

1971   Bill Wright: GRIP – molecular model plus electron density maps (computer-generated "Electronic Richards Box")

1.5. A TAXONOMY OF DATA REPRESENTATION TECHNIQUES SINCE THE INTRODUCTION OF THE COMPUTER

The techniques for data visualization ranging from isolines to three-dimensional surfaces to volume rendering are examples of data representation of scalar properties. Though they are still evolving rapidly, it has

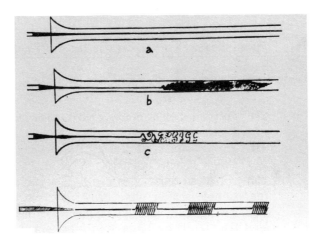

Figure 1.13. Particle traces(V): dye injection in fluid flow (1883, Osborne Reynolds).

now become possible to identify some unifying concepts and to extract a general structure; see for example Berton (1990), Earnshaw (1991), Hearn and Baker (1991) and Senay and Ignatius (1990). Figure 1.14 shows how it is possible to classify these techniques along with a number of others for scalar, vector and tensor properties and multivariables according to data type, data dimension and the primitive used.

The techniques can be classified according to the dimension of the primitive, shown as a 0D, 1D, 2D or 3D prefix to the primitive, with the data type represented by S, V, T and MV (scalar, vector, tensor and multivariable respectively; Figure 1.14).

0D *Point:* scatter plot (S, MV), dot isosurface(S), particle trace(V).
1D *Line:* line chart(S), contour map(S), wire isosurface(S), arrow plot(V), stream/streak line(V).

Dimension of the Primitive used for Data Representation			
3D			Volume rendering(S) Cuberille(S) Texture map(S,MV)	Glyph(T) Icon(MV)
2D		Colour map(S) Height map(S)	Tiled isosurface(S) Flow ribbon(V)	Attribute map(S,MV)
1D	Line chart(S)	Contour map(S) Arrow plot(V)	Wire isosurface(S) Arrow plot(V) Stream line(V) Streak line(V)	
0D		Scatter plot(S,MV) Particle trace(V)	Dot isosurface(S) Scatter plot(S,MV) Particle trace(V)	
	1D	2D	3D	nD
Data Dimension (Spatial, Temporal, Spectral) $\longrightarrow$				
Data Types - Scalar(S), Vector(V), Tensor(T), MultiVariable(MV)				

Figure 1.14. Data representation – classification (after Earnshaw).

2D *Polygon:* height map(S), tiled isosurface(S), flow ribbons(V).
Pixel: color map(S), attribute map(S, MV).
3D *Voxel:* volume rendering(S), Cuberille(S), texture map (S, MV).
Other: glyph(T), icon(MV).
Some of these techniques can be used in more than one data dimension, for example scatter plot, arrow plot and particle trace. In the following lists, descriptions will only be given for the highest data dimension, shown as a 1D, 2D, 3D or *n*D prefix to the technique.

1.5.1. Scalar

1D *Line chart:* a traditional mathematical graph of a property, frequently a time-line (see Cleveland, 1985).
2D *Contour map:* a set of isolines connecting points with the same data values.
Height map: data values, in a two-dimensional (x,y) cubic grid, are mapped to a z-coordinate, giving the appearance of a terrain map with mountains and valleys, although the property is not always actual height (see Grotch, 1983).
Color map: data values, again in a two-dimensional (x,y) cubic grid, are mapped to a range which is typically 0 to 255. The data are displayed as an 8-bit image using a pseudo-color table which is designed to enhance some feature of the data. Other mapping ranges are used, thus 0 to 4095 yields a 12-bit image. The color table is often chosen to relate to some intuitive human perception of the property,

for example the sequence white, red, orange, yellow ... can represent decreasing temperature (see Berton, 1990). The traditional method is *luminance mapping* where bright colours are correlated with high data values, thus a gray-scale image is used for CT scans with black corresponding to 0 and white to 255 and shades of gray for intermediate values. The raw data are commonly an image collected using sensors but can also be a two-dimensional slice through a three-dimensional volume from either sensor or calculated data sources.

3D *Scatter plot:* this technique does not usually associate the traditional data dimensions with the coordinate axes, instead properties are associated with them. Thus a phase diagram of temperature versus pressure shows regions where a chemical system is either in the solid, liquid or gaseous state; and point scatter plots can highlight clustering and statistical trends (see Cleveland, 1985; Grotch, 1983). This technique is also applicable for multivariable data.

Dot isosurface: an isosurface is a three-dimensional surface within a volume on which a property has a particular value. Dot isosurfaces are formed using regularly spaced, depth-shaded points lying on the surface and were originally developed for use in chemistry to represent solvent accessible surfaces (see Connolly, 1983).

Wire isosurface: this is an isosurface represented by depth-shaded lines, which are usually connected as the edges of polygons.

Tiled isosurface: this is an isosurface represented by either flat, Gouraud or Phong shaded polygons.

Texture map: a texture map is the three-dimensional equivalent of a colour map. It maps a three-dimensional grid to a range via a pseudo-color table to a new three-dimensional "image", and thence via a projection to a two-dimensional image. The texture map is by definition solid texture.

Cuberille: used almost exclusively in medical imaging; the surface of an object is approximated by a connected set of cube faces which are shaded to give the appearance of the real object surface.

Volume rendering: this is very similar to a texture map but the final two-dimensional image has the appearance of a semi-transparent gel. This is because the data values are mapped to both a color and an opacity and all voxels contribute to the final image.

1.5.2. Vector

It is common to simplify the data types for visualization purposes, thus the scalar component of a vector property can be represented while the directional component is ignored. In which case scalar techniques would be used.

3D *Particle trace:* this involves the injection of point particles into a vector field, for example velocity, at specific locations. The characteristics of the vector field are used to move or advect the particles in space and time. This requires resampling of the vector field at locations usually not corresponding to the discrete data values. In a variation called "particle trail", old particles are displayed for a certain number of time steps.

Streamline/streakline: a streamline is the same as a particle trail except that lines join the particle locations for a certain number of time steps. Streaklines are all the streamlines that pass through one point but originate at different locations.

Arrow plot: each vector is mapped on to a single-headed arrow. The scalar value is usually represented by the length of the shaft of a fixed-width arrow or by the width of the shaft of a fixed-length arrow. The latter technique is particularly useful when there is a large range of scalar values of the vector property where long arrows would overlap neighbors. Arrow plots work well in two dimensions but can be cluttered in three dimensions where perspective can also shorten or narrow "distant" arrows.

Flow ribbon: these are streamlines represented as a flat ribbon with a leading arrow. The ribbon is rotated to show the local vorticity in the vector field.

1.5.3. Tensor

Tensors of order 3 can be simplified to a lower order; thus a stress tensor (order 2) can be contracted with a normal vector (order 1) to give a surface traction vector (order 1). In that case scalar or vector techniques would be used.

nD   *Glyph:* there are at least three glyphs which have been devised to represent tensors. *Jacks*, essentially three double-headed, mutually perpendicular arrows which represent the diagnonal tensor elements. The scalar value maps to the length or width of the arrow and the arrow direction (away from or towards the centre of each arrow) shows the sign. *Lamé's ellipsoid*, used by Johnson (1965) to represent the spatial components of thermal motion of an atom in a crystal structure. The diagonal tensor elements map to the ellipsoid radii. *Shaft-and-disk*, used by Haber and McNabb (1990) to represent a stress tensor. The shaft direction, color, length and the disk axes and color represent the tensor elements.

1.5.4. Multivariable data

In order accurately to understand certain complex application areas it is necessary to calculate or collect large number of dependent variables. Examples occur in reservoir modeling and multiple modality medical imaging (see Hu *et al.*, 1990). Innovative techniques for data representation are required to see relationships between groups of variables. This is the area where the generalities are least clear and much research is still necessary.

nD   *Icons:* the use of complex icons composed of a number of connected line segments – whose lengths, widths and angles each represent one variable – has been explored by Smith *et al.* (1991) with some success.

Attribute map: this can be viewed as a color map of one scalar property on a surface which is either an isosurface derived from a second scalar property (see Treinish and Goettsche, 1991) or the geometric surface of an object such as an aeroplane fuselage or an oil reservoir.

Van Wijk (1991) has developd a technique called *spot noise* to represent a vector property on a surface.

Other techniques: Nielson *et al.* (1991) have investigated a technique called *surfaces-on-surfaces* to represent multivariate data on scattered grids, for example measurements over the earth's surface.

Pottinger *et al.* (1990) have developed a technique using both attribute mapping and texture mapping to represent five variables derived from a chaotic system of interconnected pendula.

In contrast, the book by Banchoff (1990) assists the reader in trying to build up a mental picture of more than three spatial dimensions and in using the fourth dimension for the representation of a property.

1.5.5. Further reading

For more information on data representation techniques the books edited by Brodlie *et al.* (1992), Earnshaw and Wiseman (1992), Kaufmann (1991), Nielson, Shriver and Rosenblum (1990), and Thalman (1990) and the tutorials by Hearn and Baker (1991), Kaufman (1990) and Levoy (1991) are excellent sources. See also the present author's keyword bibliography (Collins, 1991) and Fuller *et al.* (1991) for further references to these techniques.

1.6. CONCLUSIONS AND QUESTIONS ANSWERED

The previous sections document numerous examples of data visualization from the age before computers. These provide the evidence for the answers to the questions posed in the introduction. However, before computers, data visualization was limited to data obtained from the real world. The advent of computer programs which generate data about the real world phenomena using theoretical models has been a necessary catalyst in the "re-development" of data visualization.

1. Have computers contributed to new techniques for the visual represen- tation of numerical data?

    No – all of the major techniques were invented "pre-computer" for data collected from the real world. Generally the data were in two dimensions but some extensions of the techniques were tried for higher dimensions. There are also practically no examples of the application of the techniques to theoretical world data in the "pre- computer" age.

2. Have computers made the visual representation of large amounts of numerical data tractable?

Yes – today the "old" visual techniques which were developed to represent real world data are now applied to both real and theoretical world data. Also the computer generated visual representation is more accurate mathematically especially where dimensions higher than two are involved.

Nevertheless, data visualization is more than just a new term for established methods. It brings a sharp focus to the role that the visual representation of numerical data plays in the complete scientific process.

REFERENCES

Banchoff, T. F. (1990). *Beyond the Third Dimension*. Scientific American Library, Number 33. W. H. Freeman.

Bang, B. G. and Bang, F. B. (1957). Graphic reconstruction of the third dimension from serial electron microphotographs. *Journal of Ultrastructure Research* **1**, 138–149.

Benest, I. D. (1979). A review of computer graphics publications. *Mechanical Engineering* **4**, 95–136.

Beniger J. R. and Robyn D. L. (1978). Quantitative graphics in statistics: a brief history. *American Statistician* **32**(1), 1–11.

Berton, J. A. (1990). Strategies for scientific visualization: analysis and comparison of current techniques. Proceedings of SPIE Conference, Vol. 1259, 14–16 February 1990, Santa Clara, CA, pp. 110–121. SPIE, Bellingham, WA.

Brodlie, K. W., Carpenter, L. A., Earnshaw, R. A., Gallop, J. R., Hubbold, R. J., Mumford, A. M., Osland, C. D. and Quarendon, P. (eds) (1992). *Scientific Visualization – Techniques and Applications*. Springer-Verlag, New York.

Chasen, S. H. (1981). Historical highlights of interactive computer graphics. *Mechanical Engineering* **103**(11), 32–41.

Cleveland, W. S. (1985). *The Elements of Graphing Data*. Wadsworth and Brooks/Cole, Pacific Grove, CA.

Collins, B. M. (1991). Data visualization keyword bibliography. Technical Report Number 240, IBM UK Scientific Centre, Winchester, UK.

Connolly, M. L. (1983). Analytical molecular surface calculation. *Journal of Applied Crystallography* **16**(5) 548–558.

Dayhoff, M. O. (1963). A contour-map program from X-Ray crystallography. *Communications of the ACM* **6**(10), 620–622.

Earnshaw R. A. (1991). Scientific visualization – transforming numeric data into visual information. In *Graphics, Interaction and Visualization – The Challenge of the 1990's*. Proceedings of International State-of-the-Art Seminar, 4 December 1991, London, UK. British Computer Society.

Earnshaw, R. A. and Wiseman, N. (eds) (1992). *Introductory Guide to Scientific Visualization*. Springer-Verlag, New York.

Fuller, M., Hall, P. M., de Geus, K., Watt, A. H. and Maddock, S. C. (1991). Vis-Lab: visualization in scientific computing at Sheffield University. In Christie, P. and Willis, P. J. (eds), *9th Eurographics UK Conference*, Proceedings, 10–12 April 1991, Sheffield, UK, pp. 11–45. Eurographics Association, Aire-la-Ville, Switzerland.

Funkhouser, H. G. (1937). Historical development of the graphical representation of statistical data. *Osiris* **3**, 269–404.

Greenleaf, J. F., Tu, J. S. and Wood, E. H. (1970). Computer generated three-dimensional oscilloscopic images and associated techniques for display and study of the spatial distribution of pulmonary blood flow. *IEEE Transactions on Nuclear Science*, **NS-17**(20), 353–359.

Grotch, S. L. (1983). Three-dimensional and stereoscopic graphics for scientific data display and analysis. *IEEE Computer Graphics and Applications* **3**(8), 31–43.

Haber, R. B., and McNabb, D. A. (1990). Visualization idioms: a conceptual model for scientific visualization systems. In Nielson G. M., Shriver, B. D. and Rosenblum, L. J. (eds), *Visualization in Scientific Computing*, pp. 74–93. IEEE Computer Society Press, Los Alamitos, CA.

Hearn, D. D. and Baker, P. (1991). Scientific visualization. Technical Report from Eurographics '91 Conference EG-91-TN-6, Eurographics Association, Aire-la-Ville, Switzerland.

Hopgood, F. R. A. (1991). Pioneering images. In *Graphics, Interaction and Visualization – The Challenge of the 1990's*, Proceedings of International State-of-the-Art Seminar, 4 December 1991, London, UK. British Computer Society.

Hu, X., Tan, K. K., Levin, D. N., Pelizzari, C. A. and Chen, G. T. Y. (1990). A volume-rendering technique for integrated three-dimensional display of MR and PET data. In *Proceedings of NATO Advanced Study Institute*, 25–29 June 1990, Travemunde, Germany, pp. 379–397. Vol. 60. NATO ASI Series F, Computer and Systems Sciences. Springer-Verlag, Berlin.

Johnson, C. K. (1965). ORTEP: a Fortran thermal ellipsoid plot program for crystal structure illustrations. ORNL Technical Report 3794, Oak Ridge National Laboratories, TN, USA.

Kaufman, A. (1990). 3D volume visualization. Technical Report from Eurographics '90 Conference EG-90-TN-12, Eurographics Association, Aire-la-Ville, Switzerland.

Kaufman, A. (ed.) (1991). *Volume Visualization*. IEEE Computer Society Press, Los Alamitos, CA.

Levinthal, C. (1966). Molecular model-building by computer. *Scientific American* **214**(6), 42–52.

Levoy, M. (1991). Introduction to volume visualization. ACM SIGGRAPH '91 Course Number 7, ACM SIGGRAPH.

McCormick, B. H., DeFanti, T. A. and Brown M. D. (1987). Visualization in scientific computing. *Computer Graphics* **21**(6) (complete issue).

Nielson, G. M., Shriver, B. D. and Rosenblum L. J. (eds). (1990) *Visualization in Scientific Computing*. IEEE Computer Society Press, Los Alamitos, CA.

Nielson, G. M., Foley, T. A., Hamann, B. and Lane, D. A. (1991). Visualizing and modeling scattered multivariate data. *IEEE Computer Graphics and Applications* **11**(3), 47–55.

Pottinger, D., Todd, S. J. P., Rodrigues, I., Mullin, T. and Skeldon, A. (1990). Phase portraits for parametrically excited pendula: an exercise in multidimensional data visualization. Technical Report Number 213, IBM UK Scientific Centre, Winchester, UK.

Richards. F. M. (1968). The matching of physical models to three-dimensional electron density maps: a simple optical device. *Journal of Molecular Biology* **37**(1), 225–230.

Robertson, J. M. (1953). *Organic Crystals and Molecules*. Cornell University Press.

Robinson, A. H. (1982). *Early Thematic Mapping in the History of Cartography*. University of Chicago Press, Chicago.

Senay, H. and Ignatius, E. (1990). VISTA: visualization tool assistant for viewing scientific data. In Smith, M. (ed.), *State of the Art in Data Visualization*, ACM SIGGRAPH '90 Course Number 27, pp. V.21–VV.28. ACM SIGGRAPH.

Smith, S., Grinstein, G. and Pickett, R. (1991). Global geometric, sound and color controls for iconographic displays of scientific data. In Farrell, E. J. (ed.), *Extracting Meaning from Complex Data: Processing, Display, Interaction II.* Proceedings of SPIE Conference, 26–28 February 1991, San Jose, CA, Vol. 1459, pp. 192–206. SPIE, Bellingham, WA.

Thalmann, D. (ed.) (1990). *Scientific Visualization and Graphics Simulation.* John Wiley.

Tilling, L. (1975). Early experimental graphs. *The British Journal for the History of Science* **8**(30), 193–213.

Treinish, L. A. and Goettsche, C. (1991). Correlative visualization techniques for multidimensional data. *IBM Journal of Research and Development* **35**(1/2) 184–204.

Tufte, E. R. (1983). *The Visual Display of Quantitative Information.* Graphics Press, Cheshire, CT, 1983.

Tufte, E. R. (1990). *Envisioning Information.* Graphics Press, Cheshire, CT, 1990. ISBN 0-8186-8979-X.

Webb, S. (1990). *From the Watching of Shadows: The Origins of Radiological Tomography.* Adam Hilger.

van Wijk, J. J. (1991). Spot noise. *Computer Graphics (Proceedings of SIGGRAPH '91)* **25**(4), 309–318.

Weinstein, M. and Castelman, K. R. (1971). Reconstructing 3-D Specimens from 2-D Section Images. In *Proceedings of SPIE Conference*, May 1971, Vol. 26, pp. 131–138. SPIE, Bellingham, WA.

Wright, W. V. (1972). An interactive computer graphic system for molecular studies. PhD dissertation, Department of Computer Science, University of North Carolina, Chapel Hill.

About the author

Brian M. Collins obtained his doctorate in chemistry at the University of Oxford in 1973. He joined IBM and worked as a systems analyst and database specialist until 1986. He is currently engaged in research into the history and application of data visualization to scientific computing at the IBM European Visualization Centre.

Chapter 2

Get the picture – new directions in data visualization

Jeremy Walton

2.1. INTRODUCTION AND BACKGROUND

The rapid evolution of computer technology is leading to large increases in the power of computer processors coupled with a steady fall in their cost. This in turn means that we will be able to work with larger and larger amounts of data on our computers as we go through the 1990s. However, unless there is a concomitant increase in the quality of the methods which we can use for the display and interrogation of these large multidimensional datasets, the vast majority of these data will prove to be completely useless. The important role which visualization plays in the interpretation of data has been recognized for a long time. Indeed, there exist many types of data of central interest to BP (for example, seismic, environmental, well log and chemical) for which graphical display is a crucial or even indispensable step in the analysis process.

The requirement for improved techniques for interacting with data has led to the development of a variety of desktop toolkits to fulfill this role. These can be used to prototype and develop applications in a way which is much faster (and more appealing) than traditional approaches which either involve the use of a graphics library in the construction of a tailor-made display program or the purchase of a monolithic package. This paper describes some of these toolkits and the ways in which they have been used at BP Research to add value in the solution of business problems. We also discuss the way that these new methods for data visualization and manipulation fit into the broader field of human–computer interaction, which is currently undergoing a revolution with developments in the area of virtual reality.

ANIMATION AND SCIENTIFIC VISUALIZATION
ISBN 0-12-227745-7

2.2.   DATA VISUALIZATION USING A GRAPHICS LIBRARY

Data visualization is the gaining of insight by making a picture out of numbers – be they from geology, physics, chemistry, finance or architecture. Graphics libraries are collections of routines which perform simple operations on data to contribute to the synthesis of an image on a display device. Traditionally, a user would write a program in a high-level language such as FORTRAN or C which calculates or reads in the data and perhaps processes or filters them in some way. The program would contain calls to a selection of routines from the library to create the picture of the data in the form of a line chart, contour map, surface, scatter plot, volume, etc. Examples of graphics libraries include commercial products such as DI–3000 from Precision Visuals, Bradford University's SIMPLEPLOT, GL from Silicon Graphics or Hewlett-Packard's Starbase; *de facto* standards such as the X Window System's Xlib; and implementations of international standards such as GKS and PHIGS. All of these are available at the Research Centre, and we have had a lot of experience with them. Many excellent programs based on graphics libraries have been developed at BP Research for the display of specific types of data, such as *Blockfill*, by Wayne Price, Roger Sommers and Jon Barley, Brennan Williams' *Review* and Roger Sommers' *isr*.

The use of a graphics library implies the following sequence of actions on the part of the user:

conceiving the way in which the data is to be displayed;
editing, creating or modifying the source of a program to make it perform this function;
compiling the source into object code;
linking the object code with the graphics library;
running the executable;
viewing the image on the appropriate display device;
analyzing the image to see if it meets requirements;

and a return to the first step in this process if the image is unsatisfactory. This cyclical, or iterative aspect of the visualization process deserves more emphasis. At the beginning of the visualization process, the user will typically have only a vague idea of what the picture of the data "should" look like. In the first place, there could be a variety of ways in which the data could be displayed. For example, consider (Figure 2.1) some of the techniques which could be used when displaying a two-dimensional dataset.

Even when the technique has been clearly identified beforehand, there will invariably be a series of adjustable parameters such as color, texture, lighting, orientation and other attributes such as text labeling which must be – implicitly or explicitly – selected to produce the "best" picture possible. Clearly, one technique will be more apposite (or pleasing, or useful) for certain types of data than others. The important thing is to be able to have the flexibility to choose the technique for the dataset, and to see the results with the shortest possible delay. What is more, this flexibility must be made available in some way to the end-users, since it is they who are making the judgment as to what is the "best-looking" representation of their data.

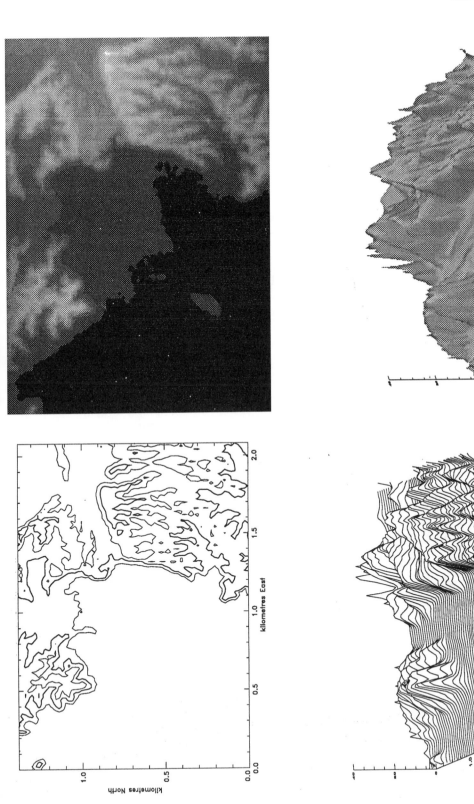

Figure 2.1. Four ways to display a two-dimensional dataset – in this case an array of topographic heights – as a contour plot, an image, a hidden line surface, or a shaded (illuminated) surface.

The use of graphics libraries, with the inherent time-lag between conceiving what is to be done, and analysing the results is unsatisfactory in this respect, because of the large number of steps that need to be taken in between the beginning and the end of the process.

Visualization applications which have been written using a graphics library can be hard to maintain and modify, which means that, unless the user can find an application which is exactly fit for purpose (such as one of those mentioned above), there will be a necessity – or a temptation – to write it from scratch. Although instructive, this can be time-consuming, and will inevitably lead to multiplication of effort as users find themselves writing the same code over and over again. Finally, it should be noted that, unless the user is also a programmer, code development will be tiresome, difficult and an inappropriate use of resources.

2.3. A SIMPLE VISUALIZATION ENVIRONMENT

One step beyond the use of graphics libraries was taken by Precision Visuals Inc. with the release of *PV~Wave*. This is a software system designed for the analysis of scientific and technical data, a programming language and a plotting and image display package. Commands to PV~Wave may be entered from the keyboard, when they are immediately executed, or they can be combined into programs and compiled and executed. PV~Wave contains a large number of high-level graphics, image processing and numerical analysis functions as well as useful routines for the control of the application's "look and feel" (i.e. the layout of windows, the use of menus or buttons in a point-and-click user interface, etc.). Finally, from the programmer's point of view, PV~Wave provides a sophisticated and compact programming language which has many of the features of FORTRAN and C, but with some extensions that can facilitate code development.

To illustrate its use, the contour plot in Figure 2.1 was made using the PV~Wave command.

contour, heights, xdist, ydist, levels = [5, 10, 20, 30]

while the shaded surface plot was created using the even simpler command

shade_surf, heights, xdist, ydist

Here, heights is the two-dimensional array of height values while xdist and ydist are one-dimensional arrays giving the locations of columns and rows of the height array. The height values at which the contours are to be drawn are specified using the levels parameter to the contour command. The important point is that both of these commands can be entered from the keyboard so that the different techniques for displaying the data can be tried out with the minimum delay between deciding what to do next and seeing the results. This trend has continued with the release of a variant of PV~Wave where the interface is of the so-called point-and-click variety. Here, the command language is hidden from the user, which makes the product easier to use, but less flexible and extensible.

We have been using PV~Wave at the Research Centre for over two years and have found it to be particularly well suited for the rapid prototyping, modification and development of visualization programs. Some of the applications which we have developed using PV~Wave include:

a program for the display and analysis of data from a major environmental project for monitoring atmospheric emissions from BP Oil and BP Chemical plants;

an application for the rapid visualization, manipulation and analysis of two-dimensional sections from X-ray computer tomographs of core samples;

a program for viewing orthogonal slices through three-dimensional seismic data.

2.4. AN OFF-THE-SHELF THREE-DIMENSIONAL VISUALIZATION PROGRAM

Our experience has been that PV~Wave is a very good tool for visualising one-dimensional and two-dimensional datasets, but that it is rather more limited in the number of ways in which it can deal with three-dimensional datasets, because of the comparative paucity of relevant routines which are provided in the product. When working in this area, we have therefore often made use of other packages, notably Wavefront's *Data Visualizer*. This is a self-contained program which is specifically aimed at the display of three-dimensional scalar (e.g. temperature, density or porosity) and vector (e.g. velocity, force or flux) datasets. It offers a range of special visualization techniques such as isosurfaces, cutting planes, and particle tracking (Plates 4–6 in color section), as well as supporting functions like lights, titles and labels, and the control of orientation and animation sequences. All options are accessed through a point-and-click interface so that, once again, a variety of ways of viewing a dataset can be quickly tried in the search for the best display, which may ultimately involve an amalgam of several techniques. A command-line interface is also available. Three examples of the way in which we have used the program are displayed in Plates 4–6. Other examples of off-the-shelf programs for visualization include *VoxelView* from Vital Images and Cognivision's *FOTO*.

2.5. DATAFLOW TOOLKITS

Powerful though they are, the Data Visualizer and other packages of this type have the same advantages and disadvantages which have previously been noted for the point-and-click variant of PV~Wave. They are user-friendly and present the user with rapid feedback on the results of their actions when selecting or modifying the parameters of the display, but they are somewhat limited in their functionality because they cannot be reconfigured, reprogrammed or extended. In particular, the user is usually only able to visualize the data – there is no capability in the program for data interrogation, although the Data Visualizer does provide a somewhat limited ability for calculating new datasets from values that have previously been read into the program.

A method which has been quite successful as a paradigm for data visualization/interrogation which is flexible and yet still powerful is the so-called dataflow model. In this approach, the user interactively creates the application in the form of a network of modules (Figure 2.2). Each module is a software routine that performs a specific function on its input data, and produces some output. The network controls the way in which data flow between modules, i.e. how the output from one module is the input to another. A module will usually perform a substantial amount of data processing, which means that typical networks need only contain a small number of modules to do useful work (Figure 2.2).

Modules may be procedures to (a) read the data into the network (from a file, or another application which is running simultaneously); (b) modify or filter the data (e.g. clamping of values, normalization, edge detection of an image, etc.); (c) transform the data into geometric objects which can be displayed (e.g. slice, isosurface, contours, etc); or (d) output the final image to a display device or file. A particular feature of the toolkit is that it is extensible – users have the facility to create their own, supplementary, modules which can be added to the default set.

The creation of the network is performed interactively using a point-and-click interface where the user first selects the modules that are to compose the network from a palette and drags them onto a work area. The user then makes or breaks connections between the modules using the same type of interface. Each module usually has a set of parameters which control some aspect of its behavior (for example, the value at which an isosurface is to be displayed, the form of a colormap, the angle of a cross-section plane or rotation, etc.). These are the "control knobs" for the module (and so, for the whole application) and the user is able to alter these while the application is running via a familiar set of widgets (dials, buttons, sliders, file browsers, etc.). Three of the dataflow toolkits which are currently available – *apE* from TaraVisual Corporation, Advanced Visual Systems' *AVS* and *IRIS Explorer* from Silicon Graphics – are displayed in

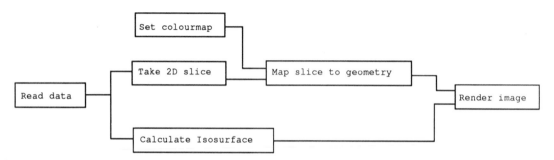

Figure 2.2. An example of a dataflow network for the display of a three-dimensional scalar dataset, composed of a few modules. The dataflow is from the left of the network (where it is read in) to the right (where the image is rendered).

Plates 7–12. We have used all of these packages at BP Research, along with other toolkits such as IBM's *Data Explorer*.

Once the network has been configured, it may be used immediately. This two-stage build/execute process is the key to the success of toolkits in creating visualization applications, and may be contrasted with the more lengthy approach of using a graphics library (above). What is more, it is usually possible to reconfigure the network while the application is running, to quickly see the effect which the addition or subtraction of modules has on the final image. This suggests the possibility of extending this general approach of interactively shaping the form of the application "on the fly" (a method of working which has been referred to elsewhere as visual programming) to other areas of computation in which the task under consideration can be broken down into a series of well-defined stages with a variety of options for each stage. One example of such an area could be, say, modeling. As a user interface, visual programming is strongly appealing, because it is based on the familiar desktop metaphor of windows and pointers, combines a clear, predictable cognitive model with ease of navigation through the system, and offers powerful user control.

2.6. CONCLUSIONS. VISUALIZATION AND VIRTUAL REALITY

The use of dataflow toolkits to create visualization applications represents a significant step beyond previous approaches in which a display program would be hand-built on top of a graphics library, or a package would be purchased off-the-shelf. They can be used to prototype and develop programs quickly in which there is a strong degree of user feedback and interaction with the data. As a result, the user feels more in control of the data, begins to grasp its significance more rapidly and so is able to make better decisions. This heightened degree of interplay between the user and the data is especially important when the dataset is large, multidimensional or complicated – for example, an isosurface, a CAD model, a flow pattern or a reservoir model. The ever-increasing requirements for better ways to visualize and handle data has led to the development of the field of virtual reality. Here, the display of the data achieves the illusion of a surrounding medium into which the user is immersed, i.e. the display screen and the mouse are replaced by a head-mounted display and hand-based sensors. Then, head-tracking and other motion detection systems monitor the bodily movement of the user, which is used to update the display and other aspects of the system. The result is that the user has the impression of traveling through a computer-based three-dimensional model, which may be directly hand-manipulated. Thus, for example, objects in the virtual world may be transformed as the user "touches" them. It has been predicted that virtual reality could revolutionize the world of the scientist in the same way that the spreadsheet changed the world of the financial planner, by making it easier to view and manipulate data in an interactive fashion. The development of virtual reality has been viewed as part of a process which has seen the progressive lowering of the barriers which separate users from their data – leading to faster, more direct interaction with them.

At BP Research, we have been studying both the technology and the possible applications of virtual reality. The systems which are available today demonstrate both the potential of the methods and the distance which is still to be travelled before hardware and software technology can provide useful environments for the solution of practical problems. Yet the notion of being surrounded by an environment that contains both a scene and the controls to change the scene's parameters has a strong appeal for those interested in the visualization and interrogation of data, and the ever-increasing power of computing technology makes it almost inevitable that this nascent field will affect all of us who work with computers sooner or later.

ACKNOWLEDGMENTS

I thank my colleagues, past and present, at BP Research for helpful discussions concerning this work. I am particularly grateful to Margaret McCabe, Ian Beaver, Dave Davis, Bill Christmas, Jon Barley, Richard Noble and Brennan Williams. Finally, I thank the British Petroleum Company plc for permission to publish.

About the author

Jeremy Walton obtained a B.Sc. (1st class Hons) in Chemistry from Imperial College, London in 1980. He received a D.Phil. in Physical Chemistry from Oxford University in 1984, before carrying out a year's post-doctoral research at Cornell University, USA, on molecular simulation of fluids in pores. He joined BP Research in 1985 to study the computer modeling and display of molecular processes in Applied Physics Branch. Dr Walton moved to the Information Science and Engineering Branch in 1990 to initiate the work on visualization, and to form a team which developed visualization applications for clients from all over BP. He joined NAG in 1993 to lead their new development effort on SGI's IRIS Explorer. His research interests are data visualization and manipulation, graphical toolkits, virtual reality and human–computer interface design and construction.

Chapter 3

Advanced research and development topics in animation and scientific visualization

José L. Encarnacao, Detlef Krömker,
José Mario de Martino, Gabriele Englert,
Stefan Haas, Edwin Klement, Fritz Loseries,
Wolfgang Müller, Georgios Sakas and
Ralf Rainer Vohsbeck Petermann

3.1. INTRODUCTION

The term animation has a Greek (*animos*) as well as a Roman (*anima*) root. To animate is, literally, to bring to life. The main aspect of life is that it changes over time. Modern definitions based on the role in computer graphics are as follows:

Animation 1: The application of computer graphics for the preparation of moving sequences for commercial advertising, education, or other purposes; often in video format and usually having the sequence as the end product. 2: Any graphic method where the illusion of motion is produced by rapid viewing of individually generated frames in a sequence (Latham, 1991).

These definitions are too narrow to the role of animation, as it has developed over recent years. Since its beginning in the early 1930s animation has been, on the one hand, an application in its own right. This is covered in the above definitions: nowadays, on the other hand, animation provides a set of tools, or is the basic technology for several other applications of computer graphics and related areas. These include:

Scientific visualization: "having the objective of representing data so that visual patterns will show relationships between the data" (Latham, 1991). Much of the data is time-dependent and thus animation plays a role.
Visual simulation (CGI Systems): broadly used as real-time systems for

ANIMATION AND SCIENTIFIC VISUALIZATION
ISBN 0-12-227745-7

training purposes in flight or traffic simulations. Animated objects like walking figures, etc. and other more realistic illusions of a reality taken from animation technology gain more and more importance.

Virtual reality (coined by Jaron Lanier in 1987): a new term for visual simulation focusing on user interaction through the use of helmet-mounted displays, for example and interaction devices, like the data glove. Techniques are taken from either visual simulation systems or animation systems.

Multimedia: after having completed the device-dependent early stages of development (such as Digital Video Interactive (DVI) or Compact Disc Interactive (CDI)), this area has nowadays gained device-independence. Moreover, animation is in the process of becoming an integral part of multimedia. User interaction is crucial for this application.

Model-based image coding and tele-presence have gained much attention because they promise an optimal coding and interchange of real images, based on techniques originally developed for animation systems (Plate 13, color section).

All the applications listed above, and many others, share a principle objective: to communicate information via images. If this is not limited to static frames, then animation techniques play a role. Animation principles are now a basic technology and research basis for many applications.

Existing animation systems, which have been well established at a product level for purposes of communication design over the last ten years, do not fulfill the genral requirements for a tool box to be used in many applications and circumstances. Usually these systems are more or less closed and focus on one application only.

The purpose of this chapter is to show the basic importance and relevance of animation for many modern applications. It is organized in accordance with the traditional animation process (Figure 3.1). Each level of this process is briefly described and attention is focused on the relationship with other areas, particularly integration issues and/or how to use those functions in other applications. Finally for one application area, scientific visualization, the many relationships with animation are highlighted as an example.

3.2.   GEOMETRIC MODELING

The geometry of objects forms the basis for computer animation and visualization. For representing geometric objects, many different data models are developed. Animation and visualization systems have to handle and interchange this information. Geometric information is not only needed in these areas but also for simulations and computer-aided design and manufacture (CAD/CAM). The choice for a data model is dependent upon the application requirements. Concerning the demands of an application, the implementation of the chosen model is realized. The data exchange between different applications has to be done by a conversion. Due to the

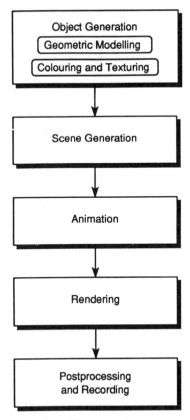

Figure 3.1. The animation process.

specialized realizations, a lot of information will get lost in the course of conversion; more over, certain information is just not available. Thus the more abstract a model and the assigned data structure are the more powerful they can be. The higher the abstraction degree is, the more consistently applications can communicate.

A geometric model is defined as follows (Foley, 1990):

Geometric models are collections of components with well-defined geometry and, often, interconnections between components, including engineering and architectural structures, molecules and other chemical structures, geographic structures, and vehicles. These models are usually depicted by block diagrams or by pseudorealistic 'synthetic photographs'.

In the first part of this section we will give a brief overview of the different geometric models in current use. The second part will concentrate on the usage of CAD data in animation and visualization systems.

3.2.1. Data models and data structures

A wide range of geometric models exists. Historically the development of data models started with simple graphical models and expanded to more and more sophisticated geometric models. They are usually classified into the following representation models:

1. Graphical models, consisting of the entities point, line and polygon. These models are used for very simple low quality visualization.
2. Decomposition models, consisting of a collection of basic elements and the glue operation. These models are used for constructing very simple objects with two or three dimensions. In these models very fast visualization algorithms exist.
3. Constructive models, which also consist of a set of basic elements, but have more powerful combination operations compared to decomposition models, such as union, intersection and difference. The amount of data for describing a complex object is compressed by using a binary tree. Very efficient algorithms can be developed, especially for ray tracing.
4. Boundary models, which represent a geometric object by its (bounding) surface. With this representation a wide range of complex operations can be introduced. All models except simple graphical models can be converted to this. The representation of volumes (solids) is easier than in the other models because only the boundary is considered.

Any combination of the four models above results in a hybrid model. Most problems with these models occur in practice – to be specific, in the process of conversion. A detailed overview of the models is given in Mäntylä (1988) or Foley (1990).

Above all, in the case of boundary models there is a subdivision of geometrical and topological models which has the advantage of separating analytical and algebraic models and operations. The geometrical part is classified into polygonal, parametrical, and analytical models. For topological models we distinguish between wire frame models, surface models and solid models. With the separation of topological and geometric information it becomes easier to solve problems, especially of solid modeling, like completeness, integrity, complexity and geometric coverage.

Based on the topological models, different data structures have been developed:

The *polygon-based* data structure contains very poor topological information. Every polygon is described for its own sake. This is typically used in graphics systems for fast rendering.

The *vertex-based* data structure has information about vertices and simple connected polygons. This data structure is a good compromise between the polygon and the edge-based data structure in the area of animation and visualization. However, it is not possible to describe free form models.

The *edge-based* data structure can hold information about multiple connected faces for any geometrical model. The best known is the winged-edge data structure (Mäntyla, 1988). With the radial-edge data structure developed by Weiler (1986) a first approach for handling hybrid models (nonmanifolds) was established.

With the *double-winged* data structure developed by Wu (1991) the first formalized approach for a complete handling of hybrid models was found.

Besides the traditional geometric modeling techniques, a lot of specialized advanced modeling techniques for creating physical-based or dynamic objects which follow special rules have been developed. A good overview is given in (Foley, 1990).

3.2.2. Object creation

The creation of the geometry of objects on a detailed level in any geometric modeler is usually quite time consuming. Thus, a common idea is to import already existing geometry. In this chapter the main emphasis is given to the problems of importing CAD data in practice. CAD systems are an important source for geometric objects for the following reasons:

CAD systems are widely accepted and available;
animation systems play the role of "post-processing" tools for presentation purposes;
scientific visualization plays the role of analyzing relationships between data.

Using CAD data for visualization and animation should facilitate the state of creation of geometric objects. But only for objects constructed with CAD modelers relying on solid modeling features is this assured. With the partially graphics entity based CAD modelers one encounters a lot of inadequacies in the area of animation and visualization.

In practice it is often easier to reconstruct the model than to convert and post-correct the CAD data. Thus for future development of modeling systems, international standards like IGES, STEP, VDAFS or SET should be taken into account to improve the exchange of data. But this will not really solve the problems because these standards:

have no concept for an integrated solution of handling hybrid models;
will not fundamentally change the practice of constructing objects in all application areas;
do not concern already constructed geometric data.

Taking especially the practice aspect into account, we can state that many constructions are achieved with pure graphical entities or at least hybrid models. Based on this fact, a solid model, or at least an adequate model for visualization, should be developed in a post-process with the support of an analyzing tool.

The following problems with CAD data can occur, based on experiences with the data exchange format DXF (ACAD):

topological adjacency: CAD systems based on graphical entities have no adjacency defined between those entities;
face normals: without topological adjacency information it is not guaranteed that the orientation of faces is correct;
transformation inaccuracy;
useless or undesired entities: in a drawing additional entities for analyzing the construction are inserted;

missing entities: faces which are important for the visualization can be useless for the construction itself.

The redesigning or refining of the above data is time consuming. Thus it is necessary to use a data model with an adequate data structure and algorithms which can automatically solve those problems or at least support the designer in analyzing and refining the data. Plate 14 shows a CAD-constructed object before (left) and after (right) the analyzing process.

Some methods for solving the problems mentioned above are:

Glue vertices with same geometrical location in an epsilon environment and delete degenerated polygons. After this step a very simple topology is built.

Snap vertices on edge or face, snap edges on face and glue entities. Most problems in transformation inaccuracy can be solved by this step.

The first step can easily be solved by a vertex-based data structure. For the second step an edge-based data structure is required. Beside these methods it is necessary to have analyzing capabilities for topological structures. For CAD data, in the most general description, these features can only be guaranteed with a data model for hybrid objects (Wu, 1991).

At the end of the post-process the CAD data should be refined so that solids or important data for the visualization exist. For this, analyzing capabilities such as the following are used:

find all faces belonging to a shell (skin of a solid);
find all edges constituting the border of a surface (Plate 15);
find all edges belonging to several shells or surfaces (Plate 15);
find all vertices which are the only adjacent entities between two surfaces.

Based on the above, additional nonmanifold operators are required to rebuild solid objects (Wu, 1992). At the end the orientation of the faces belonging to a shell or surface can be easily corrected.

3.3.   COLORING AND TEXTURING

Real objects are not determined sufficiently by their three-dimensional geometry, but need additional surface information. In the most simple case, the object's surface is covered with a constant color. Fundamental principles as well as common techniques and still remaining problems of coloring are described rigorously in, e.g. Durrett (1987) and Hall (1989). However, as a rule, the surfaces of objects are not structureless, but have location-dependent variations in color, transparency, surface roughness, or even in geometry, which give the characteristic appearance of materials like stone, sand, marble and textile surfaces. These properties are summarized in the term "texture".

In contrast to constant colors, which could be defined easily by means of color editors, texture specification, synthesis, and processing, meaning rendering, are more complex and produce a lot of difficulties and unsolved problems. Thus, we shall concentrate on the modeling and processing of textures.

3.3.1. Definitions

In the original meaning the term "visual texture" describes a sensory impression. It is considered to be that visual perception by which two neighboring, possibly structured, parts of the visual field may be separated without effort. Therefore, regions with homogeneous coloring represent a special case of visual textures.

One can distinguish between the "texture structure", the "texture image" and the "texture sensation" Figure 3.2. The texture structure is formed by the natural phenomenon and is generally represented by

surface structures of three-dimensional objects, like metal or stone surfaces;
geometric, periodic patterns;
distant objects which can no longer be distinguished individually (e.g. a
    forest seen from far away);
a large number of small objects (i.e. pebble beach, leaf covered ground).

The term "texture image" stands for the projected image of the texture structure on the observer's retina. Thus, the texture image is determined by

the texture structure itself;
the viewing conditions, including the illumination and the distance between
    the structure and the observer;
the eye-sight of the observer.

Texture sensation is the interpretation that the observer derives from the texture image.

3.3.2. Textures and colors in computer graphics

In this context the aim of texturing is to generate a texture image on the final display, which evokes an identical texture sensation to that caused by

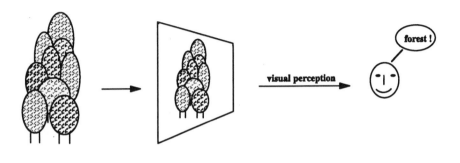

texture structure   texture. image   texture interpretation

Figure 3.2. Texture perception and interpretation.

the original, natural texture structure. In other words, instead of a physically correct model of the above mentioned phenomena, visual structures are produced, which cause the same texture impression.

In modern computer graphics, textures are used for the layout and modeling of scenes that appear real. Other application areas such as product design, architecture, fashion and textile design use textures during the actual design process in order to increase the quality of visual representation. Textures are used increasingly as support in scientific applications for perception of space and therefore of shape and form of three-dimensional objects, and as the basic primitive of visualization of datasets with multiple parameters.

In order to achieve this, textures, like any other component of an animated scene, are created in two essential steps: first, they are modeled or specified; second, the result of the specification is processed during the rendering in order to generate the final, realistic image (Figure 3.3). As discussed in detail below, both modeling and rendering of textures have their own specific difficulties and problems.

In computer graphics, textures are handled as "appearance parameters" of three-dimensional geometric objects including light sources as well as background information (e.g. forests) and grounds (e.g. lawn, pebble beaches, water surfaces). Appearance parameters comprise all material and surface properties which concern the light–material interaction. Examples

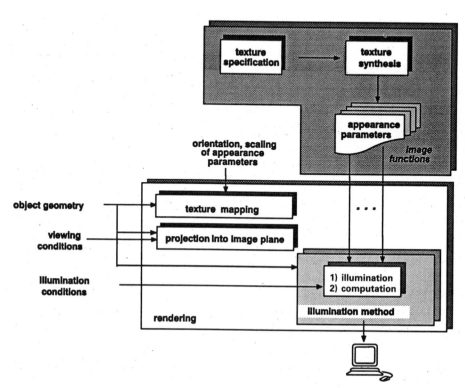

Figure 3.3. Modeling and processing of color and texture.

are color, surface roughness, shininess, reflection properties as well as local deviations of the surface normal (contour mapping).

3.3.3.   Texture modeling and specification

Usually, appearance parameters are input to the renderer in form of constant values as in the case of homogeneous colors or in the form of discrete two- or three-dimensional pixel fields, as in the case of structured textures. Only in closed rendering systems are special texture synthesis algorithms able to serve functional renderer interfaces. Thus, texture modeling and synthesis means modeling and generating those suitable structured pixel fields.

In contrast to the specification of color, which could be easily achieved by means of a capable color editor, it is very difficult to define a texture, which is perceived by the observer as the desired texture sensation. Texture pixel arrays are obtained by digitizing photographic patterns or by the use of complex mathematical methods. Indeed, the use of digitized photographs guarantees a high preservation of reality, but restricts texture specification and synthesis to the selection of one out of a set of samples. The only way to modify raster pictures is by using image processing methods. Raster images are resolution dependent, which increases the aliasing effects during the rendering process. As a rule, they are nonperiodic, which leads to artifacts on continuous object surfaces. Indirectly digitized texture samples include lighting information like shadows, which stand in contrast to the illumination of the computer-generated scene.

The application of texture synthesis algorithms demands fundamental knowledge about the implemented mathematical method and the effects of its parametrization. Thus, controlled texture generation is usually only performed by people with mathematical or technical education. However, as mentioned above, the users of textures come from artistic professions such as architecture, industrial design, or picture animation. Tools like conventional texture systems try to overcome this gap. In most cases, they offer a user interface to select and parametrize a certain selection of synthesis algorithms. They do not support a consistent image of an individual texture during the complete specification and synthesis process. Moreover, the systems do not permit the definition of correlations between different appearance parameters or provide a hierarchical texture description which is a convenient tool to achieve a high reusability of partial texture specification.

3.3.4.   Texture synthesis

In the following we compare some common texture synthesis techniques. Statistical texture synthesis methods interpret "texture" as an array of pixels filled with fixed intensities. Statistical evaluations calculate meaningful measures for the judgment of a given texture sample. Based on these texture measures, in a second step a new texture field is generated, which hopefully invokes the same visual sensation as the original sample does.

The realization of texture may be produced with a new image size or altered measurements.

Common mathematical models for texture fields are two-dimensional intensity arrays (first order statistics: Rosenfeld and Davis (1979), Gonzalez *et al.* (1987); second order statistics: Haralick (1979), Galagowicz and Ma (1985, 1986), Lewis (1987), Conners and Harlow (1980), Gool *et al.* (1985); local dependencies: Gonzalez and Wintz (1987), Kass and Witkin (1987); two dimensional stochastic processes (Gauss processes: Rosenfeld and Davis (1979), Schachter (1980); Marcov processes: Kashyap (1981), Monne *et al.* (1981), Cross and Jain (1983); autoregressive processes: Rosenfeld and Davis (1979), Deguchi and Morishita (1982), Gool *et al.* (1985), Kashyap and Khotanzad (1986), Kashyap and Eom (1989), and spectral description methods, including fractal texture synthesis (general spectral synthesis: Conners and Harlow (1980), Chen (1982), Gonzalez and Wintz (1987); fractal synthesis: Pentland (1984), Keller *et al.* (1989), Sakas (1992)).

The definite disadvantage of statistical methods lies in their inability to react to irregularities in the texture sample, such as faults in the material, which influence the statistics and lead to unwelcome effects.

Structural texture models assume that a texture contains homogeneous-appearing primitives, so-called texture elements, which are distributed on the texture field by means of placing rules. Texture elements are closed geometric regions, which are defined by their content, shape and size. This approach completely describes textures by the definition of the texture elements and their placing rule. Texture specification and synthesis can be carried out without the analysis of existing texture samples. Therefore structural models are suited to the generation of complex patterns.

Examples of structural textures are stochastic scatterings of texture elements (Schachter and Ahuja, 1979) wherein constraints may be considered (Reeves, 1983), tiling of the plane (survey: Grünbaum and Shephard, 1987), fractal Iterated Function System (IFS) methods (Smith, 1984; Demko *et al.*, 1985; Barnsley, 1988) and packing of the plane (Pickover, 1989).

The last group of texture synthesis algorithms define texture by means of specialized stochastic functions. Examples are spectral synthesis for fractal variations (Sakas, 1992), solid noise algorithms (Lewis, 1989) and noise functions with predefined properties in frequency and spatial domain. Because of the abstract parameters and complex mathematical methods of these algorithms, it is very difficult for the user to control the texture generation.

3.3.5. TexME: an example of integrated texture specification and synthesis

The texture and material editor TexME is a software system supporting the user during all phases of the texture generation process:

description and generation of textures;
visualization of textures;
management of textures;
archiving of textures.

TexME constantly provides the user with a consistent view of a clear and well-defined texture model. It is therefore much easier for the user to understand even the most complex processing steps and to use the system in a much more efficient way.

TexME tackles the problems of texture generation systems listed above by means of introducing new concepts and new tools in the area of texture generation. One of the main approaches of TexME is to describe textures on a higher level as common texture editors. TexME and all its components are based on HiLDTe, a hierarchical language for the description of textures (Englert and Sakas, 1989; Englert and Schendel, 1992). By using this language TexME can provide solutions to many of the above mentioned problems:

resolution-independent texture description;
specification of texture attributes (appearance parameters) for any available
    lighting model;
highly extendable functionality;
explicit description of correlations between different kinds of appearance
    parameters (texture layers);
high reusability of texture description components;
application specific texture parametrization.

A second very important concept of TexME is to provide various levels of views and abstractions in the process of development and manipulation of textures. The following list contains the different layers of abstraction and the corresponding manipulation actions:

catalogue, i.e. selection of textures from the texture archive (Köhler *et al.*,
    1990);
abstract (application specific) representation, i.e. simple manipulation of
    textures by reparametrization;
structural representation, i.e. simple structural manipulations and extensions
    of textures by exchanging specific texture description blocks;
development of new texture descriptions by combining existing texture
    description blocks;
HiLDTe representation, i.e. development of new texture description frag-
    ments in HiLDTe;
low-level representation, i.e. introduction of new generation methods by
    extending the language layer.

TexME consists of an extendable set of tools which are made available via a central management tool. The following list gives an overview of the currently available tools:

specialized text editor (HTE) for HiLDTe texture specifications;
HiLDTe compiler and executer;
texture library with various description fragments including stochastic
    processes descriptions and filter operations;
icon editor for graphical presentation of texture descriptions and for visual
    programming in HiLDTe (GraphEd);

texture parametrization tools for the manipulation of textures with dials, sliders, etc.;

an integrated color editor, providing various color models;

visualization tools for the representation of raster images of different texture layers;

texture archive (TexAr), which gives easy access to the texture library;

interfaces to different renderers in order to generate textures in relevant example scenes;

a central management tool (TexMan) controlling all the above parts.

New tools may easily be introduced into the system. It is therefore possible to provide special manipulation tools for specific application tools, like parametrization tools using a weaving metaphor for applications in the area of textile design.

3.3.6. Texture processing

Texture processing during rendering includes

the mapping of the local texture coordinates to the object space – the coordinate system object geometry (texture mapping);

the projection of the three-dimensional object space to the two-dimensional image space;

the computations of the pixel intensity values, mainly determined by the shading or illumination method.

Each of these steps influences the resulting texture image on the final display. One can distinguish between primary and secondary influences. Primary influences are

scaling of the texture caused by the mapping of the texture field onto the object's surface and subsequently by the object's projection onto the image plane;

distortions of the texture structure caused by mapping of the plane texture structure to non-developable three-dimensional objects;

illumination effects (specification of the incoming light, properties of the applied illumination model).

Secondary influences are aliasing effects invoked by mapping the texture structure to discrete object surfaces and respectively to the discrete image plane.

Techniques which handle both the primary as well as the secondary influences are well known and comprehensively described for instance in Foley *et al.* (1990) and Nadas and Fellous (1991). Nevertheless the problems still remain: Texture images in the final picture depend on the applied rendering method and on the illumination model within this method.

In modern computer graphics, coloring and texturing of three-dimensional objects are common elements of realistic image generation. However, there are still unsolved problems. One of these concerns the controlled specification and synthesis of complex textures. In this context, new types of texture synthesis systems like TexME may be an acceptable alternative to techniques used at present.

Other problems have to do with texture and color processing during rendering: texture mapping as well as the selected lighting conditions and the applied illumination model distort color and texture of the final image display. Thus, further research into these topics is highly desirable.

3.4.   SCENE GENERATION

The task of scene assembling in the animation process is to set up a scene using the objects of the previous process stages. In comparison to these stages scene objects are coarse-grained instances that form snapshots for the animation definition. Each instance in this scene is characterized by few animatable parameters, e.g. transformation or color which can be stored as key frame data by the animation system (Gomez, 1984). This strategy enables direct influence on complex scenes as typically needed for key frame animations (see Chapter 3.5 and Figure 3.4).

3.4.1.   Objects of a three-dimensional scene

The most elementary object in a three-dimensional (3-D) scene is the synthetic camera which opens up the view on any other object. Thus, at least one camera is supplied as default by the scene assembler. Often, further views could be accomplished by additional cameras. This overcomes the restriction of perceiving scene manipulations by a single 2-D projection, e.g. translation along the camera axis or complex lighting effects.

A synthetic camera may be defined in various ways, e.g. as an eye point and center of interest which defines the center of the camera image (Gomez, 1984). Another approach uses an eye point and viewing direction which makes it easy to follow a certain direction or a view around (Pixar 1988). Additionally, a view angle or focal length has to be specified, ranging from extreme close ups ($\leq 1°$) to wide angle views ($>180°$). Furthermore, a tilt angle or up vector may define a camera rotation around the view

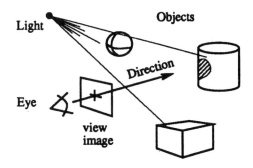

Figure 3.4. Components of a three-dimensional scene.

axis. Unfortunately, none of these simple models is sufficient for animation purposes, as they cause problems with zenith crossing of the camera.

Through the view of a synthetic camera the geometric objects as modeled by a geometric modeler or as a result of a surface reconstruction can be seen. Each object's geometry is a mesh of polygons, triangular or quadrilateral nets, free-form surfaces and sometimes annotation texts. The collection of geometric elements into objects makes it easy to handle complex-shaped objects by just a few parameters, e.g. transformation values.

Another very important class of objects in a 3-D scene are the light sources. The colors in the camera image are determined by light–object interactions according to the light distribution and the object's material properties. For synthetic image generation, various types of light sources are known as approximations of real lights. Each of these light sources realizes a specific distribution. Mainly, light sources are either virtual or real area lights (Figure 3.5). Virtual light sources describe ideal light emitters without spatial extent, simplifying the illumination equations drastically. For more realistic lighting effects, e.g. soft shadows, the spatial extent of a light source geometry has to be taken into account.

The virtual space of a 3-D scene outside objects is, unlike reality, empty and clean. As modeling of the in between is expensive compared to the resulting effect, simple definitions are used for things such as the background or the global environment. Most of the atmospheric effects can be covered with some colors, washes and attenuations, depending on the rendering package used to generate the camera views.

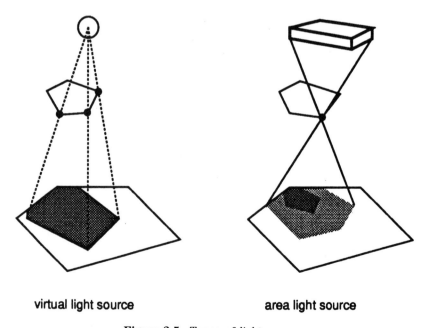

virtual light source   **area light source**

Figure 3.5. Types of light sources.

3.4.2. Assembling a scene

In the beginning, the virtual world is empty. Assembling means to fill it up with different components, describing spatial extent, material properties and constraints between them. Each of these factors needs careful modeling, usually accomplished by special editors.

Once they are finished for a certain set of modeling elements, an object in the animation sense can be defined as their summary. From now on, instances of this object can be handled as a whole. Besides geometry and material parameters, transformation parameters are introduced by the scene assembler, describing each instance's role in the scene.

Basically, a fixed set and sequence of scaling, translation and rotations can be used to put an object into its place in the scene. More complex transformations, e.g. bending and twisting, yield shape variations as well. Arbitrary shape changes, e.g. for a metamorphosis, may be realized by geometry interpolators. Unlike the geometric modeler, usually all of these transformations have in common, that transformation parameters are only specified for the whole object, not for any of its geometric elements.

This strategy enables the animation of any object changes, e.g. in place, rotation or scale, with very little data to be interpolated by the (key frame) animation system. Groupings, e.g. of elements into objects or between objects, allow efficient handling of highly complex scenes as needed to represent realistic looking scenarios. Hierarchical grouping supplies the flexibility to use a minimum of control parameter for the desired object animation.

The specification of appropriate parameter data for the object setup can be done by various input devices. Numerical data can be entered via the keyboard, e.g. for script-controlled systems. Alternatively, interactive input devices, such as mouse, dials, spaceball or data glove deliver continuous data streams. Most systems use channels (Wavefront Technologies, 1991) or handles (TDI, 1991; Pixar, 1988) with additional handle icons to define the desired parameter for the current manipulation.

Fast graphics response makes the user feel as if the real object would follow the user's directives. This enables a trial-and-error strategy for scene assembling with the risk of numerically incorrect data, e.g. for placing an object precisely onto another one. Especially for correlated multi-dimensional input devices, e.g. mouse or data glove, this risk reduces the assembling efficiency heavily. Thus, to suit differently skilled users most commercial systems offer both ways, interactive as well as numerical input.

The graphic output of the scene assembler is needed to check whether an object manipulation matches the desired effect. According to the effect, various output methods are appropriate. Basic transformations, e.g. rotations or placement, need only basic output quality, e.g. wire frame display. For light source handling, shaded images are necessary to see the lighting effects, while shadowing effects may only be seen in fully rendered images (Plate 16).

This image detail oriented output quality may contradict with the fast image generation requirement of interactive working. Most systems allow a user selection between few different output qualities. This covers all basic work to be done in a scene assembler.

3.4.3. Advanced requirements for complex usage

The technology-driven development of animation systems leads to further requirements towards more distinguished tools and presentation strategies in the scene assembler. The basic idea of transformations as numerically controllable manipulators makes it hard to interact with complex scenes intuitively as many natural constraints, e.g. rotation about arbitrary axes or with respect to other objects, have to be simulated and followed manually. In general, this leads to constraint-based manipulations, e.g. placement of an object onto another one (Vertigo, 1992).

As animation systems are no longer highly sophisticated tools for few specially trained animators, but enter the desktop domain of architects, engineers and artists, care has to be taken in the selection and usability of manipulation tools. Besides, the strict difference between scene assembling and geometric modeling in terms of object definition and manipulation tools is questionable, as both tools can no longer be based on the individuality of distinct objects but tend towards within- and inter-object related manipulations.

In parallel with this similarity of the tools, the previously presented graphic output flexibility that is required between scene assembler and material editor increases. Interactive placement of light for example is hard to predict from light cone icon only. Thus, higher quality output is needed to see the incremental changes due to interactive manipulations with the light or illuminated objects, whilst an intermediate camera change needs much less output performance (Haas, 1989; Encarnacao and Strasser, 1993).

For effective working, flexible control means have to be incorporated most of the time whenever a 3-D view is generated. If this optical output filter is linked to the manipulation tools, each tools individual quality demand may vary (Schmidt, 1991). This may lead to mixed quality images (Plate 17) in which the visualization tool can deliver any demanded quality in real time.

Besides the multiple camera feature that allows synchronous views of the scene, asynchronous snapshots for the comparison of different constellations is very important. Unlike another camera, a snapshot represents the scene at a specific time in the past. Thus, the progress in the assembling can be kept and different variants may be compared against each other. If a snapshot is taken in the parameter domain, all (relevant) scene data has to be stored. If the snapshot is taken in the image domain, only the resulting image has to be stored, but it will be difficult to recover the scene state.

3.5. ANIMATION

Literally, to animate means to bring to life. In practice it means to define changes of parameter over time. Research on computer animation also means research on the ways people deal with computers, on animators interacting with the animation systems. Manipulating graphical input devices like tablet, dials, mouse, buttons or data glove requires real-time response. This provides visual feedback. The dynamic binding of an input device to any of the desired parameters to be changed is one of the basic concepts (Gomez, 1984).

Computer animation is interdisciplinary, using methods from different fields. It has been widely influenced by computer sciences, representational art and traditional film techniques. An important feature for accepting an animation system in applications, such as in commercial art and design, is not to constrain the animator's imagination.

What should be animated? A simple answer is: any parameter which defines and manipulates objects and scenes and even parameters which control the rendering, special effects and post-processing (see below). Basically this means that all manipulation functions of the other subsystems of the animation process (e.g. geometric modeling, scene assembling, texture generation, etc.) need to be reimplemented in the animation system in some ways. This extreme position has at least two major difficulties:

1. It is much too complex to implement all these subsystems.
2. Control by the user becomes extremely difficult.

The second issue is more important than the first one. For these reasons all animation systems usually limit the capabilities in some way, often to the parameters of the scene assembling stage and add special methods to make it easier for the user to define complex relationships between different parameters. These relationships are controlled by physical laws, dynamic models, deformation models, kinematic models, or general "simulation outputs" (Foley *et al.*, 1990).

An animation is an application of operations to objects over time, using a discrete time model. Normally time is continuous. This means that between any two points of time there is always another one. A discrete time model is based on a method dividing continuous time into a series of intervals, which are in general of constant length. With respect to what is usually the final recording medium (film, video tape) the frame rate is 24, 25 or 30 frames per second or, using fields, 50 or 60 fields per second. This fact has to be considered in the design phase of the animation.

Traditionally, animation is based on a story written down on a storyboard. It describes the ideas and actions during the animation (Lasseter, 1987). Using computers to produce an animation, certain key frames are generally made. These are frames in which the objects are placed at extreme or characteristic positions. In the worst case every frame must be animated. Therefore every object must be correctly placed for every picture of the animation. Key frames contain all parameters of the special frame. They can be defined by the user interactively or as the results of simulations or measurements (e.g. by rotoscoping; see Figure 3.6).

The key-frame technique saves a key frame for the specified time. This frame controls later interpolation using the total state of the frame. Given the values of the object at the keys, the in-between frames are generated

Figure 3.6. "I'm walking".

using some kind of interpolation functions. These are different types of interpolation techniques. The easiest one is linear interpolation, but it results in abrupt changes. Splines can be used to generate smooth changes in space and time. To get a smooth transition between rest and motion, a standard sine interpolation technique often called "ease in–ease out" is used. For special interpolation between the key frames, a predefined path can be used (Gomez, 1984).

The method of interpolation is simple, but it produces many problems (Foley, 1990). One problem arises during the interpolation of the orientation. Using Euler angles (rotation about the three prechosen axes in a fixed order) results in some cases in the loss of one degree of rotational freedom. Interpolating the transformation matrix directly produces strange deformations between the key frames. An elegant method of defining and interpolating rotations is the use of quaternions, where three coordinates describe the axis of rotation, while the fourth is determined by the angle though which the rotation occurs. But this method is difficult to imagine in general and for the presentation the parameters usually have to be converted into Euler angles or into a transformation matrix. As a result, each method has its own particular advantages and disadvantages and its use depends on the application.

Computer animation has generally addressed the problem of the interpolation between objects A and B with different constructions. The most significant problem with interpolation is that A and B may require entirely different constructions. The two keys generally have a different total number of vertices and a different total number of faces. If B has a lesser number of surface elements, then the designer has to specify how some of A's surfaces are to disappear or combine. If B has a greater number, the designer has to specify how they evolved. In either case, a great deal of tedious work is required. Some algorithm exists to do this automatically using the criterion of minimal dynamic displacement (Magnenat-Thalmann and Thalmann, 1985).

Some motion based on physical laws can be used to generate motions that would be difficult to specify through explicit control (e.g. Newton's law of gravity). Other physical based models such as the human walk are extremely complex and must be described in a multitude of equations. But these equations may contain a number of interrelated variables, and result in many solutions.

Computer animation is a very intensive computational task. Increasing the quality of the animation increases dramatically the amount of CPU time. Ultimately, animation will be filmed (or taped) and viewed in the mode that was originally intended. Designing an animation with no steps between storyboard and footage is rather difficult. The animator must be able to generate intermediate images to try to get an idea of what the animation will look like when it is filmed. To do this, the animator must be able to specify what a frame looks like at some point in time (Hofmann *et al.*, 1989).

Therefore the animation has to be controlled in a simple way to eliminate mistakes efficiently. The term "previewing" summarizes all kinds of methods which allow for the checking, control and steering the generation of a computer animation before it is finished. At least three different methods are used in most animation systems.

Storyboards are usually hand drawn or painted; they show a first impression of the concept of the planned film.

Wire frames are the most simple and therefore the fastest way to render an image. Therefore, many workstations are able to display wire frames in real time. Wire frames show the geometry and the motion of objects, but no color or texture feature of the object. Wire frames allow for the controlling of the right geometry, the movement of objects and the correct perspective viewing of the camera in the scene.

Frame buffer animation is a technique which makes use of the zoom and the scroll (offset) of the frame buffer against the monitor screen. A sequence of pictures is loaded into the frame buffer. Each of them has usually a low geometric resolution. By using the hardware zoom capabilities, one of these small pictures may fit the monitor screen. Now, the screen origin of the frame buffer is altered through the whole sequence of all the small pictures in the buffer; this may be done in real time. The technique allows control of, e.g. illumination, color, motion and hidden surface removal for a sequence of limited length in time at a very low resolution per frame.

Besides this, an advanced system should have much more flexibility to preview animated sequences. An example of these capabilities is described in the previous section.

3.6.   RENDERING

The rendering phase of the animation process converts the scene description of single frames into raster images. Nowadays, it is possible to identify three different rendering techniques: (1) projective; (2) ray-tracing and (3) radiosity. A rendering technique is composed of a hidden-surface elimination procedure and a shading model. The hidden-surface elimination entails displaying only those parts of surfaces that are visible to the viewer. The shading model determines the final appearance of each surface on the screen, evaluating an illumination model, which takes into account the lighting condition of the environment, the optical properties of the surfaces (color, texture, reflectance, etc.), and the position and orientation of the surfaces with respect to light sources, other surfaces, and the viewer. Also associated with a shading model, there is a shading technique. A shading technique determines how the illumination model is to be applied.

The hidden-surface elimination problem received a lot of attention in the computer graphics community, especially in the 1970s and early 1980s. Basically, an algorithm for hidden-surface elimination exploits the fact that a surface is totally or partially hidden when another surface projects to the same position on the screen. The visible surface is the closest to the viewer. In the projective technique, the distance to the viewer is calculated after the perspective projection of the scene into the screen plane. An alternative to this technique is the strategy used in ray-tracing. Ray-tracing projects points of the screen plane into the scene.

The hidden-surface elimination problem was once considered to be the main concern in the generation of computer synthesized images, but the myriad of well established hidden-surface elimination algorithms (Sutherland *et al.*, 1974; Rogers, 1985; Foley, 1990) and the increasing power of the available hardware shifted this concern to the problem of correct shading, texturing and display of colors. This led to the development of illumination models with increasing complexity, that more and more approaches the rigorous simulation of the physical phenomenon of light reflecting around an environment. Early illumination models such as those of Bouknight (1970) and Phong (1975) constitute rough approximations of the physics involved. These illumination models were developed in the context of the hidden-surface elimination problem and were originally applied using incremental shading techniques (Goraud, 1971; Phong, 1975), which exploit scanline coherence as some hidden-surface algorithms do. Later, texture mapping (Catmull, 1975; Blinn and Newell, 1976; Blinn, 1978), recursive ray-tracing (Whitted, 1980), distributed ray-tracing (Cook *et al.*, 1984), and illumination models based on previous work in physics and optics (Blinn, 1977; Cook and Torrance, 1982; Hall and Greenberg, 1983) indicate an increasing concern for visual detail and realism. This tendency is also present in the radiosity approach (Goral *et al.*, 1984; Cohen and Greenberg, 1985; Nishita and Nakamae, 1985; Immel and Cohen, 1986), which applies energy equilibrium techniques to evaluate the final appearance of the objects in a closed environment. Unfortunately, the price of increased realism is a huge increase in computation costs (Whitted, 1982).

Another aspect that can greatly improve the appearance of an image is the reduction of the aliasing phenomenon. This holds especially true for animated sequences, because some distracting effects become much more visible in moving images and some others occur only here. Aliasing arises from the failure to reproduce accurately a continuous signal from its digital samples, if the signal is sampled with a frequency lower than twice the highest frequency present in the original signal (Shannon's theorem). In computer graphics, aliasing manifests itself notably in form of spatial aliasing and temporal aliasing. Spatial aliasing gives rise to staircase effects, jagged highlights, disappearing details, Moiré patterns, and, in animated sequences, flickering of edges, moving textures, and flashing on and off of small objects. Temporal aliasing results in the jerky motion of the objects.

There are three recognized approaches to reduce the aliasing problem. The first is to limit the bandwidth of the signal by low-pass filtering the image before sampling. This strategy is mostly used in the projective rendering technique. Many filters and filtering strategies have been proposed and used to satisfactorily cut down the effects of spatial aliasing (Catmull, 1978; Crow, 1981; FeLC, 1980; Gupta *et al.*, 1981; William, 1983; Crow, 1984; Carpenter, 1984; Amanatides, 1984; Forrest, 1975). Unfortunately, this filtering tends to be complicated and time consuming. The second approach is to increase the sample rate, leading to supersampling. This method is more suitable for ray-tracing. Unfortunately, supersampling can be a rather costly solution. To overcome this cost problem, variations of the supersampling strategy such as adaptive supersampling (Whitted, 1980) and statistical supersampling (Lee *et al.*, 1985) are actually used instead. The third approach is stochastic sampling (Dippe and Wold, 1985; Cook, 1986), which trades off the objectionable artifacts of aliasing for the less noticeable artifacts of noise. Distributed ray-tracing (Cook, 1984) explores the base concepts of stochastic sampling in order to sample other aspects of the scene, including the time, permitting the production of motion blur (Potmesil and Chakravorty, 1983), meaning temporal anti-aliasing. Although proper anti-aliasing can improve the appearance of an image, there is a computation cost involved that cannot be ignored.

Concerning rendering, the two most important requirements refer to the quality of the generated image (shortly image quality) and the interaction capability supported. Although the term "image quality" can be related to structural aspects as content and form, in computer graphics, image quality usually refers to the degree that a computer-generated image mimics a photograph. Photorealism is often the main goal in the creation of computer-generated images. The degree of photorealism achieved is fundamentally laid down by the applied rendering technique. Moreover, different rendering techniques can imply disparate computation times. Of course, this is paid for with a decrease in the interaction capability. In this sense, image quality and interaction are conflicting parameters. The point here is the integration of the different rendering techniques in a homogeneous system, that permits the user to find a good compromise between these two parameters. Figure 3.7 depicts some possible combinations of the basic tasks of a rendering technique and their impact on the image quality/interaction capability, as supported in our approach: the rendering system DESIRe (Distributed Environment System for Integrated Rendering) (Haas, 1989). Plate 18 shows some illumination models supported in DESIRe.

In the context of producing a high-quality computer-generated film, the whole process can be seen as being composed of two distinct phases: design and production. Basically, the design phase is an interactive process involved with the definition of the geometry and attributes of the objects, their movements, and the lightning conditions of the environment. During this phase, the initial ideas that motivated the film are refined until the final shapes, colors and movements are established. Here, as in other

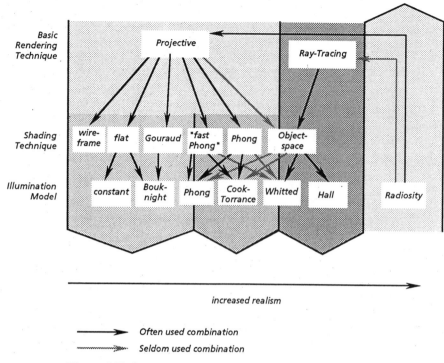

Figure 3.7. Image quality/interaction capability compromise.

computer-aided design activities, designers and animators need quick visual feedback to prove and evaluate the intermediate results of their work. For the visual feedback, real-time interaction capability is ideally requested. Unfortunately, today's graphic hardware cannot provide real-time feedback for complex images with realistic features as reflection, refraction, shadow, texturing and anti-aliasing. To bridge the gap, the so-called previewing techniques, such as wire-frame representation, rendering at lower resolution, the use of simple illumination models, reduction of the complexity of the image to match the power of the available graphic processor, etc., are often used. Basically, these techniques trade speed for quality. The key is to provide a fast visual feedback that generates images only with the necessary information, that allows evaluation of the design. Once the intermediate results of the design phase are judged to be acceptable, the production phase begins.

The production phase is, computationally strictly demanding. Often hundreds of thousands of frames need to be computed. Since the early years of animation a "rule of thumb" still holds: it takes about 20 minutes to compute one frame. Each advance in speed has been invested in increasing the scene complexity and realism. In contrast to the design phase, more stress is laid on quality than on response time during production. Now all frames of the animation are rendered at required resolution and in full quality. Depending on the complexity of the animation, this task can take days, weeks, or even months. Since the probability of a failure during such long processing cannot be neglected, we advocate a fault-tolerant distributed solution to approach the problem. Distributed systems are inherently more reliable than centralized ones. Systems relying on single critical resources, such as CPU, disk, or even software process and data structures, have a low reliability, since they depend directly on whether or not these critical resources are operational. If processors cooperate in a decentralized way, it is possible to explore hardware and software redundancy in order to implement a system that keeps on running (perhaps in a degraded form) even in case of failures. In addition, a distributed system offers potentially increased performance and extensibility (Lelann, 1981).

Roughly speaking, the real-time interaction requirement of the design phase has led to two different approaches, both concentrated upon exploiting parallelism: specialized hardware and general-purpose parallel computer architectures. Aiming at reducing the generation time of an individual frame, the granularity used in these solutions is finer than a frame (e.g. subframes, scanlines, single pixels, or primitives, spans, etc.). Without real-time interaction capability, we argue that the problem of the parallelization of the production rendering process can be shifted to a coarse-grained approach, at the frame or sequence of frames level, aiming at shortening the processing time of the whole animation and not of an individual frame. We advocate the use of this level of granularity rather than a finer one for several reasons:

There are enough frames in an animation to be processed in parallel.

Such a coarse granularity requires little or no communication between rendering tasks and, therefore, one can afford to implement it on a local area network with a theoretical bandwidth of 10 megabits per second.

Beside the communication costs, a finer grained approach needs additional synchronization overheads during the rendering of a frame.

Considering that it is not practical to manage subframes, bunches of scanlines or pixels during post-processing and recording, a granularity finer than a frame eventually leads to the definition of centralized collectors for composing the frames from their pieces. A centralized collector can represent a critical resource, thus decreasing the reliability of the system.

A description of the basic concepts of our system can be found in De Martino and Koehling (1992).

3.7. SPECIAL EFFECTS

The term "special effects" is used to define several techniques used within the visualization process, which go beyond the standard possibilities offered by geometric modeling, texturing, illumination, or rendering. As an example, the modeling of moving clouds or rising flames can hardly be achieved using only the above mentioned techniques. In cases where such "custom specific", or "application specific", effects are desired, nonstandard solutions are tailored to fulfill these requirements. Special effects may be applied at every stage of the animation process; several examples are presented here for all process stages.

Generating terrain with traditional geometric modeling techniques (see Section 3.2) is a nontrivial, time-consuming task: the high geometrical complexity and a certain degree of randomicity required for a realistic terrain appearance can not be modeled manually. Specialized fractal algorithms are involved to enhance automatically a crude initial shape to an arbitrarily complex geometric model. Plate 19 shows an example of an automatically generated mountain. Fractals and related techniques may be used for modeling different objects such as trees and plants, clouds, water waves, etc.

Similar problems appear with surfaces like marble or stone. Although scanned photographs may be texture-mapped on the objects to simulate the desired surface appearance, not all desired surfaces may be achieved by this technique. A parametrized algorithmic texture generation may be used to synthesize surface textures desired by the user. Beyond being independent of the image resolution and the size of the textured object, the main advantage of such special-purpose synthetic textures lies in the ability of the user to design a desired texture by manipulating the algorithmic parameters, colors, etc. The marble used for the pool in Plate 20 is an example of a synthetic texture.

Creating a realistic scene requires more than geometric objects and lighting effects. Several natural "objects" like wind-driven clouds, rising smoke, or flames, may be seen everywhere in outdoor scenes, and are therefore essential not only for a high-quality, realistic looking image, but also for increasing the capabilities of visual simulators like flying, driving, or ship simulation. Contrary to static entities like geometric models or surface patterns, such objects show a characteristic dynamic behavior over space and time: their shape is random and fuzzy and they do not possess anything like a sharp boundary or a surface; in addition, they change shape over time in a chaotic, turbulent, and more or less unpredictable manner. As a result, the modeling and visualization of such "objects" within synthetic scenes is not possible using the traditional animation techniques. Specialized algorithms are used to generate such effects. These techniques are based on heuristic methods (Perlin, 1985), on particle systems (Yaeger *et al.*, 1986), on fractals (Sakas and Westermann, 1992) or on spectral synthesis (Sakas, 1993). A common characteristic of all methods mentioned above is their ability to model such fuzzy phenomena. In addition, the two latter ones are able to model the random motion and the turbulent shape variation in a realistic and physically consistent way. The cloud around the mountain peak in Plate 19 and the moving flames in Plate 21 are generated by a fractal method. For the steam rising from the pool, as well as for the moving water waves in Plate 20, the spectral method has been used.

In addition to the definition of special effects, the rendering of such non-standard objects often require specialized techniques, also. As an example, the standard polygon-oriented rendering techniques presented in Section 3.6 are not sufficient to render fog, smoke, flames, steam, clouds, etc., since such objects are not described by standard modeling techniques and they do not possess a polygonal representation. Specialized techniques have been developed for rendering particle systems (Reeves and Blau, 1985) or cloud densities using ray tracing (Kajiya and Herzen, 1984), radiosity (Rushmeier and Torrance, 1987), or projective scanning (Sakas, 1990; Sakas and Gerth, 1991). The employed volumetric illumination models simulate the effects or absorption and scattering of light within a participating volume (Blinn, 1982) and are therefore completely different from the surface reflection models commonly used with geometric objects. Such specialized rendering and illumination techniques have been used for the clouds on Plates 19 and 20.

3.8. POST-PROCESSING AND RECORDING

The increase of performance of computer graphics hardware during recent years has been tremendously high. Nevertheless there are some essential reasons for the need for a real-time medium like videotape, cine film or others.

1. The necessary transfer rate, e.g. for digital video is higher than 20 Mbytes/ s. Graphic workstations may achieve 1/10th of it when reading the images from the disk-drive.
2. For ease of presentation it is important not to be dependent on a computer. The appropriate medium must fulfill the requirements concerning image quality and availability.
3. For many applications it is necessary to combine/integrate animation sequences with/in real scenes from the camera.

Depending on the application, there are mainly two "physical media" that cover the above-mentioned demands. One is the family of magnetic videotapes used in the area of television broadcasting. The other is cine film, an optical medium with a variety of formats ranging from 16 mm, 35 mm (the most common family) to 70 mm. Both solutions take advantage of widely spread reproduction facilities but require adapted signals and a specific recording process. The fundamental differences between film and video are the spatial resolution and the frame repetition rate. Cine film works with 24 frames per second where every frame is displayed twice. Video deals with different repetition rates: 25 frames per second in the European standard and 30 frames per second in the American and Japanese standards. Due to the 2:1 interlace used in the video technology in order to reduce the perception of flicker on the display while sticking to the same bandwidth it is recommended, for animation sequences with high-speed motion, to work with field rendering in order to achieve smooth movements.

Recording itself is not a technical problem any more. The exposure cine film is a well-known process, but when coming from the digital side it is slow and expensive. A problem arises in the video area concerning the magnetical tape material. The dynamic range compared to the optical medium is rather poor. Another difficult item is the reproduction of correct colors because usually there is no callibration on output systems. In addition there are limitations on the composite video signal. In order to limit the level of the signal to a maximum value all colours saturated more than 70% will be clipped. This restriction has a strong influence on the reproduction of yellow and green.

The following paragraphs look more closely at the details of recording technologies. Note that a video line is an analog signal, for square pixels the number of samples should be ($4k/3$), where k is the number of active lines, because of the aspect ratio of a video display. Besides the image contents, a video signal contains synchronization signals which mark the beginning of an image (vertical synchronization) and the image rows (horizontal synchronization). These signals are used to synchronize frame buffers with a so-called Genlock option via a phase-locked loop (PLL). Various vendors offer plug-in video boards for almost any system from PCs over Macintosh to workstations like SUN, SGI and so on.

Computer graphics usually employs three channel signals for red, green and blue (R, G, B.) A component video signal consists of one channel for the luminance (Y) and two color difference channels (C_r, C_b). Because of the low sensitivity of the human eye regarding color detail resolution the bandwidth (spatial resolution) for the C_r, C_b signals can be reduced (usually by factor 0.5). Due to broadcast requirements, a television signal must be transmitted in one channel only. This composite video signal carries the color information coded on top of the luminance signal. For this purpose there are several types of encoding and decoding equipment available on the market (Table 3.1). The transformation matrix between R, G, B and video color space is (Wendland and Schröder, 1991)

$$\begin{matrix} Y \\ C_r = \\ C_b \end{matrix} \quad \begin{pmatrix} 0.299 & 0.587 & 0.114 \\ 0.615 & -0.514 & -0.101 \\ -0.147 & -0.288 & 0.436 \end{pmatrix} \quad \begin{matrix} R \\ G \\ B \end{matrix}$$

A typical videotape is divided into different areas depending on the kind of signal to be recorded. Most formats consist of two longitudinal audio tracks, the diagonally written video tracks plus an additional longitudinal

Table 3.1. Selection of videotape formats and recorded signals.

Tape format	Signal
1″ analogue composite (1″C)	Composite (obsolete)
$\frac{3}{4}$″ U-Matic SP, high-band, low-band	Composite (obsolete)
$\frac{1}{2}$″ Betacam SP	Component
$\frac{1}{2}$″ M II	Component
$\frac{1}{2}$″ VHS (consumer)	Composite
$\frac{1}{2}$″ S-VHS	Y/C
1″ D1 (digital)	Component
1″ D2 (digital)	Composite

track for the time code. The time code marks every frame on the tape and allows correct positioning of the VTR throughout the whole animation. The process of recording a single frame is accompanied by a preroll of the tape (rewinding a few seconds) to ensure the machine works at a synchronous speed. Every step can be remotely initiated by an animation controller, who is responsible for the dialogue between workstation (frame buffer) and video equipment.

In order to minimize mechanical stress on the tape as well as on the VTR a technique called "Delta-t" recording was developed. The head wheel can be adjusted to a certain angle relative to the tape to permit recording of a single frame without motion of the tape. This feature was realized on some 1″CVTRs (Table 3.1) but the expenditure was rather high so there were only a few systems installed.

Compared to the single frame recording a much more elegant solution is to record sequences. Therefore either the frame buffer has to be large enough to store several frames (up to 1.2 Mbyte for each red, green and blue image) or a fast intermediary device must be used. A real-time-disk (Abekas or others) is special purpose hardware with two (or more) fast hard-disk drives. The rendered frames can be transferred offline from the workstation via a local network. In order to achieve the required output data rate the image data is divided into luma and chroma parts, each stored on a separate disk. An appropriate reading algorithm allows displaying/recording of sequences in real time. Additional advantages are: any kind of time behavior like movements of objects and camera paths can be assessed regarding their smoothness before anything is recorded on tape; multiple copies can be generated without losing quality; and an additional A/D converter allows the digitizing of camera sequences or tape material. Another product suitable for recording computer animations with video resolution is the family of optical disk drives. The Sony LVR 6000 (Laser Videodisk Recorder) for example works with a 12″ write once disk capable of 36250 images on either side (approx. 50 min duration).

For high-quality image presentations with a higher spatial resolution than standard video, either high-definition television technology must be used, where the image quality is comparable to 35 mm film, or the use of cine film itself becomes necessary. Because of the higher resolution (2000 to 8000 lines) the geometric modeling of the objects may have to be more detailed (increasing number of polygons). Rendering time rises with the number of pixels to be calculated. The exposure equipment consists of a pin-registered film camera mounted in front of a monochrome CRT. By means of a rotatable color filter wheel, red, green and blue exposures are made successively and line by line sequentially. Therefore the structure of the image data has to be in channel form instead of pixel form. The duration of one exposure can be up to 20 min, depending on the hardware and the size of the picture.

Traditional post-processing usually consists of three steps:

1. recording as described above;
2. adding sound (music and voice) to the visuals;

3. working with different kinds of effects like blends, wipes and keying or layering.

During the last 15 years post-processing has evolved greatly. In former times it was strongly governed by a real-time philosophy. With the advances in development of digital video equipment, plain effects likes wipes could be calculated in quasi-real time. Special purpose hardware like Quantel became popular. To satisfy the needs of rising complexity in special effects, offline image processing on general purpose workstations has become more and more attractive. Software tools like Eddie, Flame, Liberty and many others offer a variety of effects like composing, morphing and rotoscoping. The frontiers between 2-D image processing and 3-D animation seem to vanish and melt together. From the artistic point of view both tools should be used complementarily.

3.9.   THE RELATIONSHIP TO SCIENTIFIC VISUALIZATION

Besides applications in design, architecture, and entertainment, animation and animation techniques are now used intensively in the area of scientific visualization. Scientific visualization describes the application of computer graphics techniques for the visualization of data and information in science and engineering. The purpose of visualization is the exploitation of the phenomenal visual skills of man in the fields of pattern, structure and object detection in images for the analysis of abstract data.

Initially, visualization may be considered as a simple technical problem of how to map information into visual forms. In fact, it involves a communication problem of great significance. The mapping process needs to be adapted to the specific goals of the visualization. Moreover, mechanism must be provided to support the exploration of generated visual forms.

Animation is important for sicentific visualization because many results of modern research cannot be expressed in still images – DNA sequences, molecular models, medical imaging scans, terrain information, simulations of fluid flow, and so on (McCormick *et al.*, 1987). The change of a scene over time is inherent to animation and applying the parameter time to a visualization can help in many situations to enhance the quality of a visual presentation and to display more information.

Three different aspects of the application of time and, hence, of animation for visualization purposes can be distinguished.

Time can be used to map another dimension of a datset, in general time for time-dependent processes, but any other continuous channel of the dataset may be used also.

Time in correspondence with navigation makes a more intensive exploration of spatial correlations possible. Especially in a three-dimensional scene, depth and perspective as well as the form of objects can be perceived much better if the observer can move around, even if the freedom of movement is very limited.

Last but not least, time-varying visual attributes, like flashing spots or moving particles, may be applied to enhance visualizations and to emphasize specific aspects of the visual presentation (Freeman *et al.*, 1991).

Moreover, various techniques developed in the history of animation have useful applications in the field of scientific visualization. In fact, scientific visualization borrows to a very large extent from techniques and methods developed in the field of animation in recent years. For other techniques, it is obvious that an increased exchange will develop in the near future. From this aspect, the most important animation techniques for scientific visualization are:

rendering;
texture synthesis and texture mapping;
kinematics and dynamics.

The influence of animation in the field of scientific visualization can be observed very clearly in the area of rendering. In recent years, better and better global and local lighting models have been invented for the generation of photorealistic images. The new techniques were primarily developed with applications like design and architecture in mind. Now, these inventions are being increasingly applied in science and engineering to produce high-quality images from filtered data.

The relationship between scientific visualization and animation in the area of texturing is not as obvious. While texture synthesis and texture mapping are common techniques in animation (Perlin, 1985; Englert and Sakas, 1989; Heckbert, 1986), the application of textures in the area of scientific visualization is fairly new. This is quite surprising since textures have been used for a long time for visualization, for instance in design, cartography and business graphics (Bertin, 1983; Tufte, 1983). A reason for this might be that in the field of animation the selection and synthesis of textures is controlled by aesthetic criteria from the start. This can be proven especially for texture mapping, where most mapping techniques for general objects only produce aesthetically good results with respect to distortions (Bier and Sloan, 1986; Heckbert, 1986). In scientific visualization, however, only efficiency criteria are valid: all of the given information must be visualized in an optimal way and no artificial structures may be introduced. Hence, texture mapping is applied rarely in scientific visualization, although there is a high potential of useful applications in scientific visualization. For instance, surface texture is an important cue for form, distance, and orientation of a three-dimensional object in space (Buelthoff, 1991). Thus, the perception of these attributes can be strengthened by a careful application of texturing. Unfortunately, satisfactory mapping methods for this kind of application do not exist yet and one has only very little experience with the application of textures for this purpose.

Texture synthesis for visualization purposes is directly connected to the field of retinal techniques (Senay and Ignatius, 1990), where new approaches try to exploit the resources of man's visual capabilities with a maximum of effectiveness. For instance, man's abilities in the area of texture recognition and discrimination are addressed by mapping information entities into icons or glyphs (Grinstein *et al.*, 1989; Levkowitz, 1991) or other texture characteristics (Wijk, 1991). Following this approach, information is presented in a very abstract way, but since important parts of texture segregation are performed spontaneously in the human visual system, structures in data can be discovered by an observer very easily, and above all very fast (Bergen and Julesz, 1983). However, methodologies for the application of retinal techniques as well as unifying models are missing.

On the other hand, more developed concepts for texture synthesis techniques exist in the field of animation. Here, complex models and description languages (Perlin, 1985; Englert and Sakas, 1989; Sims, 1990) have been developed in order to generate high-quality surface textures for different application fields. However, approaches and algorithms developed in this area have, up to now, only been applied to a very limited degree in the field of visualization.

The connections between animation and scientific visualization are more obvious in the field of volume textures and time-variant textures. Rendering of volume textures and rendering of scientific volume data are strongly related. Thus, a broad exchange of techniques can be observed in this area (Sakas, 1993; Sakas *et al.*, 1993). An example of the application of time-variant volume textures for scientific visualization is presented in Plates 22 and 23.

Simulation plays an ever increasing role in animation, as well as in visualization systems. The difficulty in describing complex and natural motion for animation purposes has led to various developments in the areas of kinematics, dynamics, and physically based modeling (Barr, 1989). Here, animation objects are interpreted as physical entities which act under physical laws. Key frames are calculated semi-automatically with respect to the global forces and object interactions. Similar techniques can be found in visualization systems. Here, animation objects, generally particles, are used as probes which are introduced into vector fields. From the behavior of the probes a user can draw conclusions about the structure of the data field.

Today, a number of the introduced animation techniques can be found in commercially available visualization systems, such as AVS (Upson *et al.*, 1990), apE (Anderson *et al.*, 1989; Dyer, 1990), IRIS Explorer (Silicon Graphics, 1991), and Wavefront Data Visualizer (Wave-front Technologies, 1990). All of these systems allow the generation of animation scripts and support time-varying behavior of their functional elements.

3.10. CONCLUSION

A problem which today's animation and visualization systems have in common is their ever-growing complexity. Besides the software engineering problems which such large programs produce, it is also very difficult for a user to manage these tools. The number of available methods and techniques is overwhelming and thus it is very difficult to determine which technique is appropriate in a given situation and which combination of functions gives the desired result. In scientific visualization, visual programming of dataflow pipelines using icons and the object-oriented paradigm does not improve the situation significantly.

Consequently, more research is being conducted in order to support the user by some kind of automatic generation of an appropriate visualization pipeline (MacKinlay, 1986; Beshers and Feiner, 1992).

Therefore, the relations between animation and scientific visualization are obvious. There are already certain animation methods and techniques in use for the visualization of scientific data. Others do exist which certainly will improve scientific visualization once adoption has reached adequate sophistication. Furthermore, both areas have some problems in common. This recommends stronger cooperation between the animation and the scientific visualization communities; this might bring about further unification of animation and visualization systems.

If we look at other application areas, such as visual simulation, virtual reality and multimedia, we would very likely draw similar conclusions. This means that computer animation has developed from a simple application to a basic technology within computer graphics.

REFERENCES

Amanatides, J. (1984). Ray tracing with cones. *ACM Computer Graphics (SIGGRAPH '84)* **18**(3), 129–135.

Anderson, H. S., Berton, J. A., Carswell, P. G., Dyer, D. S., Faust, J. T., Kempf, J. L. and Marshall, R. E. (1989). The animation production environment: a basis for visualization and animation of scientific data. Technical Report, Ohio Supercomputer Graphics Project.

Barnsley, M. F. (1988). Fractal modelling of real world images. In Peitgen, H.-O. and Saupe, D. (eds), *The Science of Fractal Images*, pp. 219–239, Springer-Verlag, New York, Berlin, Heidelberg.

Barr, A. H. (ed.) (1989). *Topics in Physically Based Modelling*. Addison-Wesley, Reading, MA.

Bergen, J. R. and Julesz, B. (1993). Rapid discrimination of visual patterns. *IEEE Transactions on Systems, Man and Cybenetics* **SMC-13**(5), 857–863.

Bertin, J. (1983). *Semiology of Graphics*. The University of Wisconsin Press.

Beshers, C. and Feiner, S. (1992). Automated design of virtual worlds for visualizing multivariate relations. *Proc. Visualization '90*, Boston, pp. 283–290.

Bier, E. A. and Sloan, K. R. Jr. (1986). Two-part texture mappings. *Computer Graphics and Applications* **6**(9) 40–53.

Blinn, J. (1977). Models of light reflection for computer synthesized pictures. *ACM Computer Graphics* (SIGGRAPH '77), **11**(2), 192–198.

Blinn, J. F. (1978). Simulation of wrinkled surfaces. *ACM Computer Graphics* (SIGGRAPH'78) **12**(3), 286–292.

Blinn, J. F. (1982). Light reflection functions for simulation of clouds and dusty surfaces. *ACM Computer Graphics* (SIGGRAPH-82) **16**(3) 21–29.

Blinn, J. F., Newell, M. E. (1976). Texture and reflection in computer generated images. *Communications of the ACM* **19**(10), 542–547.

Bouknight, W. J. (1970). A procedure for generation of three-dimensional half-toned computer graphics presentations. *Communications of the ACM* **13**(9), 527–536.

Buelthoff, H. H. (1991). Shape from X: Psychophysics and computation. In Landy, M. S. and Movshon, J. A. (eds), *Computational models of visual processing*, pp. 305–330. MIT Press, Cambridge, MA.

Carpenter, L. (1984). The A-buffer, an anti-aliased hidden surface method. *ACM Computer Graphics* (SIGGRAPH '84) **18**(3), 103–108.

Catmull, E. (1975). Computer display of curved surfaces. In *Proceedings IEEE Conference on Computer Graphics, Pattern Recognition and Data Structures*, pp. 11–17.

Catmull, E. (1978). A Hidden-surface algorithm with anti-aliasing. *ACM Computer Graphics* (SIGGRAPH '78) **13**(3), 6–11.

Chen, C. H. (1982). A study of texture classification using spectral features. In Lang, M. (ed.), *Proceedings IEEE 6th International Conference on pattern recognition*, Munich, Germany, pp. 1074–1077.

Cohen, M. and Greenberg, D. (1985). The hemi-cube, a radiosity solution for complex environments, *ACM Computer Graphics* (SIGGRAPH '85) **19**(3), 31–40.

Conners, R. W. and Harlow, C. A. (1980). A Theoretical comparison of texture algorithms. *IEEE Transactions on Pattern Analysis and Machine Intelligence*, **PAMI-2**(3), 204–222.

Cook, R. (1986). Stochastic sampling in computer graphics. *ACM Transactions on Graphics* **5**(1), 51–72.

Cook, R. and Torrance, K. (1982). A reflectance model for computer graphics. *ACM Transactions on Graphics* **1**(1), 7–24.

Cook, R., Porter, T. and Carpenter, L. (1984). Distributed ray tracing. *ACM Computer Graphics* (SIGGRAPH '84), **18**(3), 137–145.

Cross, G. R. and Jain, A. K. (1983). Markov random field texture models. *IEEE Transactions on Pattern Analysis and Machine Intelligence*, **PAMI-5**(1).

Crow, F. (1981). A comparison of anti-aliasing techniques. *IEEE Computer Graphics and Applications* **1**(1), 40–48.

Crow, F. (1984). Summed-area tables for texture mapping. *ACM Computer Graphics* (SIGGRAPH '84), **18**(3), 40–48.

Deguchi, K. and Morishita, I. (1982). Two-dimensional auto-regressive model for the representation of random image fields. In Lang M. (ed.), *Proceedings IEEE 6th International Conference on Pattern Recognition*. Munich, Germany, pp. 90–93.

Demko, S., Hodges, L. and Naylor, B. (1985). Construction of fractal objects with iterated function systems. *ACM Computer Graphics* **19**(3), 271–278.

Dippé M. and Wold, E. (1982). Anti-aliasing through stochastic sampling. *ACM Computer Graphics* (SIGGRAPH'85), **19**(3), 69–78.

Durrett, H. J. (ed.) (1987). *Color and the Computer*, Academic Press, Orlando, FL.

Dyer, D. S. (1990). A dataflow toolkit for visualization. *IEEE Computer Graphics and Applications* **10**(4), 60–69.

Encarnacao, J. L. and Strasser, H. (1993). *Computer Graphics*. Oldenburg-Verlag (to be published)

Englert, G. and Sakas, G. (1989). A model for description and synthesis of heterogeneous textures. In Hansmann, W., Hopgodd, F. R. A. and Strasser, W. (eds), *EUROGRAPHICS '89*, pp. 245–256. Elsevier Science Publishers B. V., North-Holland, Amsterdam/London.

Englert, G. and Schendel, M. (1992). Fractals and formal texture specification. In Encarnacao, J., Peitgen, H.-O., Sakas, G. and Englert, G. (eds), *Fractal Geometry and Computer Graphics*, pp. 83–102. Springer-Verlag, Berlin/Heidelberg.

Feibush, E., Yeuog, M., Cook, R. (1980). Synthetic texturing using digital filters. *ACM Computer Graphics* (SIGGRAPH'80) **14**(3), 294–301.

Foley, J. D., van Dam, A., Feiner, St. K. and Hughes, J. F. (1990). *Computer graphics; principles and practice*, 2nd edn. Addison Wesley, Reading, MA.

Forrest, A. (1975). Anti-aliasing in Practice. In Earnshaw R. (ed.), *Fundamental Algorithms for Computer Graphics*, Springer-Verlag, 1975, 111–133.

Freeman, W. T., Adelson, E. H. and Heeger, D. J. (1991). Motion without movement. *Computer Graphics*, **25**(4), 27–30.

Gagalowicz, A., and Ma, S. (1985). Sequential synthesis of natural textures. *Computer Vision, Graphics, and Image Processing* **30**(3), 289–315.

Gagalowicz, A. and Ma, S. (1986). Model driven synthesis of natural textures for 3D-scenes. *Computer and Graphics* **10**(2), 161–170.

Gool, L., van Dewaele, P. and Oosterlinck, A. (1985). Survey; texture analysis 1983. *Computer Vision, Graphics, and Image Processing*, **29**, 336–357.

Gomez, J. E. (1985). A 3D animation system, *Computer and Graphics*, Vol. **9**(3), 292–298.

Gonzalez, R. C. and Wintz, P. (1987). *Digital Image Processing*, 2nd edn, Addison Wesley, Reading, MA.

Goral, C., Torrance, K., Greenberg, D. and Battaile, D. (1984). Modelling the interaction of light between diffuse surfaces. *ACM Computer Graphics* (SIGGRAPH '84) **18**(3), 213–222.

Gouraud, H. (1971). Continuous shading of curved surfaces. *IEEE Transactions on Computers*, June, **C20**, 623–629.

Grinstein, G., Pickett, R. and Williams, M. (1989). EXVIS: an exploratory visualization environment. In *Graphics Interface '89*, 254–261.

Grünbaum, B. and Shephard, G. C. (1987). *Tilings and Patterns*. W. H. Freeman, New York.

Gupta, S., Sproull, R. and Sutherland, I. (1981). Filtering edges for gray-scale display. *ACM Computer Graphics* (SIGGRAPH '81) **15**(3), 1–5.

Haas, X. (1989). Stefan Haas, Entwicklung eines Rahmensystem für Renderer, Diplomarbeit, TH Darmstadt, Fachgebiet Graphisch-Interaktive Systeme (GRIS), Darmstadt.

Hall, R. (1989). *Illumination and Colour in Computer Graphics*. Springer-Verlag, Berlin/Heidelberg.

Hall, R. and Greenberg D. (1983). A testbed for realistic image synthesis. *IEEE Computer Graphics and Applications* **3**(8), 10–20.

Hall, R. (1981). *Illumination and Color in Computer Graphics*. Springer-Verlag, Berlin/Heidelberg.

Haralick, R. M. (1979). Statistical and structural approaches to texture. *Proceedings of the IEEE* **67**(5), 786–804.

Heckbert, P. S. (1986). Survey of texture mapping. *Computer Graphics and Applications* **6**(11), 56–67.

Hofmann, R., Klement, E. and Krömker D. (1989). Computeranimierte realitätsnahe Bilder. In *Graphik in Industrie und Technik*, Springer-Verlag, Berlin/Heidelberg.

Immel, D. and Cohen, M. (1986). A radiosity method for non-diffuse environments. *ACM Computer Graphics* (SIGGRAPH '86) **20**(4), 133–142.

Kajiya, J. T. and von Herzen, B. (1984). Ray-tracing volume densities. *ACM Computer Graphics* (SIGGRAPH-84), **18**(3), 165–174.

Kashyap, R. L. (1981). Analysis and synthesis of image patterns by spatial interaction models. In Kanal, L. N. and Rosenfeld, A. (eds), *Progress in Pattern Recognition*, Vol. 1, 149–186. North Holland.

Kashyap, R. L. and Eom, K.-B. (1989). Texture boundary detection based on the long correlation model. *IEEE Transactions on Pattern Analysis and Machine Intelligence* **11**(1) 58–67.

Kashyap, R. L. and Khotanzad, A. (1986). A model-based method for ratation invariant texture classification. *IEEE Transactions on Pattern Analysis and Machine Intelligence* **PAMI-5**(4), 472–481.

Kass, M. and Witkin, A. (1987). Analyzing oriented patterns. *Computer Vision, Graphics, and Image Processing* **37**, 362–385.

Keller, J. M., Chen, S. and Crownover, R. M. (1989). Texture description and segmentation through fractal geometry. *Computer Vision, Graphics, and Image Processing* **45**, 150–166.

Köhler, D., Baumann, P. and Englert, G. (1990). Das Texturarchiv als Beispiel für den Einsatz nichtkonventioneller Datenbanktechniken. In *Proceeding Int. Workshop on Integrated Intelligent Information Systems*, Schloß Tucczno, Pila, Polen, pp. 156–175 (in German).

Lasseter, J. (1987). Principles of traditional animation applied to 3D computer animation. *ACM Computer Graphics* **21**(4), 35–44.

Latham, R. (1991). *The Dictionary of Computer Graphics Technology and Applications*. Springer-Verlag, New York.

Lee, M., Redner, R. and Uselton, S. (1985). Statistically optimized sampling for distributed ray tracing. *ACM Computer Graphics* (SIGGRAPH '85) **19**(3), 61–65.

Lelann, G. (1981). Motivations, objectives and characterization of distributed systems. In Lampson, B. W., Paul, M. and Sieger H. J. (eds), *Distributed System – Architecture and Implementation* pp. 1–9. Springer-Verlag, Berlin.

Levkowitz, H. (1991). Color icons – merging color and texture perception for integrated visualization of multiple parameters. *Proc. Visualization '91*, Boston, pp. 164–170.

Lewis, J. P. (1987). Generalized stochastic subdivision. *ACM Transactions on Graphics* **6**(3), 167–190.

Lewis, J. P. (1989). Algorithms for solid noise synthesis. *Computer Graphics* **23**(3), 263–270.

Mackinlay, J. (1986). Automating the design of graphical presentations of relational information. *ACM Transactions on Graphics* **5**(2), 110–141.

Magnenat-Thalmann, N. and Thalmann, D. (1985). Computer Animation, Springer-Verlag.

Mäntylä, M. (1988). *An Introduction to Solid Modeling*. Computer Science Press, Rockville, MD.

De Martino, José M. and Koehling, R. (1992). Production rendering on a local area network. *Computer and Graphics* **16**(3), 317–329.

McCormick, B. H., DeFanti, T. A. and Brown, M. D. (1987). Visualization in scientific computing. *Computer Graphics* **21**(6), 1–14.

Monne, J., Schmit, F. and Massaloux, D. (1981). Bidimensional texture synthesis by Markov chains. *Computer Graphics Image Processing* **17**, 1–23.

Nadas. T. and Fellous, A. (1991). Rendering techniques. In Hewitt, W. T., Grave, M. and Roch, M. (eds), *Advances in Computer Graphics IV*, pp. 213–247. Eurographics Seminars, Springer-Verlag.

Nishita, T. and Nakamae, E. (1985). Continuous tone representation of three dimensional objects taking account of shadows and interreflection. *ACM Computer Graphics* (SIGGRAPH '85) **19**(3), 23–30.

Pentland, A. P. (1984). Fractal-based description of natural scenes. *IEEE Transactions on Pattern Analysis and Machine Intelligence* **PAMI-6**, (6), 661–674.

Perlin, K. (1985). An image synthesizer. *ACM Computer Graphics* (SIGGRAPH-85) **19**(3), 287–296.

Phong, B. T. (1975). Illumination for computer generated pictures. *Communications of the ACM* **18**(8), 311–317.

Pickover, C. A. (1989). Circles which kiss: a note on osculatory packing. *Computer and Graphics* **13**(1), 63–67.

Pixar, (1988). RenderMan Interface. Description, San Rafael.

Potmesil, M. and Chakravarty, I. (1983). Modelling motion blur in computer-generated images. *ACM Computer Graphics* (SIGGRAPH '83), **17**(3), 389–399.

Reeves, W. T. (1983). Particle systems – a technique for modeling a class of fuzzy objects. *ACM Computer Graphics* **17**(3), 359–376.

Reeves, W. T. and Blau, R. (1985). Approximate and probabilistic algorithms for shading and rendering structured particle systems. *ACM Computer Graphics* (SIGGRAPH-85) **19**(3), 313–321.

Rogers, D. (1985). *Procedural Elements for Computer Graphics*. MacGraw-Hill, New York.

Rosenfeld, A. and Davis, L. S. (1979). Image segmentation and image models. *Proceedings of the IEEE* **67**(5), 764–772.

Rushmeier, H. and Torrance, K. (1987). The zonal method for calculating light intensities in the presence of a participating medium. *ACM Computer Graphics* (SIGGRAPH-87) **21**(4), 293–302.

Sakas, G. (1990). Fast rendering of arbitrarily distributed volume densities. In *Proceedings EUROGRAPHICS '90*, Montreux, Switzerland, pp. 519–530. North-Holland.

Sakas, G. (1992). Modeling turbulent gaseous motion using time-varyuing fractals. In Encarnacao, J., Peitgen, H.-O., Sakas, G. and Englert, G. (eds), *Fractal Geometry and Computer Graphics*, 173–194. Springer-Verlag, Berlin/Heidelberg.

Sakas, G. (1993). Modeling and animating 3-D turbulence using spectral synthesis. *The Visual Computer* **9**(4), 200–212.

Sakas, G. and Gerth, M. (1991). Sampling and anti-aliasing discrete 3-D volume density textures. *IEEE Computer and Graphics* **16**(1), 121–134, *Proceedings EUROGRAPHICS'91*, Vienna, Austria, 87–102. North-Holland.

Sakas, G. and Westermann, K. (1992). A functional approach to the visual simulation of gaseous turbulence. *Computer Graphics Forum* **11**(3), C107–C117.

Sakas, G. Schroeder, F. and Koppert, H.-J. (1993). Pseudo-satellite film – using fractal clouds to enhance animated weather forecasting. Submitted to *Eurographics*.

Schachter, B. (1980). Model-based texture measures. *IEEE Transactions on Pattern Analysis and Machine Intelligence* **PAMI-2**(2), pp. 169–171.

Schachter, B. and Ahuja, N. (1979). Random pattern generation processes. *Computer Graphics and Image Processing* **10**, 95–114.

Schmidt, E. (1991). Stageman – Konzeption und Realisierung einer graphish interaktiven Visualisierungsoberfläche. Master's Thesis, Technische Hochschule Darmstadt, FG GRIS.

Senay, H. and Ignatius, E. (1990). Rules and principles of scientific data visualization. In *SIGGRAPH '90 Course Notes #27, State of the Art in Data Visualization*, pp. V-1–V-20.

Silicon Graphics Inc. (1991). IRIS Explorer™, Technical Report. Silicon Graphics Inc., Mountain View, CA.

Sims, K. (1990). Particle animation and rendering using data parallel computation. *Computer Graphics* **24**(4), 405–413.

Smith, A. R. (1984). Plants, fractals and formal languages. *ACM Computer Graphics* **18**(3) 1–10.

Sutherland, I., Sproull, R. and Schumacker, R. (1974). A characterisation of ten hidden-surface algorithms. *Computing Survey* **16**(1), 1–55.

TDI (1991). *TDI Explore Training Manual*.

Tufte, E. R. (1983). *The Visual Display of Quantitative Information*. Graphics Press, Cheshire, CT.

Upson, C., Faulhaber, T. Jr., Kamins, D., Laidlaw, D., Schlegel, D., Vroom, J., Gurwitz, R. and van Dam, A. (1990). The application visualization system: a computational environment for scientific visualization. *IEEE Computer Graphics and Applications* 30–42.

Vertigo (1992). Vertigo animation system.

Wavefront Technologies (1990). *The Data Visualizer Version 1.0 User Guide.* Wavefront Technologies Inc., Santa Barbara, CA.

Wavefront Technologies (1991). *Wavefront: The Advanced Visualizer User Guide.* Wavefront Technologies Inc., Santa Barbara, CA.

Weiler, K. (1986). Topological structures for geometric modeling, Ph.D. Dissertation, RPI, Troy, NY.

Wendland, B. and Schröder, H. (1991). *Fernsehtechnik,* Band II. p 87 ff. Hüthig-Verlag.

Wijk, J. J. van (1991). Spot noise: texture synthesis for data visualization. *Computer Graphics* **25**, 309–318.

Whitted, T. (1980). An improved illumination model for shaded display. *Communications of the ACM* **23**(6), 3443–3449.

Whitted, T. (1982). Processing requirements for hidden surface ellimination and realistic shading. *Digest of Papers, COMPCON,* Spring.

William, L. (1983). Pyramidal parametrics. *ACM Computer Graphics* (SIGGRAPH '83) **17**(3), 1–11.

Wu, S. T. (1991). Topologie von Hybriden Objekten, Ph.D. Dissertation, THD, Darmstadt, Germany.

Wu, S. T. (1992). *Non-Manifold Data Models: Implementational Issues.* MICAD, Paris.

Yaeger, L., Upson, C. and Myers, R. (1986). Combining physical and visual simulation – creation of the planet Jupiter for the film "2010". *ACM Computer Graphics* (SIGGRAPH-86, **20**(4), 85–93.

About the authors

José Encarnacao is a professor of computer science at the Technical University of Darmstadt, head of its Interactive Graphics Research Group, chair of the board of the Darmstadt Computer Graphics Center, and director of the Darmstadt R&D institute of the Fraunhofer Research Society. He serves as a consultant to government, industry, and several international institutions, and was a founder of Eurographics. Encarnacao holds a Dipl.-Ing. and a Dr.-Ing. in electrical engineering from the Technical University of Berlin. He is a member of GI, VDE, ACM, ACM Siggraph, IFIP WG5.2, and IFIP WG5.10.

Detlef Krömker is the head of the animation and high-definition image communication department of the Darmstadt R&D institute of the Fraunhofer Research Society. He chairs both the GI (Gesellschaft für Informatik) special interest group on simulation and animation (GI-FG 4.1.4), and the DIN group on imaging. He is Convenor of the ISO/IEC JTC1/SC24 Working Group 7 that currently prepares the ISO/IEC Standards 12087 and 12089 on Image Processing and Interchange (IPI). Krömker received his degree in electrical engineering (Ing.-grad.) from the FH Bielefeld in 1975 and a university degree (Dipl.-Ing.) in computer science from the Technical University of Darmstadt in 1982. He completed his Ph.D. work (Dr.-Ing.)

on the analysis of visualization systems, focusing on modeling and performance evaluation issues.

Part II
Techniques

Chapter 4

Development of a procedure for generating graphical computer animations

Giuseppe Fenini

4.1. INTRODUCTION

Graphical visualization of computed results is the technique most commonly used by researchers for numerical analyses of the majority of the dynamic phenomena affecting industrial and civil engineering structures. Above all, graphical animation represents the ideal means of fulfilling the need for a full and concise understanding of the most significant factors of the complex problems analysed.

Techniques for setting up graphical computer animations have been developed at the Structural and Hydraulic Research Center (CRIS) at ENEL since the second half of the 1970s (Fenini, 1979).

Since the software tools have not been acquired outside of the Center, but instead have been developed internally and independently, it has been possible to plan their growth according to specific needs which have gradually emerged and define their characteristics so as to obtain codes having maximum versatility and efficiency, and which are easy to update as production requirements alter and to insert in generalized procedures.

Almost all of the graphical animations produced by CRIS refer to the visualization of three-dimensional models defined via techniques of second-order isoparametric finite-element discretization. As a result, the software prepared for the static and dynamic analysis, for generating operational databases and for graphical visualization, is based on the use of three-dimensional finite-element meshes with these characteristics (Zienkievicz, 1972).

ANIMATION AND SCIENTIFIC VISUALIZATION
ISBN 0-12-227745-7

4.2.   METHOD

The complex process of graphical computer animation can be divided into four basic phases, each of which relates to different activities with specific objectives.

Plate 24 (see color section) shows the sequence of these phases and the links between the various activities, some of which can be performed in parallel, while others require a predefined time sequence. Some of the activities are critical, and subsequent activities can only be started after their completion.

The first working phase relates to:

(a) Definition of the meshes for geometric discretization of the continua studied, bearing in mind the description requirements of the model and the geometric conditions of its boundary (activity 1).
(b) Definition of the observer's navigation path, which is in the same three-dimensional space where the model is defined (activity 2).
(c) Acquisition of the data describing the external actions studied, such as earthquakes, impulsive actions etc. (activity 13).

The second working phase is composed of the following:

(a) Numerical analysis of the problem presented, by means of computation programs which, by using the geometric data and the boundary conditions defined mechanically and physically, supply the eigenshapes and eigenvalues of the structure and the participation coefficients of the components of the seismic or impulsive actions (activities, 6, 7, 10, 15).
(b) Checking the ability of the numerical model to reproduce accurately the behavior of the real structure, comparing the experimental data collected from measurement campaigns (activity 8).
(c) Definition of the harmonic components of the data describing the external dynamic actions occurring on the structure (activity 14).

In the third working phase, the actual animation process is performed, consisting of:

(a) Generation of databases relating to the geometric description (instant by instant during the occurrence of the phenomenon in question) of modal shifts and shifts due to external actions, using the nondeformed geometry, the eigenshapes and eigenvalues and the participation coefficients (activities 5, 11, 12, 16, 17).
(b) Assembly of the global database to integrate those generated previously with the data of the observer navigation path (activity 18).
(c) Use of the programs of graphical visualization and synchronization of the peripheral activities to produce the final videotape (activity 19).

Finally the fourth phase is performed at the end of each of the previous phases with feedback actions. They consist of work to adjust the parameters of the numerical model in order to bring it into line with the effective real conditions, or the parameters applied to generating animation, in order to achieve the optimum conditions for understanding the problems studied.

4.2.1. Mesh definition

This is the main activity of the first working phase and can be considered one of the most critical points in the whole method.

There are several tools able to produce data representing any kind of finite-element mesh and there is no problem about the one used, but the user's attention must be focused on the size of the mesh and its suitability to obtain fast computation and believable results. In dynamic computation, meshes with plenty of nodes and elements may not be fit for an accurate investigation of the behavior of numerical models used, even if they seem suitable for better visualization.

The user must then find meshes of the right size, managing the best compromise between the need to get correct numerical results and good detail in their representation, avoiding both redundancies and lack of description in critical points of the model.

4.2.2 Navigation path

This second activity, even if it is not as critical as the previous one, should be performed with attention given to forecasting the most significant sections of the model for a more detailed observation.

As the observer's navigation path is generated by means of some fixed points, connected with a cubic spline line, it is important to define with plenty of information each point given.

For each point the following information are required:

(a) three space coordinates defining the position of the observer;
(b) three space coordinates of a point to which the observer's sight is directed;
(c) the value of the viewing angle;
(d) the instantaneous velocity of the observer on the path.

The observer is supposed to be in a upright position, no head rotation in his frontal plane being allowed.

All these quantities are used in the parametric equation

$$\mathbf{r} = k_1\,\mathbf{r}_1 + k_2\,\mathbf{r}_2 + k_3\,\mathbf{r}_3 + k_4\mathbf{r}_4$$

where $\mathbf{r}_1$, $\mathbf{r}_2$, $\mathbf{r}_3$, $\mathbf{r}_4$ are position vectors in the multidimensional space defined above and

$$k_1 = (1-t)^3, \quad k_2 = 3t(1-t)^2,$$
$$k_3 = 3t^2(1-t), k_4 = t^3$$

assuming t variable from 0 to 1 between two contiguous defined points.

Then, referring $\mathbf{r}_1$ to the defined point i and $\mathbf{r}_4$ to the defined point $i + 1$, $\mathbf{r}_2$ and $\mathbf{r}_3$ are respectively computed on the entity connecting the defined points $i-1$ with $i+1$ and i with $i+2$ in order to get tangential values at $t = 0$ and $t = 1$ (Shimada, 1984).

By means of the above equations, and taking into account the space covered by the observer's movement (using the given speed in Newtonian motion equations) it is possible to define for every instant of the animation (say 1/25 of a second), the position of the observer and all the other parameters necessary for the perspective transformation of the space seen.

Plates 25 and 26 show two projections, respectively on the planes x, y and x, z of the studied model and the defined points of the observer's navigation path. The green lines connect the observer position and the point seen: this allows control of the movement of the hypothetical camera used to see the model in order to avoid unrequested rotations, both in the vertical and the horizontal plane.

This method has two remarkable advantages:

1. changes of the given values for a point take effect on the spline only for two sections before the modified point and two sections after it;
2. any modification to a single value in the path results as a soft global variation as it involves the participation of the whole group of defined quantities.

4.2.3. External actions

Two external actions are considered: earthquakes and impulsive actions. For earthquakes the user action consists of collecting the data of a seismic oscillograph in order to obtain, using Fourier harmonic analysis, the values of the most significant components which will be applied to the computed eigenvalues, obtaining by superposition the parameters of the solution to the model.

With impulsive actions it is necessary to define an external action time history and submit it to the computer program, evaluating subsequent displacements of the numerical model modes.

4.3. NEW CODES

The phase which leads to the generation of the global animation database is thus composed of activities performed by means of a set of dedicated codes for defining geometries which describe the evolution of the structure's movements, referred to the eigenshapes and eigenvalues, or to the effect of the external dynamic actions.

In order to meet the representation requirements of each class of the problems tackled, they are constantly updated or integrated with new versions or implementations.

Two of the requirements which have recently emerged have led to the development of new programs for assembling geometries, suitable for treating different geometries simultaneously and to which independent actions are applied, and for treating heterogeneous geometries where the external actions have different effects on the types of component materials.

4.3.1. Homogeneous multiple geometries

It is often necessary to examine simultaneously the behavior of a structure according to different eigenshapes and eigenvalues, in order to be able to evaluate the differences between the deformations, phases and amplitudes.

The new code is able to copy the topological and numerical elements of the original nondeformed geometry several times, distancing each copy appropriately and assembling the whole in a single group in order to be utilized by the visualization programs to create the required global effect.

For each copy of the original geometry, the algorithm which describes the harmonic motion representing each eigenshape and eigenvalue considered is applied simultaneously but with different working parameters. The start, amplitude and duration of the motion of each individual copy is suitably parametrized to take into account the different scales of representation and the phase differences calculated previously.

Plate 27 shows an animation frame produced to compare six different vibration modes of the same structure simultaneously.

4.3.2. Heterogeneous geometries

When the numerical model used for dynamic analysis is composed of different materials, each with a different dynamic behavior according to their nature, the codes generating the movement geometries must be able to represent these differences realistically.

A typical case is the study of a dam, bearing in mind the presence of the retained liquid basin, given the compressibility of the liquid. The effect of the participation of the liquid mass in the dynamic events is indicated by the change in amplitude, form and phase of the eigenshapes and eigenvalues of the dam, while pulsating pressures occur in the liquid basin, with similar frequencies to those of the structure, but with different phases.

The new code utilized to generate the motion geometry represents the pressures in the liquid mass with shifts proportional to it, on a scale which takes adequate account of the shifts of the dam. The representative shift vector has a constant orientation chosen at random in order to highlight the shift itself as far as possible without interfering with the movement of the structure.

The algorithm used in the same code to represent the surface waves caused by movements of the dam is, however, more complex. This is not shown in the computation of the eigenshapes and eigenvalues, since the liquid mass is considered to participate by means of the pressures induced and the movement of the structure produces lengthening of the order of micrometers, which renders the surface movements imperceptible. In animation visualizations, the lengthening of the structure must be emphasized considerably so that surface movements can be seen (they are normally a sixth of the maximum dimension of the figure), and thus, with similar shifts, the formation of surface waves in the liquid mass could not be ignored.

The movement of the boundary nodes between the mesh of the liquid basin and the dam, defines the changes in the positions of the remaining surface nodes of the basin mesh.

The vertical shifts of the dam are transformed, using a predetermined parameter which represents the viscosity of the liquid, into increments of the horizontal movements occurring at the basin surface.

The movements of each node of the free surface is obtained by summing the components due to each boundary node. The components are proportional to the cosine of the angle formed by the vector of movement of the boundary nodes and the links with the individual nodes of the free surface.

In order to construct a time "history", account should be taken of the speed of propagation of the wave which is a result of the speed of motion of the boundary nodes and of the damping parameter affecting the space covered by the wave calculated. Any reflected waves are not taken into account.

This procedure allows the propagation of the waves during and after the dam shifts to be represented, obtaining a sufficiently realistic effect from a quality point of view.

The assembler program for the database relating to the representations both of the modal movements and those caused by external actions, thus incorporates the movements of the dam and those of the surface of the liquid mass for visualization by means of the graphic plotting program.

Plate 28 shows an animation frame for indicating the first eigenshape, with enlarged displacement values of the dam with the movement of the basin surface.

4.4. FRAME GENERATION AND VIDEO RECORDER SYNCHRONIZATION

The generation of a graphic animation in real time is quite impossible with current standard graphic workstations if the numerical model is represented with a large number of finite elements, even if all graphic data are stored after computation and then just displayed.

As every frame of the animation is finally projected in 1/25 or 1/30 of second, corresponding to the television frame frequency, shorter visualization time is necessary, currently available only with very big and expensive machines.

To make an offline time-independent generation, a frame-by-frame approach is necessary; in this way every frame of the animation is generated, no matter how long the visualization process lasts, and then stored on a video recorder.

Using a videodisk recorder, every frame can be immediately stored as soon as it is visualized on the graphic workstation screen, but the capacity of a professional videodisk recorder is limited to 1500 frames, that is 1 min of animation. This requires recursive generation of groups of frames and transferral to a videotape recorder.

A videotape recorder may be used unattended if the whole process is controlled by means of software synchronizing the rendering activities and the recorder.

Normally there is a hardware tool interposed between the graphic workstation and the videotape recorder, in order to convert the high resolution video signals into PAL or NTSC as necessary and to control the videotape movement. This interface may thus be driven by means of a link with an asynchronous port of the graphic workstation.

A script running on the graphic workstation can then synchronize the dialogue between the converter and the graphic rendering software, following all the mechanical movements of the videotape recorder as prerolling, positioning, inserting of the frame and postrolling of the tape, utilizing all the time necessary for these video tape activities to compute and render every frame.

Most of the animations carried out using this approach were obtained using continuous videotape movement, inserting all the frames generated without any operator action. The whole animation process could operate continuously 24 h a day up to completion.

4.5. THE ANIMATION PRESENTED

The subject of this animation is the study of the eigenshapes and eigenvalues and the seismic behavior of the Talvacchia dam, situated in central Italy in the Province of Ascoli Piceno, taking into account the participation of the retained liquid basin. The dam, built in 1960, is a concrete arch-gravity structure, with a volume of approximately $100,000 \, m^3$, a height above the foundations of 77 m and a development at the crest of 224 m. The artificial basin has a volume of 15 million m^3.

The numerical model is composed of a finite-element mesh of 1650 elements and 5100 nodes, for a total of *ca* 8000 degrees of freedom.

In the first part of the animation an observer follows a navigation path around the model as shown in Plate 29. The aim of this journey is to allow participation in the consistency of the structure in all its details.

The first seven eigenshapes and eigenvalues are later shown in sequence, with deformations suitably emphasized and alterating time scales to facilitate observation.

The first four shapes and eigenvalues are typical of the dam structure; from the fifth onwards the effects of the participation of the retained liquid mass are mainly apparent.

An overview summarizing the first eigenshapes and eigenvalues on six copies of the dam is then shown, indicating the differences between the modal forms and their frequencies, also taking into account compression of the time scale.

Finally, after having shown the oscillograph of an earthquake recorded on 4 September 1987 at the base and crest of the dam, the seismic behavior of the model is represented, visualized with deformations having the same scale used for the eigenshapes and eigenvalues and with different time scales to allow the observer to appreciate the phenomenon as a whole.

Plate 30 shows the animation frame at the instant corresponding to the maximum deformation during the earthquake.

4.6. APPLICATIONS CARRIED OUT

Various animations relating to structural and dynamic hydraulic problems have been carried out to date in the scientific–engineering field.

The visualization techniques adopted initially were based on wire-frame representations by means of COM graphics tools and a later reversed version on videotape (Fenini, 1979; Piatti, 1986; Crutzen *et al.*, 1987; Fanelli, 1989; Fenini, 1989a).

The advances in graphical plotting devices and graphical visualization codes have led to products of higher graphical quality using representation techniques based on rendering for sculptured surfaces, where a source for lighting the model exhibited is also included (Fenini, 1989b, 1992).

The methods used to solve the problems encountered have become a reference standard for subsequent projects (Fenini, 1989a) and the diagrams adopted facilitate updating and development of the working procedures.

4.7. CONCLUSIONS

Scientific research methods for dynamic structural problems are developing continually, thanks to greater understanding of the results provided by visualization via animation. The importance of graphical representation has become such that it must be considered essential for this type of analysis. At the same time the visualization techniques must evolve constantly in order to provide tools which are even easier to use and more effective, thus allowing an increasingly broad range of situations and aspects of the problems dealt with to be explored. The new possibilities demonstrated in this presentation are only a small step forward towards increasing knowledge.

Many problems involved in an increasingly realistic representation of the models used have still to be solved both in the field of analysis (taking into account more complex boundary conditions, examining nonlinear situations, etc.) and in graphics, where representations of more sophisticated quality (based for example on ray-tracing techniques) enable greater realism to be achieved for better understanding and communication.

Further consideration can be made of the importance of the commitment required to improve the quality and performance of the software adopted. With the availability of efficient graphical codes and compact databases it will be possible in the near future, when the performance of graphics hardware has reached the expected levels, to try to obtain good quality animations in real time for complex problems.

REFERENCES

Crutzen, J., Piatti, E. and Fenini, G. (1987). Engineering animation on the structural response of NET First Wall under vibration modes and electromagnetic-mechanical transient. Videotape presented at SMIRT Conference, Section 52. Lausanne, ORA 33630.

Fanelli, M. (1989). Ecoulements stationnaires et instationnaires, et cavitation. Videotape, presented at XXmes Journees de l'Hydraulique, Lyon.

Fenini, G. (1979). Animazione grafica mediante computer output microfilm. *Quaderni di Informatica* **11**(1).

Fenini, G. (1989a). Esperienze di animazione grafica computerizzata. Videotape, submitted to the Posters section of the Workshop Conoscenza per Immagini, Roma.

Fenini, G. (1989b). Esperienze di animazione grafica computerizzata. Problemi e metodologie nella tecnica delle animazioni. *PIXEL* **10**(12).

Fenini, G. (1992). Indagini dinamiche sui resti del Tempio di Marte Ultore al Foro di Augusto in Roma. Videotape, submitted to the Secondo Convegno Nazionale Conoscenza per Immagini. C.N.R., Roma.

Piatti, E. (1986/7). Animazione computerizzata di stutture soggette a transitori elettromagnetici: applicazione allo studio di un reattore a fusione Termonucleare. Tesi di laurea al Politecnico di Milano.

Shimada, S. (1984). *Computational Geometry for Structural Engineering*. Nagoya University.

Zienkievicz, O. C. (1972). *The Finite Element Method In Engineering Science*. McGraw-Hill.

About the author

Giuseppe Fenini graduated as Building Expert in 1954 and started his career in an architectural project management company. At the end of 1955 he joined the Edison Spa where he was engaged in a research branch devoted to hydraulic and hydrologic activities in order to develop projects for new hydro-electric power plants. In the 1960s, when the company became a National Electricity Power Board, he started his informatics activities, creating and managing a departmental computing center and leading a team of researchers with the aim of developing computing programs in the fields of stress analysis and fluid dynamics using a finite-element approach. At the same time he started a wide activity in the field of computer graphics representations using several output media and creating techniques of visualization by means of computer animations.

Chapter 5
Animation aerodynamics

Jakub Wejchert and David Haumann

5.1. INTRODUCTION

Every year leaves fall from trees and gather on the autumn ground; winds blow and scatter them in currents, whirlpools and eddies; it seems as if it were the last magical dance of leaf life. This charming motion is a consequence of aerodynamics: the description of fluid flow and its relation to the motion of solid objects. To animate and control such motion by computer proves an intriguing and rewarding task.

5.1.1. Relevant models

The motivation of physical realism has driven computer animators to design a variety of models of natural phenomena, some of which are relevant to our goal. Particle-based systems have mimicked the visual appearance of fire (Reeves, 1983), waterfalls (Sims, 1990) and viscous jets (Miller and Pearce, 1989). Although these models have produced stunning effects, they are quite difficult to control, and they cannot account for the extra degrees of freedom associated with solid objects. Models of bird flocking (Reynolds, 1987; Amkraut and Girard, 1989) were successful at drawing many independent objects in motion with some degree of control, but were not strictly based on physical laws. Models of fluids, such as ocean foam (Fournier and Reeves, 1986) and shallow water (Kass and Miller, 1990) have displayed the visual appearance of liquid surfaces, but are not useful for representing air currents for aerodynamics. Simulations of flexible objects (Platt and Barr, 1988; Terzopoulos *et al.*, 1988; Haumann and Parent, 1988; Norton *et al.*, 1990) have typically displayed the elasticity of one solid object; related models of flags (Terzopoulos *et al.*, 1987; Haumann and Parent, 1988) could exhibit flapping motion without reference to external wind. In summary, not any one of these models addresses the dynamics of fluid flows combined with the motion of flexible solid objects. Furthermore, the models do not provide a consistent approach for controling the simulations.

Usually, models of natural phenomena are too complex to be applied by an animator using traditional techniques (Lasseter, 1987; Barr, 1989). A number of researchers have addressed this problem. Pintado and Fuime,

1989) describe a kinematic approach using dynamic splines that allows the interactive control of object motion in nonphysical two-dimensional fields. Methods based on constraints allow animations to be controled by specifying the geometric relationships between rigid objects (Barzel and Barr, 1988). By applying optimization techniques, physically based motion can be keyframed (Platt and Barr, 1988; Witkin and Kass, 1988; Brotman and Netravali, 1988). However, these techniques can be numerically intensive and become unwieldly for controling collections of objects with many degrees of freedom.

5.1.2. An aerodynamic model with control

In this chapter, we describe a fast aerodynamic way of modeling and controling the motion of many flexible objects in fluid currents in three dimensions. Usually, just concentrating on the physics results in lack of control. Surprisingly, in this case the formalism, provides convenient handles for the design and control of animation sequences.

In principle, the physics of the problem should require numerical solutions of the Navier–Stokes equations for fluid flow with immersed solid objects. To avoid this computational expense, we divide the system into two parts: a linear flow regime and an object boundary regime. The first ranges over all space and the second is used in the vicinity of solid objects. In the linear flow regime we use the analytical solutions of the equations instead of solving the flow numerically. These solutions define a set of flow primitives, which are given as fluid velocity fields. Solutions such as vortices, sinks and uniform flows, can be linearly mixed so as to create a complex flow scenario, which is still an actual solution of the Navier–Stokes equation. The second part of the physical model is the interaction between the flow and the objects. This is based on simplified boundary effects, which describe the forces exerted on object surfaces. Once the forces acting on objects are known, object motion is governed by Newtonian mechanics. With the appropriate adjustment of parameters, such as density and viscosity, the methods can be used to represent the motion of objects in liquids or air.

The methodology naturally presents a design and control mechanism for animation, by providing a set of building blocks for constructing flows. In the same way as complex geometrical objects can be built from geometrical primitives, one can create complex flows from a set of flow primitives. The methods are also useful because they can be used to create realistic flow around obstacles, and using time-dependent flows the timing of animation sequences can be directed. Norton's model (Norton *et al.*, 1990a) has the capability of modeling many solid objects simultaneously and thus provides a convenient framework for the integration of the methods into an existing physically based simulator.

5.1.3. Overview

This chapter is organized as follows. First we give a background to fluid mechanics, and show how the relevant equations can be linearized. We introduce the use of flow primitives as a motion design tool, and then discuss object boundary effects and define a fluid–object interaction. We then show how the methods are integrated into an existing physically based simulator. Finally, we describe how the methods were used in making an animation called "Leaf Magic" (Norton *et al.*, 1990b).

5.2. Linearized fluid mechanics

The Navier–Stokes equation is the standard and general way of expressing . the mechanics of a fluid (Batchelor, 1967; Feynman *et al.*, 1965; Patterson, 1989). It can be grouped into two parts that correspond to Newton's second law $F - ma = 0$. The Navier–Stokes equation may be written as

$$\frac{\partial \mathbf{v}}{\partial t} + (\mathbf{v}.\nabla)\mathbf{v} + \frac{1}{\rho}\nabla p + \nabla\psi - \frac{\eta}{\rho}\nabla^2\mathbf{v} = 0. \tag{1}$$

A solution of this is $\mathbf{v}$, the velocity field of the fluid. This is a vector field: for every point in space there is a velocity vector giving the magnitude and direction of the fluid at that point (Bourne and Kendall, 1977; Feynman *et al.*, 1965). The fluid density is given by ρ, η is the viscosity, p and ψ are the scalar fields of pressure and gravitational potential. The equation can be greatly simplified with the assumption that the flow is (a) inviscid, $\eta = 0$; (b) irrotational, the curl $(\nabla \times \mathbf{v})$ of the velocity is zero; and (c) incompressible, $\nabla.\mathbf{v} = 0$. This idealized flow can exhibit a variety of motions. It is a reasonable model for air at normal speeds when it does not exhibit turbulence. With condition (a) the last term in eq. (1) disappears. Next we rewrite the remainder of eq. (1) so that (b) and (c) can be easily imposed. First, let us use the relation that

$$(\mathbf{v}.\nabla)\mathbf{v} = (\nabla \times \mathbf{v}) \times \mathbf{v} + \frac{1}{2}\nabla(\mathbf{v}.\mathbf{v}). \tag{2}$$

Defining the rotation as $\Omega = \nabla \times \mathbf{v}$, eq. (1) reduces to

$$\frac{\partial \mathbf{v}}{\partial t} + \Omega \times \mathbf{v} + \frac{1}{2}\nabla(v^2) = -\frac{1}{\rho}\nabla p - \nabla\psi. \tag{3}$$

By taking curl of both sides and since $\nabla \times \nabla\psi = 0$ for any scalar field ψ, we get

$$\frac{\partial \Omega}{\partial t} + \nabla \times (\Omega \times \mathbf{v}) = 0. \tag{4}$$

So, if we impose condition (b) then a solution of the Navier–Stokes equation satisfies

$$\nabla \times \mathbf{v} = 0. \tag{5}$$

Physically this means that infinitesimal fluid volume elements do not rotate, but motion of the fluid as a whole may circulate. This coupled with the continuity condition (c) for an incompressible fluid results in our simplified system that is inviscid, irrotational and incompressible. As a result of imposing the conditions, it is also steady in that the fluid moves along paths that do not change with time. It remains to show that with condition (c) it is a linear system. Equation (5) implies that **v** can be written as the gradient of a scalar field (since $\nabla \times \nabla\phi = 0$), that is

$$\mathbf{v} = \nabla\phi. \tag{6}$$

Then from the continuity condition (c) we must have

$$\nabla.\mathbf{v} = \nabla.\nabla\phi = \nabla^2\phi = 0. \tag{7}$$

This is Laplace's equation; it is a linear second order differential equation which implies that if we find any two analytical solutions to this equation then their linear combination is also a solution. The application of boundary conditions then results in a physical solution. Typically, this requires that the flow should (a) be uniform at infinity and (b) have no normal component at obstacle boundaries. In this way we bypass the task of solving the fluid equations numerically, and we are guaranteed that the fluid motion will be physically correct if we linearly add the solutions. This provides a fast and simple technique for creating fluid flows for animation.

5.3. Flow primitives

From eq. (6) the fluid velocity v describing a flow is given by $\nabla\phi$ for a field ϕ. We call a velocity field that satisfies the Laplace equation and also satisfies the boundary conditions a flow primitive. Given a set of flow primitives, an animator can construct complicated flows from these basic building blocks. The simplest primitive is uniform flow. Consider a potential field given by

$$\phi = ax + by + cz, \tag{8}$$

which is obviously a solution of eq. (7). The velocity field is given by

$$\mathbf{v}_x = a, \mathbf{v}_y = b, \mathbf{v}_z = c, \tag{9}$$

in which case the velocity lines follow straight lines and a, b, c are constants that give the fluid speeds in the respective directions. Other primitives include source, sink and vortex flows. A source is a point from which fluid moves out in all directions; a sink is a point to which fluid flows uniformly in all directions and disappears, and fluid moves around a vortex in concentric circles. It is more convenient to write the remaining primitives in cylindrical coordinates (r, θ, z). For example, the potential and the velocity field for a line of source at the origin, with strength a, can be written as

$$\phi = \frac{a}{2\pi}\ln r; \mathbf{v}_r = \frac{a}{2\pi r}; \mathbf{v}_\theta = 0; \mathbf{v}_z = 0. \tag{10}$$

For a sink the constant a is set negative. A vortex at the origin with strength b is given by

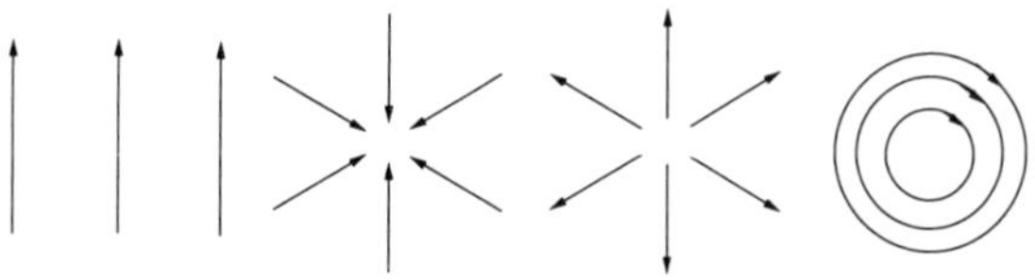

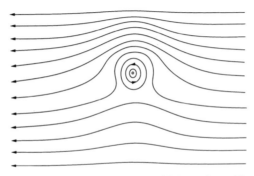

Figure 5.1. A schematic diagram of the flow primitives.

$$\phi = \frac{b}{2\pi}\,\theta;\, \mathbf{v}_r = 0;\, \mathbf{v}_\theta = \frac{b}{2\pi r};\, \mathbf{v}_z = 0. \tag{11}$$

It is straightforward to show that these scalar fields satisfy the Laplace equation in cylindrical coordinates. Figure 5.1 shows streamline diagrams of the primitive flows, showing the paths the fluids follow.

5.3.1. Addition of flows

Because the system is linear we can add the basic flows together:

$$\mathbf{V} = \mathbf{v}_{\text{vort}}(x, y, z) + \mathbf{v}_{\text{sink}}(x, y, z) + \mathbf{v}_{\text{source}}(x, y, z) + \ldots \tag{12}$$

thereby creating a more complicated velocity field, V. Figure 5.2 shows the result of adding a uniform flow with a vortex. This corresponds to a fluid velocity field given by $\mathbf{v}_r = a\,\cos(\theta);\, \mathbf{v}_\theta = -a\,\sin(\theta) + b/2\pi r$. The method of adding elementary flows to obtain a more complex flow is used extensively in aerodynamics (Anderson, 1985).

A fluid velocity field depends on the absolute position in space (x, y, z) and parameters such as fluid speeds or positions of the flow primitives. We write this as $\mathbf{v}(x, y, z, \Lambda)$, where Λ refers to the parameters. Thus from eq. (12) the fluid flow built out of primitives is described by

$$V = \sum_k \mathbf{v}_k(x, y, z, \Lambda). \tag{13}$$

Here each $\mathbf{v}_k$ refers to any of the basic flow types, each with a set of parameters Λ that are available to the user. Thus, the methods naturally

Figure 5.2. Streamlines that result from the addition of a uniform and vortex flow.

present a design tool, by providing a set of building blocks of flows whose positions and strengths can be chosen. Just as complicated geometrical objects can be built from primitives, complex physically correct flows can be designed from a set of flow primitives. The flow defines the whole temporal path of the fluid at the beginning, middle and end of the motion. It enables a simple physically based way of designing the paths of solid objects, instead of using trial and error from initial conditions. Once objects are placed in the fluid, their trajectories have already been designed by the user to a first approximation. However, the degree to which objects follow the flow lines depends on the fluid–object interaction.

5.3.2. Flow obstacles

We can also use flow primitives to design flows around large solid obstacles, and to bound the spatial extent of a flow. Obstacles can be built out of primitives that are strong enough to cause a main flow to be directed from certain regions. Similar methods are used in aerodynamics to study the flow around obstacles such as airfoils (Anderson, 1985). Figure 5.3 shows the effect of adding together a uniform flow with a point source. This can be taken to represent flow around a solid object, since no fluid flows across the streamline shown in bold. This approach is faster than normal collision detection algorithms and allows the smooth and natural motion of the objects as they interact with obstacles. The method was used to show the motion of leaves around obstacles such as slides or walls. We also used primitives to build flow fields that are bounded in spatial extent. For example, to create a bounded field, a set of sources was placed on a plane A and a set of sinks (of equal strength) on a parallel plane B. To a first approximation this results in a nonzero field between A and B and zero everywhere else. We could use bounding fields to confine objects in space in a natural way.

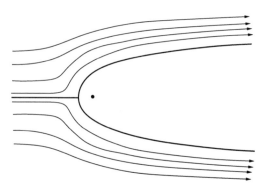

Figure 5.3. Creating solid obstacles to flow using the addition of primitives. The solid line represents a stagnation boundary across which no fluid can travel.

5.3.3. Time-varying flows

Since the above flows have no time dependence, they can only be used to build a velocity field with spatial variation. We can also model some time-dependent flows that are physically correct to within the approximations used. The required condition is that the flow cannot be not influenced by itself or the objects therein, and changes to the primitives are directed externally. This can be interpreted as the evolution of a number of time-dependent linear solutions:

$$V = \sum_k \mathbf{v}_k(x, y, z, \Lambda, t). \tag{14}$$

Time-varying fields enable a user to change the flow lines, by directing the positions of the primitives defining it with time. This gives a further degree of control on top of the time independent situation. It allows obstacles to move and events to occur at specific times. Coupled with bounded fields, it enables the control of collections of objects to follow specified paths.

5.4. FLUID–OBJECT INTERACTION

The division of fluid flow into two regimes, linear flow and boundary layer, simplifies our general problem. For the major part, the fluids are taken to behave as a linear inviscid system as described in the previous section. However, in the vicinity of objects we have to include boundary effects: viscous drag and pressures differences. In this way, forces exerted on the objects may be calculated.

5.4.1. Particles in flows

We consider two cases: the first is when the fluid exerts forces on particles, the second when the fluid acts on surface areas of larger objects. The first can be based on the Stoke drag equation. This gives the force exerted on a spherical particle with radius a, moving with relative velocity $\mathbf{v}^r$ in a fluid with viscosity η as

$$\mathbf{F} = 6\pi a\eta\mathbf{v}^r. \tag{15}$$

Given a mass particle i at position x, y, z, with velocity p, the relative velocity with respect to a fluid velocity field v is

$$\mathbf{v}_i^r = \mathbf{v} - \mathbf{p}_i, \tag{16}$$

where $\mathbf{v} = \mathbf{v}(x, y, z)$. So from eq. (15), we define the force on the particle i as

$$\mathbf{F}_i = \alpha\mathbf{v}_i^r, \tag{17}$$

where α is a constant that represents a coupling strength between the fields and the particles. This is a physically based equation that describes dynamic control. If particles are not moving at the field velocity they will experience large adjustment forces until they do so. The coupling strength α is related to the viscosity through eq. (17). If α (and therefore η) is large then we have a strong coupling between the particles and field. This will result in particles being forced to follow the flow quite closely, as they would in a viscous fluid. If α is small this coupling is weaker and if $\alpha = 0$ then the fluid fields have no effect on the particles. It turns out that the form of eq. (17) is similar to a control-based system used to direct the motion of particles along two-dimensional spline fields (Pintado and Fuime, 1989).

5.4.2. Objects in flows

Representing an object as a mass particle does not result in any rotational effects. To account for the fluid acting on an area, a more sophisticated surface model has to be used. In this case, forces acting on a surface depend on its area and orientation with respect to the relative velocity vector. Surfaces defining an object are divided into triangular patches with a mass point at each vertex. The relative velocity of any of the three particles is resolved into the normal and tangential components with respect to the triangular surface (Figure 5.4):

$$\mathbf{v}_i^r = \mathbf{v}_i^n + \mathbf{v}_i^t, \tag{18}$$

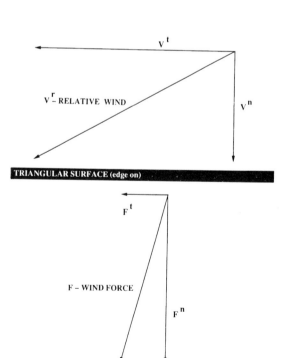

Figure 5.4. Side view of a triangular area in a fluid. An object surface is made up out of many triangular patches.

where $\mathbf{v}_i^n$ is the normal component and $\mathbf{v}_i^t$ is the tangential component. The normal component of the force is due to pressure differences in front of and behind the object. Consider the case of a uniform flow that impinges on a flat surface. The speed of the fluid is v and has density ρ. Thus the mass of fluid impinging on the area A is $\rho A v \delta t$. The force on the area is given by the momentum change

$$F = \frac{\delta m}{\delta t} = \rho A v^2 . \tag{19}$$

To calculate the tangential component, we consider the force exerted laterally on the surface due to the viscosity of the fluid. This is given by the viscous shear stress times the area:

$$F = A\eta \frac{dv}{dy}, \tag{20}$$

where y is measured from the object surface into the fluid. For a nonslip condition we have at $y = 0$, $v = 0$ and for $y \rightarrow \infty$, $v \rightarrow v^t$. Typically the velocity profile is parabolic, but in the vicinity of the surface we may take it to be linear:

$$F \sim A\eta \mathbf{v}^t . \tag{21}$$

Therefore we write the normal and tangential forces as

$$\mathbf{F}_i^n = \alpha^n A v \mathbf{v}_i^n , \tag{22}$$

$$\mathbf{F}_i^t = \alpha^t A \mathbf{v}_i^t . \tag{23}$$

$\mathbf{F}^n$ is the force experienced by a surface facing into the fluid, while $\mathbf{F}^t$ is due to the viscous drag of fluid flowing across the surface; A is the area of the triangular element. This may be interpreted as a generalization of eq. (17): a set of physically based dynamic control equations, that determine the degree to which objects follow the fluid. Finally, it remains to point out that the fluid description can be used to represent the motion of solid objects in liquids or air by the appropriate adjustment of masses, density and viscosity.

5.4.3. Overall approximations

In our model we have chosen a balance between physical exactness, execution speed and control. For example, linearized air flow cannot exhibit turbulence – but if we used a nonlinear system: (a) mixing flow primitives would give nonphysical solutions, (b) it would be numerically intensive. Objects in wind exhibit complex motion mainly due to their geometry and fluid–object interaction (little is due to the local turbulence of the fluid itself) so using a linear fluid is not unreasonable. It should also be understood that dividing the system into two parts results in the flows affecting the objects and not vice versa. This holds better for small objects, spaced relatively wide apart.

5.5.   SIMULATION

We integrated the methods into an existing simulator, that models the flexibility and fracture of solid objects (Norton, 1990a). In the simulator, flexible and brittle objects can be built of masses and springs that are governed by Newtonian mechanics. For example, a three-dimensional mesh of interconnected masses and springs can be used to model a flexible sheet. This can be molded into geometrical shapes such as cylinders or spheres. The flexibility of an object can be changed by altering the spring constants; to simulate breaking or tearing, springs can break if stretched beyond a given threshold.

The evolution of a collection of objects with time is carried out by integrating Newton's second law, $\mathbf{F} = m\mathbf{a}$. At each time step Δt, and for each mass particle i of mass m, making up an object, the total force $\mathbf{F}$ acting on the point is computed. The total force is made up of contributions from gravity, spring stretching and external fluid flows

$$\mathbf{F}_i = \mathbf{F}_{\text{grav}} + \mathbf{F}_{\text{spring}} + \mathbf{F}_{\text{fluid}} + \dots . \tag{24}$$

This determines the acceleration a_i of that particle as $\mathbf{a}_i(t) = \mathbf{F}_i/m_t$ from which the extrapolated velocity $p_i(t + \Delta t)$ and position $r_i(t + \Delta t)$ can be calculated using a Runge–Kutta method. Once all the positions have been updated the same cycle is repeated for N time steps, making up a full simulation sequence.

It can be seen that the introduction of forces due to a fluid interaction is straightforward, as these are simply added into the sum given by eq. (24). In this way we could simulate the motion of solid objects in liquid or air currents. The simplicity of the fluid field description allows it to be easily incorporated into the simulator, thereby extending the range of natural phenomena modeled.

5.6.   MOTION DESIGN

We return to our original theme: the motion of leaves in gentle or sometimes turbulent winds. To design an animation showing a collection of objects (leaves) being blown by wind, we followed a number of steps.

1. Design of leaf geometries and construct them out of masses and springs in the simulator.
2. Design a set of wind fields that will define the motion paths of the objects during a sequence.
3. Simulate the motion and preview results using a field visualizer and animation previewer.
4. Make changes to the wind velocities, fluid–object interaction, position of flow primitives, or number of objects.
5. Finally, ray trace a sequence.

Our user interface mainly consisted of a previewer that could perform rapid rendering and real-time animation. This was useful for visualizing the flows by using point particles and studying the effects of the fluid–object interactions by doing a rapid rendering of solid objects in motion.

The subsequent examples describe animation scenes, each of which used some aspect of the techniques discussed in this chapter. Our animation story described playful autumn leaves in a playground with a garbage bin.

5.6.1. Object geometry

Our first test leaves were simply point particles, whose motion in air was directed by eq. (17). These were useful for seeing the overall motion of collections of leaves in air currents. To exhibit individual rotational motion, a leaf was built out of masses and springs using the geometry of seven triangles. The leaf was duplicated with slight variations in geometry, mass distribution and stiffness. The fluid–object interaction equations (22) and (23) cause thin objects to glide and twirl, because of the different forces experienced in the lateral and tangential directions. Leaves which exhibited interesting, lilting, fluttering motion were selected for the animation sequences. Plate 31, color section shows a shot from the animation of leaves gently floating in a breeze. The leaves are covered with texture maps using transparency to define the irregular leaf boundary. In this case the field is uniform and it is the object geometry and the nature of the fluid–object interaction that causes individual motion.

5.6.2. Obstacles and flow strengths

By combining field primitives as described by eq. (13), complex motion paths could be designed. This enabled us to build large obstacles to flow around which the leaves would travel. An animation sequence required leaves first to be blown over a wall by strong winds and then to swirl around in a playground. Part of this sequence included leaves blowing up a slide. To do this, a uniform field was used as the main driving flow and leaves then passed over an obstacle wedge made out of fields that directed the flow lines from penetrating the slide geometry. This enabled the smooth motion of leaves blowing over the solid obstacle (Plate 32). The second part of the sequence required leaves to be blown by a whirlwind and then float towards the ground as the wind subsided. The whirlwind action was based on a set of vortex primitives set at different angles, which were then decreased in strength over time, allowing gravity to dominate (Plate 33).

5.6.3. Bounded and time-varying flows

Later in the animation, the appearance of a group of leaves hovering in the wind was achieved by using a uniform flow acting vertically so as to cancel the effect of gravity. This was combined with a bounded field to keep the leaves hovering within a desired volume. A strong wind gust was required to move rapidly upward through the hovering leaves. This was achieved by successively moving the two bounded flows up through the collection of leaves with time (eq. (14)). The first flow had a strong upward component causing the leaves to rise momentarily and to collect near its upper boundary. The second flow contained a strong downward component designed to pull the leaves rapidly down to the ground.

5.6.4. Adding flow primitives

Turbulent-like and directed motion could be achieved by mixing and positioning flow primitives, as in eq. (13). In the animation, the frivolous behavior of the leaves could not be tolerated by the garbage bin and a chase resulted. Once the leaves landed on the ground, a uniform horizontal field caused the leaves to be blown away from the bin as if escaping. Plate 34 shows these leaves tumbling along the ground to escape the pursuit of the garbage bin in the background. Later, after a fruitless chase, the bin inhales all the leaves flying above it. The combination of a vortex, sink and uniform flow was used. For dramatic effect the leaves were pulled in by a cyclone consisting of vortex and sink primitives coincident with the bin mouth (Plate 35). The strength of a sink was set so as to make the flow lines converge into the mouth of the bin at the end of the sequence, causing the leaves to be funneled in and down (Plate 36).

5.7. CONCLUSIONS

We have described a methodology based on aerodynamics and fluid mechanics that can be used for object motion simulation and control. We took care to design a model that was physically consistent, and could also meet some of the requirements of animation, such as speed and control. The approach is much faster than the numerical solution of the Navier–Stokes equations with immersed objects. Furthermore, it allows the creation of fluid currents from flow primitives, which can be used to design flows and object motion paths both in time and space. Coupled with the fluid–object forces, the methodology provides a way of both simulating and controlling the motion of multiple objects in the physically based paradigm.

Future extensions to the project could include physically based aerodynamic flight of birds or airplanes; leaves are just one example. Another extension would allow the objects to affect the fluid fields in a physically based way, so as to create more accurate motion. Although we have given a theoretical basis to our work, the actual applications of the methods are quite simple. We hope that the methods could be integrated by others into their physically based simulation systems.

ACKNOWLEDGMENTS

We wish to give credit to the members of the Animation Systems Group Alan Norton, Bob Bacon, Paula Sweeney, Kavi Arya, Al Khorasani and Jane Jung, without whom the realization of the ideas would not have been possible. Thanks to Tim Kay, Greg Turk, John Snyder and John Hart for software support; to Mike Henderson for useful discussions on fluid mechanics; to staff at Winchester for encouragement and support; and to Roz Boland for proof reading.

REFERENCES

Amkraut, S. and Girard, M. (1989). Eurhythmy. *Siggraph Video Review*, Issue 52, selection 8 (SIGGRAPH '89 Film and Video Show, and supplement to *Computer Graphics*).

Anderson, J. (1985). *Fundamentals of Aerodynamics*. McGraw-Hill.

Barr, A. (1989). Teleogical modeling. In *SIGGRAPH '89 Course Notes on Topics in Physically Based Modeling*.

Barzel, R. and Barr, A. (1988). A modeling system based on dynamic constraints. *Computer Graphics (SIGGRAPH '88 Proceedings)* **22**(4), 179.

Batchelor, G. (1967). *An Introduction to Fluid Mechanics*. Cambridge University Press.

Bourne, D. and Kendall, P. (1977). *Vector Analysis and Cartesian Tensors*. Thomas Nelson.

Brotman, L. and Netravali, A. (1988). Motion interpolation by optimal control. *Computer Graphics (SIGGRAPH '88 Proceedings)* **22**(4), 309.

Feynman, R., Leighton, R. and Sands, M. (1965). *The Feynman Lectures on Physics*. Addison Wesley.

Fournier, A. and Reeves, W. (1986). A simple model of ocean waves. *Computer Graphics (SIGGRAPH '86 Proceedings)* **20**(4), 75.

Haumann, D. and Parent, R. (1988). The behavioral test-bed: obtaining complex behavior from simple rules. *The Visual Computer* **4**(6), 332.

Kass, M. and Miller, G. (1990). Rapid, stable fluid dynamics for computer graphics. *Computer Graphics (SIGGRAPH '90 Proceedings)* **24**(4), 49.

Lasseter, J. (1987). Principles of traditional animation applied to 3D computer animation. *Computer Graphics (SIGGRAPH '87 Proceedings)* **21**(4), 35.

Miller, G. and Pearce, A. (1989). Globular dynamics: a connected particle system for animating viscous fluids. *Computers and Graphics* **13**, 305.

Norton, A., Turk, G. and Bacon, R. (1990a). Animation and fracture by physical modeling. *The Visual Computer*.

Norton, A., Arya, K., Bacon, R., Haumann, D., Khorasani, A., Sweeney, P. and Wejchert, J. (1990b). *Leaf Magic*. Computer Generated Film.

Patterson, A. (1989). *A First Course in Fluid Dynamics*. Cambridge University Press.

Pintado, X. and Fuime, E. (1989). Gradfield: field-directed dynamics splines for interactive motion control. *Computers and Graphics* **13**, 77.

Platt, J. and Barr, A. (1988). Constraint methods for flexible models. *Computer Graphics (SIGGRAPH '88 Proceedings)* **22**(4), 279.

Reeves, W. (1983). Particle systems – a technique for modeling a class of fuzzy objects. *Computer Graphics (SIGGRAPH '83 Proceedings)* **17**(3), 359.

Reynolds, C. (1987). Flocks, herds and schools: a distributed behavioral model. *Computer Graphics (SIGGRAPH '87 Proceedings)* **21**(4), 25.

Sims, K. (1990). Particle animation and rendering using data parallel computation. *Computer Graphics (SIGGRAPH '90 Proceedings)* **24**(4), 405.

Terzopoulos, D. and Fleischer, K. (1988). Deformable models. *The Visual Computer* **4**, 306.

Terzopoulos, D., Platt, J., Barr, A. and Fleischer, K. (1987). Elastically deformable models. *Computer Graphics (SIGGRAPH '87 Proceedings)* **21**(4), 205.

Witkin, A. and Kass, M. (1988). Spacetime constraints. *Computer Graphics (SIGGRAPH '88 Proceedings)* **22**(4), 159.

About the authors

Jakub Wejchert is currently Project Officer with ESPRIT Basic Research at the European Commission. Present work involves the coordination of a number of research projects throughout the EC. He has worked in the areas of visualization and computer graphics simulation at the IBM Scientific Centre Winchester and at the IBM TJ Watson Research Center in New York. He obtained his PhD in simulational physics from Trinity College Dublin in 1988.

David Haumann's primary interest is in the use of computer graphics for creative and artistic purposes. He received his Batchelor of Science in Applied Mathematics from Brown University and his Ph.D. in Computer Science from The Ohio State University in 1989, where he concentrated his research efforts in graphics and animation. David is currently a research staff member at the IBM T. J. Watson Research Center in Yorktown Heights, NY, USA.

Chapter 6
Visual programming using high-level visualization motif widgets

Mikael Jern

6.1. INTRODUCTION

A key trend has emerged in the 1990s: application builders, programmers and users are looking for a fundamentally different approach to software development. They are looking for interactive construction of programs using highly graphical tools and reusable "standard" software components rather than the traditional process of software program development consisting of an iterative cycle of FORTRAN or C based source-code development, compilation and linking.

Interactive visual constructions of programs speeds development and increases productivity.

The favored phrase and solution is composed of two simple words: object and oriented. The term has been adopted by so many people in so many contexts that it is already beginning to lose some of its meaning. In this chapter, the focus will be on the first word "object" and I hope to provide you with a clear understanding of why this paradigm is so significant in our future application development.

The evolution of an object component industry seems like a natural consequence of the adoption of object technology. The whole idea of object-oriented (O-O) software development is to "program" by assembling rather than writing new software from scratch. This new development approach needs to recognize that not all application programmers will become O-O wizards and, furthermore, that it is not even desirable for all programmers to become experts. For many people on a development team, there is really no reason to be doing sophisticated O-O design. These people should use existing components designed and developed by experienced

ANIMATION AND SCIENTIFIC VISUALIZATION
ISBN 0-12-227745-7

O-O graphics developers. The point of reusable components is to provide a way of shielding non-O-O application programmers from the large complex class hierarchies and event handling typical of O-O development environments. These non-O-O developers have no need to use most of the classes in the hierarchy. Perhaps more important, they should not be messing around with the classes provided to them.

When you develop your new application, you do not have to replicate all the low-level work. You automatically get the benefits of that effort, when you used the reusable components, and most important: you are reusing not just the code but the results of the entire life cycle in a development process. There is a great variety of generic objects that could be used by developers in thousands of companies. Why should all these objects be developed simultaneously in every company?

The approach in this paper has numerous advantages, but it does require a ready supply of reusable objects. Where do these objects come from? This is an exciting commercial opportunity for specialty companies with expertise in particular areas to develop components and sell them to many different companies.

6.2. SOFTWARE DEVELOPERS FACE A VERY STEEP LEARNING CURVE

Although many software developers would like to jump on the "X/Motif bandwagon" immediately, they have discovered a number of obstacles. Initially, there was a problem over the choice of "look and feel". During 1990–91, there was some uncertainty about the likely success of OPEN LOOK or Motif. If you started developing using the wrong user interface style, you might end up with a noncompatible and unusable application. This uncertainty is now over; Motif is the obvious choice unless you are looking to address a "SUN only" policy. However, even SUN has now finally acknowledged Motif as the "standard" graphical user interface (GUI) toolkit.

The Motif toolkit provides the programmer with a library of C routines used to generate the GUI of an application. The programmer provides callback routines that are called when the user clicks on pushbuttons, makes selections from menus, or interacts in some other way. The callback routines will execute the code that makes the application do its job, for example, draw a contour map.

Qualified X and Motif expertise is still rare. This means that existing programmers have to learn a new programmer paradigm, and it will take a minimum of six to nine months before a programmer can even start doing any serious work with X and Motif, assuming he/she can pick up the new skills. Software developers face a very steep learning curve and must obsorb:

several programming layers, toolkits and GUI libraries;
hundreds of C function calls;
thousands of parameters and resource definitions;
an entirely new technical vocabulary;

event-driven architecture *vs* command-driven;
radical departure from linear logic programming to object-oriented;
at worst, a new programming language (C, C++).

The dramatic change in this new programming paradigm can be confusing for those new to X and Motif and require frequent reprogramming in application development.

The biggest problem of programming directly using the Motif toolkit is the large amount of knowledge required for a programmer to be productive and the amount of source code that has to be written to generate anything but the simplest application program. (Anderson, 1992).

The magic bullet to solve this problem can be found in using any of the excellent range of high-quality GUI builder products, user interface management systems (UIMS), to build interactively the Motif user interfaces. These products include TeleUSE from Telesoft, UIM/X from Visual Edge and Builder Xcessory from Integrated Computer Solutions.

These UIMS tools provide a palette of standard widgets and a layout area for arranging interface objects. Some UIMS tools also have a built-in C interpreter that allows the application code to be written, loaded, and linked with the user interface while the interface is being developed. Customized widgets can also be accessed inside a UIMS. This integrated development facility forms the framework for the visual programming concept described below.

6.3. LACK OF GRAPHICS WIDGETS IN MOTIF

The Motif widget set introduced by Open Software Foundation (OSF) has become the industry standard. The Motif widget set implements user interface components, including scroll bars, menus and buttons.

The Motif widget set supplies a set of components, which encapsulate a user interface standard as defined by the Motif Style Guide, which is sufficient for implementing an application interface. However, even with the richness of Motif, the functionality of its widget set remains at a fairly low level. Significant of its code must be written for any application to make use of the Motif widget set, and its underlying style. A simple form with a name, address, a query field and a response field may take several hundred lines of code just to manage the widget set and its inter-relationships. This fact has not gone unnoticed by the C community as a whole.

Given the current standard of the widgets supported in Motif, it is clear that the majority of development projects are likely to require development of customized widgets (Mikes and Keller, 1991, p. 30).

One of the more interesting ironies of Motif programming is that Motif, a tool designed for implementing GUI, has no drawing commands. It is nothing more than a set of user interface widgets and convenience functions.

If you want to create computer graphics in a Motif program, you have to drop down two levels and talk directly to the X library.

Many expert programmers have therefore chosen the X library (Xlib) as a base to build their visualization applications on. This low-level library can be tedious and difficult to use correctly. The X library provides a very low-level set of graphics drawing primitives such as draw dots, lines, arcs and text. Any attempt to draw an application object, such as a contour map, requires an excessive amount of calls to these low-level routines.

Some application programmers therefore prefer to use higher-level graphics libraries, designed to be used together with the X Window System. TOOLMASTER/agX from UNIRAS, DI-3000 from Precision Visuals and GL from Silicon Graphics are examples of such high-level visualization tools, which extend the low-level functionalities in X to a more comprehensive graphics library. (Note that the ISO standard graphics libraries GKS and PHIGS are not suitable to be used in an integrated X environment.) It is however, still cumbersome to develop an event-driven interactive graphics application at this level.

The evolution of an object component visualization industry therefore represents a solution to the problem. UNIRAS is the first graphics software company to provide standard, Motif-compliant, high-level *interactive* visualization components to the UNIX programming development environment (TOOLMASTER/Xplore).

The TOOMASTER/Xplore object-oriented user interface approach emphasizes a elaborate direct manipulation user interface technique. The visual programming components, i.e. "customized visualization widgets" allow developers to build graphics applications much faster than using convential graphics library programming techniques by fitting together screen jigsaw puzzle pieces into an application.

Customized visualization widgets represent a greater level of specialization than the Motif widget set. These widgets are generally enough for the user to reuse throughout their custom environment, yet also specific enough to solve their needs readily, easily and without a great deal of supporting code.

A custom widget is an object which encapsulates a particular behavior and its supporting data into a single abstract entity. It may inherit its attributes from the Motif widget set, another custom widget or the X toolkit as is appropriate.

The good news about high-level customized widgets is that the application programmer only needs to understand a widget's external, public interface to use a widget in a program.

6.4. THE IMPLEMENTATION ENVIRONMENT OF THE TOOLMASTER/XPLORE WIDGETS

The TOOLMASTER/Xplore visualization widgets are designed to provide professional application builders with a "programless" access to sophisticated visualization methods. The system includes numerous visualization objects for exploring data using two-dimensional (2D) and 3D contours, grid maps, X-Y-Z scatter maps and X-Y curves, profiles, histograms, color legends and spreadsheet.

The high-level components provide a coherent set of visualization widgets, that not only draw, but also provide a wide range of interactive behavior that is traditionally the responsibility of the application. Because these widgets manage themselves, application programmers can concentrate on developing the application code rather than visualization code.

The customized Xplore widgets provide an object encapsulation of C libraries on top of the TOOLMASTER/agX visualization C-based function libraries. The Xplore widgets represent a family of "super" widgets for the interactive visualization of various types of technical and commercial data.

The central paradigm of the Xplore widgets, which was used as a framework for the widget development, is that of an O-O Model view controller (MVC), originated as a Smalltalk 80 user interface model. The MVC model promotes intimate integration of the dataset (model), the graphical presentation (view), and user interaction devices such as a mouse (controller). Under this paradigm, changes in the behavior of the phenomena serving as the model can be reflected immediately in the graphics display, and user requests to cause changes in or to query the model can be indicated through graphics events.

Visualization objects are not merely graphics effect, they are expression of the behavior of the information.

The use of the Xplore widgets reduces the effort in programming graphics in a striking way. Instead of providing higher-level routines for graphics components within the display, the complete display itself is encapsulated. In this method, the developer only specifies the display types and the attributes of the display (axis, ticklines, etc.). The advantage is that these attributes are specified as values, not as lines of code which then must be debugged. All the sections of code exist within the widget and are provided for use to the application developer, not to rewrite each time. These values, called resources, are often true/false values. For example, if ticklines are wanted, setting the tickline resource to "true" will enable its display – no code to write or debug.

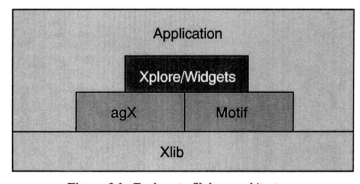

Figure 6.1. Toolmaster/Xplore architecture.

The other way that the Xplore widgets are different from traditional X graphics is in the interactivity with the data displayed. X has both input (mouse, keyboard, etc.) and output (graphics) mechanisms built within it, but they are not tied together. If you wanted, for example, to know the value of a graphics surface by clicking on it, you would have to:

1. Write all the code that would connect the mouse click to the graphics drawn.
2. Relate it back to the original data to get its value.
3. Finally, the action to be performed with the value must be executed (e.g. display it to the user).

Again, this is code which must be written, debugged, and maintained. The Xplore widgets have encapsulated this function within the widget. Clicking within the widget causes the execution of the routine which specifies the action to be performed (display the value). Only the application-unique third part needs to be written each time. This is specified by setting the resource for the action name. When the user clicks the mouse over the graphics area, the action routine is automatically called. The routines that are called in such a manner are called callbacks.

Each of the widgets can also invoke another stand-alone widget. For example, the user can open the ContourXplore widget on a 2D regular data set, display and edit that data as a contour plot, and from that widget control panel, spawn a 3D ContourXplore widget on the same data. One can also spawn a spreadsheet, profile, slicer, etc. from the ContourXplore widget.

Each widget is fully autonomous. The user can make use of all its features and interact between the different widgets at the same time. The total repertoire of each widget is accessible at any time and ready to perform in reponse to a proper request. This is one of the most powerful features of O-O environments.

The ContourXplore widget can also spawn subviews of selected regions of their own data. Using a "zoom cursor", the widget collects the selected view coordinates and does a transform between display space and data space. The model creates a new subdata set and spawns a new ContourXplore widget in another view, showing this portion of its data. Zoomed regions can be zoomed themselves until resolution of their data is exhausted. As a visualization widget, the zoomed view is independent of its parent view and is capable of all functionalities, including selecting and spawning a zoomed view of its part of the model.

Callback requirements and translation behaviors are a dynamic part of the coding standard implemented in the Xplore widgets. The goal of these features is to facilitate the use of the widgets throughout a generic user community. A callback is used to inform the parent of some updating of an item of interest, like adding or editing a point of interest. A large number of convenience functions are provided to code a specific behavior into a widget, based on a user event.

The Xplore widgets provide a functionally rich set of tools that allow you to build highly interactive graphics applications quickly and effectively.

Because all resources of each widget can be specified or modified at runtime, the interaction can be very dynamic. The numerous callbacks and convenience functions provide the necessary flexibility required for flexible customized solutions.

The Xplore widgets include both "utility" widgets for the experienced X and Motif developers and "super" widgets for the application developers. The utility widgets can be used to build compound widgets. The following initial set of high-level application widgets are available in the Xplore widget set: Contour Xplore2D, ContourXplore3D, GridXplore, X-Y-Z ScatterXplore, X-Y CurveXplore, Histogram, EditTable, ColorScale, ClassLimits, Profile, Slicer and Legend.

The Xplore widget set provides complete data interactivity for manipulating data in 1D, 2D and 3D, i.e. the user can view and edit data in all dimensions. The data manipulation widgets also offer "data zoom" interaction suitable for operation with large datasets.

Plate 37 (see color section) shows the Contour widget, a widget based on a regular 2D array, that uses a sophisticated color-shaded contouring visualization technique, sometimes referred to as "color imaging". This display technique provides an effective means of analysing large volumes of scientific data. The contour map on the left shows the entire dataset with a user-designated region (a rubber band) specifying the parameters for a zoomed view. The user selects the zoomed region by moving the mouse. In this case, the user has selected a region of high values for further inspection. The view on the right is the result of the selection process. To improve further the readability of the data, the user has selected a 3D visualization technique (3D Contour widget) for the zoomed data set. The Profile widget is spawned on top of the contour widgets, showing a selected profile of the zoomed data set.

Plate 38 shows the same data represented by the 2D and 3D Contour widgets. A zoomed data region is also represented in another version of the 3D Contour widget.

In Plate 39, the Contour widget is shown together with the Table widget (spreadsheet). The actual data values behind the contour map can be viewed and edited. Plates 40–42 are additional examples of widgets in the Xplore widget set.

6.5. VISUAL PROGRAMMING FOR X ENVIRONMENT

As shown in Figure 6.2, the population of software developers and users resembles a pyramid. At some point in the pyramid, there is a dividing line separating those able to create programs using available programming tools from those unable to build their own applications, the "programmer's line". Those at the very top of the pyramid represent the programming experts ("gurus") and are very familiar with the more complex programming environment including languages like C, C++, low-level graphics libraries (GKS, PHIGS, Xlib) and GUI tools (Xt and Motif). Those just above the line are the application programmers with only a minor knowledge about

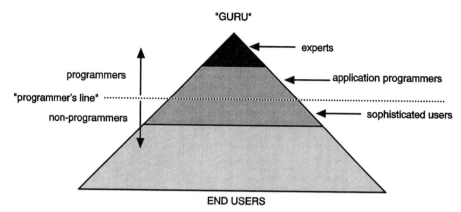

Figure 6.2. The population of software developers and users resembles a pyramid.

the X and Motif programming environment. The sophisticated users reside just below the "programmer's line" and represent an attractive new group of possible application builders, if the right development environment could be provided to them.

The O-O Visual Programing for X (VPX) technique should improve the productivity of the gurus, but most benefits are provided to the vast majority who "live close to the line", above and below, i.e. the application programmers and the sophisticated end users.

The challenge is to use the VPX technique to lower where the "programmer's line" is drawn in the pyramid and expand the number of nonprogramming application builders and increase the productivity of the many "high-level" application programmers.

What/who are the primary elements of a "component-based" visualization software development "VPX" environment? The future model of a VPX environment is shown in Figure 6.3 and will consist of five key elements:

Application builders are represented by all application developers, including

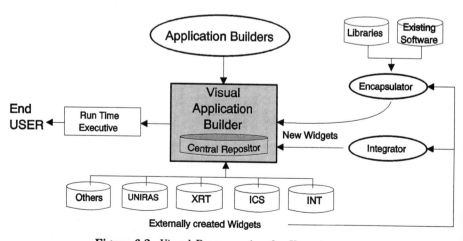

Figure 6.3. Visual Programming for X environment.

the experts ("top of the pyramid"), application programmers (above the "programmer's line") and sophisticated end users (just below the "programmer's line").

Integrators, represented by the experts and application programmers, retrieve components from the central repository, graphically interconnect them into more complex components or even a complete application, and save them back into repository. The integrators will use the Visual Application Builder to interactively build new components from the existing components.

Encapsulators represented by the programming gurus, provide new standard components based on requests from the application builders using low-level function libraries (agX, X, Motif, ...) and/or existing components. The encapsulators will also add the standard component interface framework around already existing "classic" software. The encapsulators will program at a low level, using a programming language like C or C++ together with the GUI toolkits X, Xt and Motif. The new developed components are placed in the central repository.

Visual Application Builder represents the core of the VPX environment with its interactive construction of application programs from components in a central repository. The encapsulated high-level application components ("customized widgets"), as described in Section 4, are integrated into the interactive Visual Application Builder (advanced GUI builder). The components are then represented and interactively manipulated iconically as objects in the Visual Application Builder.

Central repository for components (capsules, widgets, etc.) provided by external vendors (like widgets customized from ICS, INT, XRT and UNIRAS) or the in-house expert programmers ("encapsulators").

The O-O components on their own do not help the nonprogrammers. It is through the fusion of O-O components and an interactive "visual programming" environment that the number of nonprogrammers capable of producing their own applications can be increased.

The technical heart of this solution is therefore an advanced Visual Application Building supporting all capabilities of a full UIMS environment, like the TOOLMASTER UIM/X product, developed by the Montreal company, Visual Edge. This Visual Application Builder will represent the framework "engine" for application program development.

By augmenting UIM/X with the Xplore customized visualization widgets and the agX graphics library, UNIRAS has taken a first step towards an integrated VPX environment.

Augmenting a GUI builder with standard customized widgets, would be analogous to retrofitting your family automobile with a space shuttle rocket booster (Mikes and Jern, 1992).

The additional functionality gained by integrating customized widgets and a graphics library into UIM/X, far exceeds the original scope of most builder tools and can often yield more professional results with a great savings in development effort and cost.

UIM/X is relinked into a new executable program, which can resolve all references to any customized widget, its resources, callbacks, and actions, just like any of the standard Motif widgets.

The "Xplore" components represent the first generation of a TOOLMASTER family of visualization application widgets and will be followed by more components in the future. Future component development will also include components for presentation graphics, plot server (networked hardcopy distribution) and data server (visualization data management). Components from other vendors like ICS, XRT, INT, etc. can also be integrated.

The available components will not satisfy entirely the need for building new applications. The encapsulators (gurus) will therefore focus on developing new O-O reusable components from low-level function libraries (APIs) like agX graphics library from UNIRAS (Figure 6.4), or using existing components to provide new more specified high-level application components, "compound widgets".

The benefits of VPX can be summarized as:

Increases the ability of application programmers and "nonprogrammers" to build applications using standard GUI technology, breaking the software bottleneck.

Promotes the reuse of existing and newly developed code modules, dramatically increasing the traditional programmer productivity.

Provides an easy way to distribute large programming projects over larger groups of developers and still allow individual creativity.

Allows applications to be transparently distributed across a local area network by partitioning of a module-based application.

Standardized interfaces allow for the creation of a market mechanism for reusable software components.

Testing and quality assurance is an inherent part of the development process, resulting in increased reliability of the completed application.

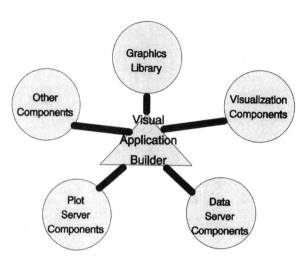

Figure 6.4. Visual Programming for X in a UNIRAS environment.

6.7.   CONCLUSION

Object-oriented (O-O) technology will continue to improve over the next decade. Efforts toward standardization with groups such as Object Management Group, combined with the competitiveness of the marketplace, will ensure continued improvements. The most important improvement is the enhancements to object components. These components are the major leverage point in O-O programming because you do not have to reinvent the wheel every time you program. Instead, you can inherit automatically from components provided by third-party sources.

Most of the component libraries in use are foundation libraries. That is, they supply generic components such as the Motif objects. While these are important building blocks, I believe that we shall see the emergence of a high-level component industry to supply objects for vertical market applications.

For many types of software development, a "visual" approach with the right O-O methodology could help eliminate the traditional programming bottleneck. When we have visual components as sophisticated as the applications themselves, we do not have to write large amounts of code to combine them into complete systems.

The Xplore widgets are specialized visualization components, which can be integrated into a broad range of applications and will provide a base for visual programming.

The concept of a Visual Programming for X environment includes another key element, the Visual Application Builder. By augmenting the Application components into an interactive application builder like UIM/X, the productivity of the application programmer is further increased and the number of "nonprogrammers" building applications can be expanded.

REFERENCES

Anderson, R. (1992). An easy route to X. *The X Journal*, March/April 1992.

Cunningham, Brown, Craighill and Fong (1992). *Computer Graphics Using Object-Oriented Programming*. John Wiley.

Mikes, S. and Jern, M. (1992). *TXJ Special Report*.

Mikes, S. and Keller (1991). The fact and fictions about X Window System GUI development tools. *The X Journal* 1, 28–35.

Jern, M. (1992). Evolution of a visualization object component industry. *The X Journal* **2**(1), 42–46.

ICS (1992). *ICS Widget Databook*.

About the author

From 1969–79, Mikael Jern was a senior researcher and professor at the University of Lund, Sweden. His research interests included computer graphics technology, where he was a pioneer of raster technology. He worked with Professor Hertz at the University of Lund. Together they invented a color graphics system based on the first ink jet plotter for raster-based visualization software. The first high-resolution color images (200 dots/inch) were produced in 1972 using a memory paging and dithering technique. The application software included basic graphics, charting 2D and 3D shaded contouring, imaging and seismic plotting. In 1976, Dr Jern and Dr Hertz sold the right to manufacture and distribute the color graphics plotting systems to the US-based CAD company Applicon. More than 300 systems were installed world wide and used extensively by major oil companies for producing color seismic displays. In 1980, Dr Jern founded UNIRAS, where he has since served as the Vice President of Technology. UNIRAS is a major supplier of visual data analysis and presentation graphics software for scientists and engineers. The UNIRAS fundamental raster technology was developed by Dr Jern.

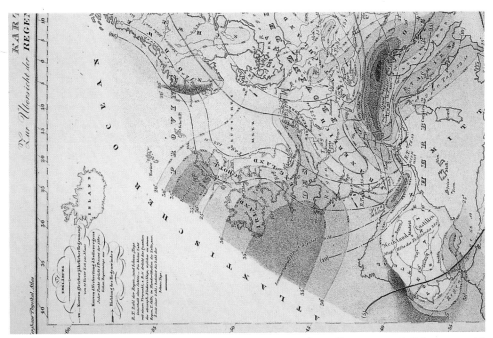

Plate 1 Contour maps(S) with hypsometric tinting: first European rainfall map with hypsometric tinting (1841, Heinrich Berghaus).

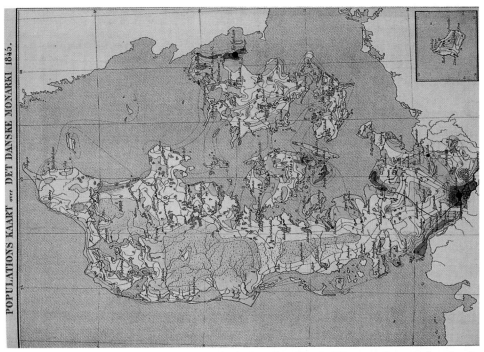

Plate 2 Contour maps(S) with hypsometric tinting: first "isopleth" maps of population density (of Denmark) (1857, Nils Ravn).

Plate 3 Icons(MV): number of rainy days in year in Britain (1851, unknown).

Plate 4 Using the Data Visualizer to display an isovolume for the (scalar) potential energy field for three atoms – placed at the two nearest corners of the bottom face of the box, and in the middle of the far edge on the top face. The isovolume encloses all points where the potential is less than −0.0191. The Data Visualizer's control panels can be seen to the left and bottom of the main image.

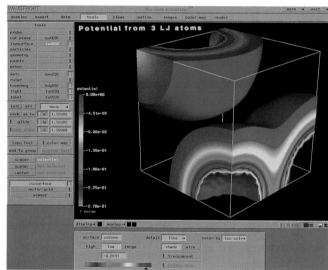

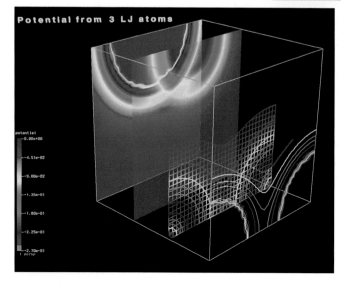

Plate 5 Using the Data Visualizer to display the dataset of Plate 4 using cutting planes. These can be rendered in a variety of styles – working from the back of the box to the front, these are: solid, transparent, wireframe and contour. The last two have also been thresholded, so that only a subset of data values are displayed.

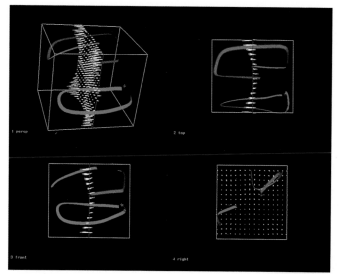

Plate 6 Using the Data Visualizer to display a vector dataset – in this case, air flow in a furnace, as calculated using CFD. The velocity is displayed using a vector grid on a cutting plane in the middle of the box, plus three ribbon tracers which show the local form of the velocity field. The four images are four different views (three orthogonal, and one perspective) of the same scene.

Plate 7 Running a network in apE. The palette of modules (which are represented by icons) is at the top left, and the network has been assembled in the work area in the middle. The widgets (dials and push-button menus) for the control of the modules are in the area beneath this; the control panel for one of the modules (a color-map editor) is in a separate window, at bottom left. The image appears in the display window (bottom right), created by the final module in the network (dataflow is left to right in apE), while the window at the top gives summary information about individual modules as the user clicks on them in the network. This network is displaying contours of pressure from a numerical simulation of a jet exhaust.

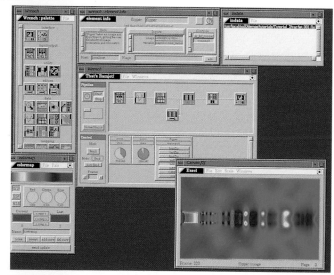

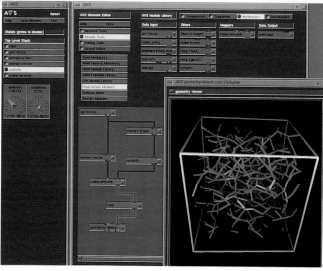

Plate 8 The network builder in AVS. At the top on the right is the palette of modules, from which the user selects the constituents of the network by dragging them down onto the work area (bottom) where they are connected together. The widgets (dials in this case) for the control of one of the modules appear on the network control panel, at left. The image appears in the display window (bottom right), created by the final module in the network (dataflow is top to bottom in AVS). This network is displaying the lines of force in a geomechanical numerical simulation of stresses in a rock. The system is modeled as an assembly of spheres (see Plate 9); the lines connect the centers of all spheres which touch, and are colored according to the force which act along them. The user can interactively select the range of forces to be displayed using the dial widgets.

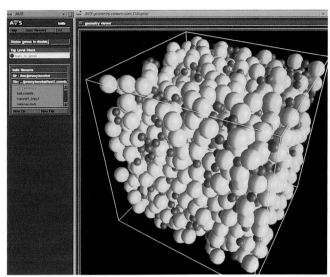

Plate 9 Using AVS to display the spheres in the configuration from the geomechanical stress modeler corresponding to the forces in Plate 8.

Plate 10 Building the network in IRIS Explorer. The palette of modules is on the top left (partially obscured by the display window at bottom left). The work area is in the middle at the top. The widgets which control the modules actually appear on the representation of the modules themselves when they are in the work area. The image appears in the display window, created by the final module in the network (dataflow is left to right in IRIS Explorer). This network is displaying a two-dimensional section through the potential field for a methane molecule in a zeolite (see also Plate 11), both as a contour plot in three-dimensional space and as an elevated, colored surface.

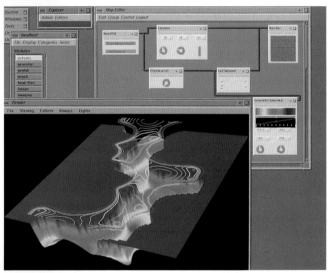

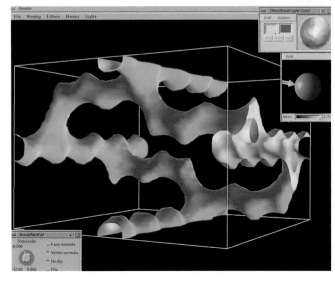

Plate 11 Using IRIS Explorer to display the potential energy field for a methane molecule inside a zeolite as an isosurface. Note the use of multiple colored light sources (controlled by some of the widgets which surround the main image) to highlight different parts of the surface.

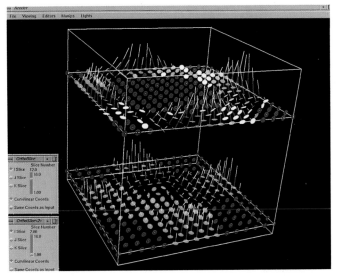

Plate 12 Displaying a vector field – in this case, the flow of a fluid through an assembly of spheres – using IRIS Explorer. There is a single sphere at the center of the box, and one at each corner. The velocity of the fluid is displayed using a vector grid on two cutting planes; the discs help to indicate the orientation of the vectors. The scaling of the vectors in the display is controlled by the widgets at the bottom left.

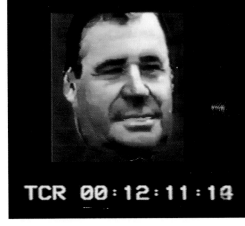

Plate 13 Tele-presence, an example of new applications based on animation techniques.

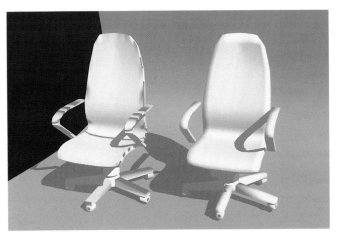

Plate 14 Visualization of CAD data (dataset was provided by Königin-Neurath).

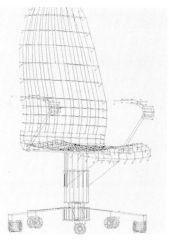

Plate 15 Analyzing CAD data.

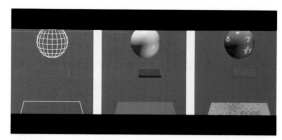

Plate 16 3-D visualization with wireframe (left), shaded (middle) and high quality rendering (right).

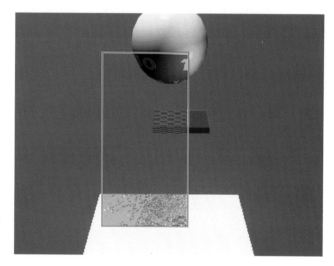

Plate 17 Visualization with mixed-quality rendering.

Plate 18 Variation of illumination models.

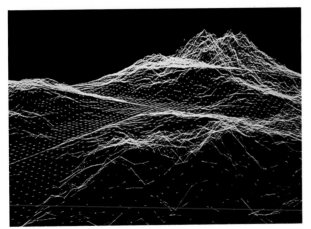

Plate 19 Automatically generated fractal mountain. On the right a 3-D fractal cloud has been placed around the mountain peak.

Plate 20 Three-dimensional steam rising from a pool. Special techniques have been used for the marble, steam, water waves and tree.

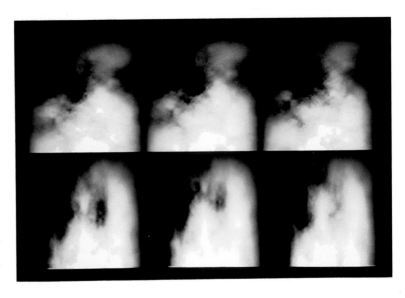

Plate 21 Moving flames generated by a fractal method having a "bulky" (upper) or a "striped" (lower) appearance.

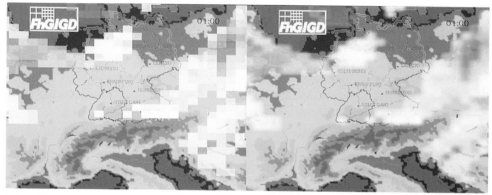

Plate 22 (Left) Original weather simulation data. (Right) Bicubically smoothed data.

Plate 23 Stills of a 10 h weather simulation visualized as pseudo-satellite film.

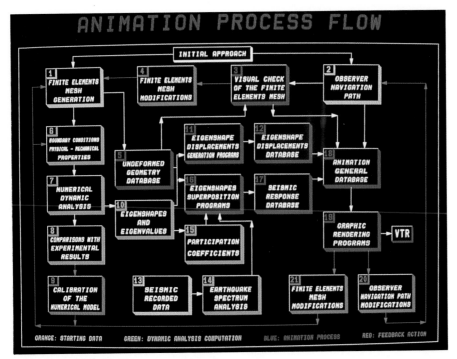

Plate 24 Block diagram of the animation process.

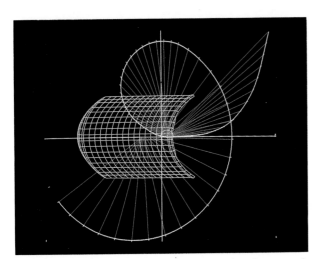

Plate 25 Navigation path. Projection on the plane x,y of the given points and the finite element model studied.

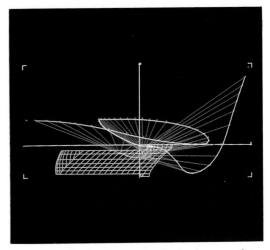

Plate 26 Navigation path. Projection on the plane x,z of the given points and the finite element model studied.

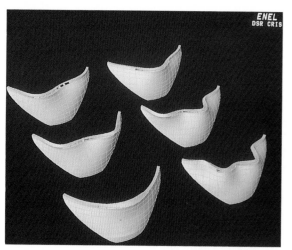

Plate 27 Comparison between six different vibration modes simultaneously shown.

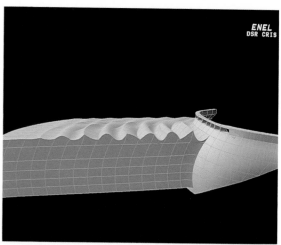

Plate 28 Surface waves and the dam deformations in the first vibration mode.

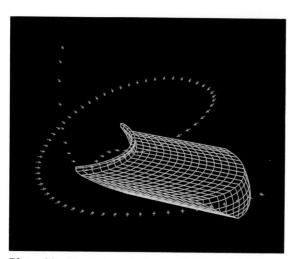

Plate 29 Navigation path. Arrows indicate the observer position at every second.

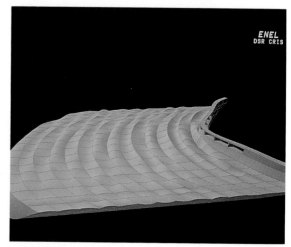

Plate 30 Surface face and dam deformations during the earthquake.

Plate 31 Leaves gently floating in the wind. The leaves are not flat but slightly distorted, giving rise to their interesting motion.

Plate 32 Leaves being blown up and over a slide. The slide was built out of collection of sources and sinks, thereby creating an obstacle to the flow.

Plate 33 Having blown over the slide, the leaves swirl around a playground.

Plate 34 Leaves tumbling along the ground to escape the garbage bin.

Plates 35 and 36 A sequence showing leaves being sucked in by a garbage bin. The motion was set up with the addition of vortex, sink and uniform flows.

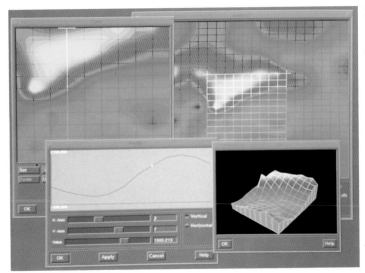

Plate 37 Contour widget (see chapter 6) using color imaging showing entire data set, zoomed view of region and 3D Contour widget. © 1993 David Lawrence.

Plate 38 The same data set as in Plate 37 with the zoomed region also represented in another version of the 3D contour widget. © 1993 David Lawrence.

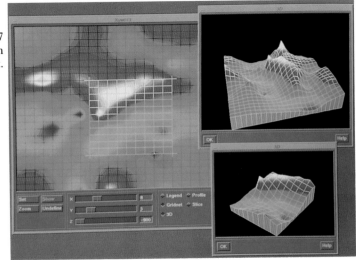

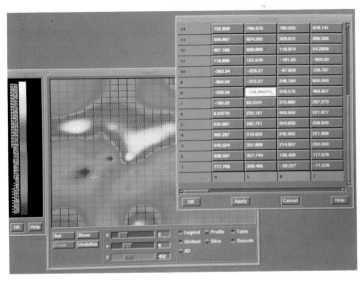

Plate 39 The Contour widget is shown together with the Table widget (spreadsheet). © 1993 David Lawrence.

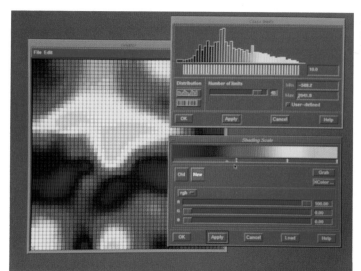

Plate 40

Plate 41

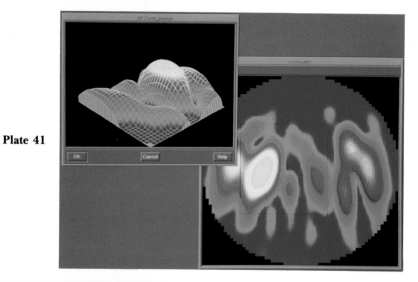

Plate 42

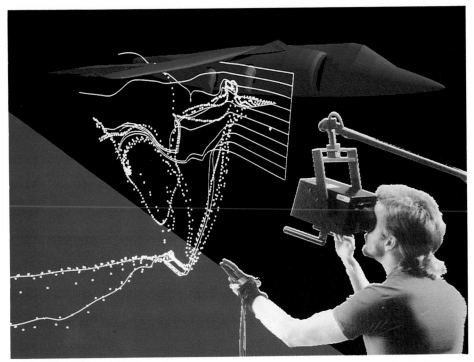

Plate 43 The virtual windtunnel in use, with the flow around a simulated harrier aircraft in hover (Smith *et al.*, 1991).

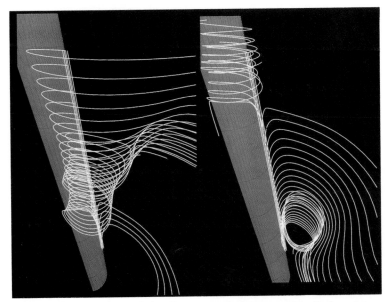

Plate 44 Streamlines of the flow around the tapered cylinder at two successive moments of time (Jespersen and Levit, 1991).

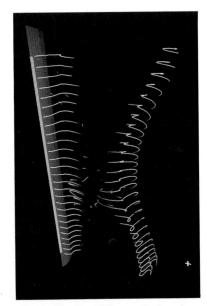

Plate 45 Streaklines of the flow around the tapered cylinder rendered as smoke (Jespersen and Levit, 1991).

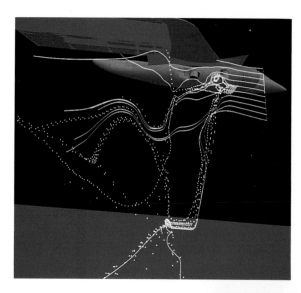

Plate 46 The user environment in the virtual windtunnel, showing a rake of streaklines rendered as bubbles used in combination with a rake of streamlines in the harrier dataset (Smith *et al.*, 1991).

Plate 47 Boom and glove hardware interface to the virtual windtunnel.

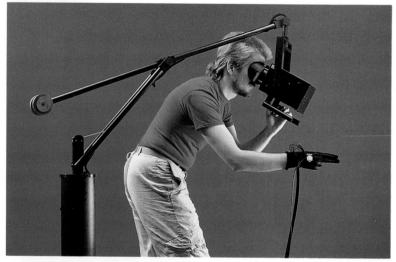

Plate 48 An illustration of virtual spacetime in use. The user is manipulating a spray of geodesics in a curved spacetime with an instrumented glove while observing the results in a head-tracked, wide field of view stereo display.

Plate 49 Heights on the Earth's surface.

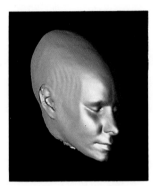

Plate 50 MRI head.

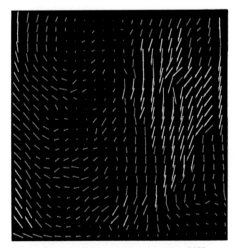

Plate 51 Surface winds over the UK.

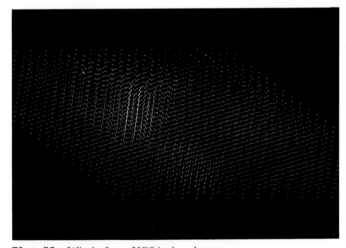

Plate 52 Winds from NCSA thunderstorm.

Plates 49–52 Data sets used for bench-marking.

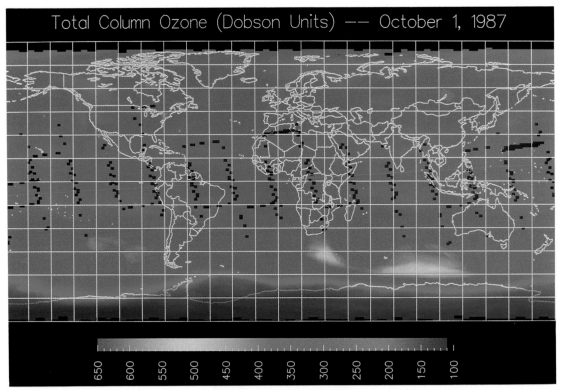

Plate 53 Pseudo-color-mapped global column ozone on 1 October 1987. © 1992 IBM.

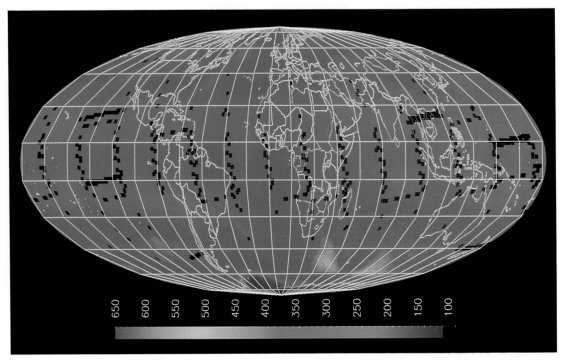

Plate 54 Mollweide warped pseudo-color-mapped and contoured global column ozone on 1 October 1987. © 1992 IBM.

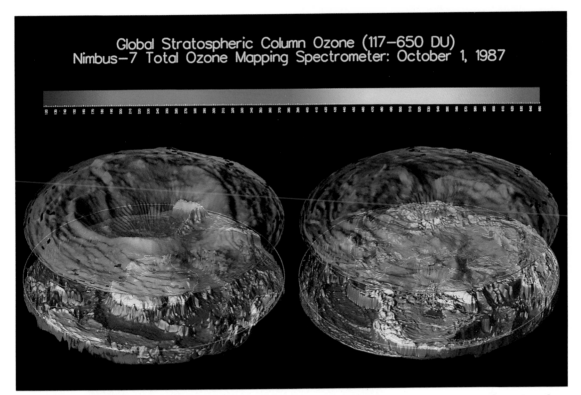

Plate 55 Southern and northern hemisphere orthographic warped pseudo-color-mapped deformed surfaces of global column ozone on 1 October 1987. © 1992 IBM.

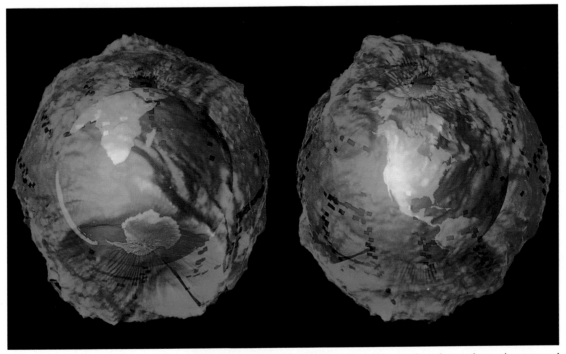

Plate 56 Southern and northern hemisphere views of radially deformed pseudo-color and opacity-mapped spherically warped surfaces of global column ozone on 1 October 1987. © 1992 IBM.

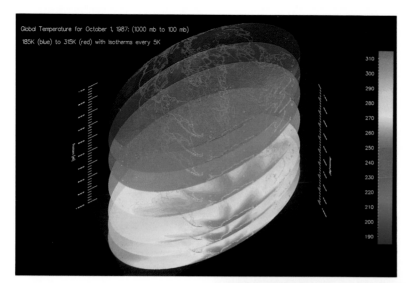

Plate 57 Mollweide warped pseudo-color-mapped and contoured global atmospheric temperatures stacked by pressure and opacity-mapped for 1000 mb to 100 mb on 1 October 1987. © 1992 IBM.

Plate 58 Volume rendering of pseudo-color-mapped global atmospheric temperatures for 1000 mb to 100 mb on 1 October 1987. © 1992 IBM.

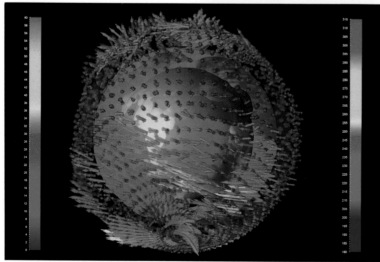

Plate 59 Isosurfaces of pseudo-color and opacity-mapped global atmospheric temperatures at 200 K, 250 K and 300 K for 1000 mb to 100 mb and wind vector glyphs on 1 October 1987. © 1992 IBM.

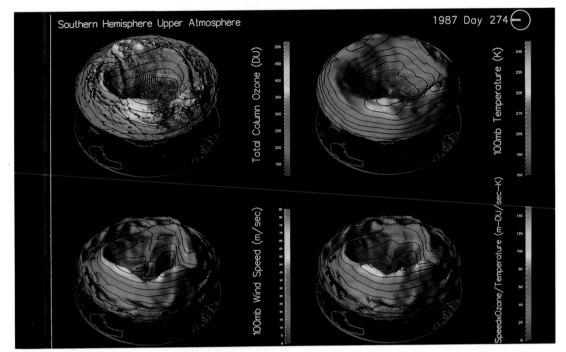

Plate 60 Southern hemisphere orthographic warped pseudo-color-mapped deformed surfaces with iso-contours of global atmospheric data on 1 October 1987: column ozone with contours every 50 DU from 100 to 650 DU (upper left), 100 mb temperature with contours every 5 K from 180 to 245 K (upper right), 100 mb horizontal wind speed with contours every 10 m/s from 0 to 85 m/s (lower left), column ozone × 100 mb (wind speed/temperature) with contours every 20 m-DU/s-K from 0 to 150 m-DU/s-K (lower right). © 1992 IBM.

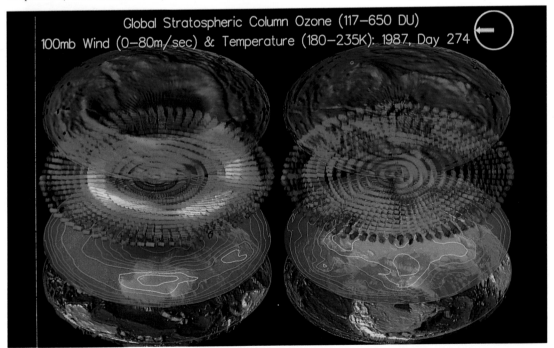

Plate 61 Southern and northern hemisphere orthographic warped global column ozone as pseudo-color-mapped deformed surfaces, 100 mb horizontal wind velocity as vector arrows pseudo-colored by speed and 100 mb temperature as pseudo-color-mapped disks with contours every 5 K on 1 October 1987. © 1992 IBM.

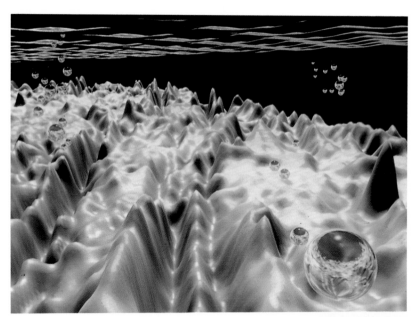

Plate 62 A frame from an animated "swim-around" in a reconstructed underwater gravity field. The gravity field correlates with bathymetry, enabling the identification of underwater geophysical features (McLeod and Small, C., 1992).

Plate 63 A typical Sea Beam mapping scenario. Parallel tracks of swath bathymetry are collected (bottom left to top right). A perpendicular track "ties" the data together at a time of day when accurate navigation information is available. Note also how the track becomes narrower in the region of the Seamount (underwater mountain). This illustrates a second problem in bathymetric mapping: obtaining fewer data than usual in those regions that are most interesting.

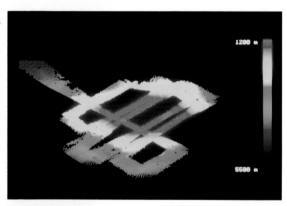

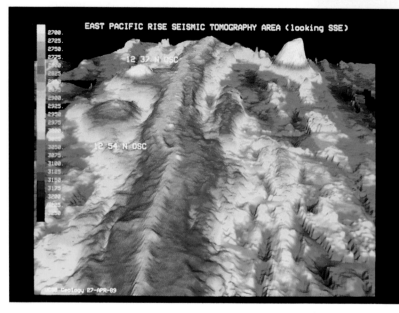

Plate 64 Color-depth encoded perspective view of a mid-ocean ridge generated from Sea Beam bathymetry. The vertical scale is exaggerated to emphasize relief (Toomey and Foulger, 1989).

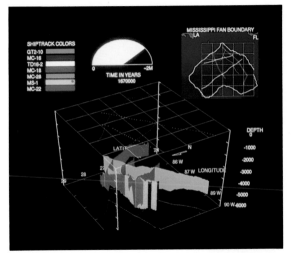 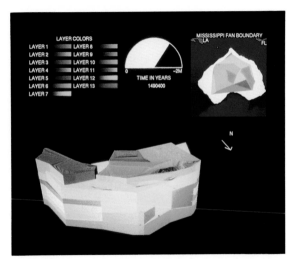

Plate 65 A frame from an animation sequence that relates the growth process of the Mississippi Fan with the seven ship's tracks used to acquire the data. The ships' tracks are color coded and the 3D display integrates the track information with the 2D bitmapped display in the upper right that shows the evolutionary process at a given time: As the animation proceeds (one frame is equal to 800 years), the growth and consolidation along all ships' tracks are observed by representing them as height that changes with time (Parmley *et al.*, 1993).

Plate 66 A frame from an animation sequence (one frame equals 1200 years) where each layer is represented as a 3D layer. The Mississippi Fan is represented as a 3D solid with distinguishing interconnected layers that illustrate the growth of the fan as the animation proceeds (Parmley *et al.*, 1993).

Plate 67

Plate 68

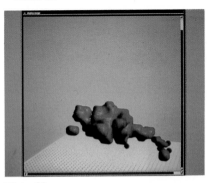 

Plate 69

Plate 70

Plates 67-70. Volume rendered reconstruction of PLUTO. (67) after thresholding - single pass; (68) after thresholding and additional data filtering - single pass; (69) using four passes over PLUTO without registration; (70) after registering the four passes over PLUTO.

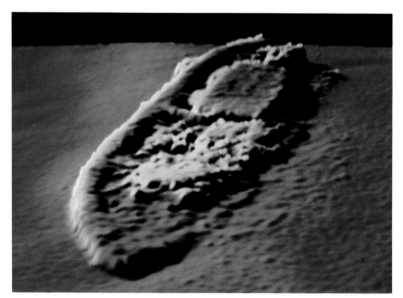

Plate 71 A 3D estimate of the most probable shipwreck form of the USS Monitor. Color-coded perspective provides redundant elevation information (red is the highest, blue the deepest).

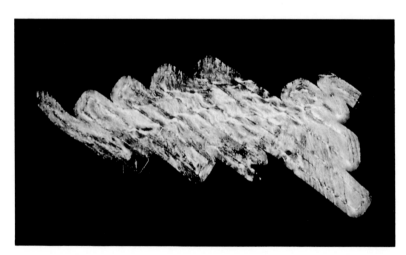

Plates 72 and 73 Sea MARC II maps of the Siqueiros Transform; (72) the imagery shows fine structure; (73) bathymetry has less detail but provides quantitative shape information.

Plate 72

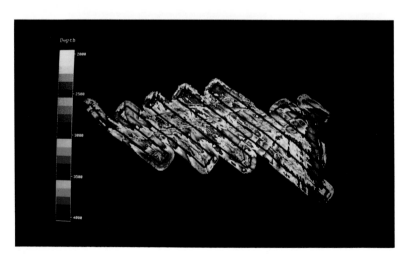

Plate 73

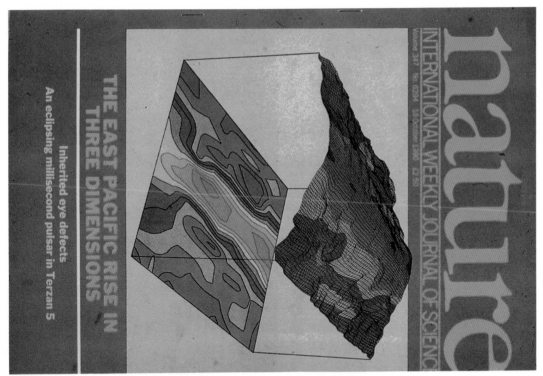

Plate 74 Combined depiction of seismic-velocity structure (lower) with overlying seafloor morphology (upper). The velocity "hot spot" corresponds to high temperatures and magma injection at a site of seafloor spreading on the East Pacific Rise (Toomey *et al.*, 1990).

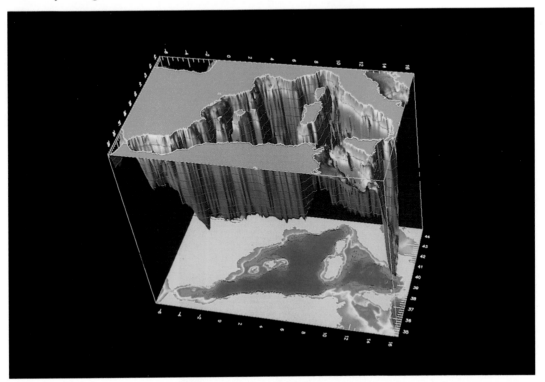

Plate 75 The Western Mediterranean basin, viewed from the south-east.

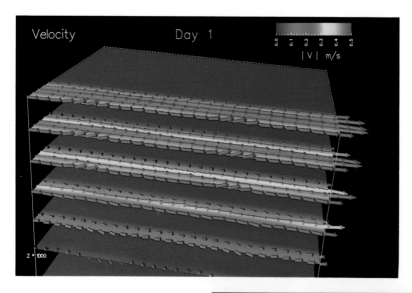

Plate 76 Velocity field at day 1.

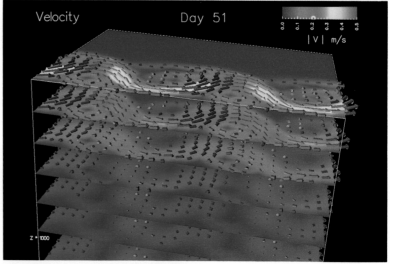

Plate 77 Velocity field at day 51.

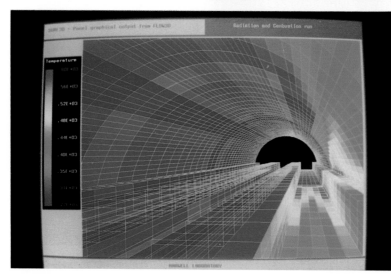

Plate 78 A simulation of the disasterous fire in King's Cross Underground Station produced for the public enquiry. The coloration is according to surface temperature. The results are from FLOW3D. Courtesy of CFDS (AEA Technology, Harwell).

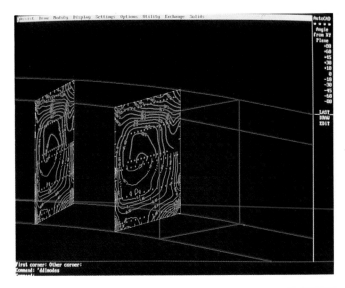

Plate 79 Study of flow in a duct. The results are contours showing velocity perpendicular to the axis of the duct and show evidence of a vortex. The green isolines are the result of laser Doppler anemometry; the blue isolines are the simulated output of FLOW3D. Courtesy of Flow Dynamics Measurement Service (AEA Technology, Harwell).

Plate 80 A flow field with a vortex visualized as stream-line ribbons colored according to velocity. Courtesy of AVS Inc.

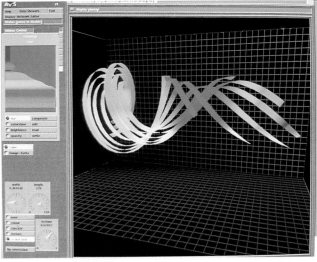

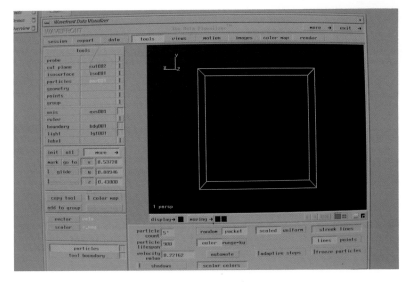

Plate 81 General view of system environment.

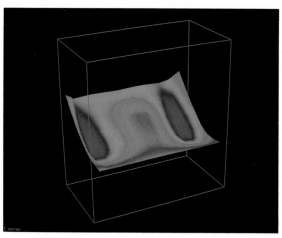

Plate 82 Elevated cutplane, showing scalar velocity magnitude mapped onto the resulting surface.

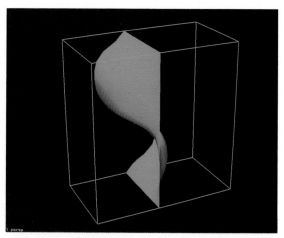

Plate 83 Isosurface showing the scalar temperature.

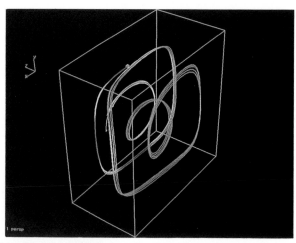

Plate 84 Particle streamlines colored by the scalar velocity magnitude.

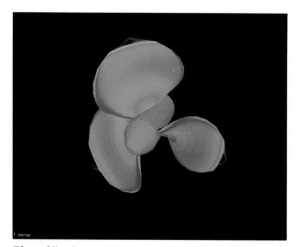

Plate 85 Computer generated geometry of a three-bladed ship propellor.

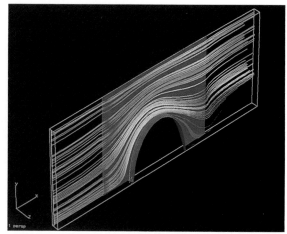

Plate 86 Streamline flow over a tube/fin heat exchanger (streamlines colored according to the scalar temperature).

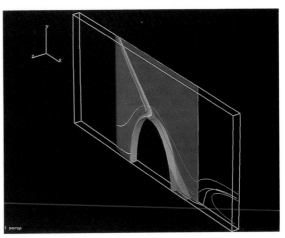

Plate 87 Probe tools using the sheet subtool positioned close to the forward stagnation point.

Plate 88 Isovolume tool using temperature as the mapped scalar, partially erased and transparent with streamlines.

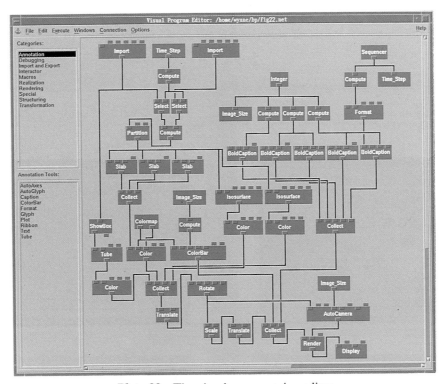

Plate 89 The visual programming editor.

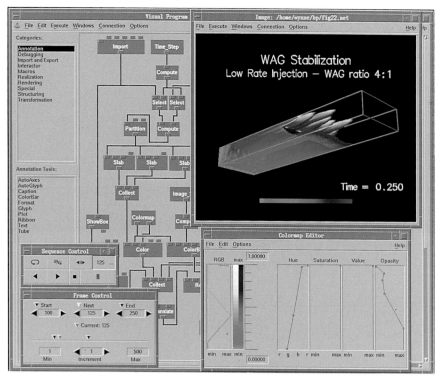

Plate 90 The sequencer module (two windows at lower left), colormap editor (window at lower right) and rendered image (window at upper right).

Plates 91–110 Images rendered using the visual programming editor.

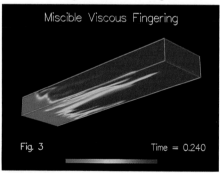

Plate 91

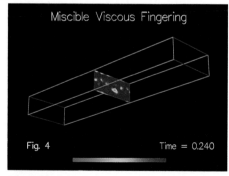

Plate 92

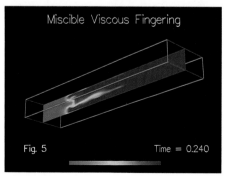

Plate 93

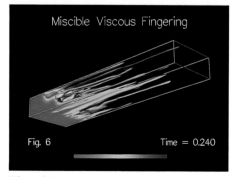

Plate 94

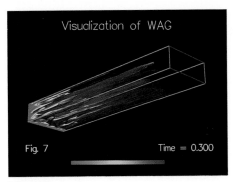

Plate 95

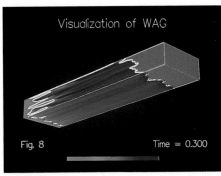

Plate 96

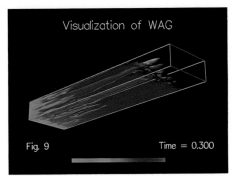

Plate 97

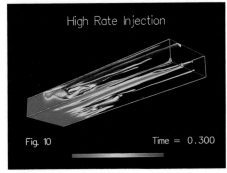

Plate 98

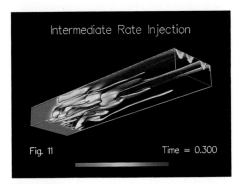

Plate 99

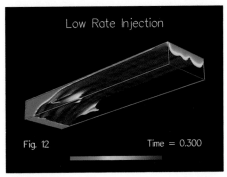

Plate 100

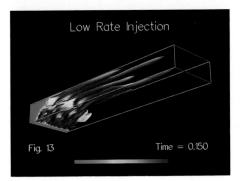

Plate 101

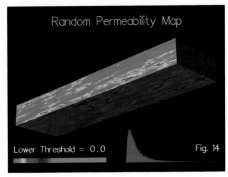

Plate 102

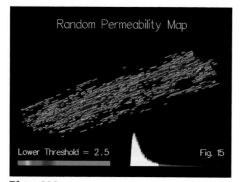

Plate 103

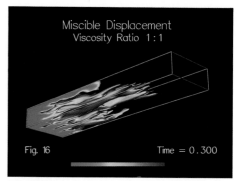

Plate 104

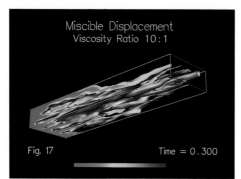

Plate 105

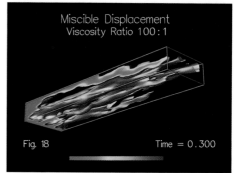

Plate 106

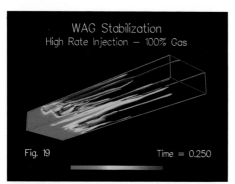

Plate 107

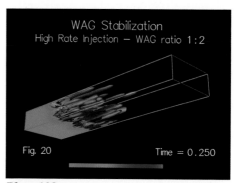

Plate 108

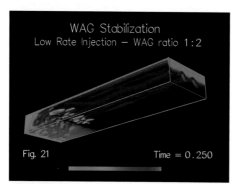

Plate 109

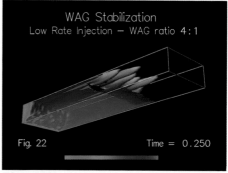

Plate 110

Chapter 7
Virtual environments in scientific visualization

Steve Bryson

7.1. INTRODUCTION

Scientific visualization is the use of computer graphics in the investigation of scientific phenomena (McCormick *et al.*, 1987; Smarr, 1991). Some investigations involve large amounts of data arising from observation or from numerical simulation. Other problems, such as the structure of an exact solution in general relativity, are understood in principle but not in detail. Computer graphics assists the researcher's understanding of the qualitative structure of phenomena by drawing pictures which can be obtained in no other way. Interactive computer graphics, which allows real-time control over how the graphics are generated, further enhances the researcher's ability to explore a phenomenon through the computer. In conventional real-time computer graphics systems, a mouse and keyboard can be used to control, for example, the initial position of a streamline in a fluid flow. When the phenomenon under study is three-dimensional, the display is projected onto the two-dimensional display screen and the two-dimensional mouse movements are mapped into three-dimensional control. The mouse typically controls both the view point of the projection and the position of the objects in the view.

Virtual environments provide a fully three-dimensional interface for both the display and control of interactive computer graphics (Bryson and Levit, 1992). A wide field of view stereoscopic head-tracked display system presents a compelling illusion of a three-dimensional world generated by the computer graphics. The researcher feels immersed in this world, which is populated by computer-generated objects which appear and behave as if they were real (Plate 43, see color section). This three-dimensional display provides many of the depth cues that we use in the real world, such as binocular disparity and head-motion parallax, providing a display of three-dimensional structures that overcome many of the ambiguities that occur on two-dimensional screens. The display device tracks the user's head and controls the point of view of the computer-generated scene. Using an instrumented glove, the researcher can reach out and directly manipulate virtual objects' position and orientation in three dimensions. The glove also

ANIMATION AND SCIENTIFIC VISUALIZATION
ISBN 0-12-227745-7

senses the user's fingers, allowing the computer to interpret hand gestures. A virtual object can be "picked up" by simply closing the fist over the object, just as in the real world. Another object can be indicated for some action by literally pointing at it in the virual environment. Using these techniques, virtual environments attempt to create the illusion of a computer-generated reality so compelling that one naturally interacts with it as one interacts with the real world. Virtual environments do not attempt to mimic the real world, rather they provide a natural, intuitive interface to computer environments. The goal is to present a researcher with a virtual object for study, as opposed to a picture of an object.

Virtual environments have found a fruitful application in the field of scientific visualization. When the scientific phenomena under study are three-dimensional and contain complex structures, virtual environments provide a natural way to display them. Virtual environment control via the glove and other input technologies allow simple, intuitive control of the three-dimensional position and orientation of the displays involved in the visualization of phenomena. The researcher need not remember things like "when the control key is pressed the mouse motion is mapped into roll and yaw". This control capability is particularly useful when the richness of the phenomena allows only partial display at any one time. Using virtual environment control techniques, the researcher can rapidly change what and where data is displayed, allowing the exploration of complex data environments. We feel that it is this exploration capability which brings out the real power of virtual environments. As Brad Comes of the Army Corps of Engineers Waterways Experimental Station exclaimed when he first tried a virtual environment, "with this kind of interface, you can get inquisitive!".

Virtual environment interfaces are very striking, but the advantages of this interface are apparent only for those using the virtual environment system. For this reason, virtual environment interfaces are not particularly useful for the presentation of scientific results. They are useful, however, for the exploration and, hopefully, discovery of phenomena which can then be presented in more conventional ways.

Research in the use of virtual environments in scientific visualization is underway at several locations. NASA Ames Research Center is pioneering these applications in several areas of scientific investigation, particularly fluid flow visualization. The Army Corps of Engineers Waterways Experimental Station has duplicated the system at NASA Ames for research in water flow visualization. The National Center for Supercomputing Applications at the University of Illinois at Urbana-Champaign is developing several virtual environment setups, including a duplicate of the system at NASA Ames. They are investigating applications in cosmology, magnetohydrodynamics, and medical imaging. The University of North Carolina at Chapel Hill is investigating several applications of virtual environments in such fields as molecular modeling and medical visualization. SRI International is also evaluating the use of virtual environments for the study of molecular models. NASA Goddard Spaceflight Center is investigating the use of virtual environment techniques for the visualization of magnetohydrodynamic problems and data from the Earth Observation Satellite. Other institutions are acquiring or thinking seriously of acquiring virtual environment systems.

While virtual environments are rather new, there have been interesting applications developed for scientific visualization. After describing a major example, we will discuss what makes a virtual environment work and how to evaluate whether a visualization problem is suited for a virtual environment with current technology. This technology certainly has a long way to go before the full potential of virtual environments is realized, but it has matured to the point where significant scientific visualization problems can be addressed.

7.2. THE VIRTUAL WINDTUNNEL

The virtual windtunnel is an application of virtual environments to the problem of fluid flow visualization developed by the author, Creon Levit and Michael Gerald-Yamasaki at the Applied Research Branch of the Numerical Aerodynamic Simulation Systems Division at NASA Ames Research Center (Bryson and Levit, 1992). It is designed to visualize precomputed simulated unsteady three-dimensional fluid flows which are the product of computational fluid dynamics (CFD) calculations. These calculations are typically performed on supercomputers and provide velocity, energy and pressure data of fluids on curvilinear multiple-zone numerical grids. Visualization of these unsteady flows are difficult due to their often extremely complex time-varying three-dimensional structures. There are many methods for visualizing these flows using computer graphics, such as isosurfaces of scalar quantities, cutting planes rendered with color maps that indicate scalar quantities, and streamlines of the flow. Due to the inherently three-dimensional structure of flow phenomena, virtual environments were expected to be useful.

The virtual windtunnel visualizes the fluid velocity vector field using streamlines, streaklines and particle paths. Streamlines (Plate 44) are the integral curves of the velocity vector field given an initial position or seedpoint, and provide insight into the field's geometrical structure. A streakline is a collection of particles which are repreatedly injected into the flow, and correspond to a smoke or bubble source in the flow. Streaklines (Plate 45) are particularly useful in the observation of vortical structures and recirculation regions. Particle paths are the actual paths of the particles injected into the flow over time. In the case of steady flows these three techniques coincide. These visualizations are rendered either as lines connecting the points of the paths or as disconnected points. They are controlled by rakes, which are linear collections of seedpoints that are moved by the user's hand via an instrumented glove. A rake is simply picked up and moved to the new, desired location. Several rakes with different visualization techniques can be operated at the same time (Plate 46).

By creating the illusion that the researcher is immersed in the flow under study with real rakes "out there" within reach, the researcher can concentrate on the science of the problem, and not worry about the details of the interface. By waving a rake of streamlines around, the interesting areas of the geometry of the flow can be quickly identified. By watching a streakline develop, vortical structures can be identified which can then be explored with streamlines. The passage of time can be speeded up, slowed down, stopped or reversed. The scale of the display and interaction can be controlled at will, as can the display of objects inside the flow.

The design and implementation of the virtual windtunnel involves several constraints. The most severe constraint is the requirement that as the user's head moves the scene must update sufficiently quickly so that the illusion of viewing a real environment is not destroyed. Slow update causes the display to look like a series of still pictures rather than a dynamic view of a three-dimensional world. Experience has shown that to maintain the illusion an update rate of about 10 frames/second is required. The control, computation, and rendering in stereo of the environment must take place in less than 0.1 s for the illusion of reality to be compelling. It is also important that interactive aspects of the environment take less than 0.1 s from when the user requests the action to when the action is completed. Longer delays significantly impede the ability of the user to perform interactive tasks.

In choosing the visualizations, it was important that the computation and rendering involved could be performed fast enough for the virtual environment scene to be updated faster than the required 10 frames/second. Streamlines and their unsteady generalizations based on simulated particles were chosen as they can be made to satisfy this constraint. Computation of streamlines involves only simple numerical integration of the vector field and the rendering of streamlines involve drawing simple lines in the three-dimensional environment. The accuracy of the computation was also determined by performance considerations. The second order Runge–Kutta integration technique was chosen as a good compromise between performance and accuracy.

The display device was constrained by the demand that it provide the highest quality display possible. Many wide field of view stereoscopic head-tracked displays use a pair of four-inch diagonal liquid crystal displays (LCDs) worn on the head. These LCD systems were, however, judged to provide too low a resolution to be acceptable. The Fake Space Labs (Menlo Park, CA) Binocular Omni Orientation Monitor (BOOM), a device using a pair of four-inch diagonal monochromatic NTSC cathode ray tube (CRT) monitors supported on a counterweighted yoke assembly (Plate 47), was chosen because of its superior display quality. This was later upgraded to the Fake Space Labs BOOM IIC, which uses 1000×1000 resolution monitors with two color channels. A standard shadow-masked three-color CRT display was rejected because the shadow mask degraded the image and because of safety uncertainties. Head tracking on the BOOM systems is performed by providing the computer system with the angles of the joints in the counterweighted yoke assembly, which are detected via optical encoders.

The Dataglove Model II developed by VPL Research, Inc. (Redwood City,

CA) was chosen for the control device (Plate 47). The dataglove uses a magnetic tracking system built by Polhemus Inc. (Colchester, VT), which provides the absolute position and orientation of a sensor relative to a source. While somewhat inaccurate, this tracker is sufficient for our purposes. The glove itself uses specially treated optical fibers at 10 finger joints to measure the finger bend angles of the user's hand. These angles are interpreted as gestures by the computer system, which cause different things to happen depending on where the gesture is performed. For example, if the closed fist gesture is performed at the center of a rake, that rake is picked up and moved with the user's hand until the closed fist gesture is released. A closed fist gesture in the open air allows the movement of the entire display relative to the researcher. Another gesture combined with hand motion controls the scale of the environment.

Finally, the computation and rendering platform must be sufficiently powerful to integrate the computation, control and display of all the elements of the virtual environment. For small unsteady flows, we use a Silicon Graphics (Mountain View, CA) Iris 380 GT/VGX system, which has eight MIPS R3000 processors for a total 37 megaflops performance and a VGX high-speed three-dimensional graphics geometry engine capable of drawing 800,000 small traingles/second. Our system contains 256 Mbyte of physical memory. The Iris system reads the control devices to determine the position of the user's head and the state of the user's hand, computes the visualizations for the current display, and renders the display in stereo from the user's point of view (Figure 7.1). This system is sufficient for unsteady data sets which involve less than a total of 250 Mbyte of data and visualizations involving up to about 20,000 integrations of the vector field.

On the Iris, sufficient speed is attained by storing the entire data set in memory so it can be very quickly accessed. Most interesting unsteady flows involve more than 256 Mbyte of data, however, and so will not fit into the Iris' memory. Storing the data on disk and reading each timestep's data when it is needed is too slow on the Iris to allow the system to run at 10 frames/second. For this reason, a distributed architecture has been

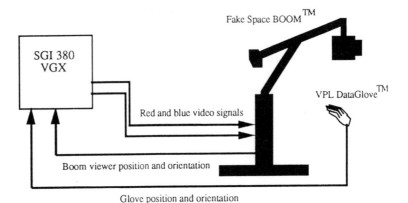

Figure 7.1. The system configuration of the virtual windtunnel.

implemented where the flow data and computation of the visualizations all take place on a remote supercomputer (Bryson and Gerald-Yamasaki, 1992). We currently use a Convex 3240, which has four vector processors and a gigabyte of physical memory. This allows four times as much flow data to be visualized, but many unsteady datasets are larger still. A disk bandwidth of about 50 Mbyte/s allows the dynamic loading of data stored on disk so long as the size of one timestep's worth of data does not exceed 5 Mbyte. One might expect that the computational performance of the Convex 3240 would also provide advantages, but particle integration is not well suited to vectorized computation due to the constant access of memory, and the performance of the Convex with four processors is comparable to the Iris with eight processors.

Because the virtual environment display fills the user's field of view, shutting out the real world, virtual environments are a highly personal experience. An advantage of a distributed architecture is the ability to build shared virtual environments, where two or more users using different virtual environment systems can view the same dataset that is resident on a remote supercomputer. The UltraNet network system has sufficient bandwidth to transmit the visualization data. By sending the user's commands directly to the supercomputer, each of the users can interact with the same virtual environment and see the effects of the other user's actions. The virtual windtunnel is being developed into a shared facility.

Unsteady data sets can involve considerably more data. A typical example is a computation of a hovering Harrier jump jet (Smith *et al.*, 1991) which contains hundreds of timesteps containing 36 Mbyte of velocity vector data each. The virtual windtunnel currently under development at NASA Ames has as its eventual goal the interactive investigation of such large data sets.

7.3. OTHER APPLICATION EXAMPLES

The techniques developed in the virtual windtunnel have been applied to the visualization of curved spacetime in the general theory of relativity (Bryson, 1992a). The flow data in the virtual windtunnel is replaced by geometry data in the form of the metric of spacetime. The streamlines are replaced by geodesics in the geometry data (Plate 48). Geodesics in spacetime require an initial speed, direction and position as opposed to the initial position required by streamlines of a flow. The user's hand position and orientation are used to supply this initial position and orientation for a preset speed. This application is being developed jointly by the Applied Research Branch at NASA Ames and the numerical relativity group at NCSA to study the results of numerical spacetime simulations.

At NCSA, the BOOM has been used to provide a display of static three-dimensional map of galaxy distribution due to Margaret Geller. The data in this application are the measured three-dimensional positions of galaxies on a very large scale. This application was very successful in bringing out structures in the galaxy distribution that were not previously perceived. Another application under development at NCSA is the investigation of large scale cosmological structures that are the result of n-body simulations.

At the Army Corps of Engineers Waterways Experimental Station in Vicksburg, MI, virtual environments are being used to explore fluid dynamics in explosives studies and water channel design.

A somewhat different application that has been explored is the use of interactive virtual environments to allow the manipulation of mathematical surfaces to illustrate geometrical and topological concepts. This application involves some rather difficult questions of how the surface is to react to the user's inputs (Bryson, 1992b). The visualization of mathematical concepts leading to the discovery of the remarkable properties of four-dimensional spaces is one possible application (Freedman and Quinn, 1990).

7.4. CONSIDERATIONS IN THE DEVELOPMENT OF VIRTUAL ENVIRONMENTS

From the virtual windtunnel example, we can draw several conclusions about what makes a virtual environment useful. The three-dimensional control and head-tracked display in real time are crucial to the illusion of a real virtual world. While the virtual objects must be meaningful to the researcher, it is not important that elements of the virtual world look like anything in the real world. The sense of presence that the virtual objects have, due to the head-tracked display and user interaction, compel the illusion of reality. This sense of presence allows the researcher to interact with the objects exactly as if they were objects in the real world. When the researcher says "I want to move the streamline over there", the researcher simply reaches out and grabs the seedpoint of that streamline and moves it there. Asking "I wonder where the vortices are in this time frame", the researcher grabs a rake of streamlines and waves it about in the virtual space watching the resulting streamlines to look for signs of vortical structure. This kind of exploratory interaction requires fast update rates in the virtual environment.

The control and display devices are also critical. The control device must track the user's body in such a way that the user can forget that the device is there. We wish to make the interface to the virtual environment as invisible as possible. The magnetic trackers and gloves used in current virtual environments have serious accuracy problems and are functional within only a limited range. The display devices suffer from a severe resolution restriction, due to the fact that a four-inch display is blown up to a typically 100° image to cover the user's field of view. Pixels become large with this kind of magnification, and even in the highest resolution systems with 1000 pixels on a side the pixels are plainly visible. In this case the pixels are as large as 0.1° across, which is one fifth of the full moon. Stereoscopic display and color rendering help considerably. The CRT systems used in the boom have enough resolution to be useful, but higher resolution is highly desirable.

Virtual tools in the virtual environment can alleviate many of the control problems. Simple menus and sliders can be used to control many aspects of the visualization environment. Using these virtual tools the user can operate with very few hand gestures. Hand gestures will pass different commands to the system depending on which tool the gesture is operating on. In the current version of the virtual windtunnel, only two gestures are used, grab and point. In combination with various virtual tools, many different commands may be given to the system with these two gestures. A challenge for future development is the exploration of virtual tools that take advantage of the three-dimensional interface. Explorations in this area are part of the virtual windtunnel development project. The Applied Research Branch at NASA Ames, where the virtual windtunnel is being developed, is also working closely with the computer graphics group under Andy van Dam at Brown University on the next generation of three-dimensional virtual tools.

Other control and display devices would also be useful. The virtual windtunnel system contains only the minimum control and display capability for a viable virtual environment. An obvious addition would be a voice recognition system. This would allow the researcher to talk to the system directing various aspects of the environment. While the glove is appropriate for "manual" tasks such as the movement of a rake, it is less suited for the control of more abstract quantities such as the type and number of seedpoints on a rake. A voice recognition system will be integrated into the virtual windtunnel this year for additional control. Other possible controls include the six-degree-of-freedom spaceball, which senses the force and torque applied by the user about a point. The force and torque can be interpreted as six numbers that are used to control various aspects of the environment. One use of the spaceball is to control the user's position and orientation within the virtual environment.

The computational platform for the virtual environment must be capable of performing the computations involved in the desired visualizations. Isosurfaces, for example, are computationally intensive and require more computational speed for real-time interaction than is available in most graphics workstations. The computer platform must, on the other hand, read the interface devices and render the graphics associated with virtual environments. Workstations are typically well suited for this task. The further development of high-power graphics workstations will enable a wider variety of applications of virtual environments to scientific applications. Distributed architectures when available are often desirable, where the workstation reads the interface devices and renders the graphics, while a remote supercomputer performs the computations.

The most severe problem is that of large amounts of data. The nature of interactive exploration requires that the data be accessed at high speed in unpredictable ways. This problem was already discussed in the context of large unsteady flows in the virtual windtunnel. Interesting datasets besides fluid flow have this problem in very severe ways. Numerical spacetime data are on grids of size comparable to those in fluid flow, but each grid point has much more data. Data returned by the Earth Observation Satellite (EOS) will be massive. The ability to quickly get at large amounts of stored data is one of the primary bottlenecks in the use of virtual environments for the visualization of large datasets.

7.5.   FUTURE DIRECTIONS

The advantages of virtual environments in the unambiguous display of three-dimensional structures and the intuitive three-dimensional control of objects in the virtual environment can potentially be of great use in scientific visualization. The ability to explore complex data by selectively displaying aspects of that data is the most dramatic aspect of these advantages.

The real power of virtual environments comes when abstract concepts which have no tangible real world counterpart such as streamlines in an unsteady flow are used to create virtual objects. By making these abstract concepts tangible their investigation is greatly facilitated. One is tempted to call this process "scientific reification". The examples above take physical quantities such as airflow and render derived structures such as vortices as real things with tangible properties. The same principles can be applied to more abstract quantities, such as statistical data or mathematical models. This would aid the pedagogical presentation of abstract concepts as well as the investigation of abstract phenomena.

What kinds of applications are virtual environments suited to? At this stage of development, virtual environment technology is "clumsy", full of difficulties and limitations which must be worked around to provide a viable application. There are undoubtedly several interesting applications that can be developed now with the current technology. As the technology advances, qualitatively different applications may appear that are as far beyond the current systems as the current systems are beyond early computer plotter drawings.

Given the current state of the art, any visualization that involves complex three-dimensional data which is moderately computationally intensive will probably benefit from a virtual environment interface. While the current cost in both hardware and labor of virtual environment development is high, research in the effective use of virtual environments in scientific visualization is needed. The few successful examples that exist only hint at the usefulness and limits of virtual environments.

7.6.   CONCLUSIONS

Virtual environments, at least at the current level of technology, are not intended to be a panacea for every computer graphics interface problem. Virtual environment interfaces are a tool and like all tools have their place. Ultimately, it may be that virtual environments will include all other interface paradigms as subsets, but that day is far in the future. In the meantime, however, there seems to be a class of problems, particularly in the scientific visualization of complex three-dimensional phenomena, where virtual environments provide significant advantages.

ACKNOWLEDGMENT

This work was supported under government contract NAS 2–12961.

REFERENCES

Bryson, S. (1992a). Virtual spacetime: an environment for the visualization of curved spacetimes via geodesic flows. In *Proceedings of IEEE Visualization '92*, Boston, MA.

Bryson, S. (1992b). Paradigms for the shaping of surfaces in a virtual environment. In *Proceedings of the 25th Hawaii International Conference on Systems Science*, Poipu Beach, Hawaii.

Bryson, S. and Gerald-Yamasaki, M. (1992). The distributed virtual windtunnel. In *Proceedings of Supercomputing '92*, Minneapolis, MN.

Bryson, S. and Levit, C. (1992). The virtual windtunnel: an environment for the exploration of three-dimensional unsteady fluid flows. *Computer Graphics and Applications.*

Freedman, M. H. and Quinn, F. (1990). *The Topology of Four-Manifolds.* Princeton Mathematical Series 39, Princeton University Press, Princeton, NJ.

Jespersen, D. and Levit, C. (1991). Numerical simulation of flow past a tapered cylinder. Paper AIAA-91-0751, American Institute of Aeronautics 29th Annual Aerospace Sciences Meeting, Reno.

McCormick, B., DeFanti, T. A. and Brown, M. D. (1987). Visualization in scientific computing. *Computer Graphics* **21**(6).

Smarr, L. (1991). Visualization captures the imagination of physicists. *Computers in Physics*, Vol. **5**(6).

Smith, M., Chawla, K. and Van Dalsem, W. (1991). Numerical simulation of a complete STOVL aircraft in ground effect. *AIAA-91-3293, AIAA 9th Applied Aerodynamics Conference*, Baltimore, MD.

About the author

Steve Bryson is an employee of Computer Sciences Corporation working under contract for the Applied Research Office of the Numerical Aerodynamics Simulation Systems Division at NASA Ames Research Center. In this position he is researching the use of virtual environment technology in various fields of scientific visualization, primarily the visualization of fluid flow. Prior to this position, he worked at the NASA Ames VIEW lab developing the first fully integrated virtual environment facility. Prior to that he worked for VPL Research, Inc., a small company devoted to the development of virtual environment technology.

Part III
Theory and Models

Chapter 8
A classification scheme for scientific visualization

Ken Brodlie

8.1. INTRODUCTION

Scientists and engineers have long used visualization as a tool in understanding complex phenomena. Historical research (West, 1991) shows that many notable scientists such as Faraday and Clerk Maxwell have relied on visual thinking in their work. From the early days of computing, researchers in computational science and engineering have provided the stimulus for the development of data plotting tools – for example, GHOST was developed at the United Kingdom Atomic Research Authority's Culham Laboratory in the 1960s, to support the needs of computational physicists.

However, the recent thrust in scientific visualization is often attributed to the publication of the NSF Report on Visualization in Scientific Computing (McCormick *et al.*, 1987). This report made the case for attention to be given to visualization, as a way of capitalizing on two major technological developments of the past decade: first, the increasing computing power for numerical simulation, and second, the increasing bandwidth of sensing equipment. Both of these developments have led to significant increases in data collection throughout basic and applied science. The NSF report argued that visual techniques were necessary, first of all to understand and explore such datasets, and secondly, having understood, to communicate and educate.

Publication of the report sparked the development of a new era of visualization systems. Many are based on a dataflow paradigm: the system offers a variety of building blocks which can input data, transform it and display it. To visualize a dataset, a scientist will select a particular combination of modules and connect them together in a pipeline. Data flows from one module to another. Well known examples are AVS (Upson *et al.*, 1989); apE (Dyer, 1990), Khoros (Rasure *et al.*, 1991), IBM Data Explorer (Lucas *et al.*, 1992) and Iris Explorer (Edwards, 1992). These systems are now in common use, but it is important to note that some

ANIMATION AND SCIENTIFIC VISUALIZATION
ISBN 0-12-227745-7

more traditional approaches have remained popular: the subroutine library approach (such as UNIRAS, GHOST, GINO and NAG Graphics); the menu driven systems (such as the UNIRAS interactives); and command driven systems (such as PV-WAVE).

The scope of visualization software has also been extended in recent years. Early systems provided visualization in one or two space dimensions; three-dimensional (3D) volume visualization is now common place, and flow visualization using particle traces and streamers is increasingly common.

Visualization is therefore an expanding subject, driven by the demands of users in a variety of application areas. It is the task of the computer scientist to develop a sound underlying methodology for the new "science of visualization".

Several authors have built models of the visualization process and how it fits into an overall problem-solving environment (Upson *et al.*, 1989; Haber and McNabb, 1990). In particular, a view has emerged that sees the visualization process divided into a number of logical steps. In Section 8.2, we review this work and suggest a variation that may be closer to a mental model of the process.

We then seek some means of classifying visualization techniques. This is work that has evolved over a number of years (Brodlie, 1992, 1993) and to which various people have contributed. The aim is to define a structure on the subject that can be the basis of a taxonomy of visualization.

8.2.   THE VISUALIZATION PROCESS

8.2.1.   The data flow model

An important paper by Upson *et al.* (1989) has set out a model of the visualization process, which has had a major influence on the development of visualization. It is a data-oriented model in which data is transformed in a number of logical steps on its way to display. Thus the model assumes there is a source of data – this may be a simulation or a set of observations. The steps in the visualization process are then described as follows (Figure 8.1):

Filtering: in this step, data of "interest" are derived from the raw input data. This step can involve a variety of operations: it could involve an interpolation from scattered data to a regular grid; or extracting a cross-section of data; or performing some smoothing operation.

Mapping: in this step, a geometrical representation of the data is constructed. For example, if a contour map is being drawn from 2D height data, this will involve constructing isolines as a set of polylines, or curves.

Rendering: in this final step, the geometric representation is converted to an image which can be displayed.

A further elaboration of this model is given by Haber and McNabb (1990). The model has been the basis of several visualization systems, including

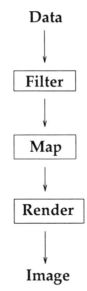

Figure 8.1. Data flow model.

AVS and Iris Explorer. These provide a library of modules, each categorized as one of the three types. The application developer picks an appropriate combination of modules and "wires" them together in a network. As data is read in, it "flows" through the network, from filter modules to map modules to render modules – hence the term "dataflow system".

Although this model has been successful, it can be argued it gives a false view of the world because it is data-centered. It is rarely the data which one wants to "visualize" – rather it is the underlying field from which the data has been sampled. It is the job of visualization to reconstruct this field from the data, and then to use different techniques to display the field. For example, in the simple case of a topographic map, one would be disappointed to see only the spot heights marked – it is the behavior over the entire area of interest that one wishes to see displayed.

8.2.2. Not the data

In this section we give a simple example which hopefully proves the point. We consider the observed oxygen levels in flue gas when a batch of coal undergoes combustion in a furnace. At ignition, the oxygen level is 20.8% and it rapidly falls to 4.2% after 4 min have elapsed. Eventually the oxygen level rises again as the combustion process is completed.

The data values are shown in Table 8.1. Visualizing the "data" produces the plot shown in Figure 8.2. Of course, this is not what we are really interested in – we want to know the behavior where we do not have data! A typical approach found in visualization systems is to fit a cubic spline interpolant (see, for example, Lancaster and Salkauskas, 1986), and this has been done to construct the curve shown in Figure 8.3.

The resulting visualization has no credibility whatsoever. Negative

Table 8.1.

		x (time in mins)					
	0	2	4	10	28	30	32
y (% of oxygen)	20.8	8.8	4.2	0.5	3.9	6.2	9.6

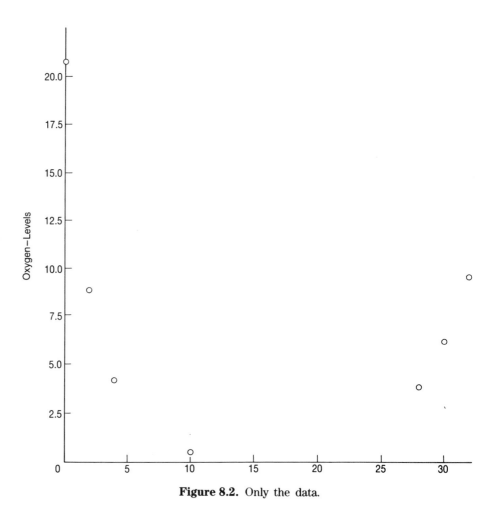

Figure 8.2. Only the data.

percentages of oxygen are physically impossible. Failure occurred because the wrong empirical model was used to define the underlying field. If the scientist knows the field is everywhere positive, then this information must be built into the interpolation process. Recently there has been work on preserving different shape properties in interpolation – for example, monotonicity (Fritsch and Carlson, 1980), convexity (Brodlie and Butt, 1991) and positivity (Butt and Brodlie, 1993). Here it is positivity we require in the underlying model, and Figure 8.4 shows the results we get from the

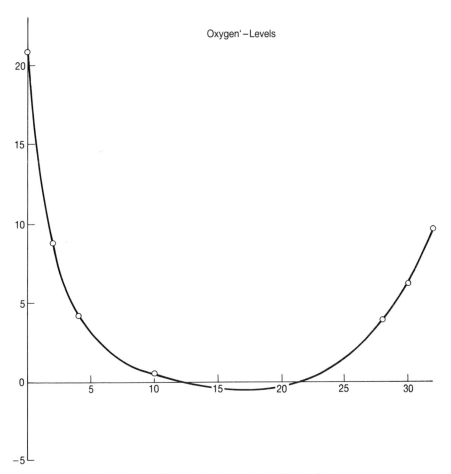

Figure 8.3. Not only the data, but also in between.

Butt–Brodlie interpolation method. (The slopes at data points are calculated by cubic spline interpolation, but additional knots are inserted to maintain positivity.)

8.2.3. Importance of a model

The previous example has underlined the importance of basing a visualization on a valid empirical model. In this section we develop the idea further by looking at two common visualization techniques which use no underlying model of the data whatsoever, and hence suffer serious flaws.

A very simple approach to contour plotting is the following. Suppose the data are defined on a regular rectangular mesh, and suppose we look in particular at the grid cell shown in Figure 8.5. The contour level to be drawn is of value h. The value at A is $\geq$ h, and at B, < h; inverse linear interpolation along the side AB gives an intersection point T.

Now consider Figure 8.6: the values at C and D indicate an intersection point S. It is common practice to join T and S by a straight line; most

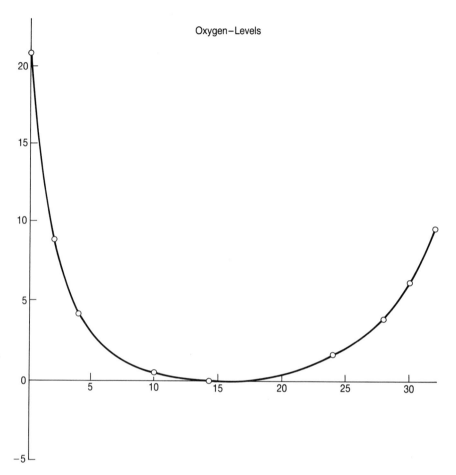

Figure 8.4. Not only the data, but also a sensible curve.

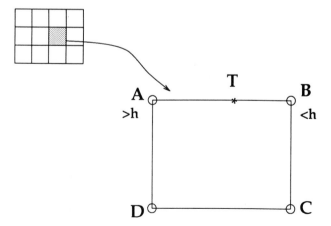

Figure 8.5. Contouring: calculating intersection point.

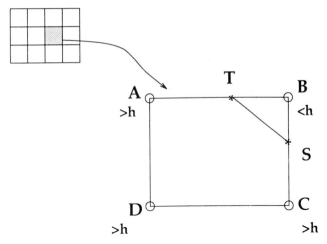

Figure 8.6. Contouring: drawing a section of contour line.

other arrangements of data at C and D admit similar solutions to the problem. But consider Figure 8.7: there is an ambiguity with three possible solutions – which to choose?

The difficulty is that the method has no underlying model of the data to help it choose. The four data values at the grid points would allow a bilinear function to be constructed:

$$F(x,y) = a + bx + cy + dxy.$$

This is linear along the cell edges, so the intersection points are correct, but it is not linear within the cell – so it is quite incorrect to join the intersection points with straight lines.

It is time consuming to track the contours of the bilinear function F within the cell, but there is a simple way out. One can use the function F

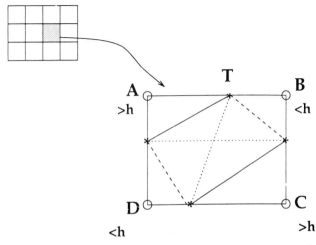

Figure 8.7. Contouring: ambiguities – which lines to draw? (——, solution 1; – – –, solution 2; ....., solution 3).

to estimate the value at the centre of the cell, and then construct a St Andrews cross of four triangles (Figure 8.8). A linear function

$$G(x,y) = a + bx + cy$$

can be fitted to each triangle; the contours of this function are straight lines and so no ambiguity occurs.

This is no new discovery – see for example Sutcliffe (1980). But the lessons are not always learned, and it is not uncommon to find visualization systems using the ambiguous method (and using some rule of thumb to resolve the ambiguity rather than a sound alternative as just described).

Indeed one can see the same thing happening in volume visualization. The 3D analog of the simple contouring method is the marching cubes algorithm of Lorensen and Cline (1987), which is very widely used in modern visualization systems as a means of drawing isosurfaces. Rather than a grid cell, we now have a voxel as shown in Figure 8.9. Each grid point can be either greater than or less than the isosurface level h – giving 2^8 or 256 different arrangements. Lorensen and Cline show that there are in effect only 14 canonical forms, and for each of these they show the triangular facets of the isosurface that will result. Figure 8.9 shows the two triangles generated for one of the 14 forms.

It will come as no surprise now to find that this arrangement is ambiguous – the triangles could be as in Figure 8.10. The ambiguity is because there is no underlying model. Again the solution is to construct a trilinear interpolant over the voxel

$$F(x,y,z) = a + bx + cy + dz + exy + fyz + gzx + hxyz$$

in order to estimate the value at the centre; the voxel can then be split into 24 tetrahedra within each of which a unique linear underlying model can be defined:

$$G(x,y,z) = a + bx + cy + dz .$$

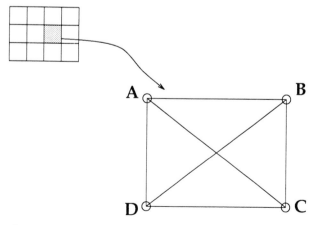

Figure 8.8. Contouring: subdivision into four triangles, to allow consistent bilinear interpolation.

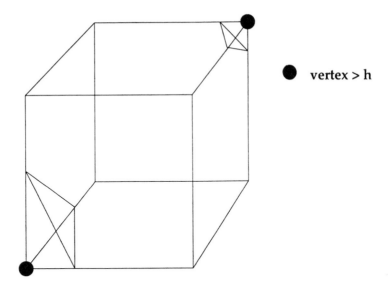

Figure 8.9. Marching cubes: triangular facets for one canonical form.

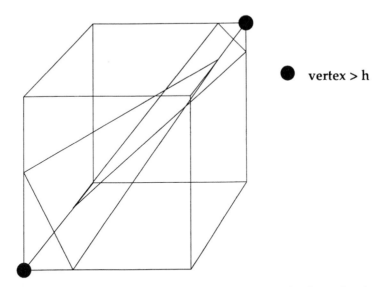

Figure 8.10. Marching cubes: an alternative pair of triangular facets for the same canonical form.

This has triangular facets as isosurfaces and so there is no problem; see Wilhelms and van Gelder (1990) for a fuller discussion.

8.2.4. Model-centered approach

The above examples have shown the importance of the underlying model in obtaining an accurate and valid visualization. This suggests that any view

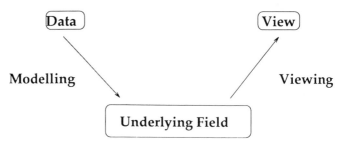

Figure 8.11. Model–centered approach.

of the visualization process should have the model as a central concept. This leads us to propose an alternative view of the visualization process to the conventional data flow paradigm described earlier: the steps are (see Figure 8.11):

Modeling: in this step we construct an empirical model from the data samples. This will involve interpolation if the data are assumed exact, and approximation if the data are in error.
Viewing: in this step a particular view of the model is constructed.

In the example of drawing a contour map from scattered data, the modeling step is the use of one of a number of possible interpolants to define the value of the function at all points in the region of interest. The viewing step will then choose one of a number of techniques for displaying the function – a contour map, or a surface view, say.

How does this approach compare with the conventional filter, map, render sequence? The modeling stage in our approach corresponds to part of the filter operation; the viewing stage corresponds to the remainder of the pipeline. It can be argued that this gives a better logical separation. The filter operation, as currently defined, is a combination of two operations that should be seen as distinct: first, building the empirical model, and then extracting data from the model for display.

In our approach, the map and render steps are not distinguished. While in some visualizations such a separation may be useful (for example, in isosurfacing, where an intermediate geometric representation is indeed constructed), in others it is an irrelevance (for example, in volume rendering by ray casting).

Thus we would claim our approach gives a high-level view of visualization that is a useful mental model for the scientist or engineer to follow. The filter, map, render sequence on the other hand could be regarded more as an implementation model to support dataflow systems.

8.3. DEVELOPING A CLASSIFICATION SCHEME

In this section, we seek a notation that we can use to describe concisely a particular instance of the visualization process. This is work which began at the AGOCG Workshop on Scientific Visualization (Brodlie *et al.*, 1992).

At that workshop, a notation was developed to describe different visualization techniques. However, it failed to distinguish properly between the nature of the underlying field and the means of looking at that field. Thus here we prefer to start with a classification of the underlying field, which is at the heart of our approach.

The notation was further influenced by two other workshops: Visualization in Geographic Information Systems (Brodlie, 1993) sponsored by AGI, and Data in Visualization (Gallop *et al.*, 1992) sponsored by SERC EASE Visualization Community Club – and no doubt will evolve further!

There are other important influences. Butler and Pendley (1989) have described an elegant mathematical approach called fiber bundles. This aims to describe the underlying field in terms of two spaces: a base space which defines the range of the independent variables; and a fiber space which defines the range of the dependent variables. Suppose we are drawing a simple xy graph. The base space will be the range of x; the fiber space will be the possible range of y – say, from $-\infty$ to $+\infty$.

Imagine now the fiber space being attached to each point of the base space. This product space defines an envelope of all possible realizations of the underlying field (i.e. in our case, all possible xy graphs): a cross-section through this space gives an instance of the entity (in our case, a single xy graph). Butler and Pendley call this cross-section a fiber bundle.

The elegance and power of this description becomes evident when the base space is a complicated region – say, an aircraft wing – and the fiber is, say, a 3D vector defining a flow direction. This complex field is concisely described. Moreover, different operations on bundles can be defined: for example, a bundle restriction will select a subset of the base space – taking in effect a cross-section through the fiber bundle.

A different treatment is given by Haber *et al.* (1991), extending the fiber bundle theory to fields described in piecewise fashion – for example, over a finite element mesh. This work has been used as the basis of the datatypes in the IBM Data Explorer visualization system (Lucas *et al.*, 1992).

Our approach here is similar in that we are concerned with the underlying field rather than the data. However, we are aiming to extract the key factors so that we have a concise notation to describe a field and its possible views. We are aiming then to classify types of field and view, rather than precisely describe a particular field.

8.3.1. Classifying the underlying field

In general terms, the underlying field can be regarded as a function of many variables: say,

$$f(x)$$

where

$$f = (f^1, f^2, \dots f^m) \,,$$

$$x = (x_1, x_2, \dots x_n) \,.$$

The range of the independent variables x will typically be restricted to some domain R, which may be of lower dimension – for example, in visualizing the temperature across an aircraft wing, the three independent space variables are restricted to a 2D domain, namely the surface of the wing.

We shall be interested in classifying the type of the function, that is, the type of the dependent variable; and in classifying the type of the independent variable.

Type of dependent variable

Consider first the type of the dependent variable. We can identify two distinct cases: first where the data type is ordinal (O), that is the values can be put in order; second, where the data type is nominal (N), that is the values are essentially names with no associated ordering. For example, if the underlying field is height over a region, that is clearly of type O; on the other hand, if the underlying field is the make of car parked at points in a region, that is of type N.

In addition, the dimension of the dependent variable will be of interest. The common terminology is to talk of scalar, vector and tensor fields: a scalar field will be indicated by S; a vector field by V_m, where m is the number of components of the vector; a tensor field by $T_{m:m:...m}$. This can be applied as a superscript to the basic data type; thus, a second-order tensor of dimension 6 would be coded as $O^{T_{6:6}}$ for example. Likewise, N^S would represent a field which can take one of a set of names, say, place names in the UK.

Type of independent variable

The type of the independent variable can again be either ordinal or nominal. For example, if the underlying field is height over a region, then as with the dependent variable, the independent variable (position in space) is also of type ordinal; on the other hand, if the field is the number of cars of a particular type, the type of the independent variable is nominal. The dimension of the independent variable can be attached as a suffix; thus, positions in 2D space could be coded as O_2, for example. Similarly, N_1 would be a 1D list of names.

In addition, it is useful to introduce two "operators". The first is an aggregate, where the independent variable does not take single values, but instead is defined as a range of values. For example, one might be interested in the number of cars within a specific area: the independent variable here is an area, an aggregate of points. This will be denoted

$$[O_2]$$

the [...] notation indicating a range.

The second operator is a restriction, where the independent variable is restricted to some lower-dimensional subspace. The notation we use is {...}. Thus, if an entity is defined over a curve in 3D space, we would write

$$\{O_3\}_1 .$$

Composite notation

We can now put the two parts of the notation together. Corresponding to the mathematical notation $f(x)$, we can write the notation for the independent variables within parentheses following the notation for the dependent variables. Thus, the height over a 2D region can be written as

$$O^S(O_2);$$

a vector field in 3D as

$$O^{V_3}(O_3);$$

the number of cars of a particular type as

$$O^S(N_1);$$

and so on. Often the field will be a combination of different quantities: for example, in a CFD application, one can have pressure, density and velocity as dependent variables – this can be coded as

$$O^{2S+V_3}(O_3)$$

if it is to be seen as a unified entity, or as

$$O^S(O_3) + O^S(O_3) + O^{V_3}(O_3)$$

if the quantities are to be considered separately.

To illustrate the restriction operator, suppose we are interested in depicting the temperature on an aircraft wing: this is coded as

$$O_S(\{O_3\})_2,$$

that is, a scalar of ordinal type over a domain which is a 2D subset of 3D space.

8.3.2. Classifying the view

In our approach, we see viewing as an operation on the underlying field to produce a pictorial representation. The view may not depict the entire field, but only some subset. The notation described above can also be used to describe this subfield. Therefore a useful way of characterizing a view, or indeed a visualization technique, is to express it in terms of the field it operates on and the subfield which results.

An example may help to make this clearer. Consider the case where we are given heights at a number of positions in 2D space, and wish to visualize the surface from which these height values are sampled. The modeling step will generate by means of interpolation a scalar 2D field, that is

$$O^S(O_2).$$

If a line contour map is chosen as the view, then isolines are constructed for a specified set of heights. These isolines are essentially a subfield of the original model, with independent variable of dimension 1. The subfield is therefore

$$O^S(O_1).$$

On the other hand, if a continuously shaded image is to be created as the view, then the subfield is identical to the original field.

Some views involve applying the aggregate operator. For example, in a histogram display, the independent variable is an aggregate, or range, of values, even though the underlying field is defined at single values. Using the notation for aggregates, a histogram is represented as

$$O^S([O_1])$$

Scatter plots provide an interesting case study. A 2D scatter plot is based on a model:

$$O^{V_2}(N_1)$$

that is, an unordered set of points; the view could be coded as

$$\{O_2\}_0$$

that is, a restriction of 2D space to 0D space, i.e. points.

8.4. A TAXONOMY OF VISUALIZATION TECHNIQUES

We are now in a position to develop a taxonomy of techniques based on our notation. Table 8.2 lists a number of common visualization techniques, and characterizes them by the field which they operate upon and the view which results. This is just a preliminary exercise to show what is possible; it should be feasible to extend this to a more complete set of techniques.

8.5. CONCLUSIONS

Conventional models of the visualization process are based on a dataflow paradigm, in which data is filtered, then mapped, then rendered. This

Table 8.2.

Field	Display technique	View
$O^S(O_1)$	Line graph	$O^S(O_1)$
	Histogram	$O^S([O_1])$
$O^S(N_1)$	Bar chart	$O^S(N_1)$
$O^S(O_2)$	Contourline plot	$O^S(O_1)$
	Surface view	$O^S(O_{29})$
$O^S(O_3)$	Isosurface	$O^S(O_2)$
	Volume rendering	$O^S(O_3)$

chapter has presented an alternative model in which the emphasis is not on the data, but on the underlying field from which the data are sampled. It has been argued that it is this field which one wants to visualize, not the data. This has motivated the new approach in which two steps are identified: a modeling step in which the empirical estimate of the underlying field is created; and a viewing step, in which some aspect of the model is depicted.

These ideas have been used to further develop a notation for classifying visualization data and display techniques – work which has evolved over a number of recent workshops. Finally this notation has been proposed as the basis of a taxonomy of display techniques.

Is the classification simply an interesting exercise, or has it greater value? One clear benefit is that it establishes equivalence classes of techniques, thus providing an immediate set of alternative views for any given model–view pairing. There is also the possibility in the future of developing an automatic selection of visualization technique, given the model and view.

The notation will surely evolve further – for example, is the notation for scatter plots suggested earlier the correct one, or are there other interpretations? How is a pie chart denoted?

Hopefully, however, this is a small contribution towards establishing a sound methodology for visualization as a science.

ACKNOWLEDGMENTS

The work on developing a good notation has evolved over a number of workshops and I would like to thank all who have helped even though they are too numerous to name individually. Particular help with this paper has come from Lesley Brankin and Helen Wright – many thanks.

REFERENCES

Brodlie, K. W. (1992). Visualization techniques. In Brodlie, K. W. *et al.* (eds), *Scientific Visualization – Techniques and Applications*, pp. 37–86. Springer-Verlag, New York.

Brodlie, K. W. (1993). A typology for scientific visualization. In Hearnshaw, H. and Unwin, D. J. (eds), *Visualization in Geographic Information Systems*. Belhaven Press.

Brodlie, K. W. and Butt, S. (1991). Preserving convexity using piecewise cubic interpolation. *Computer and Graphics*, **15**(1), 15–23.

Brodlie, K. W., Carpenter, L. A., Gallop, J. R., Earnshaw, R. A., Hubbold, R. J., Mumford, A. M., Osland, C. D. and Quarendon, P. (eds) (1992). *Scientific Visualization – Techniques and Applications*. Springer-Verlag.

Butler, D. M. and Pendley, M. H. (1989). A visualization model based on the mathematics of fibre bundles. *Computers in Physics* **3**, 45–51.

Butt, S. and Brodlie, K. W. (1993). Preserving positivity using piecewise cubic interpolation. *Computer and Graphics* **17**(1), 55–64.

Dyer, D. S. (1990). A dataflow toolkit for visualization. *IEEE Computer Graphics and Applications* **10**(4), 60–69.

Edwards, G. (1992). Visualization – the second generation. *Image Processing*, 48–53.

Fritsch, F. N. and Carlson, R. E. (1980). Monotone piecewise cubic interpolation. *SIAM Journal of Numerical Analysis* **17**, 238–246.

Gallop, J. R., Hewitt, W. T. and Larkin, S. (1992). Report on data in visualization workshop. SERC EASE Visualization Community Club.

Haber, R. B. and McNabb, D. A. (1990). Visualization idioms: a conceptual model for scientific visualization systems. In Shriver, B., Nielson, G. M. and Rosenblum, L. J. (eds), *Visualization in Scientific Computing*, pp. 74–93. IEEE Computer Society Press.

Haber, R. B., Lucas, B. and Collins, N. (1991). A data model for scientific visualization with provisions for regular and irregular grids. In *Visualization '91 Proceedings*, pp. 298–305. IEEE Computer Society Press.

Lancaster, P. and Salkauskas, K. (1986). *Curve and Surface Fitting: An Introduction.* Academic Press, London.

Lorensen, W. E. and Cline, H. E. (1987). Marching cubes: a high resolution 3d surface reconstruction algorithm. *Computer Graphics* **21**(4), 163–169.

Lucas, B., Abram, G. D., Collins, N. S., Epstein, D. A., Gresh, D. L. and McAuliffe, K. P. (1992). An architecture for a scientific visualization system. In Kaufman, A. E. and Nielson, G. M. (eds), *Visualization 92 Proceedings*, pp. 107–114. IEEE Computer Society Press.

McCormick, B., DeFanti, T. A. and Brown, M. D. (1987). Visualization in scientific computing. *ACM SIGGRAPH Computer Graphics* **21**(6).

Rasure, J., Argiro, D., Sauer, T. and Williams, C. (1991). A visual language and software development environment for image processing. *International Journal of Imaging Systems and Technology.*

Sutcliffe, D. C. (1980). Contouring over rectangular and skewed rectangular grids – an introduction. In Brodlie, K. W. (ed.), *Mathematical Methods in Computer Graphics and Design*, pp. 39–62. Academic Press, New York and London.

Upson, C., Faulhaber, T., Kamins, D., Schlegel, D., Laidlaw, D., Vroom, J., Gurwitz, R. and van Dam, A. (1989). The application visualization system: a computational environment for scientific visualization. *IEEE Computer Graphics and Applications* **9**(4), 30–42.

West, T. G. (1991). *In the Mind's Eye.* Prometheus Books.

Wilhelms, J. and Van Gelder, A. (1990). Topological ambiguities in isosurface generation. Technical Report UCSC-CRL-90-14, CIS Board, University of California, Santa Cruz.

About the author

Ken Brodlie is Senior Lecturer in the School of Computer Studies at the University of Leeds, and Deputy Head of the Division of Computer Science. He has had a long involvement with international standards for computer graphics, and presently chairs the group looking at the revision of GKS. His interest in scientific visualization began with an involvement in the NAG Graphics Library, and has extended to research into more general problem solving environments. He was founding chairman of the UK Chapter of Eurographics, and is on the editorial board of Computer Graphics Forum and Computers and Graphics.

Chapter 9
Unifying principles of data management for scientific visualization

Lloyd A. Treinish

9.1. BACKGROUND

Obviously, data management is critical for appropriate and effective utilization of large volumes of data. For example, such data may come from sources as diverse as

remotely sensed or *in-situ* observations in the earth and space sciences;
seismic sounding of the earth for petroleum geophysics (or similar signal processing endeavors in acoustics/oceanography, radio astronomy, nuclear magnetic resonance, synthetic aperture radar, etc.);
large-scale supercomputer-based models in computational fluid dynamics (e.g., aerospace, meteorology, geophysics, astrophysics), quantum physics and chemistry, etc.;
medical (tomographic) imaging (e.g. CAT, PET, MRI);
computational chemistry;
genetic sequence mapping;
intelligence gathering;
geographic mapping and cartography;
census, financial and other "statistical" data.

The instrumentation technology behind these data generators is rapidly improving, typically much faster than the techniques available to manage and use the resultant data. In fact, an onslaught of data orders of magnitude greater from these and other sources is expected over the next several years. Hence, greater cognizance of the impact of these data volumes is required. For example, NASA's Earth Observing System (Eos), which is planned for deployment in the late 1990s, will have to receive, process and store up to 10 Tbyte (10^{13} bytes) of complex, interdisciplinary, multidimensional earth sciences data per day, for over a decade. Given the fact that such datasets are or will be generated, what can be done to cope

ANIMATION AND SCIENTIFIC VISUALIZATION
ISBN 0-12-227745-7

with this deluge from the perspective of their access, management and utilization?

The ability to generate pictorial representations of data is currently in vogue as being the answer. This concept of (scientific) data visualization really implies a method of computing that gives visual form to complex data using graphics and imaging technology. It is based upon the notion that the human visual system has an enormous capacity for receiving and interpreting data efficiently. Despite the advancement of visualization techniques for scientific data over the last several years, there are still significant problems in bringing today's hardware and software technology into the hands of the typical scientist. Some of these same problems do occur in more general processing and analysis of scientific data in many disciplines. For example, data management is required to make such computing effective, which can be expressed by the need for a class of data models that is matched to the structure of scientific data as well as how such data may be used. The critical component of data management is typically missing in many such computing efforts. When this concept is scaled to support large datasets (e.g. a few gigabytes), several critical problems emerge in the access and use of such data, which brings the problem back to the data level. This circular reasoning does not imply that applications such as visualization are not relevant, but the challenge is more complex than simply flowing data for storage and looking at the pictures or even "pointing" back to the numbers behind the pictures. This requirement for scientific data models extends beyond the definition and support for well-defined physical formats. It must include the logical specification of self-documenting (including semantics) scientific data to be studied via a visualization system and data derived through the operation of the tools in such a system.

Recently, considerable attention has also been placed on metadata support for the management of current and past large data streams, because through it a scientist would be able to select data of interest for analysis. However, if adequate mechanisms for use of the actual data that meet the requirements and expectations of the scientific users of such data are not available, then the efforts to generate and archive the data and supporting metadata management will be for nought. Although it is beyond the scope of this discussion, advances in visualization and data structures can also be applied to metadata management in the form of browsing, support of spatial search and selection criteria, etc.

What can be done? A place to begin is a discussion about solutions for how data should be organized, managed and accessed, which is often not adequately addressed in visualization and related software. The following is a survey of some of the methods and requirements for data management in visualization. It is hardly meant to be either exhaustive or definitive, but merely an introduction to an important topic.

9.2. DATA CHARACTERISTICS

There are a tremendous number of sources of scientific data, be they computed or measured. Even from a single source there can be a wide variety of datasets. Each such dataset typically contains several independent variables such as time, one or more spatial, spectral, etc. variables, and of course, many dependent variables, where the interesting science is stored. There can be a bewildering range of underlying formats, structures, arrangements and access methods for these data. To attempt to bring some simplifying order to this chaos, consider the following categories for describing data, where data implies a field or parameter of one or more (dependent) values that is a function of one or more (independent) variables:

physical data type primitives (e.g. byte, int, float, ...) – how the values are stored on some medium;

dimensionality (e.g. spatial, temporal, spectral) – the size, shape and organization of the values;

rank (e.g. scalar, vector, tensor, ...) – the number of values per element;

mesh description (e.g. regular, irregular, curvilinear, ...) – the size, shape and organization of how the values map to some physical domain for each element;

aggregation (e.g. hierarchies, groups, series) – any collection or organization of a set of functional values.

Such a taxonomy typically does not include those data directly associated with graphics, which is beyond the scope of this discussion. The appendix contains a table which outlines the extent of support of these characteristics by various implementations. An important point to consider is that these characteristics should be considered more or less independently of each other to maximize flexibility in actual visualization software. For example, a distinction can be made between a 2-vector, 3-vector and two scalars in 2-space vs. a 2-vector, 3-vector and 3-scalars in 3-space independently of data type primitive or underlying mesh structure, if any. In this context, rank implies tensor rank (e.g. rank 0 is a scalar, rank 1 is a vector, rank 2 is what is commonly considered a tensor, etc.). Scalars are single-valued functions (e.g., temperature). Vectors of size, n, are n-valued functions (i.e. there is magnitude and direction, e.g., velocity). A rank 2 tensor in n-dimensional space is a $n \times n$ matrix of functions (e.g. stress).

Table 9.1 illustrates some of the diversity of visualization techniques that may be required in a system when only considering the earth and space sciences. Examples are listed with different dimensionalities and rank. The number of elements in a particular quantity is d^r, where d is the dimensionality and r is the rank. The suite of techniques should accommodate time-dependent quantities as having another scalar dimension, which can be mapped into a specific visualization primitive or "axis". In a complementary fashion, animation should be treated as an additional scalar "axis" for sequencing of other visualization primitive(s) in either a discrete or continuous fashion, which may be hardware dependent. It should be noted that the example data types are not intended to be all encompassing and

Table 9.1. Visualization primitives.

Dimension/ rank	Example data types	Discrete visualizations	Fully continuous visualizations
0/0	Flat (point)	Histogram	
1/0	Time histories Profiles Zonal means Particle spectrum	xy (scatter, bar) 2D histogram	xy (line)
1/1	Currents	Arrows	
2/0	Grid/image Zonal profiles Particle spectra	Multiple xy xyz (scatter boxes) xy pseudo-color	Contours Wire-frame surface Shaded surface Pseudo-color image
2/1	Surface winds	Arrows	Ribbons Particle advection Streamlines
2/2	"u-v" currents	Pseudo-color arrows Pseudo-color streamlines	Pseudo-color ribbons
3/0	Grids/images Gridded profiles Zonal profiles	xyz pseudo-color Sliced isosurfaces Transparent isosurfaces "Solid" contours	Pseudo-color-shaded surface 3D contours Volume (voxel)
3/1	Winds	"Solid" arrows	Ribbons Particle advection Streamlines
≥3/2	Electromagnetic field (3/2) Relativistic electromagnetic field (4/2)	Multiple techniques Animation Scatter diagram matrix Glyphs Retinal encoding	Multiple techniques Animation

the specific visualization methods are not meant to be definitive mappings for specific data types nor exhaustive, but only to impart the notion of the amount of diversity.

9.2.1. Data meshes

Perhaps the class of characteristics for which there is the most confusion is the specification of mesh or grid types because of the typical use of domain-specific terminology. In general, a mesh describes the base geometry for the mapping of the functions or dependent variables to some (physical) coordinate system. Such a mesh may be explicitly or implicitly positioned. In the latter case, it is preferred to store the positioning information implicitly. Some implementations may store it explicitly. In most cases there is a topological relationship or cell primitive connecting these positions. For example, consider the following:

1. *Regular grid with regular positions and regular connectivity.* In this case, the two-dimensional primitive is a rectangle while the three-dimensional primitive is a parallelpiped. Usually, this case would imply cartesian coordinates. The mesh may be implicitly stored in a compact fashion via a specification of an ordered pair for each dimension (i.e. the origin and spacing in some coordinate system). The entire mesh may be formed by taking a product of the specifications across each dimension.

2. *Deformed regular or curvilinear or structured grid with irregular positions and regular connectivity.* In this case the primitives are the same as in case 1. Non-cartesian coordinates may be implicitly supported through such a deformed structure. Generally, the mesh is explicitly stored via a specification of a node position along each dimension (axis) in some coordinate system. The entire mesh may be formed by taking a product of the specifications across each dimension. A variation in this case and in case (1) would be a partially regular grid, which has one or more dimensions being regular (i.e. case (1)) and the balance being irregular.

3. *Irregular "regular" or structured grid with irregular positions and regular connectivity.* In this case the primitives are the same as in cases (1) and (2) but with irregular sizing and spacing, which may include holes. Positions are specified explicitly. Sparse matrices, grids or meshes can also be considered in this category. However, indexing schemes can be introduced to eliminate wasted storage.

4. *Unstructured or irregular grid with regular or irregular connectivity.* In this case, the two-dimensional primitive is typically a triangle while the three-dimensional primitive is typically a tetrahedron. However, it may be prismatic, icosahedral, hexahedra, etc. or even variable. Positions of each node are specified explicitly while a connections list identifying the relationship and order of each node on each primitive is generally required.

5. *No grid with irregular positions and no connectivity.* In this case the data are scattered or available on specific points, which are explicitly identified.

The notion of taking a product to form a mesh from vectors of positions can be applied to connections between positions. For example, regular connections of n points is defined by a set of $n-1$ line segments. A product of two sets of connections is a set of points obtained by summing one point from each of the terms in all possible combinations. Hence, a product of two regular connections composed of line segments would be a set of squares. A product of a regular connection of line segments and an irregular one of triangles would be a partially regular set of prisms.

Some of the two-dimensional mesh structures are shown in Figure 9.1. However, conventions are required for the specification of where the data (function is applied) with respect to the connection elements or topological

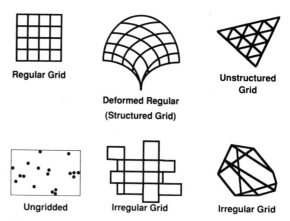

Figure 9.1. Example two-dimensional mesh types.

cell primitives. The data may apply to each node or position of a grid. Alternatively, the data may apply to a cell center or face, or even an edge. Although many cases usually apply only one convention for an entire mesh, it is not always true. Some finite element meshes may use more than one type of primitive and convention.

9.2.2. Data aggregates

Often there is a need to form aggregates of data. In dependent-variable space, one could have a collection of parameters or fields over the same or different grids that could be treated as single entity. In that sense, an aggregate or group could be composed of members that are either a single field or another group. This mechanism can be used to define simple tree structures. In independent-variable space, one could have a collection of meshes. For example, in aerospace fluid dynamics simulations, a computation is often performed over several intersecting grids. Such a multigrid solution permits the definition of variable grid resolution and regularity around airframe structures such as an engine nacelle or a wing. In this case, one could treat the collection of meshes as a single entity, although a mechanism must be defined for accommodating regions of invalidity where grids may intersect. A similar problem occurs with observational data, where there may be no data for some grid nodes. Another type of mesh aggregate can result from a hybrid collection of meshes of different cell primitives, where within each mesh, the cell is the same.

A special case of aggregates can be called series, where the tree structure has only one level of children. The classic example is a time series, where there is multiple instances of some field or aggregate over a constant or changing mesh. Generically, such a series does not have to depend on time, but could apply to any sequencing of events.

9.2.3. Temporal data

The support of temporal data as time series is an interesting matter. How should time be handled? There are two types of temporal support: as a running clock and epoch-based. In either case, time tags could be viewed like an additional dimension in the position component of a field with "linear" connectivity. One could then use a compact representation for constant Δt. Otherwise, each time tag (position) could be specified individually for irregular spaced time steps. Obviously, the other method of supporting time tags would be associating each tag with a member of a (time) series.

The running clock approach supports elapsed time from some base (i.e., such as the origin of a position component dimension) like time of launch or start of simulation. The simplest implementation would be the use of a floating point representation of linear time in user-defined units (e.g., milliseconds, seconds, minutes, hours, days, years). Optionally, the elapsed time could be a clock or calendar representation as a float (e.g. HHMMSS.s, YYDDD.d, where HH = hour [0–23], MM = minute [0–59], SS = second [0–59], s = fractional second, YY = year, DDD = day of year [0–365 or 366], and d = fractional day).

Epoch-based time tags represent an "absolute" standard time from a standard reference epoch in a linear, clock or calendar representation. Such tags are more common with observational than simulated data since the former often require a link to the real world as well as registration with other observations. Generally, Greenwich Mean Time (GMT) is used as the standard time frame (at least for the earth). Example reference epochs often start exactly at midnight on 1 January of some specific year (e.g. 0, 1900, 1950) according to an accepted (i.e. European) calendar. Some example conventions for representation include the following:

milliseconds since midnight, 1 January 0 AD (double);
year/month/day since midnight, 1 January 0 AD:YYYYMMDD (long);
time of day: HHMMSS (long);
year/month/day since midnight, 1 January 1900: YYMMDD.d (float);
year/day of year since midnight, 1 January 1900: YYDDD.dd (float);
year/month/day/h/min/s/ms since midnight, 1 January O AD:
    YYYYMMDDHHMMSSmmm (string).

Obviously, one can generate any number of acceptable and useful conventions *ad nauseam*. However, in almost all such cases there are significant problems in providing a 32-bit floating point representation with sufficient precision to handle both clock and calendar data together. In addition, for whatever conventions are established, efficient algorithms for calendaric and temporal manipulation will be required (e.g. unit and scale conversion, leap year calculations) to keep these conventions reasonably transparent.

9.3.   IMPLEMENTATIONS AND TECHNIQUES

Traditional methods of handling scientific data such as flat sequential files are generally inefficient in storage, access or ease-of-use for large complex datasets particularly for input/output and floating-point-intensive applications like signal processing (e.g. inverse problems) and visualization. Modern, commercial relational data management systems do not offer an effective solution because they are more oriented to business applications. The relational model does not accommodate multidimensional, irregular or hierarchical structures often found in scientific datasets. In addition, relational systems do not provide sufficient performance for the size, complexity and type of access dictated by current and future datasets and their potential usage. In contrast, these database management systems have been quite viable for a class of nonspatial metadata management (e.g. in the NASA earth and space science community). Hence, current database systems are not yet up to the challenge of supporting very large datasets.

Therefore, there is a need for some type of data (base) model(s) that possesses elements of a modern database management system but is oriented toward scientific datasets and applications. This intermediate approach should be easy to use, support large disk-based (perhaps other media as well) datasets and accommodate multiple scientific data structures in a uniform fashion. In the process of providing simple access to self-describing data, such a mechanism should match applications requirements for visualization as well as data analysis and management, and be independent of any specific discipline or source or visualization technique. Hence, data management as embodied as a data model(s) is as important a component of a data visualization system as underlying graphics and imaging technology. Its implementation, the management of and access to the data, should be decoupled from the actual visualization software. Conceptually, Figure 9.2 illustrates this notion, where the data model serves as a bridge between visual and data media. In other worlds – borrowing from the data base community, there exists a physical representation (media), a logical representation (structures) and a visual media, more simply illustrated in Figure 9.3.

Many software packages touted as supporting visualization ignore the issue of data management. Access to data is often provided via a simple flat file structure that may or may not be proprietary or left as an exercise to the user. Systems that support different classes of grids (e.g. regular/structured and unstructured) typically do not provide uniform mechanisms for their use. In any of these cases, the extensibility of such software to many, potentially very large datasets for disparate applications is extremely limited. Any process that accesses data implies the development of software that can manage arbitrary data sets and possesses different tools for displaying (or working with) data. There must be a clean interface between the data and the display of the data, so that arbitrary data can be accessed by the visualization software. As a consequence of such an approach, a software system of this design has an open framework. It can ingest arbitrary data objects for visualization, and other visualization techniques

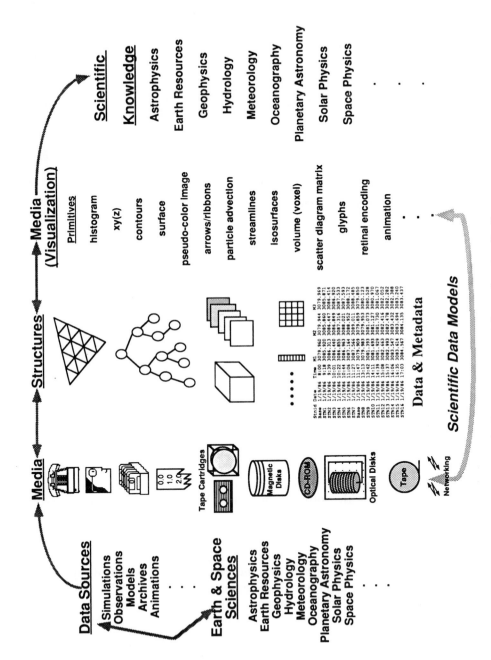

Figure 9.2. Data management layer for visualization.

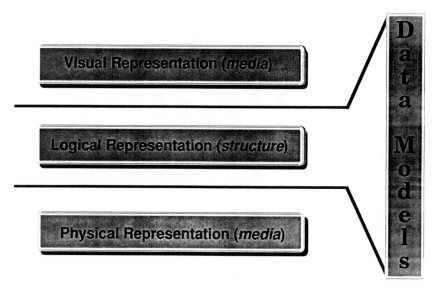

Figure 9.3. Role of data models in visualization software.

can be added independent of the application. This implies that a significant reduction in long-term software developed costs can be realized because new datasets do not require new display software, and new display techniques do not require new data access software. A recommended initial approach is to attempt to characterize and categorize the data in the domain of interest according to the taxonomy outlined in Section 9.2.

9.3.1. Implementation genre

These classic limitations have been recognized by a few groups in the support of a number of scientific applications. As a result, several data models have been defined, some within very domain-specific contexts while others being more general. Recently, a few of these models have been associated with software, including visualization and have associated language bindings that represent the implementation of one or more abstract data types. These implementations can be characterized in the following manner:

Unified – utilizes a single, generalized data model. A unified implementation includes an applications programming interface (API) and/or language bindings, which defines operations to be performed with data. This implementation is shown schematically in Figure 9.4. Such an interface may be "object-oriented", where such operations imply methods that are associated with a class of objects. However, the notion of an abstract data type is sufficient for such an implementation. Hence, the API hides the details of the physical form(s) of storage for data. In general, such implementations permit easy incorporation of new data and applications and offer the potential to develop highly optimized performance for

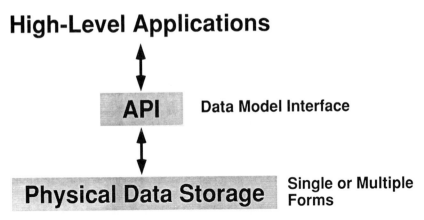

Figure 9.4. Unified implementation (interface defines operations).

generic applications. The primary limitation of this approach relates to the data model itself. Such implementations are usually hard to extend for new classes of data not considered in the original data model definition.

Diffuse – utilizes multiple data models. A diffuse implementation includes multiple APIs, which define underlying data structures. Each of these structures and hence, APIs, are associated with a single physical form of storage. This implementation is shown schematically in Figure 9.5. Usually, separate implementations of specific applications are required for each interface, which may be integrated in some fashion by a higher-level application. Such implementations permit easy incorporation of new data because a new application, interface and structure is added. Hence, it becomes difficult to operate with more than one of the types of data

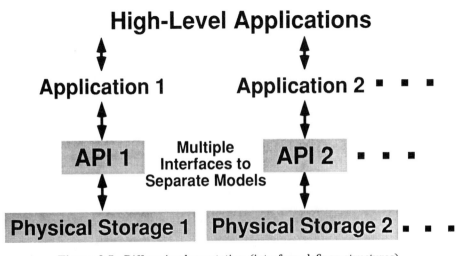

Figure 9.5. Diffuse implementation (interface defines structures).

simultaneously. As a result, these implementations are usually difficult to optimize or extend for generalized applications.

Focused – utilizes a single, domain-specific data model. A focused implementation usually does not include an API for the data model. This implementation is shown schematically in Figure 9.6. Any interface to data in such a system defines the underlying physical data format. Therefore, it becomes easy to optimize the performance for very specialized applications and quite difficult to extend to other data and applications.

To illustrate this taxonomy, a few examples of each type of implementation for data management or applications enabling and visualization are discussed briefly below. These examples are either public domain or commercial software that are used in the scientific community. The list is meant to be illustrative, not exhaustive or comprehensive. Additional details concerning these implementations are given in the appendix.

9.3.2. Implementations for data management or applications enabling

Common data format (CDF), developed at NASA/Goddard Space Flight Center, was one of the first implementations of a scientific data model. It is based upon the concept of providing abstract support for a class of scientific data that can be described by a multidimensional block structure. Although all data do not fit within this framework, a large variety of scientific data do. From the CDF effort spawned the Unidata Program Center's netCDF, which is focused more on issues of uniform data transport. Hence, CDF and netCDF can individually be characterized as being distinct unified implementations.

Both netCDF and CDF support the same data model – the idea of a data abstraction for supporting multidimensional blocks of data – since netCDF is a separate and more recent implementation of the ideas that were developed in the original VAX/VMS FORTRAN version of CDF in the mid-1980s. Although the model is the same, the interfaces are quite different. The current release of CDF is much newer than that of netCDF, where the

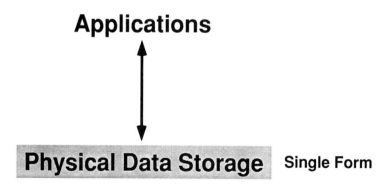

Figure 9.6. Focused implementation (interface defines formats).

latter has only had incremental improvements and new ports since its initial implementation. These systems are extensible by the user, and conventions have been established in some organizations to ensure proper interpretation when data are exchanged.

NetCDF has only one physical form – a single file written according to the IEEE standard via the eXternal Data Representation (XDR) protocol developed by Sun Microsystems and placed in the public domain. The multi-dimensional arrays are written by C convention (last dimension varies fastest). This implementation has proven to be very convenient and easy to use. As a result, the software has been ported to a number of platforms, is widely used in the atmospheric sciences and other research communities and can be employed with some independent visualization software. However, this approach does have its performance limits when scaled to large datasets, used by FORTRAN programmers or operated on non-IEEE machines. Many operating systems have relatively small limits (either actual or practical) on the size of physical files, which would require a user to implement a multiple file solution. In addition, the current software supports only limited direct editing or other transactions on the files in place (i.e. without copying). Currently, Unidata has only provided very limited generic utilities for data in netCDF. However, they are developing a number of new tools (netCDF operators) and a C++ interface.

In contrast, CDF supports multiple physical forms: XDR or native, single or multiple file (one header file and one file for each variable), row (i.e. C) or column (i.e. FORTRAN) major organization and the ability to interoperate among them, which includes compatibility with the original VMS FORTRAN implementation. This implies that for performance-critical applications, the appropriate physical form can be chosen. For example, where data portability is not critical and absolute performance is of greater importance (e.g. VMS), the support of a native physical format is critical. The CDF software has been ported to a number of platforms and is most often used in the space physics and climate research communities. The CDF software supports caching and direct utilization of the file system to provide rapid access and in-place updates. Data in CDF are supported by a large and growing collection of both utilities and sophisticated general-purpose applications (some portable and some VMS-specific).

Another important effort has been the hierarchical data format (HDF) developed by the National Center for Supercomputing Applications (NCSA) at the University of Illinois at Urbana-Champaign. This activity evolved from the need to move files of scientific data among heterogeneous machines, which grew out of the requirement to look at images and other data on personal computers, workstations, etc. that were generated on a supercomputer. HDF, which is also self-describing, uses an extensible tagged file organization to provide access to basic data types like a raster image (and an associated palette), a multidimensional block, etc. In this sense, HDF provides access (i.e. via its C and FORTRAN bindings) to a number of different flat file organizations. Hence, HDF can be characterized as being a diffuse implementation.

The HDF software has been ported to a wide variety of platforms from personal computers to supercomputers. Currently, all of HDF's data structures are memory resident. Thus, the aforementioned discussion about the relative physical organizations of CDF and netCDF and performance tradeoffs does not apply to HDF, because that level of functionality is not provided. This limits the ability of an application using HDF software to utilize effectively, or even access randomly, large disk-resident data sets. The myriad of data types that HDF supports essentially through separate interfaces is through central registration at NCSA in contrast to the CDF/ netCDF approach. There are obvious advantages and disadvantages of leaving full authority with the user or with the implementer. A particular choice of approach is highly application dependent. Thus, HDF is extensible to support additional models and formats, but only at NCSA (e.g. recent efforts to support more complex data stuctures). HDF has been an extremely successful vehicle for creating portable data sets and driving a number of popular and powerful visualization packages in the Apple Macintosh environment and more recently under XWindow, which offers further evidence as to the importance of codified data access techniques.

HDF has been extended with a new storage scheme called Vset, that is compatible with the extant HDF structures. It attempts to supersede some of the limitations inherent in the CDF/netCDF and the conventional HDF data models. It supports regular and irregular data and the ability to form hierarchical groupings. Another extension to HDF currently in development is to embody the netCDF and model and interface as an additional HDF object. This idea may be extended to the CDF model and interface as well.

The flexible image transport system (FITS) developed by the National Radio Astronomy Observatory is the standard interchange mechanism for astronomical (except for planetary) imagery and related data. It is well defined, self-describing but has no official software interface or language bindings. Hence, portability is implied at the physical byte level. Hence, FITS can be characterized as being a focused implementation.

Most databases for spherically distributed (e.g. astronomical, cartographic, climatological) data are not structured in a manner consistent with their geometry. As a result, such databases possess undesirable artifacts, including the introduction of "tears" in the data when they are mapped onto a flat file system. Furthermore, it is difficult to query the topological relationship among the data components (e.g. adjacency of connected regions) using simple and purely symbolic means, that is, without performing real arithmetic. For example, hierarchical data structures are appropriate to support spatial data. A potential solution to these problems has been developed at NASA/Goddard Space Flight Center by applying recursive subdivision of spherical triangles obtained by projecting the faces of an icosahedron onto a sphere. The collection of these spherical triangles are managed with quadtrees. These sphere quadtrees are insensitive to the familiar distortions suffered in planar representations far away from the equator. Such distortions arise from the need to project data properly (i.e. flatten the earth) by preserving shape or distance, for example, in two-dimensional visualizations. This data structure allows the representation of data at multiple resolutions and arbitrary levels and is supported with efficient searching mechanisms. It provides the ability to correlate geographic data by providing a consistent reference among datasets of different resolutions or data that are not geographically registered. The implementation of this idea represents a hybrid of the aforementioned approaches because it is very domain-specific, but possesses a well-defined data structure and interface as well as operations.

9.3.3. Implementations for visualization

The Scientific Visualization Systems Group at IBM T. J. Watson Research Center has developed a data format which is based upon a more comprehensive data model that includes curvilinear and irregular meshes and hierarchies (e.g. trees, series, composites), vector and tensor data, etc. in addition to the class of scalar, multi-dimensional blocks supported by the aforementioned implementations. Currently, the physical disk-based format, called dx, is complete and has been published, but it provides only simple sequential access. A portable, application-independent software interface for it is not yet available, and hence support for disk-based structures and database-type updates in place are not supported. The IBM Visualization Data Explorer software, developed by this same group, utilizes this format as one import/export mechanism. It is a client-server dataflow system for general visualization applications. More importantly, however, is the implementation of the data model in this software package via an object-oriented approach to management of data in memory for computation. All operations on data within this software, independent of a role in generating pictures, work with shared data structures in memory via a uniform interface. The model utilizes the fact that researchers at Sandia National Laboratories observed that the mathematical notion of fiber bundles provides a useful abstraction for scientific data management and applications. In the Visualization Data Explorer, this idea is specialized and extended to incorporate localized, piecewise field descriptions. This permits the same consistent access to data independent of its underlying grid, type or hierarchical structure(s) via a uniform abstraction. Data communication among subsequent operations is accomplished by passing pointers. In addition, sharing of these structures among such operations is supported. For example, when an image is rendered, or for that matter any computation in this system, the data structures can be lined (i.e. hierarchically) so that a path from the data to the pictures and back can be identified. Hence, IBM Visualization Data Explorer can be characterized as being a unified implementation.

The Application Visualization System (AVS) from Advanced Visual Systems, Incorporated and IRIS Explorer (or simply Explorer) from Silicon Graphics Incorporated are both distributed dataflow software packages for general visualization applications. From a data management perspective, both systems are conceptually quite similar. They incorporate separate underlying interfaces for different classes of data (e.g. structured *vs.* unstructured). As a result they often provide separate applications of similar functionality for different data (i.e. modules). Both packages also provide higher-level applications that integrate some of this functionality. Hence, AVS and Explorer can individually be characterized as being distinct diffuse implementations.

The Flow Analysis Software Toolkit (FAST) developed by Sterling Federal Systems, Incorporated for NASA/Ames Research Center is an integrated collection of tools designed for the visualization and analysis of the results of computational fluid dynamics (CFD) simulations. The performance of the tools and their interface are optimized toward researchers working on CFD problems. Hence, FAST can be characterized as being a focused implementation. More recently, researchers there have also utilized the idea of a fiber bundle to serve as an abstraction for CFD data to be visualized, and hence simplify the manipulation of large data sets. Their system, called SuperGlue, uses an interpretative language, based upon C and Scheme (a dialect of Lisp) for rapid prototyping of complex visualizations and user interfaces while effectively supporting code reuse. Therefore, SuperGlue can be considered a hybrid implementation because it uses a unified approach for handling data but within a very specific domain.

9.4   METADATA

Inherent in data models for visualization should be the ability to support self-describing scientific data structures. Generically, such self-descriptions are loosely referred to as metadata or information/data about data. Recently, considerable attention has been placed on metadata support for the management of current and past large data streams because through it a scientist would be able to select data of interest for analysis. For example, the National Space Science Data Center (NSSDC) at NASA's Goddard Space Flight Center among others has been instrumental in the implementation of several systems that provide metadata management services to the earth and space science research communities. Such support has primarily been for characteristic (i.e. directories and catalogs), physical inventory and temporal information with more recent efforts looking at problems in spatial (e.g. geographic) information. Unfortunately, most efforts at metadata management, including many of those within NASA have been divorced from the data themselves. An exception to this was the development of an information/analysis system for atmospheric research in the early 1980s. An attempt to bridge this gap between metadata management and data was one of the factors that lead to the initial development of the CDF, from which spawned (for some similar reasons) netCDF. It is in such a context that this discussion about metadata – that is for the data themselves, what information is required to make the data sufficiently scientifically self-descriptive for "visualization".

In addition to self-describing data structures with well-defined software interfaces such as CDF, netCDF and HDF that support metadata at some level, there are a number of more traditional approaches bundling useful scientific information with data. Typically this has implied sequential (i.e. magnetic tape) formats whose data contents are preceded by formatted text headers with little or no associated software. Among the better examples are ones that have been developed in the earth sciences in Europe (e.g. GF3, BUFR/GRIB) and the astronomical imaging community in the US (e.g. FITS). Recently, on-line versions of such formats have appeared as well as reading/writing FORTRAN programs and interesting applications. Although these formats were originally designed for the convenience of data producers trying to create magnetic tapes rather than more challenging applications like visualization, their developers and subsequent users have developed a rich lexicon of metadata that should not be ignored.

Database management systems (DBMS) provide a capability to find, sort, merge, organize, update and output diverse data types. However, most DBMSs have been designed primarily for archiving and managing data for a specific domain by developers with a background in computer science or related fields rather than a (physical) science discipline. The result is that these systems suffer from the intrinsic flaw of not effectively providing the capabilities needed by a casual or new user in that scientific discipline. These databases restrict the capabilities for managing the syntax of a domain as part of its data structure, have limited data structures which cannot represent explicit relationships between data classes and demand precise, mathematical query formulation for database interactions (i.e. SQL). In addition, such DBMS often exclude many of the data objects used in the scientific domain and do not efficiently store, index or retrieve (i.e. in relational systems) image or spatial data. Hence, such databases are difficult to design for scientific data and the users of existing database systems require an in-depth understanding of the database architecture, data content, location and query language in order to use the data effectively. When data structures exist in a large database (i.e. schemata), this problem is exacerbated, often making the database unusable in an operational environment. These limitations can apply for large scientific metadata bases as well as for the data themselves.

9.4.1. Classes of metadata

To help in the evaluation of what metadata is and how it should be supported, the notion of metadata must be more clearly specified. Hence, four classes of metadata are defined: (1) what is needed to access the data; (2) what information is associated with or describes the data; (3) what data are associated with or define the data; and (4) what other documentation categorizes the data.

"Database" metadata

The first class – what is needed to access the data – is essentially what is refered to as metadata in the database sense. Generically this metadata class includes data type primitives (e.g. byte, short, long, float, double, string) and structural information for each enumerated data object. The latter can include dimensionality (size, shape, [in]dependency), rank, positions, connections and any referencing or indexing to other objects. For group objects, global information on the type of group would be necessary while similar information on individual members would by definition already be supported.

Attribute metadata

The second class of metadata is various types of information that is associated with data, generally at the level of an individual data object. Consistent with the CDF/netCDF parlance this class is called attributes. The attribute class of metadata should be extensible by the user. In other words, the user is free to define new attributes, even though some application software should not be expected to operate on such user-specific information except to acknowledge its existence and be able to "list" it. A discussion of individual examples of such metadata can be seen in the user's manuals for CDF and netCDF.

Ancillary (meta)data

In addition to information about data, there may be other data associated with data that are required for a complete definition. Such (meta)data are clearly numeric and could typically include spatial, temporal and spectral tags or locations associated with data, which can be accommodated via mesh specification.

Other (documentation) metadata

The last class of metadata helps the user to identify qualitative facts about the data. Such information is typically textual and probably is best supported by free text. There are several types of documentation in this category, which include laboratory notes or logs to identify what was seen, to identify what was done, etc. Another category would include a specification of what should be done with the data by the user or someone else. A third variety would include user and dataset information to identify saved images or hardcopy, place data in the proper context, etc. These metadata are textual and could be supported in the same manner as text/string attributes. Examples of such metadata are user name, organization, the data of creation of a dataset, image, script or log, and the source, name/title, version and history (e.g. audit trail of what has been done to the data from its initial raw form) of a dataset. Without conventions for nomenclature, this category is unsupported in context – application software can only record and play back the text, not act on the stored information.

9.5. EVALUATION CRITERIA

As implementations of specific data models have matured and been used, experience in their use have led to a host of issues concerning actual applications. In this sense, an enumeration of criteria to evaluate extant implementations can be helpful. Much of the underlying issues were discussed in a workshop on "Data Structures and Access Software for Scientific Visualization" conducted at the ACM SIGGRAPH conference in Dallas, TX in 1990. From the report of that workshop these issues can be divided into two categories, access and implementation. In summary, the access issues relate to:

How should data be brought into a visualization system?
What does a system let a scientist do with the data?
What does a system let an application programmer do with the data?
How should data be described (i.e. metadata and data attributes as discussed in the previous section)?
How does a system preserve the fidelity of the data?

Given implementation approaches as outlined in Section 9.3, the issues that arise are:

How are code AND data to be portable across multiple platforms?
How is interoperability between structures to be maintained?
At what (low) level should interfaces be independent of the user?

The participants in the aforementioned workshop generally agreed that to address these issues, the following is required.

utilize well-defined layering;
employ C for coding and provide bindings to other languages as required (e.g., FORTRAN);
maintain consistent terminology in interfaces and structures and use them to define a context for functionality.

9.5.1. Scaling

A major concern for extant systems is in their practical application to a number of large datasets. These issues often relate to scaling to even modest datasets by today's standards independent of addressing raw bandwidth. The data effectiveness of a system can be measured by its ability to handle multiple datasets simultaneously of various sizes, types, structures, etc. without forcing artificial constraints that disrupt the fidelity of the original data. Systems that support different classes of data separately will have difficulty scaling to support disparate data properly at the same time. Systems that support different classes of data uniformly do not because they effectively decouple the management of and access to the data from the actual visualization software.

Another area of scaling is in performance related to aggregate data size and visual complexity (e.g. numbers of polygons, pixels, voxels, etc.). Given current and planned data rates for scientific investigations, whether computational or observational, workstation demonstrations with a few megabytes of data are hardly relevant. For real science problems, an effective system should be able to scale up to the storage capacity of a given platform (e.g. memory + swap) independent of the cpu performance. Therefore, the software should be able to generate images, for example, slowly on a small workstation, for what would seem to be large datasets for that platform while operations on small datasets would be more interactive. Higher performance should be achievable via increased aggregate CPU performance, which should include parallelism.

Therefore, one should consider the following:

Data structure residency. Are the data structures in an implementation on secondary storage (i.e. disk) and/or in primary storage (i.e. memory)?

Transaction-like processing. What types of access methods for data are supported? Is the ability to do DBMS-like operations on data provided, which can be important for datasets that are too expensive even to reproduce partially?

Physical format and file structure. How does an implementation compensate for typical limitations in conventional file systems (e.g. blocking) or operating systems (e.g. paging) for bulk data access?

Distributed access to data within visualization systems (see next subsection).

The implementations discussed in Section 9.3 address perhaps only a few of these points and are areas for which further research is required.

9.5.2.   Distributed access

Developing machine- and media-independent distribution and network services for well-structured and supported science data presents a number of difficult technical problems. In the scientific community today and especially in the future there will be strong demands for the ability to easily access and share large volumes of complex data among computational facilities, network and data servers, and user/scientific workstations. Typically data must be physically moved by low-level network transfer or via off-line media, despite the capabilities of today's computer systems. Such techniques are slow and clumsy, and will be increasingly inadequate for large data volumes.

Current Unix workstations from a number of manufacturers lend themselves ideally to the implementation of the aforementioned software. However, to be truly effective in the growing communications needs among heterogeneous scientific computing environments, other classes of systems must be accommodated. The mechanism for sharing should be driven by the scientific requirements of the applications and the structure of the data, not by the conventional limitations dictated by the architecture of the respective computer hardware and operating systems. The key to the development is the use of appropriate generic and portable techniques so that the software can operate on a wide variety of platforms that the ultimate users may have at their disposal. It is assumed that the software must utilize ANSI C as a programming language and the XDR protocol would appear to be a likely portable physical data protocol, but TCP/IP must be used as a low-level network protocol. (Many computer manufacturers, typically of Unix-based systems, have adopted XDR as their native protocol. Specific data models like netCDF and CDF utilize XDR.) However, the use of XDR does create additional overheads as the price for portability.

Work on defining the protocols for interprocess communication among heterogeneous platforms is needed. Unfortunately, many interprocess protocols are inefficient for migration of large datasets or datasets with large internal structures. For example, the network file system (NFS) developed by Sun Microsystems and placed in the public domain has been adopted essentially by all workstation, minicomputer, mainframe and supercomputer manufacturers. Since NFS provides access at the file level not the science data object level, it would have limited performance to drive data-intensive applications.

Other mechanisms under consideration would include, for example, Unix (TCP/IP) sockets, the remote procedure call protocol developed by Sun Microsystems and the network computing system (NCS) developed by (the former) Apollo Computer. All of these mechanisms are geared toward low bandwidth communications with small packet sizes. However, NCS is relatively new, it has only been adopted by a few computer manufacturers and it is still proprietary. NCS appears to offer better performance and more flexibility than NFS and XDR, but it may still be inefficient for shared, distributed access to large datasets. In addition, with the absorption of Apollo by Hewlett-Packard, there has been little new in NCS development. Hence, there is a need for further research to select an appropriate protocol.

Such a network data access protocol would be incorporated within a network shell to provide transparent access to distributed data. In this scenario, a visualization application running a workstation or a background server could have transparent access to large data sets stored on a data server, for example, at the applications programmer's level. For environments where task-to-task networking is neither available or feasible (e.g. wide-area and other low bandwidth networks, non-networked systems), transport distribution services are required to provide computer-independent mechanisms for "shipping" of data through a variety of media. Currently, visualization software systems such as AVS, IRIS Explorer and apE have a distributed execution model, in which computational tasks embodied as modules reside in separate processes, which may be on different machines. In this case, all communication among such processes is via sockets. Unfortunately, typical networking infrastructures place practical limits on this approach to relatively small datasets.

For example, NCSA has developed a data transfer mechanism (DTM) as a simplified RPC but more robust than the standard Unix RPC. It is a message passing system to support building of distributed applications. These message are classes of self-describing data types, which obviously can include scientific fields. Such messages are at least 1 Mbyte in size. NCSA provides an extensible software interface with access to the messages at multiple levels. This approach has shown some promise in on-going experiments at NCSA.

In parallel, NASA/Ames Research Center, has developed Distributed Library (dlib) as a tool to enable software developers to implement procedures on heterogeneous systems that communicate as part of distributed processing over a network. Employing only standard RPC, it takes the approach of maintaining state about the on-going processes and allocating memory for long-term communication among a client and server, for example. Dlib has been used for integrating visualization on a graphics workstation with computation on a supercomputer with packages like FAST. Hence, like DTM, one goal of dlib is to enable computational steering.

9.6.   CONCLUSIONS

An effort to create data models and associated access software, especially to support scientific visualization involves the integration of various physical science disciplines and the computational sciences. It emphasizes the development of capabilities for a researcher to concentrate on science activities, freeing him or her from the mechanism of working with specialized data structures or formats. What is important is not the details of the technology, but what that technology can easily and inexpensively provide to promote science. Such activities will further the use of computer systems to support the management, analysis and display of any scientific data of interest under the control of the scientist doing research.

ADDITIONAL READING

The following is a brief list of selected papers, documents, and other material related to scientific data structures, formats, access software and systems for data management and visualization. Apologies are given for any documentation, software or other material inadvertently omitted.

Bancroft, G. V., Merritt, F. J., Plessel, T. C., Kelaita, P. G., McCabe, R. K. and Globus, A. (1990). FAST: a multi-processed environment for visualization of computational fluid dynamics. In *Proceedings IEEE Visualization '90*, pp. 14–27.

Brittain, D. L. *et al.* (1990). Design of an end-user data visualization system. In *Proceedings IEEE Visualization '90*, pp. 323–328.

Butler, D. M. and C. Hansen (ed.) (1992). Scientific visualization environments: a report on a workshop at Visualization '91. *Computer Graphics* **26**(3), 213–216.

Butler, D. M. and Pendley, M. H. (1989). The visualization management system approach to visualization in scientific computing. *Computers in Physics* **3**(5).

Butler, D. M. and Pendley, M. H. (1989). A visualization model based on the mathematics of fiber bundles. *Computers in Physics* **3**(5).

Campbell, W. J. and R. F. Cromp (1990). Evolution of an intelligent information fusion system. *Photogrammetric Engineering and Remote Sensing* **56**(6).

Campbell, W., Short, N. and Treinish, L. (1989). Adding intelligence to scientific data management. *Computers in Physics* **3**(3).

Campbell, W. J., Cromp, R.F., Fekete, G., Wall, R. and Goldberg, M. (1992). Panel on "techniques for managing very large scientific data bases". In *Proceedings IEEE Visualization '92*, pp. 362–365.

CDF User's Guide, Version 2.1. National Space Science Data Center, NASA/Goddard Space Flight Center, December 1991.

Cook, L. M. (1990). *Mesh Types for Scientific Calculations.* Lawrence Livermore National Laboratory.

Dyer, D. S. (1990). A dataflow toolkit for visualization. *IEEE Computer Graphics and Applications,* **10**(4), 60–69.

Faust, J. T. and Dyer, D. S. (1990). An effective data format for scientific visualization. In *Proceedings of the SPIE/SPSE Symposium on Electronic Imaging.*

Fekete, G. (1990). Rendering and managing spherical data with sphere quadtrees. In *Proceedings IEEE Visualization '90*, pp. 176–186.

Implementation of the Flexible Image Transport System. NASA/OSSA Office of Standards and Technology.

French, J. C., Jones, A. K., and Pfaltz, J. L. (1990). A summary of the NSF scientific database workshop. *Quarterly Bulletin of IEEE Computer Society Technical Committee on Data Engineering* **13**(3).

Haber, R., Lucas, B. and Collins, N. (1991). A data model for scientific visualization with provisions for regular and irregular grids. In *Proceedings IEEE Visualization '91 Conference*, pp. 298–305.

Hibbard, B. and Santek, D. (1990). The VIS-5D system for easy interactive visualization. In *Proceedings IEEE Visualization '90*, pp. 28–35.

Hibbard, W., Dyer C.R. and Paul, B (1992). Display of scientific data structures for algorithm visualization. In *Proceedings IEEE Visualization '92*, pp. 139–146.

Hierarchical Data Format (HDF) Version 3.0 Calling Interfaces and Utilities and HDF Vset, Version 2.0. National Center for Supercomputing Applications, University of Illinois at Urbana-Champaign, November 1990.

Hultquist, J. P. M. and Raible, E. L. (1992). SuperGlue: a programming environment for scientific visualization. In *Proceedings IEEE Visualization '92*, pp. 243–249.

IBM AIX Visualization Data Explorer/6000 User's Guide, first edition. IBM Document Number GC38-0496-0.

IRIS Explorer. Technical Report BP-TR-1E-01 (Rev. 7/91). Silicon Graphics Computer Systems.

Lang, U., Lang, R. and Rühle, R. (1991). Integration of visualization and scientific calculation in a software system. In *Proceedings IEEE Visualization '91*.

Li, Y. P., Handley Jr. T. H., Dobinson, E. R. (1992). Data hub: a framework for science data management. Submitted to 18th International Conference in Very Large Data Bases, August 1992.

Lucas, B., Abram, G.D., Collins, N. S., Epstein, D. A., Gresh, D. L., McAuliffe, K. P. (1992). An architecture for a scientific visualization system. *Proceedings IEEE Visualization '92*, pp. 107–113.

NetCDF User's Guide, Version 2.0. Unidata Program Center, October 1991.

Pfau, L. M. (1990). *The GridFile Tool Structure of System Files.* Eidgenössische Technische Hochschule, Zürich.

Rasure, J. and Wallace, C. (1991). An integrated data flow visual language and software development environment. *Journal of Visual Languages and Computing* **2**, 217–246.

Rew, R. K., and Davis, G. P. (1990). NetCDF: an interface for scientific data access. *IEEE Computer Graphics and Applications* **10**(4), 76–82.

Schroeder, W. J., Lorensen, W. E., Montanaro, G. D. and Volpe, C. R. (1992). VISAGE: an object-oriented scientific visualization system. *Proceedings IEEE Visualization '92*, pp. 219–225.

Smith, A. Q. and Clauer C. R. (1986). A versatile source-independent system for digital data management. *Eos Transactions American Geophysical Union* **67**, 188–189.

Treinish, L. A. (1989). An interactive, discipline-independent data visualization system. *Computers in Physics* **3**(4).

Treinish, L. A. (1990). The role of data management in discipline-independent data visualization. In *Proceedings of the SPIE/SPSE Symposium on Electronic Imaging*.

Treinish, L. A. (ed.), (1991). Data structures and access software for scientific visualization, a report on a workshop at SIGGRAPH '90. *Computer Graphics* **25**(2).

Treinish, L. A. and Gough, M. L. (1987). A software package for the data-independent storage of multi-dimensional data. *Eos Transactions American Geophysical Union* **68**, 633–635.

Treinish, L. A. and Ray, S. N. (1985). An interactive information system to support climate research. *Proceedings First International Conference on Interactive Information and Processing Systems for Meteorology, Oceanography and Hydrology*, pp. 72–79. American Meterology Society.

Treinish, L. A. *et al.* (1989). Effective software systems for scientific visualization. In *Proceedings of SIGGRAPH '89 Panels*.

Treinish, L. A., Butler, D. M., Senay, H., Grinstein, G. G., and Bryson, S. T. (1992). Panel on "grand challenge problems in visualization software". In *Proceedings IEEE Visualization '92*, pp. 366–371.

Upson, C. *et al.* (1989). The application visualization system: a computational environment for scientific visualization. *IEEE Computer Graphics and Applications* **9**(4), 30–42.

Walatka, P. P. and Buning, P. G. (1989). *PLOT3D User's Manual Version 3.6*. NASA Technical Memorandum 101067, NASA/Ames Research Center, 1989.

Wells, D. C., Greisen, E. W. and Harten, R. H. (1981). FITS: A flexible image transport system. *Astronomy and Astrophysics Supplement Series* **44**, 363–370.

Yamasaki, M. J. (1990). Distributed library. RNR-90-008, NASA/Ames Research Center.

APPENDIX. TABLE OF SELECTED REPRESENTATIVE SCIENTIFIC DATA STRUCTURES, FORMATS AND ACCESS SOFTWARE

Table 9.A1 compares the characteristics of several fairly generic structures and software that are used to access and utilize scientific data in applications such as visualization. This table covers examples that provide a uniform data model, access mechanism or both, which have been used in visualization systems. Neither the characteristics nor the list is meant to be complete. It is meant to be a "living" document that serves as a point of reference on data formats for software developers as well as users and generators of data. Therefore, some of the information is likely to be out of date already. Hence, anonymous ftp addresses on the internet are provided for access to the latest material. There are innumerable omissions to keep the information succinct and useful, for which apologies are given. Some examples that are very domain-specific or no longer in widespread use or not readily available have been left out. Others are visualization or application environments/software, which may support many of the characteristics enumerated in the table. They have been omitted for either a lack of information from the developing organization, or because the support mechanism is not uniform. With regard to the latter, in other words, the software provides multiple paths for access to distinct data types rather than a single one. Many of the references in the "additional reading" list will address most of these examples.

Public domain contacts for information about data structures, formats, and access software

Name	Contact	Address	Anonymous ftp
Common data format (CDF)	Greg Goucher	goucher@nssdca.gsfc.nasa.gov	ncgl.gsfc.nasa.gov nssdca.gsfc.nasa.gov
Flexible image transport system (FITS)	Don Wells	dwells@nrao.edu	nssdca.gsfc.nasa.gov fits.cx.nrao.edu tetra.gsfc.nasa.gov
Hierarchical data format (HDF)	Mike Folk	mfolk@ncsa.uiuc.edu	ftp.ncsa.uiuc.edu
Network common data form (netCDF)	Russ Rew	rew@unidata.ucar.edu	unidata.ucar.edu

Public domain contacts for information about visualization environments and associated data structures, formats and access software

Name	Contact	Anonymous ftp
AVS	AVS via North Carolina Supercomputer Center	avs.ncsc.org
FAST	NASA/Ames Research Center	? (415-604-4444)
IRIS Explorer	SGI via Edinburgh Parallel Computing Centre	ftp.epcc.ed.ac.uk swedishchef.lerc.nasa.gov
Khoros	University of New Mexico	pprg.eece.unm.edu
SciAn	Florida State University	scri.fsu.edu
VIS-5D	University of Wisconsin	vis5d.ssec.wisc.edu
Visualization Data Explorer	IBM via Cornell Engineering and Theory Center	eagle.tc.cornell.edu

Table 9.A1. Selected representative scientific data structures, formats and access software

Name/characteristic	CDF	dx	FITS	Flux	HDF	netCDF	PLOT3D
Type	Structure	Format	Format	Structure/format "4GL"	Structure	Structure	Format
Host language interface	Yes	via Data Explorer	No	No	Yes	Yes	No
Language bindings	FORTRAN, C, IDL	C (via Data Explorer)	No	No	FORTRAN, C	FORTRAN, C	No
Applications/utilities	Yes	Yes (Data Explorer)	Yes	Yes (apE)	Yes	Yes	Yes
Translation tools	Yes	Yes	Limited	?	Limited	Limited	No?
Systems							
Alliant Concentrix	No	N/A	N/A	?	Yes	No?	Via PLOT3D
Apollo Unix	No	N/A	N/A	?	Yes	No?	Via PLOT3D
Apple MacIntosh	Yes	N/A	N/A	Via apE (A/UX)	Yes	Yes	N/A
Convex Unix	No	N/A	N/A	?	Yes	Yes	Via PLOT3D
Cray Unicos	Yes	N/A	N/A	Via apE	Yes	Yes	Via PLOT3D
DEC Ultrix	Yes	N/A	N/A	Via apE	Yes	Yes	Via PLOT3D
DEC VMS	Yes	N/A	N/A	N/A	Yes	Yes	N/A
HP-UX	Yes	Via Data Explorer	N/A	Via apE	Yes	Yes	Via PLOT3D
IBM AIX	Yes	Via Data Explorer	N/A	?	Yes	Yes	Via FAST
IBM MVS	No	N/A	N/A	N/A	Yes	Yes	N/A
IBM OS/2	No	N/A	N/A	N/A	No	Yes	N/A
IBM PVS	Planned via AIX	Via Data Explorer	N/A	N/A	No	Yes, via AIX	N/A
MS-DOS	Yes	N/A	N/A	N/A	Yes	Yes	N/A
Silicon Graphics IRIX	Yes	Via Data Explorer	N/A	Via apE	Yes	Yes	Via FAST
SunOS	Yes	Via Data Explorer	N/A	Via apE	Yes	Yes	Via PLOT3D
Other operating systems	No	N/A	N/A	Stardent, NeXT	Stellar, CTSS, …	NeXT	N/A
Regular grids	Yes, implicit	Yes, implicit	Yes, implicit	Yes?	Yes?	Yes, implicit	Yes?
Point/scattered data	Yes	Yes	Yes	?	Yes	Yes	?
Curvilinear meshes	Indirect	Yes	Limited	Limited	Via VSET	Indirect	Yes

Irregular meshes	Indirect	Yes	No	?	Via VSET?	No	No
Unstructured grids	No	Yes	No	?	Via VSET?	No	No
Sparse matrices	Indirect	Yes	No	No	No	Indirect	No
Time and other series	Yes	Yes	Limited	?	Yes	Yes	Limited
Hierarchies	No	Yes	No	Limited	Via VSET	No	Multiple grids
Dimensionality	No limit (def. ≤10)	No limit	999	?	SDS: ≤7	No limit (def. ≤32)	3
Scalar	Yes	Yes	Yes	Yes	Yes	Yes	Yes
Vector	As scalars	Yes	As scalars	As scalars?	As scalars?	As scalars	As scalars
Tensor	As scalars	Yes	As scalars	No	No?	As scalars	As scalars
Variables, fields, etc.	No limit (def. ≤128)	No limit	No limit?	?	?	No limit (def. ≤512)	?
Data type support							
Physical data level	Byte	Byte	Byte[d]	Byte	Byte	Byte	Byte
	XDR, native, ASCII	IEEE, ASCII	IEEE	XDR, native, ASCII	Multiple	XDR	Native, ASCII
Byte/logical/char	Yes	Yes	Yes	Yes	Yes	Yes	No
Integer*2/short	Yes	Yes	Yes	Yes	Yes	Yes	No
Integer*4/long	Yes	Yes	Yes	Yes	Yes	Yes	Yes
Integer*8/hyper	No	Yes	No	No	?	No	No
Signed & unsigned integers	Yes	No	No	No	No?	No	No
Real*4/float	Yes	Yes	Yes	Yes	Yes	Yes	Yes
Real*8/double	Yes	Yes	Yes	Yes	Yes	Yes	No
Complex*8/complex	No	No	Yes	No	Yes	No	No
Complex*16	No	Yes	No?	No	?	No	No
Quaternion (int, float, ...)	No	Yes	No	No	No?	No	No
Pointer	No	Yes	No	No	?	No	No
Character strings	Yes	Yes	Yes	Yes	Yes	Yes	No
Embedded metadata	Yes	Yes	Yes	Yes	Yes	Yes	No
High-level I/O access	Yes	Via Data Explorer	No	Yes	No	Yes	No
Sequential access	Yes	Yes	Yes	?	Yes	Yes	Yes
Random access	Yes	Via Data Explorer	No	?	No?	Yes	No

Table 9.A1. Continued

Name/characteristic	CDF	dx	FITS	Flux	HDF	netCDF	PLOT3D
Physical files	Single or multiple	Single or multiple	Single	Single	Single	Single	Single
Array majority	Row or column	Row	Column	Row	Row	Row	Column?
Structure driver	Data	Data	Physical	Data	Data	Data	Data
In-place edits/transactions	Yes	No	No	No	No	Limited	No
Data structure residency	Disk	Memory (DX)	N/A	Memory (apE)	Memory	Disk	N/A
Primary orientation	Application	Application	Transport	Application	Transport	Transport	Application
Transport mechanism	Copy	Copy	Copy	Copy	Copy	Copy	Copy
Disciplines							
Astronomy/astrophysics	Yes	Yes	Yes	Yes	Yes	No	No
CFD (e.g. aerospace)	No	Yes	No	Yes	Yes	No	Yes
Chemistry	Limited	Yes	No	Yes	Limited	Limited	No
Meteorology	Yes	Yes	No	Yes	Yes	Yes	No
Oceanography	Yes	Yes	No	Yes	Yes	Yes	No
Planetary sciences	Yes	Yes	No	Yes	Yes	No	No
Space physics	Yes	Yes	Yes	Yes	Yes	No	No
Other disciplines	Yes	Yes	No	Yes	Yes	Yes	Applicable

Notes

CDF – NSSDC common data format. Developed by the NSSDC and NASA/Goddard Space Flight Center and has become a standard in the NASA space and earth sciences community for storage and applications systems.

dx – Data Explorer (format). External disk representation of the data model of the IBM Visualization Data Explorer developed by IBM T. J. Watson Research Center.

FITS – Flexible image transport system. Primary standard interchange format for the astronomical community and a driver for some powerful image processing applications.

Flux – Internal general data format, which supports the animation production environment, apE, a visualization system developed by the Ohio Supercomputer Center and now owned by TaraVisuals, Inc.

HDF – hierarchical data format. NCSA initially developed HDF to facilitate the transport of data generated by supercomputer simulations to other computer systems. It is supported by a number of useful and popular scientific tools and has become widely available.

NetCDF – Network common data form. Unidata developed its own implementation of the CDF data model for the machine-independent access and transport of multidimensional data, which has become widely available.

PLOT3D. Developed to support a number of CFD visualization and analysis applications, including PLOT3D and more recently, FAST.

Type. Is the standard a format or a data structure?

Host language interface (HLI) or *applications programming interface (API).* Does the standard support a software package or other mechanism that provides access to its data structure(s) such as a subroutine package or library?

Language bindings. If the standard has an HLI or API, does that interface support extensions to a host language's data types and operations as abstractions?

Applications. Are there application software systems or utilities available that operate on the standard (e.g. visualization, manipulation)? Standards that are currently in design or development may lack such applications today, but they may be planned.

Translation tools. Are there software packages or utilities that enable different classes of data to be recast, filtered, modeled or translated into the standard?

Systems. For what computer systems is the standard implemented? For formats, as opposed to structures with access software, N/A (not applicable) is generally indicated. If there is applications software that operates on a particular system that utilizes the format directly, it is indicated.

Regular grids. Does the standard support the definition and access to regular (rectilinear) grids typically as multidimensional parameters? Is the grid structure implicit (e.g. via product or other specification) or explicit?

Point/scattered data. Does the standard support the definition and access to simple point data?

Curvilinear meshes. Does the standard support the definition and access to complex grids or meshes such as deformed or irregular grids on noncartesian topologies?

Irregular meshes. Does the standard support the definition and access to complex grids or meshes that are fully irregular?

Unstructured grids. Does the standard support the definition and access to complex grids or meshes that are unstructured on constant or irregular topologies (e.g. finite element)?

Sparse matrices. Does the standard support the definition, access and compact storage of sparse matrices?

Time and other series. Does the standard support the definition and access to series of parameters, such as a time dependency?

Hierarchies. Does the standard support the definition and access to groups, hierarchical or collections of parameters such as aggregates, geographic, tree, etc. structures?

Dimensionality. Does the standard support multidimensional parameters or fields? Any arbitrary limit or default on the number of dimensions is indicated.

Scalar. Does the standard support the definition and access of scalar fields?

Vector. Does the standard support the definition and access of vector fields? Explicit support by components as scalars is indicated.

Tensor. Does the standard support the definition and access of tensor fields? Explicit support of components as scalars is indicated.

Variables, fields, etc. Any limit on the number of distinct items supported in the standard are indicated.

Data type support. At what level does the standard provide or define access to data elements? What primitive data types are supported by the standard for the definition of data elements? "Metadata can include an algorithm for conversion to real for data and grid structure.

Embedded metadata. Does the standard support self-describing information on the data objects that it contains?

High-level I/O access. Does the standard provide access to data elements at an object level?

Sequential access. Does the standard support sequential access to the data elements that it contains?

Random access. Does the standard support random access to the data elements that it contains?

Physical files. Does the standard support each instance of itself via one or more physical files in a file system?

Array majority. How does the standard store array elements, either row major (last dimension varies fastest, the convention in the C programming language) or column major (first dimension varies fastest, the convention in the FORTRAN programming language).

Structure driver. Is the driver of the structure of data objects in the standard the data themselves or the physical organization of the data?

In-place edits/transactions. Once data are defined in terms of the standard can an application edit, extend or delete the metadata or the data elements in-place without violating the integrity of the standard or copying physical files (e.g. through the host language interface)?

Data structure residency. For standards that are associated with or only accessible via software, are the data resident in memory or on disk potentially with associated caching?

Primary orientation. Is the driver of the structure and design of the standard for building applications systems or for the transportation or interchange of data?

Transport mechanism. What is the procedure for moving data in the standard between different computer systems (e.g. offline (tape) or online (ftp) copy, remote procedure call)?

Disciplines. What scientific or engineering discipline(s) is the standard designed to support?

About the author

Lloyd A. Treinish is a research staff member in the Scientific Visualization Systems Group in the Computer Science Department at IBM's Thomas J. Watson Research Center in Yorktown Heights, NY, USA. He works on techniques, architectures and applications of data visualization for a wide variety of scientific disciplines. His research interests range from computer graphics, data storage structures, data representation methodologies, data base management, computer user interfaces, and data analysis algorithms to middle atmosphere electrodynamics, planetary astronomy and climatology. Mr Treinish is particularly interested in generic or discipline-independent techniques for the storage, manipulation, analysis and display of data. Earlier he did similar work in the development of advanced scientific data systems, including studying space and atmospheric phenomena, for over a decade at the National Space Science Data Center of NASA's Goddard Space Flight Center in Greenbelt, MD. He graduated in 1978 at the Massachusetts Institute of Technology with an S.M. and an S.B. in physics, and an S.B. in earth and planetary sciences; he has been at IBM since April 1990. He is a member of the IEEE Computer Society (IEEE-CS), the IEEE-CS Technical Committee on Computer Graphics, the Association for Computing Machinery (ACM), ACM SIGGRAPH, the National Computer Graphics Association, the Planetary Society, and the American Geophysical Union.

Chapter 10
Visualization benchmarking

David Watson, Kelvin Goodson and David Williams

10.1. INTRODUCTION

Data visualization encompasses a broad spectrum of subdisciplines ranging from computer graphics to user interface design. It is therefore no surprise that users of visualization tools exercise the full range of computer hardware in their systems from disk storage, through the CPU, to the display system. However, performance measurements for visualization tasks have not been extensively investigated. This chapter examines the background to performance measurement in visualization and reports results of a comparative study using three commercial products. The study was carried out by the authors at the IBM UK Scientific Centre using machines available on site. Whilst comments are made on the relative performance of IBM and other commercial products they are not intended to undermine the position of IBM's competitors, they are reported as examples and illustrations of the need to undertake effective visualization benchmarking.

The marketplace for visualization products in the USA alone was estimated to be 1.14 billion dollars in 1990. It is expected to rise at 18–25% per year over the coming years reaching over 3 billion dollars by 1995. With such a vast marketplace it is not surprising that numerous commercial products have appeared in recent years. The catalogue of visualization tools ranging from image processing, to specialized computation fluids dynamics visualizers, from turnkey applications to visual programming interfaces is growing steadily thicker.

In order to make comparisons between available products from this vast array of choice the user is faced with interesting questions, such as:

Does it have the function I need?
Is it easy to learn and use?
Is it flexible?
How do I get my data in?
Can I add my own functions?
How fast will it run on my system?

The questions posed are a mixture of emotive: "Is it easy to learn and use?" and quantifiable: "How fast will it run on my system?" The emotive questions can only be answered with experience of use. This chapter primarily addresses the question "How fast is it?" The discussion covers some examples of commercial visualization products with the emphasis on flexible tools.

Benchmarking of CPU performance has been with us for some time; however, it is only recently that computer graphics hardware has come under scrutiny with a unified approach to performance measurement (NCGA, 1991). The measurement of graphics hardware will be examined to illustrate the methods used. A discussion of the background to benchmarking of visualization relates the topic to the cycle of scientific investigation. This approach will ultimately lead to a more "user-based" measurement of performance, rather than the hardware-based graphics performance figures. Alternative methods of visualization benchmarking are discussed together with the relationship of graphics hardware performance to the visualization task.

During the performance measurement of the products selected for test, some degree of learning takes place as to how to use a given set of tools together with some personal comparison between the products. It is appropriate to put forward these experiences in order to help the user answer some of the emotive questions asked when examining diverse products.

The methods used to assess three visualization products for this study are detailed and the results presented. Finally a way forward for the future of visualization benchmarking is presented.

10.2.   COMMERCIAL PRODUCTS

It is hardly surprising that a marketplace of many billions of dollars has spawned the development of a multitude of visualization products. The speed at which the commercial marketplace is changing is extremely rapid. There are still users who write bespoke code using graphics application programmers interfaces (APIs) such as PHIGS and GL in order to examine data from specialized simulation or experimental codes. Conversely, there are a vast number of users who have no desire to write C or FORTRAN code at the API level. The need for every scientist to understand the intricacies of the "marching cubes algorithm" and "PHIGS structure definitions" in order to gain insight into the science which they are investigating has been made redundant by the advent of advanced visualization products.

Products available from software developers show a great variety of function, platform availability, performance, flexibility and ease of use. It is helpful to make a distinction between those products that can be regarded as "turnkey" and those which give greater flexibility to the end user. For the purposes of this discussion the graphics API interface will be discounted. In terms of visualization software the graphics API is a tool available to the product developer in order to shield the user from hardware.

10.2.1.   Turnkey visualization systems

These products can be characterized as complete packages of functions with a fixed user interface and functionality. They offer a rapid route to examine user data provided the product supports the visualization method the user wishes to use. Many products in this area are application specific and so do not map well to usage in other disciplines. A few examples of turnkey systems are:

Wavefront: Data Visualizer;
Intelligent Light: CADimator, IVIEW, 3DV, Fieldview;
Cray: MPGS;
NCSA: Xdataslice;
Precision Visuals: PV-Wave;
Sterling Software: FAST;
UNIRAS: UNIGRAPH;
Vital Images: VoxelView.

The products available in this category have reached a high level of maturity and are extensively used in scientific work. Until recently, this type of product was seen as the "state of the art" in visualization software offering high functionality at relatively low cost to a wide range of users.

10.2.2.   Application builders

The announcement of the Application Visualization System (AVS) by Stellar Computer (later Stardent and now AVS Inc.) in 1989 heralded a new era in commercial visualization software. AVS attempted to unify work in a number of areas. The hardware interfaces of graphics APIs became embedded in the tools and traditional rendering and animation environments were integrated into the package (Upson *et al.*, 1989). The most significant feature of AVS at this time was that it made available, in a commercial product, the visual programming interface. The developers drew ideas from graphics application development systems such as Grape (Nadas and Fournier, 1987), Frames (Potmesil and Hoffert, 1987), and RIVERS (Haber, 1989). Other similar interfaces being developed around this time included Conman (Haeberli, 1988) and apE (Dyer, 1990) apE is now a commercial product available from Taravisual Corp.

AVS gained rapid acceptance by users because of the flexibility of the visual programming interface. The ability to alter the visualization without having to program extensively in a standard programming language appealed to users in the scientific and engineering community. AVS runs on numerous platforms including the IBM RISC System/6000 (RISC/6000), SGi, DEC, HP and Sun.

In 1991 both IBM and Silicon Graphics (SGi) introduced visualization products with a visual programming interface. The IBM product, Data Explorer (DX) was developed by Scientific Visualization Systems, part of IBM Research, Yorktown Heights. When announced, DX ran on the IBM

POWER Visualization System and the RISC System/6000. Recently the code has been ported to SGi, HP and Sun workstations.

The SGi product, IRIS Explorer, when announced, ran on the range of SGi hardware. The product is shipped free of charge with SGi hardware. Recent statements of direction suggest SGi are to port IRIS Explorer to the RISC System/6000, HP and Sun platforms.

Another class of application builders is characterized as having a "4GL" or fourth generation language interface. Products such as IDL, Mathematica and Maple use a symbolic interface that fits the typical quantitative interaction of analysis and computation. This class of products is not examined in this chapter.

The availability of three visualization products with visual programming interfaces running on common platforms could lead to suggestions of a lack of differentiation. The products are not all the same, as this chapter will show. Differences exist in such areas as:

data model;
interface design;
functionality;
execution design (both model and modes);
performance;
use of hardware features;
extensibility.

This chapter will concentrate on a comparison of the following products:

Data Explorer from IBM;
AVS from AVS Inc.;
IRIS Explorer from Silicon Graphics Inc.

These products are, in the short term, likely to be the major competitors in the field of visualization.

The remainder of this chapter will detail approaches to benchmarking of visualization together with some general comments on the three systems based on the author's experience whilst undertaking the work.

10.3.   BENCHMARKING, THE GPC MEASUREMENT

In late 1986 the major workstation manufacturers and users met to discuss the problem of benchmarking computer graphics performance. The Graphics Performance Characterization group (GPC) was formed under the administration of the National Computer Graphics Association (NCGA). Founder members of GPC were: Alliant, DEC, Du Pont Pixels, Evans & Sutherland, HP, IBM, Intergraph, Megatek, Prime, SGi, Sun and Tektronix.

In order to characterize different hardware platforms the picture level benchmark (PLB) was developed. The PLB comprises five elements:

(1) Benchmark interchange format (BIF), geometry file;

(2) benchmark timing methodology (BTM), for standardized performance measurement;

(3) benchmarking reporting format (BRF), for consistent reporting results;

(4) PLB program to implement BIF file processing and run a test displaying and manipulating geometry on a particular graphics platform, measure performance according to the BTM and output the results in a BRF file;

(5) a suite of standard tests and a report summary sheet.

The PLB program is vendor dependent; the original work was all PHIGS based, although GL measurements have been presented by IBM and SGi. Five example tests are used by GPC to test graphics hardware performance (Table 10.1).

A report is issued quarterly by NCGA in which vendor-reported figures for hardware platform performance are detailed. A correction factor is used for each test that is divided by the elapsed time for the test to produce the GPC figure. The results allow comparison of hardware performance based at an application "like" level rather than vectors-per-second type measurements quoted by hardware manufacturers. Optimizations performed by the vendor must be reported, therefore limiting the scope of hardware manufacturers for changes that would show particular machines in a more favorable light.

The GPC figures have allowed the first sensible comparison between graphics hardware. Of course, they have not been met with total approval. Some commentators maintain that the only method of assessing graphics hardware is to test the application to be run on that platform (UNIX Today, 1991).

Table 10.1. Tests of the graphics performance characterization measurements.

Test	Description	Attributes
Printed circuit board	Pan and zoom for 560 frames	5655.3 2D vectors, 6923.3 2D markers, 882.7 characters per frame
System chassis	Pan, zoom, rotate for 500 frames	6107 3D solid polylines, 158 3D dashed polylines, total of 19,064 vectors per frame
Cylinder head	Translate, zoom, rotate for 225 frames	3621 3D Gouraud shaded polygons, 32 3D fill area sets, 3 lights per frame
Head	Rotate for 240 frames	60,000 triangles in a triangle mesh, 4 lights per frame
Modeling of astronaut using robot arm	3355 facets made from quadrilateral meshes, triangle strips, and polygons	2,283 3D markers for stars, 3 lights per frame

10.4.   BENCHMARKING VISUALIZATION

As a measure of raw graphics performance the GPC is a major step forward in standardizing results from a number of platforms. The shuttle test is designed to cover a simple simulation and the head a visualization application. However, to test only the rotation speed of a file of data such as the head is not representative of visualization tasks.

Visualization can be characterized in relation to a general model of scientific investigation shown as a cyclical process proceeding from a hypothesis. Figure 10.1 (Brodlie *et al.*, 1991) illustrates the cycle as applied to visualization. Following the display of results the user may gain some insight that refines their hypothesis or simply indicates something new to examine. User input to the computational stage may be to steer a simulation or as parameters to the production of a visualization abstraction.

The visualization process as discussed by Haber and McNabb (1990) covers a sequence of phases with transformations or mappings between phases. Simulation data are transformed by data enrichment and enhancement to derived data that are then mapped using a visualization technique to an abstract visualization object suitable for rendering to a displayed

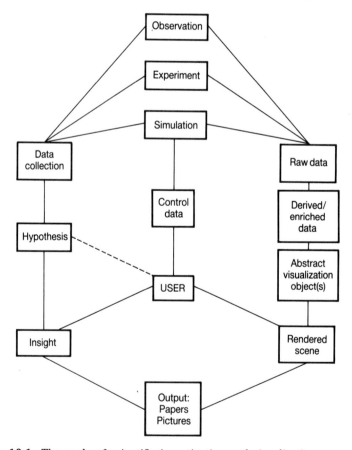

Figure 10.1. The cycle of scientific investigation and visualization.

image. This is one view of the visualization process. Upson *et al.* (1989) use a cyclical model where the user revisits the data after a picture has been presented to change the visualization representation.

Both Haber and McNabb (1990) and Upson *et al.* (1989) concentrate on data that come from computation. As can be seen in Figure 10.1, data collection in the broadest sense of scientific investigation can draw upon a number of sources. This point is important, for as visualization environments of the future develop to provide interaction in the data domain rather than the graphics domain, a more detailed understanding of data will be required.

Measurement of visualization performance that reflects the type of work undertaken by scientists and engineers requires the full process from data reading, through visualization production, to rendering to be measured. Figure 10.2 illustrates the visualization process in relation to the controls on performance and the choice of rendering technique.

The data visualization process involves the processing of data to produce visual representations. In many cases there may be a large amount of data

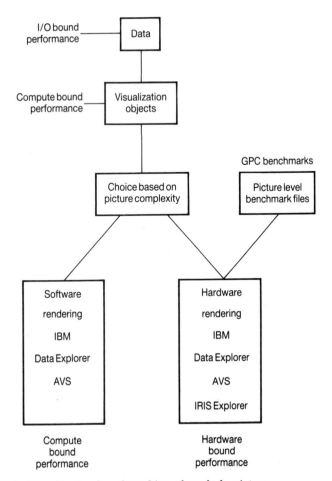

Figure 10.2. Visualization benchmarking, the whole picture.

held on disk that needs to be read for work to be done. Reading data from disk is an I/O bound operation, and the more there is, the longer it takes on any given platform. Once the data have been read in, some visualization task is performed such as making an isosurface or generating vector glyphs for display of the data. This is what Haber and McNabb call visualization mapping. The raw CPU performance and optimizations of the system are the limiting factors in this process together with the design and efficiency of the algorithms used. When the chosen visualization abstraction has been built it must be rendered for display. Figure 10.2 shows a choice being made based on picture complexity prior to the rendering phase of visualization. In reality this choice may be made as part of the selection of a suitable visualization abstraction for the data being processed. However, one must consider that a large dataset, if processed to produce, for example, an isosurface, may generate many thousands of polygons if traditional methods are used. The choice of rendering technique to be used should be based on the complexity of the visualization abstraction rather than simply on the basis of available hardware.

For many problems the number of data points and the complexity of the subsequent visualization abstraction mean that any polygons generated would be of subpixel size. Rendering these in hardware can be very expensive. A software rendering technique is more appropriate in these cases. Likewise, software rendering can be used by the visualization abstraction when volume rendering techniques are required. A number of problems remain which hardware rendering only partially addresses (Smith, 1988), such as the combination of volume rendering and geometric information. Software rendering allows the use of the CPU power of the system whilst hardware rendering relies on specialized circuitry. A forward-looking visualization system allows the user the choice of rendering technique and control over the approximations of each.

The GPC benchmark only addresses a small portion of the visualization problem, hardware rendering performance. It takes no account of the import of data from disk and the production of the visualization abstraction. A visualization benchmark must include all of these factors if a useful comparison is to be made between systems.

10.5.   PRODUCT COMPARISON

As stated in the introduction, during the period of study to obtain the benchmarking figures the products under examination needed to be used. This inevitably led both to a degree of learning, and to the formation of opinions (however subjective) as to the merits and deficiencies of individual products. Some general comments will be made about the use of IBM Data Explorer, AVS, and IRIS Explorer. Some of these are the subjective opinions of the authors and potential users are free to disagree. References to products other than those of IBM is not intended to demean or disparage competitive offerings. The comments are given as an honest assessment of the tools under examination.

User interface

The DX interface is pleasantly simple in appearance but encompasses very powerful modules. AVS is seductive in that many alternatives are presented to the user giving the appearance of a more powerful system. IRIS Explorer presents a blank window similar to DX but with less intuitive help for the new user as to where to find particular tools, only an alphabetical list is provided by default.

Turnkey aspects

AVS retains an element of its turnkey predecessors, this means that you can do things such as image or geometry viewing without the need to build a visual program.

Screen clutter

AVS uses numerous colors and a multitude of windows that change their contents as you use the system. IRIS Explorer also uses a multitude of windows as a spin-off from the manner in which the modules are presented with small interactors embedded in the tools on screen that need to be enlarged to see them clearly. The DX method of user-chosen interactors in control panels is, we believe, neater and less confusing for end users.

General purpose modules

DX excels in this area; due to the unified data model (see below) the modules in DX can accept multidimensional data and perform the correct operation based on the dimensionality and rank of the data. AVS has multiple modules exposing the data model such as isosurface and ucd iso. This illustrates the evolutionary nature of AVS; ucd, or unstructured cell data were added after the initial design. IRIS Explorer, although a recently designed product exposes the data model to the user through "duplication" of modules such as IsoLat and IsoPyr for lattice and pyramid data types respectively. The DX Compute module is of particular note in this area. Around 22 of IRIS Explorer's 103 modules could be replaced by the DX Compute, and up to 15 of AVS's 121 modules.

Port connections

The AVS port coloring is useful at first to help select what modules can be connected together. A general color informs users whether the port accepts fields or geometry, etc. but extra bands are needed to delimit this further due to the data-specific nature of AVS modules. Both AVS and IRIS Explorer light up all suitable ports in a network when an output is selected. DX waits until the user drags the connection line into the module to inform the user by a color change in the connection tab if the connection is valid.

The connection tab idea of DX is much easier to use than AVS or IRIS Explorer. IRIS Explorer requires the user to open the output port and select the output they want; then to open the input port of the target connecting module, select the input to connect to; only then is a connection made. It also allows users to fan-in to a single input that can lead to picture errors that are difficult to debug. Only one line connects any two modules in IRIS Explorer, even though multiple connections can be made on the line. This makes the flow of data in the network difficult to ascertain just from viewing the network on the screen.

System busy indication and network firing

All systems show the currently executing module but only DX shows that the system as a whole is busy. Problems due to a lack of this information do not manifest themselves until complex pictures are displayed and rotations are attempted. As the picture is rotated no information is given to users of AVS and IRIS Explorer that the system is working. IRIS Explorer fires a network as soon as it is read in. AVS allows users to disable network firing. DX has a more subtle approach, the user decides when the network is to be fired and whether it will automatically react to changes in network parameters.

Object manipulation

Both AVS and IRIS Explorer offer manipulations of the final scene for such things as lights. DX incorporates these in the network with optional manipulation via a Probe module.

Cameras

IRIS Explorer appears to have only a perspective camera; no orthogonal option can be found in the menus or manuals. This limits the user's choice as some pictures are better represented as orthogonal views, whilst others require some perspective for clarity.

10.6.   A NOTE ON DATA MODELS

Data form the fundamental element of all visualization, therefore the handling of data should be addressed as a primary objective in any system. DX is based on a sound mathematical representation of data (Haber *et al.*, 1991) around the concept of fiber bundles. This allowed code design to proceed at more abstract level than appears to have been the case in AVS and IRIS Explorer. It has already mentioned that AVS shows some of its evolutionary nature in the way data is handled. DX has a single unified data model that encompasses multidimensional scalar, vector, tensor data together with geometrical information in one abstraction. AVS has data formats for images, fields, and unstructured cell data. IRIS Explorer has images, lattices and pyramids.

10.7. DATA IMPORT

To address the problems of data import, for example IRIS Explorer has a tool called Datascribe, a window/menu-driven utility for building bespoke data readers. The IBM UK Scientific Centre has developed a general Motif/ X Windows-based tool for DX that builds DX format files from user data. DX also provides a general array import facility that can be used to describe a wide variety of data for extraction from user files.

10.8. VISUALIZATION BENCHMARKING METHOD USED

A scheme for the benchmarking of visualization should include elements from all areas of the problem (see Figure 10.2). For pure performance measurements a number of areas of real concern are not addressed. These include the conversion of data from user format to a format acceptable to the visualization system, the learning curve to write working visual programs or navigate a turnkey system, and ouput media/methods for hardcopy or video. To examine a product in a way that encompasses the problem from getting data into the system is beyond the scope of this chapter, but it is a topic for future work.

A variety of platforms were used for this study. If strict comparisons are to be made then the software should be running on identical systems – preferably the same system. The approach used for this chapter was to select data from a variety of sources at a number of dimensions with a view to producing a similar visualization on each of the three software products examined.

The datasets (Table 10.2; Plates 49–52 (see color section)) were chosen to reflect both scalar and vector data of various sizes. All of the datasets are on a regular grid; this was done for the sake of simplicity and to ensure that all systems had an equal chance of completing the set task. Future work will expand the range of datasets to include curvilinear, irregular, unstructured data over two and three dimensions. Higher resolution datasets will also be included in future work. In Table 10.2 MRI refers to Magnetic Resonance Imaging and NCSA is an abbreviation for the National Center for Supercomputing Applications.

For the purposes of this investigation a simple visualization was chosen which all systems should be capable of producing. More complex visualization abstractions could be thought of for all of the above datasets by anyone familiar with any of the tools under test. However, as will be shown in the results (Section 10.10) variations in functional capability between systems are exposed, even at this very simplistic level.

As a measure of visualization system performance, the time to first image has been used in this study. This reflects the time taken to read the data

Table 10.2. Datasets used for benchmarking.

Dimension/ rank	Description	Data size	Comments	Target visualization
2D Scalar	Heights on the earth's surface	360×180	Low resolution	Colored 'map' showing heights
3D Scalar	MRI head	$55 \times 128 \times 128$	Medium resolution	Isosurface at skin level
3D Scalar	MRI head	$27 \times 64 \times 64$	Low resolution	Isosurface at skin level
2D Vector	Surface winds over the UK	23×22	Very low resolution	Vector orientation and magnitude
3D Vector	Winds from NCSA thunderstorm	$15 \times 15 \times 15$	Low resolution	Vector orientation and magnitude
3D Vector	Winds from NCSA thunderstorm	$30 \times 30 \times 30$	Low resolution	Vector orientation and magnitude

from disk, perform the mapping to an abstract visualization object, render the scene, and display the result. In addition to this measure the time taken to perform one rotational transform was recorded to give a measure for one of the elements of scene change.

10.9. SCENE CHANGE IN VISUALIZATION

The dominance of graphics performance measurements for hardware that is expressed in the GPC has engendered a philosophy of "object spin" as the most important factor in computer graphics. In visualization the exploration of data by users is the most significant distinguishing factor between it and computer graphics. Typically a user will produce a picture, decide they wish to change a parameter controlling the production of the visualization abstraction or indeed change the whole abstraction and render the scene again. This is the computer-bound part of the visualization process and it typically takes up the majority of the user's time. It is therefore unreasonable to place undue emphasis on GPC performance figures in visualization; rather, any visualization benchmark should express both scene production and rotational capability.

10.10 RESULTS

The following tables summarize the results obtained from this visualization benchmarking study. Table 10.3 was produced using data held in ASCII form and floating point on a variety of platforms for DX and IRIS Explorer (AVS appears only in the binary test tables). Data were usually Network

Table 10.3. Comparison of data in ASCII format (results shown as seconds elapsed).

Dataset	Test	DX 1.1 IBM PVS 9570	DX 1.1 IBM PVS NFS	DX 1.2 IBM 560 512 MByte	DX 1.1 IBM 530H 96 MByte	DX 1.1 IBM 530H 32 MByte	DX 1.1 IBM 730 128 MByte	IRIS 4D/80 GT 32 MByte
Scalar 2D	Display	2	2	7.5	8	NR	7	NR
360 × 180	Image	2	2	4.5	13	13	14	59.0
	Rotation	<1	<1	2.8	5.2	NR	6.2	9.0
Scalar 3D	Read	1	3.3	4.2	8	NR	10	20
28 × 64 × 64	Isosurface	1	1	1.8	7	NR	9	10
	Image	2.8	5	10.2	17	59	23	34
	Rotation	<1	<1	0.8	2.2	NR	2.8	1.5
Scalar 3D	Read	1	27	32	64	NR	75	175
55 × 128 × 128	Isosurface	5.5	5	17.5	52	NR	70	90
	Image	6.5	32	53.2	124	894	155	292
	Rotation	1.5	1.5	2.8	7.8	NR	9.8	4.5
Vector 2D	Default	<1	1.9	NR	2.6	2.6	3	9
23 × 22	Rotation	<1	<1	0.4	1	1	1	<1
	Colored	<1	1.9	NR	2.6	2.6	3	NP
	Rotation	<1	<1	0.4	1	1	1	NP
Vector 3D	Default	1.5	1.8	NR	4.8	4.8	5	10
15 × 15 × 15	Rotation	<1	<1	0.65	1	1	1.5	<1
	Colored	1.5	1.8	NR	5	5	5.5	NP
	Rotation	<1	<1	0.65	1	1	1.5	NP
Vector 3D	Default	1.8	5	14.8	24.5	24.5	28.5	46
30 × 30 × 30	Rotation	<1	<1	1.1	1.5	1.5	1.8	<1
	Colored	2.5	5.4	14.8	25	25	29.5	NP
	Rotation	<1	<1	1.1	1.5	1.5	1.8	NP

NR: not recorded.
NP: not produced by system.

File System (NFS) mounted across a local area network (LAN) but the tests were conducted when the LAN was not being used by other users. The IBM 530, 530H, and 730 models of the RISC System/6000 range. The IRIS 4D/80 GT is manufactured by Silicon Graphics Inc. it is accepted that this machine is not from the current SGi range but it does support IRIS Explorer and is the only SGi machine at the IBM UK Scientific Centre.

It should be noted that the IBM POWER Visualization System (PVS) was designed to handle large datasets in the order of many megabytes. Some of the tests used in this study do not stress the PVS. The vector field tests are especially low resolution and therefore one should be wary of scaling workstation results to the PVS. A scalability test is give in Section 10.11, comparing DX on the PVS and an IBM RISC System/6000 560.

Scalar 2D 360 × 180

Two methods of display were used in this example, the display of the data as an image, and its conversion to a geometric object that could be rotated by the system's user interface; the speed of the IBM PVS is noticeable. IRIS Explorer takes a long time to produce the picture in this case. It should be noted that IRIS Explorer recommends a limit of 64,000 data elements for the LatToGeom module used in this test (SGi, 1991). The test dataset is 64,800 elements. The picture shown by IRIS Explorer does not have its current transform saved by default when exiting the network or map, unlike DX and AVS. The rotation figure shown for the SGi is a hardware rotation whilst the DX rotations are all software. The current level of DX (1.2) includes adaptive hardware rendering as an option on suitable workstations. For the DX 1.2 tests a hardware graphics accelerator was used known as the GTO. By using an adaptive rendering technique such that the object is represented by dots, rotation speeds of 0.6 s per frame were achieved.

Scalar 3D 28 × 64 × 64

For this test measurements were made of the read, isosurface, and cumulative time to first image on each machine. The 530H with 32 Mbyte of memory took longer than the SGi machine with the same memory. With an increase in global memory the 530H performed the task at a reasonable rate. The IBM 560 machine performs, in this case extremely well. The software rotation time is especially noticeable at 0.8 s per frame. Using hardware rotations of the GTO adapter reduces this figure only by a small margin to 0.7 s. All DX rotations were software; IRIS Explorer uses hardware rotation.

Scalar 3D 55 × 128 × 128

At this higher resolution all of the machines and software on test show significant performance degradation. The 530H with 32 Mbyte is somewhat slow with this dataset in ASCII form and floating point using DX default memory settings. This can be improved by use of extra memory and paging space as shown by comparison to the 530H with 96 Mbyte. The SGi machine takes a significant time to read the data from disk, longer than DX takes to produce the picture on the 530H with 96 Mbyte and the 730 with 128 Mybte. Using the 560 shows a dramatic performance increase over the 530H in the workstation tests. Not only is the time to image less than 50% of the 530H but software rotation is a much improved 2.8 s per frame. The read time of the dataset across NFS for the PVS highlights the need to use the fastest I/O devices for visualization data. When the data are on the 9570 Disk Array Subsystem they are read in approximately 1 s compared to 27 s over NFS.

Vector 2D 23 × 22

The two sets of results presented for all of the vector datasets show the equivalent of DX speedy glyphs, i.e. just a vector showing direction (it is possible to have the glyph show magnitude also). The default test refers to the color of the vector, colored means that the DX Autocolor module had been applied to color the vectors by their magnitude. IRIS Explorer cannot, as far as we were able to find in the system, color vectors by a color map. The IRIS Explorer vectors are red at the sample point and white at the other end. DX performs very well showing this dataset, even the with good times to first image and reasonable rotation speed in software rendering. The SGi performs expectedly well at rotating the vectors, as does the IBM 560 and GTO.

Vector 3D 15 × 15 × 15

A pattern similar to the 2D vector field emerges from this dataset.

Vector 3D 30 × 30 × 30

By increasing the density of sample points this test exposes some of the differences between the systems. The DX and RISC 6000 combinations are comparable, the faster processor of the 530H giving it an edge over the 730. The 560 reduces time to image to around 50% of the other RISC System 6000 machines under test coupled with good rotational times. Using hardware rendering in this case reduces rotations to 0.9 s per frame. NFS read time on the PVS contributes greatly to the difference in the two sets of measurements on that system. Rotation speed on the SGi is maintained but time to first image is much longer than the RISC 6000 machines.

Table 10.4 was produced using data held in byte format of DX and IRIS Explorer together with floating point binary data for AVS.

Scalar 2D 360 × 180

DX 1.2 can handle data held in byte format. This makes a dramatic improvement to the performance figures for the scalar field data. It also highlights a problem, if the data cannot be held in byte, e.g. they are actually floating point or range over zero, then this performance gain is not obtainable without manipulation of the data. The earth height data range from −7473.22 to 5731.15, for the purposes of this test a new dataset was built using DX in which the data was transformed by the Compute module using the following expression:

$$\text{byte(rint}(a + 7473.22)/52)$$

which normalizes the data between 0 and 254. A dramatic performance improvement is shown for all RISC System/6000 platforms due both to better read time and reduced rendering time. Using the Display module on PVS gives an almost instantaneous result when the data are on the 9570 Disk Array Subsystem. AVS can show this test as an image but has no simple way to convert the 2D field to a flat geometry in order to give a colored map, this limits the type of work that can be undertaken on the data.

Table 10.4. Comparison of data in byte format (results shown as seconds elapsed).

Dataset	Test	DX 1.2 IBM PVS 9570	DX 1.2 IBM PVS NFS	DX 1.2 IBM 560 512 MByte	DX 1.2 IBM 530H 96 MByte	IRIS 4D/80 GT 32 MByte	AVS 3.0 IBM 530 80 MByte
Scalar 2D	Display	<0.5	<1	NR	1.6	NR	1
360 × 180	Image	1.2	1.8	5.2	6	NR	NR
	Rotation	<1	<1	2.8	5	NR	NR
Scalar 3D	Read	<1	<1	<1	1	23	NR
28 × 64 × 64	Isosurface	1	1	1.8	4.5	12	NR
	Image	2	2	6.4	6.2	39.5	5.5
	Rotation	<1	<1	0.8	1.8	1	3.2
Scalar 3D	Read	1	1.5	1	3	110	NR
55 × 128 × 128	Isosurface	3.5	3.5	17	29	110	NR
	Image	5.5	6	21.6	39	248	42
	Rotation	1.5	1.5	2.8	6	4.5	16
Vector 2D	Default	NR	NR	NR	NR	NR	NP
23 × 22	Rotation	NR	NR	NR	NR	NR	NP
	Colored	NR	NR	NR	NR	NR	NP
	Rotation	NR	NR	NR	NR	NR	NP
Vector 3D	Default	NR	NR	NR	NR	NR	4
15 × 15 × 15	Rotation	NR	NR	NR	NR	NR	1.5
	Colored	NR	NR	NR	NR	NR	NR
	Rotation	NR	NR	NR	NR	NR	NR
Vector 3D	Default	NR	NR	NR	NR	NR	24
30 × 30 × 30	Rotation	NR	NR	NR	NR	NR	13
	Colored	NR	NR	NR	NR	NR	NR
	Rotation	NR	NR	NR	NR	NR	NR

NR: not recorded.
NP: not produced by system.

Scalar 3D 28 × 64 × 64

Again, byte data shows a dramatic improvement in read time especially on the RISC System/6000, further speedups are seen in Isosurface. The combination of these improvements makes a significant difference to the time to first image. IRIS Explorer shows a surprising tendency to go slower using byte data on this dataset. AVS is the fastest of the RISC System/6000 based systems to show the first image, although subsequent hardware based rotation speed is not as good as DX software rendering (especially on the 560) or IRIS Explorer hardware rendering. DX hardware rendering on the 560/GTO combination at 0.7 s per frame is the same as for ASCII data.

Scalar 3D 55 × 128 × 128

For ASCII data the NFS read time to the PVS was particularly slow. This is resolved by using byte data that show an 18-fold performance improvement on data read. IRIS Explorer shows an improved read time but IsosurfaceLat runs slower reducing the overall improvement in time to first image. The hardware rotation on the SGi machine remains fast, although it lags somewhat behind the 560 software rendering performance. The RISC System/6000 platforms show a range of results, the 530H improves the time to first image three-fold to 39 s (six times faster than IRIS Explorer) and maintains a reasonable rotation speed. AVS shows a good time to first image but is let down by poor rotation speed (hardware rotation with no adaptive rendering). The 560/GTO renders this test at 6.0 s per frame in hardware, less than half the machine's software rendering speed of 2.8 s. This is good example of why a choice of rendering technique is desirable.

Vector 2D 23 × 22

The conversion of the vector datasets to binary format made no difference to performance on the PVS, RISC System/6000, or SGi machines. The AVS results are presented for comparison with Table 10.3. It should be noted that AVS cannot show 2D vector fields with the hedgehog module.

Vector 3D 15 × 15 × 15

AVS shows the image in a time comparable to DX but faster than IRIS Explorer.

Vector 3D 30 × 30 × 30

After a comparable time to first image the rotation speed of this dataset by AVS is the slowest of the three products on any platform.

10.11 SCALABILITY IN VISUALIZATION

The results presented above provide a range of tests for examination of visualization performance. By using the scalar 3D field at two resolutions one can begin to observe the effects of scalability in visualization (Table 10.5). Doubling the number of points in each axis (eight times the data)

Table 10.5. Byte data at high resolution.

Dataset	Test	DX 1.2 IBM PVS 9570	DX 1.2 IBM 560 512 MByte
Scalar 3D	Read	1	1
55 × 128 × 128	Isosurface	3.5	17
	Image	5.5	21.6
	Rotation	1.5	2.8
Scalar 3D	Read	1	5
109 × 256 × 256	Isosurface	24.5	146
	Image	28.2	171
	Rotation	3.8	19

generally leads to between a 3.5.- and seven-fold increase in elapsed time to first image. It is therefore worth considering the times for the same scalar 3D field at a resolution $109 \times 256 \times 256$.

For datasets of this size the IBM POWER Visualization system begins to show its strength, remaining some six times faster than the model 560 IBM RISC System/6000. Although the number of points has been increased eight-fold the PVS time to first image is only increased five-fold. The 560 however, shows nearly an eight-fold increase in processing time for the high resolution data over that measured for the $55 \times 128 \times 128$ dataset.

10.12. CONCLUSIONS

As a first attempt at benchmarking visualization products the study has been successful. It has been shown how the GPC approach to hardware graphics performance measurement addresses only a portion of the visualization problem. When the rotation measurements alone are considered in the results the hardware rendering used by IRIS Explorer appears to offer some competitive advantage. An examination of the whole visualization problem changes the perspective on this, e.g. the time to first image of the 2D scalar problem on IRIS Explorer when compared to DX on a RISC 6000 530H with the same internal memory. There is also some evidence to suggest that software rendering can yield acceptable performance figures when undertaken on high powered workstations. To gauge accurately the relative performance of visualization products, clearly the whole process from the reading in of data, through the building of a visualization abstraction, and finally rendering/rotation must be examined and characterized. There is a need for future work to address further the assessment of visualization product performance.

10.13. FUTURE WORK

To obtain sound relative performance figures for visualization products a number of areas should be addressed in further study. Assessment of the points detailed below may lead towards the development of a visualization equivalent of the GPC (possibly the VPC – visualization performance characterization).

Comparison of products all running on one platform; this will be possible for common platforms by year end 1992.

Comparison of individual products across the range of an individual manufacturer's platforms and across a variety of vendors' machines.

A set of standard datasets that are representative in size of typical visualization tasks including nonregular grids, cell centred data, curvilinear grids, or commonly available data formats such as Plot3D.

A set of target visualizations, specified without undue emphasis on the capabilities of the products under test, e.g. colored vectors shown as cone or arrow objects.

The visualization task should be set to broaden the problem for an individual test. The test could include reading data, building the abstraction, showing the image, a number of rotations, followed by a change in abstraction parameter, e.g. a new isosurface level, and another group of rotations. These tests should run in an automatic mode without user intervention.

Further study taking into account points raised during this discussion and all elements of the above list will yield a significant comparative process for visualization benchmarking. A visualization benchmarking group analogous to the GPC would prompt vendors to address the whole problem rather than relying on graphics hardware performance as the only measure.

ACKNOWLEDGMENTS

The above discussion contains numerous trademarks; all trademarks used are hereby acknowledged.

REFERENCES

Brodie, K. W. *et al.* (1991). *Scientific Visualization, Techniques and Applications.* Springer-Verlag, New York.

Dyer, D. S. (1990). A dataflow toolkit for visualization. *IEEE Computer Graphics and Applications* **10**(4), 60–69.

Haber, R. B. (1989). Scientific visualization and the Rivers Project at the National Center for Supercomputing Applications. *IEEE Computer* **22**, Number (8), 84–89.

Haber, R. B. and McNabb, D. A. (1990). Visualization idioms. In Neilson, G. M., Scriver, B. and Rosenblum, L. J. (eds), *Visualization in Scientific Computing*, pp. 74–93. IEEE Computer Press.

Haber, R. B., Lucas, B. and Collins, N. (1991). A data model for scientific visualization with provisions for regular and irregular grids. In *Proceedings, Visualization '91*, San Diego, pp. 298–305. IEEE Computer Press.

Haeberli, P. E. (1988). ConMan: a visual programming language for interactive graphics. *Computer Graphics (Proc. SIGGRAPH)* **22**(4), 103–111.

Nadas, T. and Fournier, A. (1987). GRAPE: an environment to build display processes. *Computer Graphics (Proc. SIGGRAPH)* **21**(4), 75–84.

NCGA (1991). *The GPC Quarterly Report.* National Computer Graphics Association.

Potmesil, M. and Hoffert, E. M. (1987). FRAMES: software tools for modelling, rendering and animation of 3D scenes. *Computer Graphics (Proc. SIGGRAPH)*, **21**(4), 85–93.

SGi (1991). *IRIS Explorer. Module Definitions.* Silicon Graphics, Inc.

Smith, A. R. (1988). Geometry vs imaging: extended abstract. *Computer Graphics World*, pp. 151–156, November.

UNIX Today (1991). Graphics spec nears. *UNIX Today!* March 4.

Upson, C., Faulhaber, T., Kamins, D. et al. (1989) The application visualization system: a computational environment for scientific visualization. *IEEE Computer Graphics & Applications* **9**(4), 30–42.

About the authors

David Watson read geography at Loughborough University (1978–1981) for a B.Sc. (Hons) degree (2:1). He received a Ph.D. from Southampton University (1986) following research into the effects of aquatic plants on water flow in Chalk streams of Southern England. He joined IBM in 1984 and worked in the change teams for Screen Definition Facility and GDDM (mainframe device driver and graphics product). He moved to the IBM UK Scientific Centre in 1988 to work on Data Visualization. At the Scientific Centre he worked on interactive display of 3D solid models, and architected a visualization system for the examination of scalar fields, and mathematical functions. Recently he has worked closely with IBM Research Division on the support of the Data Explorer and IBM POWER Visualization System products. His current interests are: the application of Data Visualization to complex problem analysis, the benchmarking of visualization packages, and walkthroughs of CAD/CAM models.

Kelvin Goodson read Photographic Sciences at the Polytechnic of Central London (now University of Westminster) for a B.Sc. (Hons) degree (1st Class, 1984). He received a Ph.D. (1988) on Computer Image Interpretation of Hydrographic Charts following research at Dorset Institute (now University of Dorset). He performed postdoctoral work at Southampton University on line drawing databases for two years. As a postdoctoral fellow at the IBM UK Scientific Centre he worked on egomotion of a camera given a series of images of a rigid static object. After researching visual programming environments for data visualization he moved to join the COVIRA team (Computer Vision in Radiology) examining image processing techniques for radiation treatment planning.

Dave Williams graduated from Bath University in 1980 with a degree in Material Science. He joined IBM Hursley in 1982 as computer operator, and moved to the data processing group at the IBM UK Scientific Centre in Winchester at the end of 1985. Since 1988 Dave has worked in the Data Visualization group, specializing in applying computer graphics and data visualization techniques. He is also closely involved with IBM Research for the support of the IBM POWER Visualization System and Data Explorer.

Part IV

Applications

Chapter 11

Visualization techniques for correlative data analysis in the earth and space sciences

Lloyd A. Treinish

11.1 INTRODUCTION

In the earth and space sciences, it is very common to organize geographically located data in terms of a rectilinear grid with horizontal extent over the entire surface of the earth (i.e. latitude and longitude). In two dimensions that implies a topological primitive (cell) that is a rectangle of various sizes. In three dimensions the cell is a parallelpiped, with the height corresponding to altitude or atmospheric pressure, for example. These rectilinear mesh structures are ill-suited for the study of phenomena that occur continuously over a nominally spherical surface (as they tear the data). In addition, these grids may not be fully populated due to missing data (when observations could not be made). In such cases, the grids could be viewed as being irregular.

Whether the original grids are regular or irregular, cartographic techniques are often introduced to deform the data suitably to compensate for the problems inherent in the original structure (i.e. the use of a rectilinear representation for a spherical surface). Traditionally, such a transformation is accomplished by defining a new cartesian grid in the cartographic projection coordinate system, and then interpolating from the original rectilinear grid to the new one prior to any other operation. Figure 11.1 illustrates this operation schematically. Given the curvilinear nature of such transformations, nonlinear interpolation techniques are typically required to make the transformation of acceptable quality. In addition to being computationally expensive, such interpolation may make it difficult or impossible to preserve the fidelity of the data prior to rendering, especially if regions of no data or other discontinuities are present. Alternatively, by warping the underlying mesh structure, the geometric structure itself is

ANIMATION AND SCIENTIFIC VISUALIZATION
ISBN 0-12-227745-7

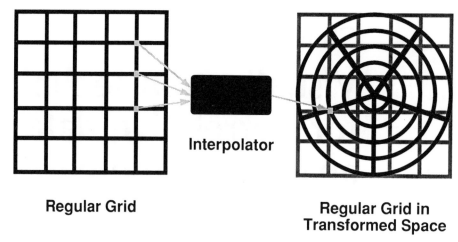

Regular Grid

Interpolator

**Regular Grid in
Transformed Space**

Figure 11.1. Interpolation of data to transformed grid.

transformed without affecting the data. Figure 11.2 illustrates this operation schematically.

Thus, any realization that is to be done to help visualize the data is independent of the choice of a specific cartographic coordinate system, the data or mesh themselves, or how the data are specified with respect to the underlying mesh (e.g. the data values are assigned at each node of the mesh or the data values are assigned to an entire cell at its center). In addition, interpolation is not required as the initial operation to be applied to the data to be visually correlated. Instead, interpolation can be isolated to be the last step in the visualization process, namely rendering (e.g. Gouraud-shaded surfaces).

The use of appropriately warped curvilinear grids can preserve the fidelity of the data prior to rendering. This does require an environment that supports direct realization (the application of one or more visualization

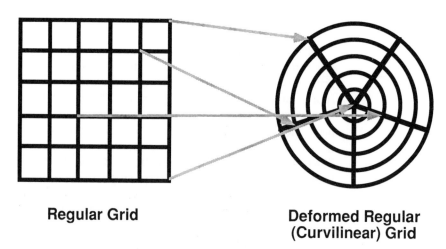

Regular Grid

**Deformed Regular
(Curvilinear) Grid**

Figure 11.2. Warping of coordinates or data mesh.

strategies that generate renderable geometry from a collection of data) and rendering of data on curvilinear grids as well as regular ones. This must be coupled with the ability to manipulate data independently and their underlying mesh structure or base geometry. In addition, the ability to render simultaneously disparate geometry (e.g. points, lines, surfaces and volumes of varying color and opacity) is very helpful in viewing the realization of multiple datasets.

Therefore, methods that support the registration of multiple datasets in geographic coordinates, using similar cartographic warping of the respective data locations for the datasets in question shows promise as an alternative to meshing, interpolating or resampling the original grids of each dataset to a common rectilinear grid in projected space. The former has been used for a number of datasets via the IBM Visualization Data Explorer (DX) developed by the Visualization Systems group at IBM's Thomas J. Watson Research Center (Lucas *et al.*, 1992) in contrast to the latter approach used by the author via the NSSDC Graphics System, developed at NASA/Goddard Space Flight Center (Treinish, 1989; Treinish and Goettsche, 1991). DX currently operates on the IBM Power Visualization System, IBM RISC System/6000 workstations and selected workstations manufactured by Silicon Graphics Incorporated, the Hewlett-Packard Company and Sun Microsystems Incorporated.

11.2   AN EXAMPLE CORRELATIVE ANALYSIS PROBLEM: STRATOSPHERIC OZONE DEPLETION AND THE POLAR VORTEX

The best way to illustrate the aforementioned approach for the analysis of multiple datasets is to discuss an example scientific problem. There is a phenomenon that occurs in the earth's upper atmosphere (primarily, the stratosphere) above Antarctica during the winter and early spring of every year known as the polar vortex (cf. Schoeberl and Hartmann, 1991). This effect is characterized by a cyclonic circulation pattern around the south pole. Many researchers believe that ozone-destroying chemicals are trapped in this vortex during the cold and darkness of Antarctic winter. Once spring begins and the polar region emerges from the long night, it is theorized that these substances react photochemically with ozone to break the molecule apart and thus, aid in the creation of the so-called Antarctic ozone hole. Hence, in late winter, regions of ozone depletion around the pole begin to form. Within a few weeks the ozone hole is completely established. By late spring the vortex weakens, causing the ozone depletion region to fragment and eventually dissipate. The question of interest is then, what are the characteristics of the south polar vortex that can be derived from diurnal observations of atmospheric dynamics and how do they relate to independent diurnal measurements of stratospheric ozone? The study of the appropriate datasets for the southern hemisphere winter and spring (June through December) are relevant. The examination of a single year, 1987, is made because that year showed the greatest amount of ozone depletion until recent years (Krueger *et al.*, 1992).

11.2.1   Total column ozone data

A very active area of atmospheric research and one that has much public interest concerns the results of the reduction in total stratospheric ozone observed annually during the Antarctic spring. Perhaps the most critical effort to study stratospheric ozone has been the observations made by the Total Ozone Mapping Spectrometer (TOMS) aboard NASA's Nimbus-7 spacecraft. Nimbus-7 is in a (polar) sun-synchronous orbit, which means that it can roughly provide global coverage of the earth for its suite of instruments once per day. Each portion of the earth that is observed is nominally under the same illumination conditions from day to day. Study of the measurements made by the TOMS instrument can be used to show the global distribution of stratospheric ozone on a daily basis. It has been operational since late 1978 and is still operating today. It measures the total column density of stratospheric ozone by observing backscattered solar ultraviolet radiation in seven spectral bands. Approximately 200,000 such measurements are made each day, which covers the entire globe (Fleig *et al.*, 1986). These data can be used to study the formation of the Antarctic ozone hole and its morphology. It should be noted that the term, ozone hole, is a misnomer. It is actually a depletion, which can be seen as a blue region or depression in various realizations discussed below. Since the instrument requires sunlight to operate there will be periods of missing data due to local polar winters (when it is dark) in addition to the usual data dropout problems associated with spacecraft observations. These regions are visible as gaps in surfaces or images in various realizations of the data. They are *not* the ozone hole. The data have been gridded in a regular lattice of 180 (1° in latitude) × 288 (1.25° in longitude) from the raw observations for daily global coverage with cells without data being flagged. The locations of missing cells are used to irregularize the data mesh prior to any realization. The total stratospheric ozone measurements are in terms of Dobson Units (DU). One Dobson Unit corresponds to a column density of 2.69×10^{16} molecules of ozone per square centimeter. For the period of 1 November 1978 to 31 December 1988 the ozone column density ranges from 117 DU to 650 DU. Plate 53 (color section) shows a traditional two-dimensional visualization of the ozone data. The data are realized with a pseudo-color map for 1 October 1987. The rectangular presentation of the data is consistent with the provided mesh in that it is torn at the poles and at a nominal International Date Line. This cartographic representation of the earth is known as a cylindrical equidistant or plate carré projection. The ozone data are overlaid with world coastlines and national boundaries as well as fiducial lines (lines of latitude or parallels and longitude or meridians), which have been registered in this same rectilinear coordinate system. The grid cells where there are no data are quite visible as gaps in the pseudo-color realization. This plate shows data acquired during the ozone depletion season. The area of low ozone is visible as a bluish band stretched across the bottom of the pseudo-colored rectangle.

Plate 54 shows the same representation as Plate 53, but transformed by the Mollweide cartographic projection. In addition, isocontour lines at every 20 DU have been overlaid to help in the interpretation of the pseudo-color image. The ozone density value for each line has been used to assign the same color to the line as the surrounding image, but at a different level of brightness. The Mollweide and similar projections are used relatively often by earth scientists as a way of preserving area in a display of the entire globe compared to the cylindrical equidistant projection. Other projections may preserve shape or linear distance, for example, on selected portions of the globe (Pearson, 1990). For the Mollweide projection, all meridians, which converge at the poles, are ellipses except for the central meridian, which a straight line and considered (a) true (representation of a line on the earth's surface). For example, the 90° meridians are circular arcs. The parallels are straight lines perpendicular to the central meridian. The equator is considered true. The Mollweide projection can be characterized by the following:

$$x = \sin(\text{latitude}) \qquad (1)$$

$$y = (\text{longitude}) \cos(\text{latitude})$$

where [latitude, longitude] represents the location of each node on the earth's surface in the original mesh and [x, y] represents the location of each node in the deformed, curvilinear (Mollweide) coordinate system.

To examine a continuous phenomenon with a central focus far from the equator and the Prime Meridian, such as the ozone hole, either a different pole point for the Mollweide projection must be used or in this case it would be appropriate to use a different map projection. Plate 55 illustrates the same data as in Plates 53 and 54 except a polar orthographic projection for both the southern and northern hemispheres is employed, which are shown in the left and right side of the figure, respectively. For the orthographic projection, all meridians are straight lines radiating from the central pole. The parallels are concentric circles, which become compressed toward the equator. The orthographic projection can be characterized by the following:

$$x = \cos(\text{latitude})\cos(\text{longitude}) \qquad (2)$$

$$y = \cos(\text{latitude})\sin(\text{longitude})$$

where [latitude, longitude] represents the location of each node on the earth's surface in the original mesh and [x, y] represents the location of each node in the deformed, curvilinear (orthographic) coordinate system.

In addition to the pseudo-color spectrum, this two-dimensional cartographic projection of the data is extended by redundant realization as a deformed surface (i.e. both height and color correspond to ozone density). The bluish contiguous area over Antarctica clearly depicts the depletion region, illustrating the advantage of choosing an appropriate cartographic coordinate system. The height mapping clearly dramatizes the concept of a hole or depression in the ozone layer while the color enhances this perception as color would enhance a topographic map. It should be noted that the use of hue-based pseudo-color mapping for realization and rendering of data as images can create problems in interpretation due to how the human visual system responds to color (Rogowitz *et al.*, 1992). For example, discontinuities may appear to be present in the pseudo-color representation that are not in the data. However, such pseudo-color maps are virtually standard in many earth and space science disciplines. The acceptance of alternative, perceptually correct pseudo-color maps (e.g. luminance-based (Lefkowitz and Herman, 1992)) would be limited in these disciplines because of their unfamiliarity. Therefore, the introduction of redundant realization techniques retains the familiar pseudo-color scale but helps to lessen their negative perceptual impact.

Daily sequencing of the data utilizing this realization strategy shows the (super)rotation of the ozone hole surrounded by an ozone high region. This ozone high or ridge corresponds to the boundary of the polar vortex. This rotation usually has a period of several days. Below each translucent surface is a hemispherical map that has been registered in the same orthographic coordinate system as the ozone data. This map consists of a pseudo-colored topographic surface, which is deformed based upon height above or below sea level. The pseudo-color scale is chosen to impart the appearance of a topographic map (e.g. the oceans are blue) for each hemisphere. This surface is created from a topographic database on a rectilinear grid at one-half-degree resolution. The grid is warped by the same orthographic projection that was applied to the ozone data, although the data were originally in a different coordinate system at different resolution. Both the ozone and topographic surfaces are Gouraud-shaded. In addition, the topographic map is overlaid with the same coastline map in magenta with political boundaries corresponding to each hemisphere that was used in Plates 53 and 54. The map geometry was transformed in a manner similar to that of the ozone and topographic data.

It should be noted that there appears to be a seam in each of the orthographic surfaces corresponding to where east longitude is either $-180°$ or $+180°$ – nominally the International Date Line. This is an artifact of the warping of the original rectilinear data onto a continuous surface, welding the discontinuity in the provided form of the data. The use of coordinate warping does preserve this inherent discontinuity in the data, which would not be the case if traditional interpolation techniques were chosen. In general this seam will not smoothly connect the surface, due to how TOMS gathers data. This scanning instrument examines each portion of the earth at a different time of day, but still covering the entire globe once per day. Hence, observations on each side of that line were taken approximately 24 h apart and usually are not the same.

Plate 56 carries this cartographic theme to a three-dimensional continuous surface by performing a cartesian to spherical coordinates transformation. For the spherical projection, all meridians are great circles converging at the poles. The parallels are also great circles, which become compressed toward the poles. The spherical projection can be characterized by the following:

$$x = (z + \text{radius})\cos(\text{latitude})\sin(\text{longitude})$$

$$y = -(z + \text{radius})\cos(\text{latitude})\cos(\text{longitude}) \qquad (3)$$

$$z = (z + \text{radius})\sin(\text{latitude})$$

where [latitude, longitude, radius] represents the location of each node on the earth's surface at its radial distance from the earth's center in the original mesh and [x, y, z] represents the location of each node in the deformed, curvilinear (spherical) coordinate system.

The ozone is now triply redundantly mapped to height (now radial), color and opacity so that high ozone values are thick, far from the earth and reddish while low ozone values are thin, close to the earth and bluish. Replacing the map is a globe in the center of this ozone surface, which is created from the same topographic data used in Plate 55. The grid is warped onto a smooth, Gouraud-shaded opaque sphere (i.e. 259,200 polygons) and similarly pseudo-colored to give the appearance of a globe by having all values around sea level and below appear light blue. As with Plate 55, southern and northern hemispheric views are shown, which are shown in the left and right side of the figure, respectively. Each spherical object gives the appearance of looking at a continuous phenomenon from two vantage points. The use of three redundant realization techniques results in patterns or textures, which are particularly effective in animation of time sequences for qualitatively identifying regions of spatial or temporal interest in the data. Therefore, this approach shows promise for data browsing. On the other hand, the orthographic projection technique does not yield such an impression, although it does impart more of a quantitative "feel" to the visualization. Hence, this projection will be revisited in the subsequent discussions.

11.2.2. Dynamics data: atmospheric temperature and winds

A good candidate to demonstrate the applicability of three-dimensional visualization techniques to the study of the earth's atmosphere is global atmospheric temperatures. In this case, data are derived from spacecraft, balloon and aircraft observations, which have been modeled and gridded on a 25° grid, originally 144 × 73 cells (longitude × latitude) at seven different levels in the atmosphere, based upon their pressure (1000 millibar [mb] – surface – to 100 mb). Hence, a two-dimensional slice of these data at a specific pressure level is organized in a torn mesh similar to that of the total column ozone, but at lower resolution and in a slightly different geographic coordinate system. It should be noted that the pressure levels are not spaced uniformly in the 1000 mb to 100 mb range.

If one considers the Mollweide cartographic projection discussed in equation (1), Plate 57 might be the result for 1 October 1987. Each of the seven pressure surfaces or slices of temperatures are independently used to define a cartographic warping, where the temperature is pseudo-colored according to a constant scale from 185 K to 315 K with isothermal contour lines every 5 K and overlaid with a coastline and national boundary map in the same manner as the ozone data were shown in Plate 54. Each of the seven Mollweide ellipses are stacked vertically according to a linear scale in pressure from 1000 mb to 100 mb, which can be seen in the axis. In addition, the opacity of each of the two-dimensional pseudo-color slices corresponds to the pressure height such that the 100 mb slice is almost transparent while the 1000 mb slice at the bottom is opaque. Since a pseudo-colored cartographic map is commonly used by climatologists to display two-dimensional data, Plate 57 could be viewed as an attempt to extend that traditional method to three-dimensional (i.e. volumetric) data. Unfortunately, it is perhaps only effective for viewing a small number of slices simultaneously.

Alternatively, if one considers the spherical projection discussed in equation (3), Plate 58 might be the result for 1 October 1987. In this case, the temperature data are treated as a true volume by warping the parallelpiped mesh representation of the atmosphere into a collection of concentric spherical shells that compose a volume of 73,584 spherical/ annular cells. The temperature data are pseudo-color and opacity-mapped, but now direct volume rendered. At the center of the volume is a globe, which is created from the topographic data as in Plate 56. The radius of the globe is chosen to be the same as the inner radius of the spherical shell corresponding to the 1000 mb level. Although this picture may be interesting, little quantitative information can be derived. In addition, a time sequence of such data on a daily basis, for example, would show only small variations. Hence, surface extraction techniques are appropriate for a more quantitative visualization.

Corresponding wind data are also available with these temperature data. However, there are many gaps in the dataset, including having only a partial value for some cells (i.e. one or more of the three vector components are missing). Plate 59 illustrates both the temperature and wind data. The temperature data are realized as pseudo-color and opacity-mapped isothermal surfaces instead of a volume rendering. The isosurfaces are at 200 K, 250 K and 300 K with the higher values being more opaque. The pseudo-color spectrum on the right corresponds to that of the temperature isosurfaces. The wind data are realized via arrows or vector glyphs, where the direction of the arrows corresponds to the direction of the wind while the length of the arrow is proportional to the wind speed. The arrows are pseudo-color-mapped to horizontal speed. In this case, the wind grid is uniformly reduced in resolution by interpolating the wind data to a grid that is smaller than the original grid by a factor of 2.5. The magnitude of the lower resolution horizontal winds range from 0 to about 60 m/s, which correspond to the pseudo-color spectrum on the left. The vertical component of the wind ranges from about -33 to about $+45$ mb/s. Further study of the data using the techniques shown in Plate 59 shows that there is a region of cold air (e.g. 200 K isosurface) over the Antarctic during this period that is concentrated near 100 mb in pressure height. The shape of this cold air mass and its diurnal variation at first glance appear to be similar to what can be seen as the depletion region in the total column ozone data.

11.2.3 Correlating ozone with temperature and winds

Two different approaches to visually correlating the ozone and dynamics data for the 100 mb level are taken utilizing the concept of coordinate warping to achieve geographic registration. The 100 mb data are the same as used in Plates 58 and 59, and hence, are of a different grid than that of the ozone data. Since the aim of this study is to examine a phenomenon that is focused on a polar region and is nearly hemispheric in geographic extent, the orthographic cartographic projection discussed in equation (3) is utilized for both approaches. They are illustrated using data from 1 October 1987 in an attempt to show the formation of the polar vortex and the ozone hole itself in Plates 60 and 61.

Plate 60 shows four separate and different data-driven representations of the atmosphere over the southern hemisphere in the same geographic coordinate system utilizing the same three redundant realization techniques: pseudo-color imagery, surface deformation and isocontouring. This is the same approach as used for the ozone data in Plate 55, except for the addition of contour lines. In the upper left is the column ozone density with contours every 50 DU from 100 to 650 DU. The upper right shows the 100 mb temperature with contours every 5 K from 180 to 245 K. The lower left shows 100 mb horizontal wind speed with contours every 10 m/s from 0 to 85 m/s. Cells where one or more components of the wind velocity or missing are shown as gaps in this surface. In an attempt to show the correlation among these observable quantities in data space, the ozone data are interpolated to the grid on which the 100 mb data are available. Hence, independent gaps in both the ozone and wind measurements are properly maintained. These quantities are arithmetically combined to yield a single scalar, such that

$$M = O\,|\mathbf{v}|/T \tag{4}$$

where M represents the combined field in m-DU/s-K, O is total column ozone in DU, v is 100 mb horizontal wind velocity (speed in m/s) and T is 100 mb temperature in K.

The lower right shows this combined quantity with contours every 20 m-DU/s-K from 0 to 150 m-DU/s-K. Each of the surfaces shows a similar structure – a depression of comparable shape and areal extent over Antarctica for low ozone, temperature and wind speed, respectively, each with a boundary corresponding to that of the polar vortex.

Plate 61 combines each of the three different atmospheric data into one visual object. As with Plate 55, southern and northern hemispheric views are shown, which are shown in the left and right side of the figure, respectively. The data are stacked vertically and shown with topographic, coastline and national boundary maps. The difference between Plates 61 and 55 are representations for the 100 mb horizontal wind velocity and temperature stacked between that of the ozone and the maps. Below the ozone surface are plates of vector arrows which correspond to the horizontal winds. The direction of the arrows correspond to the direction of the wind. The size and color of the arrows corresponds to wind speed, which ranges from 0 to 80 m/s. Below the winds and above the maps are flat, pseudo-color-mapped translucent planes corresponding to the 100 mb temperature. These disks also show pseudo-colored isothermal contour lines every 5 K, with the data ranging from 180 K to 235 K. The realization of the 100 mb data is via two-dimensional analogues of the techniques used with the full volumetric data as in Plate 59.

For both presentations of the ozone and dynamics data, an animation sequence beginning in early winter (late June or early July) through September, the availability of polar ozone data is apparent as well as the formation of the hole. Precursor and correlative signatures are visible in the temperature data as a cold air mass forms over Antarctica and persists into spring. The patterns of the wind as shown via vector arrows in Plate 61 evoke a cyclonic pattern corresponding to the polar vortex, that appears almost steady-state in the winter and early spring. As the sequences continue into late spring, the warming of the upper atmosphere over Antarctica is obvious, with direct correspondence to the dissipation of the polar vortex in the wind data and the breakup of the ozone hole.

11.3. SUMMATION AND FUTURE WORK

With easy-to-use tools to access, reorganize, realize and render, yet preserve the salient characteristics of multiple datasets, a scientist can readily and appropriately scrutinize such data at many different levels through disparate techniques. The support of a plethora of visualization strategies properly coupled with powerful manipulation functions promotes the (visual) exploration and correlation of diverse datasets and thus, enables a scientist to extract knowledge from complex data. Specifically, the application of cartographic warping to the correlation of global atmospheric datasets yields visualizations that illustrate a simple notion about the possible relationship between temperature and winds, and their contribution below the tropopause to the formation of the polar vortex and ozone depletion.

The use of interpolation prior to realization appears to be unnecessary for the visualization of gridded data in a system with a sufficiently robust infrastructure of data structure and geometric support. However, the art of good interpolation is still required for the realization of scattered or point data as well as data on grids with strange or variable topology via continuous visualization techniques. In the latter cases, however, decomposition into unstructured meshes of the same simple primitives (e.g. triangles for planes and surfaces or tetrahedra for volumes), may appear to be an acceptable compromise. Such decomposition and refinement of interpolation methods are topics for additional research.

The ideas introduced with the analysis of observational data related to ozone and tropospheric dynamics can be extended by considering the correlation between these same ozone data and objective analyses that include the entire troposphere and stratosphere as a continuum. Comparison of these data with spacecraft observations of clouds may yield additional insight into the dynamics of ozone depletion, since polar stratospheric clouds are believed to provide sites for trapping ozone-destroying chemicals during the Antarctic winter (Hamill and Toon, 1991).

ACKNOWLEDGMENTS

All of the datasets discussed above were provided courtesy of the National Space Science Data Center, NASA/Goddard Space Flight Center, Greenbelt, MD.

REFERENCES

Fleig, A. J., Bhartia, P. K., Wellemeyer, C. G. and Silberstein, D. S. (1986). Seven years of total ozone from the TOMS instrument – a report on data quality. *Geophysical Research Letters*, **13**(12).

Hamill, P. and Toon, O. B. (1991). Polar stratospheric clouds and the ozone hole. *Physics Today*, **44**(12), 34–42.

Krueger, A., Schoeberl, M., Newman, P. and Stolarski, R. (1992). The 1991 Antarctic ozone hole: TOMS observations. *Geophysical Research Letters*, **19**(12), 1215–1218.

Lefkowitz, H. and Herman, G. T. (1992). Color scales for image data. *IEEE Computer Graphics and Applications*, **12**(1), 72–80.

Lucas, B., Abram, G. D., Collins, N. S., Epstein, D. A., Gresh, D. L. and McAuliffe, K. P. (1992). An architecture for a scientific visualization system. In *Proceedings IEEE Visualization '92*, pp. 107–113.

Pearson, F. II (1990). *Map Projections: Theory and Applications*. CRC Press, Boca Raton, Florida.

Rogowitz, B. E., Ling, D. T. and Kellogg, W. A. (1992). Task dependence, veridicality, and pre-attentive vision: taking advantage of perceptually-rich computer environments. IBM Thomas J. Watson Research Center Report RC 18165.

Schoeberl, M. R. and Hartmann, D. (1991). The dynamics of the stratospheric polar vortex and its relation to springtime ozone depletions. *Science* **251**, 46–52.

Treinish, L. A. (1989). An interactive, discipline-independent data visualization system. *Computers in Physics* **3**(4).

Treinish, L. A. and Goettsche, C. (1991). Correlative visualization techniques for multidimensional data. *IBM Journal of Research and Development* **35**(1/2).

About the author

Lloyd A. Treinish is a research staff member in the Scientific Visualization Systems Group in the Computer Science Department at IBM's Thomas J. Watson Research Center in Yorktown Heights, NY, USA. He works on techniques, architectures and applications of data visualization for a wide variety of scientific disciplines. His research interests range from computer graphics, data storage structures, data representation methodologies, data base management, computer user interfaces, and data analysis algorithms to middle atmosphere electrodynamics, planetary astronomy and climatology. Mr Treinish is particularly interested in generic or discipline-independent techniques for the storage, manipulation, analysis and display of data.

Earlier he did similar work in the development of advanced scientific data systems, including studying space and atmospheric phenomena, for over a decade at the National Space Science Data Center of NASA's Goddard Space Flight Center in Greenbelt, MD. He graduated in 1978 at the Massachusetts Institute of Technology with an S.M. and an S.B. in physics, and an S.B. in earth and planetary sciences; he has been at IBM since April 1990. He is a member of the IEEE Computer Society (IEEE-CS), the IEEE-CS Technical Committee on Computer Graphics, the Association for Computing Machinery (ACM), ACM SIGGRAPH, the National Computer Graphics Association, the Planetary Society, and the American Geophysical Union.

Chapter 12

Undersea visualization: a tool for scientific and engineering progress

Lawrence J. Rosenblum, W. Kenneth Stewart and Behzad Kamgar-Parsi

12.1. INTRODUCTION

The interplay between visualization methodology and the ocean sciences is an ever-growing exploration that enables man to understand better an environment that occupies two thirds of the surface of the earth and whose depths are largely unexplored. The physical processes that define the ocean must be understood to ensure mankind's survival, for the ocean/atmospheric interface is now understood as fundamental to global-change processes. Technological advances, especially in the use of unmanned underwater vehicles (UUVs) equipped with remote sensing devices, use visualization techniques to expand our subsea exploration capabilities. Using both manned and unmanned vehicles, mapping, search and survey missions acquire data that require a variety of data visualization techniques in their processing and interpretation. Three-dimensional underwater imaging is another high-interest area growing in power and potential as volume visualization algorithms are integrated with data from sensors that just begin to provide sufficient resolution for 3D reconstruction.

What issues arise in applying data visualization to oceanic research problems? Highest on the list is the integration of computer graphics and digital imaging techniques. Much as in medical imaging, the distinction between generating pictures and extracting information from pictures is blurring. Data filtering, data registration, data segmentation and other computer vision techniques increasingly use algorithms from the computer vision toolkit that assist us in generating pictures to increase our comprehension of complex datasets. Data registration is a singularly recurrent theme, since oceanic sensors provide fewer data than typically found in other areas of experimental science. From the visualization toolkit, volume visualization techniques enable us to envisage complex three-dimensional (3D) structures and assist in algorithm development. Using animation for the perceptual gains that motion provides is a third theme that can be traced across diverse topics within ocean science.

This chapter presents examples of the interplay between scientific visualization methods and ocean engineering advances. We examine ocean mapping and imaging to illustrate how visualization techniques advance mankind's understanding of the ocean.

12.2. BATHYMETRIC MAPPING

The mapping of the ocean bottom (bathymetric mapping) emphasizes several visualization themes. Animation is useful to interpret the final product and 3D representations are replacing the contour plots of the past. However, a new theme is the ongoing merger between computer graphics, digital imaging, and machine vision. Computer graphics displays, sometimes produced in real time, provide preliminary views of data. These may assist a mapping expedition in knowing where to seek detailed data or may, back in the laboratory, be used as visual aids that initiate the map making process. From there, computer vision methodologies take over. Data may be filtered, interpolated, smoothed and/or registered to generate maps that more fully extract information from datasets. These steps require involvement of scientists who are highly skilled in underwater geophysics. The final datasets are then used graphically. Products range from 2D contour plots to 3D bathymetric reconstructions and animated "fly-throughs" (or, for the ocean, "swim-arounds") of these 3D, computer-generated models of the ocean bottom.

There are many benefits in obtaining accurate knowledge of the ocean floor. Both the US and European communities are engaged in decades-long mapping of their respective offshore economic development zones for the benefit of industries that will use these charts to exploit the ocean's mineral wealth. Scientists use such knowledge to understand seafloor morphology. For navies, the seafloor defines the operating environment. Moreover, accurate seafloor models become inputs to enhance modeling of local and global oceanic processes.

Conventional single-beam sonar systems insonify a large area beneath the ship and yield insufficient resolution for detailed mapping. The last three decades have seen significant advances in bathymetric sensors. Commercially available multibeam systems, such as Sea Beam and Hydrosweep, now operate in deep-water ocean areas and higher-frequency systems have been designed that provide even greater resolution in shallower water. A comprehensive survey of swath bathymetry systems is contained in de Moustier (1988).

Given the high cost of sending a ship to map a region, it is important to locate underwater mountains, fracture zones, and other features of geophysical interest prior to a mission. One does not want to spend precious resources and time doing a detailed survey of a flat ocean bottom! Visualization of satellite altimetry is now being used to provide a rough picture of the ocean bottom. Satellite altimetry uses microwave radar to map in detail the sea-surface height. The measured height is affected by the underlying gravity – an underwater mountain will produce a gravity peak. Although there is not an exact correlation between these gravity measurements and bathymetry, large-scale bathymetric features do correspond reasonably well with gravity data plots. Visualization and animation tools are used by scientists to analyze satellite gravity data (McLeod and Small, 1992). This analysis has provided new knowledge about the physical mechanisms by which the seafloor is formed, deformed, and transported from a ridge-axis. With the location of these new features now identified, ship-based bathymetric experiments have precise site information that allow exploring regions of known interest. Plate 62 (see color section) is a frame from an animated "swim around" in a 3D gravity map of the South Atlantic.

Sea Beam is a commonly used deep-water mapping system and we give a brief description. Two arrays are used, with 20 projectors emitting a 12 kHz wave and and a perpendicular array that contains 40 hydrophones receiving the acoustic return. Corrections are made for pitch, roll, and ray bending. After beamforming, the results are 16 discrete beams, each $2\frac{2}{3}°$ wide and are perpendicular to the ship's track. Sea Beam produces depth values at data points which almost form regular grids.

Because of limitations on ship's time, deep-ocean areas are rarely fully mapped. Instead, a series of straight line "swaths" (parallel tracks) are taken, with significant separation between them. At a time of day when accurate navigation is available using global positing system (GPS) data, a perpendicular swath ("tie line") is collected. Plate 63 illustrates the tracks taken by a mapping mission. Because (non-GPS) navigation can have sizable errors and currents alter the ship's position, the intersection of the swaths with the tie line contains significant errors, with errors of hundreds of meters typical.

The process of registering (aligning) these intersecting swaths is a roadblock in bathymetric map production. The misregistration is nonlinear with both rotational and translational components. Recent methods have entailed producing contour plots, overlaying them, and sliding them around until a navigational correction is conjectured to better align the plots. The process is then repeated until sufficient accuracy is obtained. The process can be made somewhat less tedious using interactive computer graphics (Rosenblum, 1984; Edy, 1986). While such software is of significant assistance, it is desirable to reduce or eliminate the involvement of a highly skilled bathymetrist from this process. Recent advances have included a method based on automated navigational correction (Nishimura and Forsyth, 1988), and one that we examine in some detail that uses computer vision for navigation-independent registration (Kamgar-Parsi et al., 1989).

Computer vision seeks to interpret a "scene", in our case a bathymetric image, and extract parameters (e.g. edges, features, etc.) for machine understanding. The approach taken by Kamgar-Parsi et al. (1989) is to divide the registration problem into two stages. First, individual pairs of swath intersections are registered (local matching) using a contour matching scheme. A global match is then performed based upon minimizing a cost function. Mathematically, this is the minimization of certain small angles;

physically, it is the equivalent of treating the system as spring-loaded and balancing it.

A key step in registering a pair of overlapping swaths is identifying an appropriate matching primitive. Typical matching primitives in computer vision are templates, edges, topograpic functions (e.g. ridges, peaks, saddles, hillsides, etc.), and model functions (analytic functions) that fit brightness or range values.

These have standard applications in computer vision, but, with the possible execution of topographic features, they fit this rather unusual "scene" poorly. Topographic feature matching tends to be highly computational. Also, topographic features may not fall within the swath intersections. Thus topographic feature matching was also not used. Rather, we examined contour mapping, where by contour we mean contours of constant intensity or range. In most computer vision applications neighborhoods where intensity changes gradually and where constant-intensity contours can be defined are rare. However, a swath of seafloor can be considered a "smooth" surface to within measurement accuracies. Contours, though not popular in image processing, proved to be a good matching primitive for this application.

There are several steps in local matching. These include gridding the data and extracting contours. The innovative step is in the matching of contours. We summarize this procedure: Contours (in successive depth slices) are represented as chain codes (Rosenfeld and Kak, 1976; Ballard and Brown, 1982). A chain code is generated from a contour by placing a mesh on the contour and selecting the grid point nearest each intersection as defining the curve. The match of two curves can then be quantified by the fit of the chain codes. However, there are rotational components to the misregistration and chain codes are not rotation invariant. Accordingly, we differentiate the chain code representation by taking the difference between two successive elements of the original chain code. This yields a "second-order" chain code that is rotation invariant. Two factors are now used to determine the best match of the chain code representations of contours from each swath from the intersecting pair of swaths, where fixing the depth determines the contours to be matched. These factors are the degree of match and the length of match. The process is repeated for several depth contours until a consensus match is found. Rotation components are used to test the consistency of contour overlaps. Figure 12.1 shows a pair of intersecting swaths before local registration. Figure 12.2 shows the result of applying the registration algorithm.

It is, of course, possible that the data registration process to align one pair of swaths will add to the misalignment of other pairs. Thus, it is necessary to devise a system that maximizes the benefits found by the local matching. We model the problem as a mechanical system involving many springs that can be compressed or stretched. Our "best" solution occurs when the system is in equilibrium. Hence, the cost function is derived to minimize the tension in the system caused by the violation of local matches as well as by the compression or bending of swaths. Specifically, correlated entities are joined by a spring whose strength

Figure 12.1. A swath-pair before local registration.

represents our confidence in the correlation. We seek a configuration having the lowest energy. The results of applying global matching is shown in Figures 12.3 and 12.4, where Figure 12.3 is the unregistered map and Figure 12.4 is the result after applying both local and global matching. The corrections found at the swath-pair alignment stage are maintained and even improved.

Once registration and other anomalies have been corrected, we return to the realm of visualization to understand and display final results. Plate 64 shows how Sea Beam data are represented in 3D for interpretation. Animated swim-arounds enhance our ability to "see" features in even greater detail, with visualization tools enhancing researchers' understanding of seafloor morphology in geological and geophysical research. Among several producers of these animations are Robert Tyce of the University of Rhode Island and William Ryan and colleagues at the Lamont-Doherty Geological Observatory.

In addition to bathymetric mapping, there is interest in understanding the makeup of the sub-structure of the ocean bottom. Such information helps us understand the Earth's evolution and provides us with useful information about the potential mineral content. An example is a detailed examination of the growth and consolidation of a structure located in the Gulf of Mexico called the Mississippi Fan (Parmley *et al.*, 1993). A submarine fan is an underwater structure formed during the evolution of a river system. During different epochs, different layers are added to the structure.

Figure 12.2. A swath pair after local registration.

Seismic and geophysical data produced by drilling at multiple sites provide a data base. The Mississippi Fan has been found to contain 13 distinct layers.

Computer animation and 3D displays are used to help understand the evolutionary process. Plate 65 comes from an animation sequence that relates the growth process with the seven ships' tracks used to acquire the data. The ships' tracks are color coded and the 3D display integrates the track information with the 2D bitmapped display (upper right), which shows the evolutionary process at a given time. As the animation proceeds (one frame is equal to 800 years), the growth and consolidation along all ships' tracks are observed by representing them as height that changes with time. Plate 66 shows a frame from a second animation sequence (one frame equals 1200 years) where each layer is represented as a 3D layer. The Mississippi Fan is represented as a 3D solid with distinguishing interconnected layers that illustrate the growth of the fan as the animation proceeds.

12.3. UNDERWATER IMAGING

Technology improvements in ocean engineering have placed growing emphasis on producing near photographic-quality images of underwater

Figure 12.3. 4×2 swath configuration unregistered.

objects. With the growing use and capability of both remotely operated and autonomous underwater vehicles (ROVs and AUVs) has come a new ability to approach objects of interest for "high-resolution" imaging. The goal of such imaging is to see, interpret and in some cases interact with these objects. Objects can be quite small (e.g. a valve on an oil platform) or quite large (e.g. an underwater shipwreck).

The visualization issues are similar to those discussed above. Computer graphics and digital imaging techniques merge to generate a final image. Indeed, the merger of these techniques here is more complete since the two are integrated to produce detailed images. Much of the difficulty involves an insufficient amount of data, as well as uncertain navigation. Thus, data must be interpolated at the voxel and subvoxel level and 3D filtering algorithms developed. Volume-rendering algorithms are then used for 3D reconstruction. Volume visualization tools have been especially helpful in understanding difficulties that arise and, therefore, as digital-imaging software development aids. Because a single pass over an object of interest often provides insufficient data for detailed imaging, registration of data from multiple passes assists in extracting details of interest.

Traditionally, underwater images have been produced using side-scan (side-looking) sonars. These sonars look in small azimuth angles and large elevation angles. The result is to "paint" a 2D acoustic reflectance map of the ocean, quite similar to a photograph. The result is a grid of acoustic

Figure 12.4. 4×2 swath configuration registered.

intensity values that are influenced by the geometry, the angle of incidence, and the scattering properties of the material from which the acoustic energy is backscattered. Figure 12.5 is a side-scan image of the USS Scourge (Stewart, 1991). The image was generated in real time during an archaeological survey by the Woods Hole Oceanographic Institute using a 200 kHz side-scan sonar. Notice that the ship's image is the bright portion of Figure 12.5 and contains little or no information. Rather, it is the acoustic shadow cast by the ship that provides detail in the dark portion of the image. Visible are the Scourge's two masts, the bowsprit and a dangling spar. The bright rectangles along the top rail are acoustic returns through the open gun port (Stewart, 1992). Like a photograph, this acoustic image is a 2D projection of a 3D object. Perceptually, we understand and interpret 3D images far better than we do 2D projections. For these reasons, such fields as computer vision and robotics have increasingly moved to 3D processing as advances in computer hardware enable more complex 3D computations to be performed. Also, while we can see details of a large object like the Scourge, side-scan data are insufficient for imaging small objects. An imaging capability that can distinguish a 1 m long, man-made object from a similar sized rock is useful for many applications.

For physically based reasons, underwater imaging is mainly restricted to acoustics, cameras, and lasers. Progress in sensor technology is being made in all areas. Progress is needed because sensor technology is today's

Figure 12.5. Real-time, 2D image of the USS Scourge showing the acoustic shadow.

limiting factor in underwater imaging. When usable, cameras provide images at comparable resolutions to those we are accustomed to observing. However, cameras are limited to ranges of tens of meters in clear water. In turbid water, a common condition in coastal waters or waters disturbed by man, cameras fail at centimeter range. Laser imaging devices are a relatively new development. Profiling lasers are capable of higher resolution than sonars. They can generate monochromatic images that can be combined with precision range maps (Coles, 1988). However, lasers also cannot image in turbid water.

Thus, sonar is the only practical sensor for turbid water imaging, and 3D imaging forward-looking sonars are used. Traditional forward-looking sonar systems use mechanical or electrical beamforming techniques to scan a highly directional beam over a field of view. An innovative sensor that has been used to examine the capabilities and limitations of acoustic imaging today is the acoustic lens, a sonar that operates in a manner analogous to the human eye (see Figure 12.6). The acoustic lens consists of a thin, hemispherical shell and a retina containing small ceramic transducers. A specially chosen fluid focuses incoming acoustic waves onto the retina. One of the challenges in lens manufacturing is to assure focus

Active Acoustic Lens

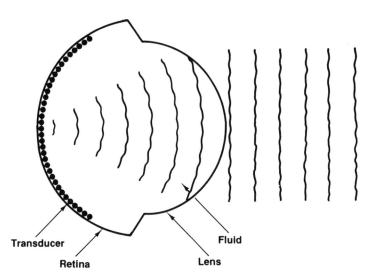

Figure 12.6. The physics of an acoustic lens. The fluid is chosen to focus the acoustic energy on the retina, yielding elevation and azimuth.

over the widest possible range of water temperatures (Kamgar-Parsi *et al.*, 1992). Range is given by the transmission time, while the location of the retina element receiving the acoustic return gives bearing and elevation. The lens is a 300 kHz sonar whose retina is populated with an 8×16 array of transducers. The very small number of transducers is due to sensor technology limitations and this lack of resolution is the fundamental difficulty today in underwater acoustic imaging. Efforts are underway to replace piezoelectric ceramic transducers with new transducer technologies that will populate a retina with more elements having narrower beam patterns. For the current lens each transducer element forms a conical beam with 1.5° resolution at the 3 dB down (half-power) point. The 128 beams thus span 48° in azimuth and 12° in elevation. The current fluid maintains lens focus over a temperature range of nearly 15°. The acoustic lens has roughly the same resolution as the best available commercial beamformed systems, and beamformed data could equally well be used for acoustic imaging, at a hardware and computational expense.

The acoustic lens is placed on a platform that passes over an object, while continually pinging and acquiring data. Typically, one ping-cycle of the lens is 0.5 to 1.0 s long. As an experiment, we passed the lens over a 1.6 m long ROV called PLUTO (Figure 12.7) to see what level of detail can be reconstructed. Recalling that the lens is an 8×16 element sensor (and actually 8×8 for the data shown), we see that far fewer samples are available than in other imaging disciplines. Also, because the platform on which the lens is mounted is moving, the data are not gridded and positional information is uncertain. Associated with each lens transducer is the 1.5° conical beam. As the lens moves, this conical beam intersects many voxels.

Figure 12.7. A picture of the remotely operated vehicle PLUTO that was used by the acoustic lens to obtain a test dataset.

Because the beam spreads with range, the number of intersected voxels increases with range. Backscatter is distributed over intersecting voxels and the (possible) multiple estimates within a given voxel are combined into a single estimate. Digital filtering algorithms are applied to remove certain spurious voxels and to fill certain undersampled regions.

Interactive volume slicing is a valued tool for understanding difficulties that arise in the software development process. When a volume rendering does not produce good results (e.g. Plate 67), it is a difficult problem to determine why. Interactive slicing through our voxel space helped us gain this understanding; these methods are applicable to a wide variety of computer vision problems. Plate 68 shows the improvements after applying additional filtering algorithms. This single pass reconstruction is adequate for extracting size and a very general shape. However, it is inadequate for extracting fine-scale details of object structure. Accordingly, registration algorithms were developed to align the data from multiple passes. Plate 69 shows the volume rendering of four data passes without performing image registration. The need for registration is clear! Feature matching offers little potential here because the low data resolutions do not provide distinguishing features. Accordingly, we performed registration by matching moments: first order image moments determined the translation parameters while the second order moments yielded the rotation parameters. Plate 70 shows the reconstruction after registration. Fine details, such as the valve on the side and the strobe lights and cameras in the head, begin to emerge as bumps in the appropriate location (Rosenblum and Kamgar-Parsi, 1992; Kamgar-Parsi *et al.*, 1992). A similar experiment was performed with small spheres whose reconstruction can be seen in Figure 12.8. Note that the closest viewing distance in these experiments were 8 m. At this distance the lens' resolution is 20 cm, which is about half the size of PLUTO's head, or nearly the size of the three smaller spheres imaged in Figure 12.8.

How we perform these tasks illustrates the substantial progress made in the last five years in commercial desktop visualization systems, particularly in the area of volume visualization (Rosenblum, 1989; Kaufman, 1991). Initially, we implemented a version of Levoy's volume rendering algorithm (Levoy, 1988) and developed in-house volume visualization algorithms for

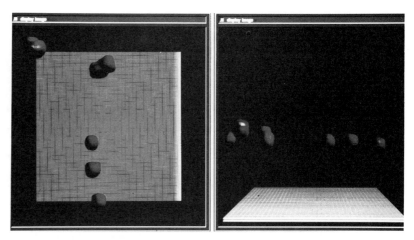

Figure 12.8. Top and side views of a reconstruction of five spheres of various sizes.

interactively slicing through data cubes parallel to the axes. When the Advanced Visualization System (AVS) arrived from Stardent, we found it met our volume visualization needs quite well. The original AVS volume renderer, based on the Upson/Keeler algorithm (Upson and Keeler, 1988), was quite slow when used in its cellular (high-resolution) mode. However, our undersampled data sets are small as volume visualization sets go, with 50-cubed points typical. So, for our applications the speed was sufficient, and faster algorithms have since been implemented within AVS. Using commercial tools that met our needs freed us to concentrate our efforts on digital imaging requirements such as gridding, filtering and data registration. While AVS and the Ohio State Supercomputer Center's ApE were the first graphical, module-based tool sets with good volume visualization, there are now a half-dozen or more systems that incorporate worthwhile volume visualization capabilities.

A somewhat different approach to 3D object reconstruction, based in part on the use of a different sensor, was used to reconstruct the famous Civil War ironclad, the USS Monitor, which sank in a storm in 1862 (Stewart, 1990, 1991). Here, a high-frequency profiling sonar was mounted on the Navy's Deep Drone ROV and used to explore the sunken wreck. Note that the Monitor is a much larger object than PLUTO. Stewart's approach is to model probabilistically the sonar return. The conical probability distribution is determined for the sonar's beam pattern and angular measurement. Position error and ranging uncertainty further smear the sensing envelopes. The approach breaks up space into volume elements. A single ping is taken to define a region that cannot be precisely determined but can be probabilistically represented using a color scale, whereby warm colors give probability values increasing close to unity. Returns are accumulated over time and when enough data samples are represented, an image emerges. The stochastic representation also provides a measure of sonar quality.

The volume-based representation is then used to extract 1D hull profiles, 2D contour plots, or 3D perspective views (Stewart, 1992) (e.g. Plate 71).

Sonar imaging has been performed for several decades, but it is only in the last few years that substantial steps have been made in obtaining 3D acoustic images with data from sonars mounted on moving platforms. The visualization problems are invariably tied to oceanic limitations: sensors that provide too little data for high-resolution imaging as well as navigation and other uncertainties that limit the value of what data does exist. Three-dimensional reconstruction, of course, requires the standard set of 3D volume visualization tools. However, probabilistic tools and/or data imaging techniques must be developed for use in conjunction with our 3D toolkit to extract meaningful 3D image reconstructions from these datasets.

12.4. MULTISENSOR, MULTIDIMENSIONAL VISUALIZATION

As our understanding of the subsea environment is refined and our questions become more subtle, the limitations of individual sensors become more apparent. Considering the full scope of a detailed site survey, for example, a suite of sensors encompassing a hierachy of range, resolution and measurement types must be accommodated. An underwater vehicle, for example, may carry different sonars (obstacle avoidance, down-look, side-look), cameras (video, film and digital still), a scanning laser, and sensors to measure gravity, magnetic fields, temperature, salinity, and so on. Such a scenario applies to different platforms including a towed instrument sled; a tethered, remotely operated vehicle; or a free-swimming, autonomous underwater vehicle. In all cases, this remote-sensing probe is capable of collecting an enormous amount of multisensor data as it moves through the undersea terrain.

To be more specific, multiple sensors are needed for underwater applications mainly because: (1) many features must be characterized to understand an environment more fully; (2) different sensors have practical limitations, in range and resolution, for example; (3) similar features, detected with different sensing modalities, may be characterized more accurately with redundant information; and (4) sensors do not always measure distinct physical properties.

First, a simple characterization, such as by surface shape alone, may not suffice in many undertakings. An AUV may need more complete information about texture, reflectance, color, hardness, and so on to discriminate adequately between different objects or regions. Scientists also need more complete descriptions to understand subsea processes. For example, a study of seafloor spreading centers could be enhanced with information about temperature, optical transmissivity and chemical constitution of the overlying water mass, as well as the shape and composition of the bottom surface (or subsurface). Such comprehensive description exceeds the capabilities of single-sensor surveys.

Second, there is often a tradeoff among different sensory capabilities. Video or still photography can supply detailed information about the seafloor, often enough to study visually the structure and distribution of geological or biological features. For fine-scale topography, a scanning laser can survey more quickly and at a higher resolution than a scanning sonar. For longer ranges, acoustic methods provide the only real alternative. Here also, different sonars offer competing options in range, resolution, speed and signal analysis (sidescan intensity versus bathymetric profile, for example).

Third, redundant information can enhance the accuracy and certainty of an underwater representation. Redundancy can also be derived from different sensing modalities as well as from multiscale surveys of the same sensor class. To determine surface shape, for example, data may be integrated from a sonar, a laser rangefinder, stereo photography, or even the touch of a manipulator. In such a scenario, the optical, acoustical and tactile surfaces may not coincide; a single surface representation would be inaccurate and misleading.

Fourth, a camera is a good example of a device that can characterize surface features only indirectly. The optical intensity measured at the sensor is a function of the surface reflectance, of the surface normals with respect to the camera and of the lighting power and geometry. Even with a perfect sensor model, it is impossible to deduce any one of these parameters without prior knowledge or simplifying assumptions about the others. To extract three-dimensional features from two-dimensional images, shape-from-shading techniques (Ballard and Brown, 1982) require a known camera and lighting geometry, and assume a uniform surface albedo. Even then, lateral dimensions are only specified relative to an unknown distance along the look axis. When complemented with laser range information, though, more complete and more accurate information can be acquired from the two sensors and with less effort than for an exhaustive analysis of the camera data alone.

To illustrate this last point, consider an acoustic-intensity image. A side-look (or side-scan) sonar, often used in a search phase to locate targets, is a relatively low-resolution sensor that generates an acoustic image similar to a photograph. Like its optical analog, a side-look image comprises a grid of intensity values. Variations in intensity are determined by acoustic "lighting" geometry, angle of incidence, and scattering properties of the target material; all are characteristic of an optical image. Also like a photograph, a side-look image is a two-dimensional projection of a three-dimensional world. Apparent shape is extracted by our human brain, with half its mass devoted to complex visual processing.

Plates 72 and 73 show two acoustic "images" created from SeaMARC II data (Stewart, 1991b). The wide-swath, phase-difference sonar (so called because its dual receivers and twin sonar beams on each side are used to extract acoustic phase differences for measuring bathymetry) can cover large areas at economic rates. The region shown is part of the Siqueiros Transform, a site where the Pacific plates are separating and sliding past one another. The acoustic imagery (Plate 72) is created by measuring the intensity (amplitude) of sound echoing back from the seafloor. Like a huge fax machine, the sonar's narrow horizontal beams, directed to either side, sweep out an image of the seafloor a 10 km line at a time. The serpentine track covers a region about 135 km in east–west (left–right) extent and required about two weeks of expensive ship's time to survey.

Though such images contain high-resolution detail and provide information about finer-scale geologic structure, they do not represent shape directly. Our impression of shape comes from a brain evolved for complex visual processing and highly adept at pattern analysis. Two-dimensional projections of a three-dimensional world can be very misleading, though, as an abundance of optical illusions confirm. Acoustic imagery can be still more difficult to fathom, even for an experienced marine geologist with eyes and brain accustomed to the task. SeaMARC II bathymetry (Plate 73), however, offers geologists and geophysicists direct measurements of seafloor morphology, adding another dimension to the information available in their quest for understanding tectonic activity.

There are two points here. First, although the governing physics of optical and acoustic remote sensing are quite different, the information ultimately extracted from the raw signals must be interpreted with similar regard to material properties, surface shape and lighting (insonification) geometry. Second, shape and intensity information are more useful than either alone and can help to identify better physical properties of interest. They can also be used in a complementary visual way as in Figure 12.9, which shows higher-resolution HMR1 sidescan (a phase-difference system similar to SeaMARC II) imagery texture-mapped onto a three-dimensional

Figure 12.9. A perspective view of higher-resolution HMR1 sidescan-sonar imagery texture mapped onto lower-resolution Hydrosweep bathymetry.

perspective view derived from coarser, Hydrosweep (a multibeam system similar to Sea Beam) acoustic bathymetry (Tucholke *et al.*, 1992). The imagery offers detail; the bathymetry provides shape cues to assist in geological interpretation. The gestalt whole is, in a sense, greater than the sum of its parts.

With the growing complexity and sophistication of marine geophysical research, three-dimensional representations are being used more often as an aid to understanding the Earth's complex internal structure. Plate 74 shows the results of an experiment by researchers at the Woods Hole Oceanographic Institution to image the subsurface composition and overlying morphology of the East Pacific Rise, a site of active seafloor spreading in the Pacific Ocean (Toomey *et al.*, 1990). The lower portion of the plate is a horizontal, subsurface cross-section through the three-dimensional seismic-velocity structure imaged by tomographic inversion of arrival times from explosive sources (similar to computer-aided tomography in medical imaging). At the top of the plate, a wire-frame representation of the overlying morphology shows the relationship of the central ridge axis to subsurface features. The "hot spot", a high-velocity region illustrated by warm colors in the seismic contour, corresponds to observed high temperatures and an upward injection of magma centered on the ridge crest.

The main point of this section is that no single tool or sensing modality suffices for all needs. Rather, we require a complete toolkit comprising low-frequency, wide-swath sensors for mapping large areas of the ocean at relatively coarse scales, and higher frequency acoustic and optical systems to provide the most detail in regions of particular interest. Other sensors to measure gravity and magnetics, for example, can provide additional information on geological processes taking place far below the seafloor crust. Similarly, the choice among different visualization techniques depends strongly on the application, and there is a critical need for a complete visualization toolkit if we are to convey effectively the massive information available today from remote underwater sensors.

12.5.   CONCLUSION

This chapter has discussed the interplay between scientific visualization and ocean engineering. We have seen that progress in new sensor and ocean platform technologies are directly tied to the development of visualization methods that extract newly available knowledge. Advances in volume visualization and 3D computer vision algorithms form the backbone of the techniques used. Data fusion has emerged as a key issue in ocean engineering and one where data visualization methods play an increasingly valuable role. The coming decade will see their use become even more widespread.

For empirical data in the physical ocean sciences (e.g. physical oceanography, ocean acoustics) similar conclusions apply. Here, though, the tools of computational physics come into play to model complex physical phenomena.

The visualization of numerical simulations requires a toolkit, including new methods for the interactive steering of computations and for searching high-dimensional spaces for regions of interest. The last half-decade has seen much progress in using visualization techniques to gain scientific understanding. However, many visualization problems remain largely unsolved and some, such as the value of immersion into a data set through virtual reality, are just beginning to be explored. The 1990s will see the fields of science and data visualization continue to march hand in hand to advance our understanding of the world around us.

ACKNOWLEDGMENTS

Many people contributed to the work discussed. The bathymetric registration algorithm was a joint project between NRL and the Computer Vision Center, University of Maryland. Much of the algorithm credit goes to Behrooz Kamgar-Parsi. Ed Belcher of the University of Washington designed and fabricated the acoustic lens as part of a joint project with NRL. We are grateful to James McLeod of the San Diego Super Computing Center, and Christopher Small and David Snadwell of Scripps Institution of Oceanography for providing Plate 62; to Toomey and Foulger (Toomey and Foulger, 1989) for Plate 64; to Parmley, Warren and Williams (Parmley *et al.*, 1993) for Plates 65 and 66; and Toomey *et al.* (Toomey *et al.*, 1990) for Plate 74. This is Contribution number 8231 of the Woods Hole Oceanographic Institution.

REFERENCES

Ballard, D. H. and Brown, C. M. (1982). *Computer Vision*. Prentice-Hall, Englewood Cliffs, NJ.

Coles, B. W. (1988). Recent developments in underwater laser scanning systems. *SPIE Underwater Imaging* **980** 42–52.

Edy, C. (1986). Automated mapping with multibeam echosounder data. *Proceedings 4th Working Symposium on Oceanographic Data Systems*, 229–238.

Kamgar-Parsi, B., Rosenblum, L. J., Pipitone, F. J., Davis, L. S. and Jones, J. L. (1989). Toward an automated system for a correctly registered bathymetric chart. *IEEE Journal of Oceanic Engineering* **14**(4), 314–325.

Kamgar-Parsi, B., Rosenblum, L. J. and Belcher, E. O. (1992). Underwater acoustic imaging. *IEEE Computer Graphics and Animation* **12**(4), 11–13.

Kaufman, A. (1991). *Volume Visualization*. IEEE Computer Society Press, Los Alamitos, CA.

Levoy, M. (1988). Display surface volume data. *IEEE Computer Graphics and Applications* **8**(5), 29–37.

McLeod, J. and Small, C. (1992). Visualizing seafloor structures with satellite gravity measurements. In *Proceedings Visualization '92*, pp. 424–427 (see also *Visualization '92 Video Proceedings*, 46:02).

deMoustier, C. (1988). State of the art in swath bathymetry survey systems. *International Hydrological Review*, **65**(2), 25–54.

Nishimura, C. E. and Forsyth, D. W. (1988). Improvements in navigation using sea beam crossing errors. *Marine and Geophysical Research*, **9**, 333–352.

Parmley, K. L., Warren, J. D. and Williams, G. N. (1993). A simulation of the formation of the Mississippi Fan. *Proceedings Offshore Technology Conference*, Houston, TX (in press).

Rosenblum, L. J. (1984). Oceanographic data profile analysis using interactive computer graphics techniques. In *Proceedings OCEANS '84*, pp. 100–104.

Rosenblum, L. J. (1989). Scientific visualization at research laboratories. *Computer*, **22**(8), 68–101.

Rosenblum, L. J. and Kamgar-Parsi, B. (1992). 3D reconstruction of small underwater objects using high-resolution sonar data. In *Proceedings IEEE AUV 92 Conference*, pp. 228–235.

Rosenfeld, A. and Kak, A. C. (1976). *Digital Picture Processing*. Academic Press, New York.

Stewart, W. K. (1990). A model-based approach to 3D imaging and mapping underwater. *ASME Journal of Offshore Mechanics and Arctic Engineering*, **112**, 352–356.

Stewart, W. K. (1991a). Multisensor visualization for underwater archaeology. *IEEE Computer Graphics and Applications* **11**(2), 13–18.

Stewart, W. K. (1191b). High-resolution optical and acoustic remote sensing for underwater exploration. *Oceanus*, **34**(1), 10–22.

Stewart, W. K. (1992). Visualization resources and strategies for remote subsea exploration. *The Visual Computer* **8**, 361–379.

Toomey, D. R. and Foulger, G. R. (1989). Tomographic inversion of local earthquake data from the Hengill-Grensdalur Volcano Complex, Iceland. *Journal of Geophysical Research* **94**(B12), 17498–17510.

Toomey, D. R., Purdy, G. M., Solomon, S. C. and Wilcox, W. S. D. (1990). The three dimensional seismic velocity structure of the East Pacific Rise near latitude 9 deg 30 min N. *Nature* **347**(6294), 639–644.

Tucholke, B. E., Kleinrock, M. C., Stewart, W. K., Lin, J., Goff, J., Jaroslow, G., Brooks, B., Lemmond, P., Howland, J., Marra, M., Reed, T., Edwards, M., Fricke, J. R. and Herzfeld, U. (1992). Geological and geophysical survey of the Mid Atlantic Ridge Flank at 25 25′ N to 27 10′ N. *EOS Transactions of the American Geophysical Union* **73** (in press).

Upson, C. and Keeler, M. (1988). V-buffer: Visible volume rendering. *Computer Graphics* **22**(4), 59–64.

About the authors

Lawrence J. Rosenblum is currently serving as Liaison Scientist for Computer Science at the Office of Naval Research European Office (ONREUR) in London, UK. In 1994 he will return to the Naval Research Laboratory in Washington, DC, where he worked as a research computer scientist prior to moving to ONREUR in 1992. His recent research has focused on applications of data visualization and machine vision to the ocean sciences. He has numerous publications in computer science, mathematics, and ocean science. He received his B.A. in Mathematics from Queens College (CUNY) and his M.S. and Ph.D. from Ohio State University with specialty in Number Theory. Rosenblum is on the editorial board of IEEE *Computer Graphics and Applications* (*CG&A*), where he edits the Visualization Blackboard Department. He has been a guest editor for special issues of *CG&A* as well as a special section of COMPUTER. Rosenblum is a former Chair and current Director of the IEEE Computer Society's Technical Committee on

Computer Graphics and he initiated the IEEE Visualization Conference Series. He is a member of the IEEE Computer Society, the IEEE Ocean Engineering Society, ACM, SIGGRAPH, the American Geophysical Union and Sigma Xi.

W. Kenneth Stewart is an Assistant Scientist at the Deep Submergence Laboratory of the Woods Hole Oceanographic Institution. His research interests include underwater robotics, autonomous vehicles and smart ROVs, multisensor modeling, real-time acoustic and optical imaging, and precision underwater surveying. Stewart has been going to sea on oceanographic research vessels for 20 years, has developed acoustic sensors and remotely-operated vehicles for 6000 m depths, and has made several deep dives in manned submersibles, including a 4000 m excursion to the Titanic in 1986. He is a member of the Marine Technology Society, Oceanography Society, IEEE Computer Society, ACM SIGGRAPH and NCGA. Stewart received a Ph.D. in Oceanographic Engineering from the Massachusetts Institute of Technology and Woods Hole Oceanographic Institution Joint Program in 1988, a B.S. in Ocean Engineering from Florida Atlantic University in 1982, and an A.A.S. in Marine Technology from Cape Fear Technical Institute in 1972.

Behzad Kamgar-Parsi is a research scientist at the Naval Research Laboratory. His research interests include computer vision, acoustic imaging, and neural networks. He received a B.A. in Physics from the University of Tehran and a Ph.D. from the University of Maryland. Before joining NRL he was a postdoctoral fellow at the Rockefeller University and a research scientist at the University of Maryland Computer Vision Laboratory. He has many publications in statistical physics, neural networks and computer vision. He is a member of the IEEE Computer Society, the American Physical Society, and Sigma Xi.

Chapter 13

Visualization of real and simulation data in physical oceanography

Jacques Haus

13.1 INTRODUCTION

13.1.1. Poor historical knowledge

Despite having been a subject of investigation for many centuries, sea behavior is still poorly understood. For the sailors who were its first explorers, knowledge often was (and still is) a matter of life and death. But as they were mostly fishermen or merchants, when not simply soldiers, information on wind or current direction, locations of fish shoals, etc., could also mean wealth and power, and was therefore not widely exchanged. Additionally they had neither real interest nor appropriate ways to investigate the vertical dimension of the sea: for long it remained a surface over an unknown world.

13.1.2. A changing situation

Hopefully, the situation has improved and due to the following facts it may yet change further:

(1) There is a greater awareness of ocean influence on climate, large heat transfers through oceanographic currents, global and regular perturbation of the general circulation (e.g. the El Nino), the roles of oceans in global change and greenhouse effect prevention (rate and limits of CO_2 absorption), etc.

(2) There are also interests in the role the ocean could play to solve some major problems like food (i.e. algae), drinking water or energy production and ocean floor mineral resources exploitation. Questions also arise concerning pollution of what has become earth's last dustbin, its limits and implications.

ANIMATION AND SCIENTIFIC VISUALIZATION
ISBN 0-12-227745-7

(3) New instruments are providing better information about the oceans.

Even if interests diverge, there is a large consensus about the need to acquire a sound knowledge of ocean behavior and eventually be able to produce reliable forecasts. To achieve this, oceanography should play a greater part in research programs.

Observation is eased by new ways of investigation such as remote sensing, although access to the ocean depth is still a problem. An opposing approach through simulation is also increasingly used. Both methods contribute to generate a large amount of data. It emphasizes the need for better results analysis and data management techniques (including storage).

13.1.3.   A challenge to face

New methods are needed to avoid being drowned in data. It is here that visualization has a major role to play. It is of course used already, but there are real possibilities to increase its role as an analysis tool besides other mainly mathematical tools, rather than focus on its use as a method of presentation.

This type of approach and history is not really specific to oceanography. But oceanographic data have their own specific characteristics that will be developed in the next sections.

13.2.   TYPES OF AVAILABLE DATA

Oceanography is a multidisciplinary science with interests ranging from sedimentology to biology, and a strong need to exchange results. The focus here is on the exploitation of physical oceanography data. Figure 13.1 shows the main analysis techniques (related to visualization).

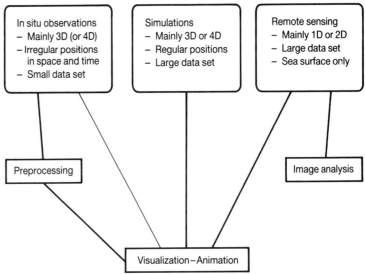

Figure 13.1. Origin of data and main analysis techniques.

13.2.1.   Real data: remote sensing

Ocean pictures taken from plane or satellite have been around for some time but the use of satellite data in oceanography is in its infancy as there has not really been permanent satellite investigation dedicated to oceanography until recently. Now operational missions (like ERS-1 or TOPEX/poseidon) produce high quality data in large quantities. But even if results are already more than satisfactory, time has to be allowed to a wide range of research teams to accept and get used to these new types of data, in addition to the necessity to master problems of access and storage.

Data visualization alone should not really be the main issue in remote sensing since data are at most two-dimensional (2D), already in the form of an image: most of the work lies therefore in the field of image analysis. But there are cases for data visualization such as deformation of surfaces to represent the elevation field, superposition of multiple data on the sea surface.

Despite their great qualities (amongst them accuracy, instantaneous coverage of large regions and access to the whole earth surface), the use of satellites is limited in oceanography by its restriction to sea surface data capture only. Instrument calibration may also appear to be a problem.

13.2.2   Real data: *in situ* observations

Acquisition

Unlike remote sensing, being on site gives direct access to the third dimension of the ocean. But there is a major drawback as information is generally collected at scattered locations. Measurements of temperature, salinity, velocity, chemical tracers, etc. are performed using a wide range of instruments. They are disposed on semipermanent mooring sites (giving time series at one point) or operated from ships during dedicated observation cruises (in which case information is collected all along the journey, but obviously not simultaneously). At each point, a vertical profile is generally obtained. Other methods of investigation include the use of tomography techniques (giving information on more than one point but rather expensive and not widely used) or drifting buoys to study currents.

In order to synthesize information, results from different sources may be gathered. But they can come from cruises that took place at different periods and/or different parts of the domain, from measurements at various locations. Also there are much more data available for the near surface zone, resulting in a completely irregular coverage (in time and space). Accuracy problems should also not be underestimated, particularly when using archive data needed to assess time evolution. Other restrictions result from the use of commercial ships for some sea surface measurements (as winds or sea surface temperature): this gives information only along trade routes (here also the advantage of remote sensing can be shown: in three days a satellite can cover nearly the whole of the earth's surface).

Analysis

Data analysis, reconstitution of spatial structures or time evolution from raw, irregularly positioned data is less than obvious and requires at least a fair amount of experience. People generally try to obtain a picture from their data using crude freehand interpolation or more elaborated optimization methods. The first step is to reconstitute 2D plane or cross sections, although the phenomena one tries to analyse are in most cases fully 3D and thus one really has to approach the problem with other methods, e.g. visualization, which allows the possibility to work directly in 3D in order to obtain the maximum out of the data.

13.2.3. Simulation data

Mathematical models deduced from theory and their numerical transcription lead to computer simulations. Their size has evolved rapidly, matching (or even trying to precede) current computer capabilities as requirements (for CPU as well as storage) are always greater than that available.

In physical oceanography, simulation systems generally contain few state variables (typically five or six). These data are, in most cases, represented along grid points regularly disposed in 3D (or 2D) domains. As in time-dependent simulations the study of the time evolution and the dynamics of the processes is of prime interest, it results in 4D data. It is a situation completely different from the one encountered with real data in the previous section: in this case it is regular in space and time and a nearly unlimited quantity is available. In fact the practical limitation comes from the storage possibilities.

Visualization is an appropriate way to explore such large amounts of data (particularly through animation of time-dependent phenomena).

13.2.4. Experimental data

For completeness, experimental data must be briefly introduced. Even if it is almost impossible to reproduce complex systems, some simple processes can be studied (at a reduced scale) in laboratory. It will probably not generate here new types of data to study: the experiments are directly filmed or photographed, in which case the visualization is already done or measurements similar to those obtained in real situations are collected.

13.3. VISUALIZATION

As a considerable part of the human brain is devoted to image analysis, it seems worth trying to use it. Better image quality, representation of 3D scenes instead of 2D, use of perspective, shading, etc., all contribute to improve image interpretation. As object detection (shape, texture) appears to be a key stage in the way the brain processes images, it is certainly an aspect to exercise. It results in a more efficient use of human capacities and allows therefore better and faster analysis, memorization and comparison. In particular, use of animation through camera displacements to explore 3D static scenes and ease detection of spatial correlation between objects is of great interest. The impressive quantity of information an image can contain makes visualization a suitable tool to analyse (very) large datasets in addition to a more traditional role of results presentation.

Two cases where 3D data have to be analysed will be presented in the next sections. Representation in a 3D physical domain is a general situation in oceanography as there are no real symmetry and the 3D evolution of depicted structures cannot be satisfactorily described by 2D sections or averages.

In both cases animation offers an excellent solution to increase perception of 3D objects (as example performing a rotation) and obtain an unmatched representation of time evolution, allowing a good comprehension of the dynamics of involved phenomena (particularly for the representation of simulation results).

13.3.1. Material description

All visualization work has been performed using IBM Data Explorer (DX) visualization software running either on IBM RISC System/6000[1] workstations or on the IBM POWER Visualization System (PVS). Following preliminary research and exploration of the effects of different views, lights, colors and variables, animation has been performed exclusively on the PVS. Sequences were recorded in real time, using the High Performance Parallel Interface (HiPPI) to send compressed images to a screen via the video controller attached to the PVS. Screen red, green and blue (RGB) images were captured and transmitted to a scan-converter, adapted to the television format and eventually sent to a video recorder. Short sequences were produced and stored in the internal PVS memory before being played back, while longer ones were temporarily stored in the adjacent disk array before being played back (Figure 13.2).

13.4. ANALYSIS OF REAL DATA IN WESTERN MEDITERRANEAN SEA

The Mediterranean Sea is interesting in many ways:

1. It is a semi-enclosed sea having well defined natural boundaries (Plate 75, color section). It can be studied as a whole or separated into its two basins: Western (WMED) and Eastern Mediterranean. There are few open boundaries (Straits of Sicily and of Gibraltar for the WMED) within which exchanges are quite well known, helping to establish (and verify) general balances and to model the domain with reliable boundary conditions.

---

[1] RISC System/6000 is a Trademark of International Business Machines Corporation.

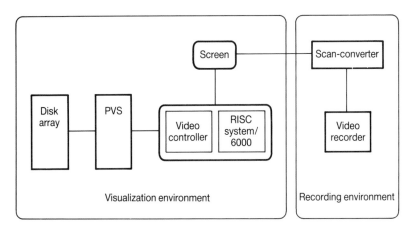

Figure 13.2. Representation of the environment used to create videos.

2. It can be seen as an example of a global ocean on a reduced scale, the complex dynamics of which provide a test case for models; the small scale could help make climatological changes more apparent.
3. It is a region of importance for many of its numerous surrounding countries, for economical as well as historical reasons (e.g. tourism, fishing, transport, pollution).

Consequently there is a reasonable amount of available data, including some historical series.

13.4.1. Characteristics of the domain

Exchanges through straits and surfaces (evaporation, heat gain or loss) have a large influence on the WMED behavior. It can simply be seen as a concentration basin: evaporation strongly increases salinity, causing a water deficit which is solved by river run-off and an inflow from the Atlantic Ocean, while salt equilibrium is reached by outflow of salt to the Atlantic. We have thus a two way exchange through the Gibraltar Strait: cold and low saline water enters the WMED at the surface while hotter and more saline water finds its way to the Atlantic at greater depth (the higher salinity makes it more dense).

Water in WMED can be differentiated into three masses of different salinity and temperature, which can be described according to their origins. As they are also of different density, they can be found more or less in superposed horizontal layers in the WMED (Figure 13.3):

Atlantic Water (A/W) enters the WMED through the Gibraltar Strait (as was explained before). It is a low saline water that lies at the surface. After some initial gyration, it flows easterly along the Algerian coast (in what is called the Algerian Current). Part of it is then deflected to the North while the other part continues its way to the Eastern Mediterranean.

Levantine Intermediate Water (LIW) originates in the Eastern Mediterranean and enters the WMED (through the Sicily Strait) where it flows at intermediate depth (between 200 and 700 m), moving to the north and the west. It is the most saline water in the WMED.

Deep Water (DW) has nearly constant properties, slightly less saline and colder than the LIW under which it resides. It is mainly formed in winter in the Gulf of Lion (in the South of France) where strong wind conditions help to increase the surface water density (via evaporation and intense cooling): it homogenizes the water column and strong vertical exchanges can take place.

Each water mass progressively loses its characteristics (mainly through mixing) in its evolution across the WMED, where there is a general anticlockwise circulation (in addition to lots of smaller scale processes). There is also an important seasonal cycle, particularly visible in the temperature evolution (summer warming of the surface layer that creates a vertical stratification, inhibiting exchanges). For a general description of the WMED circulation, see Millot (1991) or Hopkins (1985).

13.4.2. Data

In this case there is a climatological dataset which originates from the BNDO (Banque Nationale de Donnees Oceanographiques, Brest, France). It consists of a series of about 8000 casts located all across the WMED. Vertical profiles of salinity and temperature are stored for each station. It nearly covers the whole century but most data are post 1946. The distribution is irregular: there are more summer than winter data, except in the Gulf of Lion where lots of measurements were taken in winter (related to the observation of DW formation). In general more data were collected near the straits and in the northern part of the WMED.

The objective of this analysis is to try to represent average situations, permanent structures and water masses (as described earlier) using all information contained in that (irregular) dataset. It is also of interest to

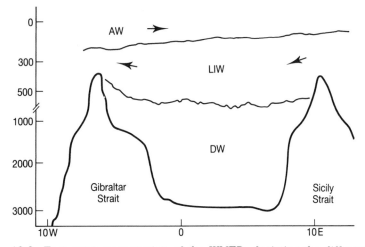

Figure 13.3. East–west cross-section of the WMED, depicting the different water masses (from Hopkins, 1985).

represent the annual cycle and seasonal or month to month variations (using for each period the corresponding part of the dataset).

In order to be visualized, data have to be processed and computed onto a regular grid. As the problem is underdetermined or overdetermined following the region, and as a straightforward interpolation is not possible (interpolation between points located on opposite sides of an island or a peninsula such as Italy is meaningless), an optimization procedure was used. It was performed at the GHER (GeoHydrodynamics and Environment Research, University of Liège) using the Variational Inverse Model: it produces a solution under constraints to ensure the smoothness of the field and of its gradient, obtain a solution close to the original data and introduce information contained in the velocity field when available. The problem is expressed under a variational principle, solved with a finite element method on a mesh adapted to the topology and eventually data are produced on a regular grid by the inverse model (Brasseur and Haus, 1991).

13.4.3. Visualization

The positioning of data in their physical context helps the interpretation. Data are thus shown jointly with a bathymetry field. But due to the sometimes complicated shape of the sea bottom, its representation can seriously impair the vision of the data. Care must therefore be taken in the choice of a good view angle or in cutting off a part of the domain. Another solution is to use a semitransparent representation of the sea bottom. More information is added about the depth using isobaths regularly spaced on the representation of the sea bottom.

Raw data (i.e. irregularly positioned points) may be represented with techniques allowing its location in the sea (in 2D or 3D) and representation of data values by colors or/and point size. But limitations remain that show the advantages of having data on a regular grid: too much data in a small region makes representation difficult as well as comparison of different situations or representation of a time evolution using points not exactly located at the same place.

Additionally, it is possible with a regularly connected grid to use more advanced visualization techniques like isosurface or volume rendering which both have their advantages:

An isosurface shows a clear shape, so that information concerning another data can be presented by mapping it on the isosurface, but it does not provide information about the rest of the volume. Experience shows that in most cases representation of more than a very few number of isosurfaces (two or three) gives a very confusing image.

Volume rendering does not define clear contours but it gives an image of the whole field and it is quite a good way to detect water masses. Parameters like colors or luminosity can also be used to add more information to the picture.

With intricate shapes and representation of 3D fields containing lots of information, ways to increase realism (e.g. surface shading, good light positioning) have been found to be very helpful. But animation (even a simple rotation) is probably the most convenient way to extract the maximum information out of a 3D scene by the depth it gives to the image. It is particularly useful (and a complementary technique) with volume rendering (or every situation where transparency makes more than one plane apparent in an image).

Sophisticated techniques are not always needed to provide first-rate results. For example, a 2D temperature–salinity diagram (where each point shows the characteristics of a part of the domain) contains adequate information for the detection of water masses of similar characteristics. Here also animation is a valuable tool to represent annual evolution; note again the advantage of having a regular grid (each point of the diagram represents the same volume of water) and the same grid all along the year to show evolution.

13.5. ANALYSIS OF SIMULATION DATA: ALGERIAN CURRENT'S INSTABILITIES

13.5.1. Simulation

As explained in the previous section, Atlantic water that enters the WMED forms a strong easterly current along the Algerian coast. Observations show that this current is unstable: it meanders and large gyres get created. Cyclonic gyres (anticlockwise rotation) slowly disappear while anticyclonic gyres (clockwise rotation) grow, move downstream along the coast and finally go to the large where they can persist a long time, interacting with other patterns and contributing to the mixing of waters of different origins (Millot *et al.*, 1990). Strong vertical movements are associated with those gyres but are not easily quantifiable.

The simulation tries to reproduce those gyres and to find the causes of the instabilities. It was done at the GHER, University of Liège (Beckers, 1992; Beckers and Nihoul, 1992) using a primitive equation, fully three-dimensional, time-dependent nonlinear baroclinic model with a turbulent closure. Conditions were set up to represent an idealized situation: a 200 km wide and 125 km long domain (with 2.5×2.5 km horizontal grid). The vertical distribution (17 levels and a maximum depth of 1000 m) is irregular with the majority of levels concentrated near the surface. The length of 125 km is assumed to be the wavelength of the dominant unstable perturbation. The coast is represented by a lateral rigid-wall boundary, while cross-flow boundary conditions are periodic. Two distinct water masses are present in the initial conditions: the Algerian Current flows along the coast at the surface; it is a low density (low saline) water. The rest of the domain is composed of more saline water at rest. Temperature does not play a role in this simulation and density is a direct function of the salinity. Small perturbations (of the salinity field) are introduced at the initial stage and a 75-day evolution is then simulated. This leads to a complete development of instabilities in good agreement with observations.

13.5.2.   Data

A set of data was stored after every 24 h of simulated evolution throughout the 75 days. Significant variables used for results interpretation are salinity and the three velocity components. In general two periods are represented (102 × 80 × 17 grid points) which lead to an overall dataset of around 170 Mbyte. Surface elevation is another significant variable but due to the simulation conditions it is strongly correlated to the salinity field and does not provide additional information here.

One particularity of the velocity field is that horizontal components (about 0.5 m/s) are far larger than the vertical one (about 0.00005 m/s). As one has to respect the aspect ratio between the vertical amplification of the domain and the vector (to keep images of vectors oriented in the real direction), even under a 1000 times vertical amplification (which is appropriate to show the interesting part of the domain) the vertical velocity remains nearly indiscernible and must be represented under different ways. There is also an interest for the representation of data under different forms and fields derived from the original data (like vorticity or gradients).

Two periods are represented, 200 km long, 125 km wide, of the upper part of the domain (approximately 150 m) with a 1000 times vertical magnification, viewed from the South through the Algerian coast boundary. Velocity is shown by arrows and coloration of regularly spaced levels (every 28 m). Colors represent the absolute value of the velocity (in m/s).

Day 1 (Plate 76): original velocity distribution clearly showing the current position near the surface and along the coast.
Day 51 (Plate 77): meandering of the current, anticyclonic (clockwise, along the coast) and cyclonic gyres.

13.5.3.   Visualization

Many ways have been explored. The first step is the study of each variable separately.

Salinity has been represented either by plane sections at different depth or by an isosurface. The principal information this field contains is the characterization of two different water masses (with a strong saline gradient in between). An isosurface is thus carefully selected to represent precisely the separation surface. Two close isosurfaces give in addition an idea of the salinity gradient (linked to the mixing of the water masses). It shows the development of oscillations at the interface, formation of gyres and their downstream movement followed by a move to the large of the anticyclonic gyre. It also shows the general upward vertical movement of the separation surface.

The velocity field is represented by vectors which provide the same kind of information and clearly show the opposite evolution of cyclonic and anticyclonic gyres.

The vertical velocity field is rather difficult to picture as it is very irregular. The main interest being to locate strong upwelling and downwelling areas, isosurfaces have been represented for characteristic positive and negative vertical velocities.

Finally, representation of trajectories is also very useful and rich in information concerning long term evolution of particles.

The next step is to show multivariable representations: each variable strengthens comprehension of the others. It helps to assess the spatial correlation of the different phenomena (for example, location of a strong downwelling upstream of the frontal zone associated with the cyclonic circulation, or the spatially large but less intense upwelling associated with the anticyclonic circulation). Great care is needed for this type of analysis as it has been proved that small changes in colors, types of representation, etc., lead to very clear or very confusing images.

Having different types of data and enough visualization tools, ways to show results are nearly endless. Time (and sometimes imagination) is needed to explore large datasets and find the best image. Animation has proved very useful in this case to explore the complete time series and be sure not to miss any important process. It is also indispensable to study and show the dynamics, the succession and the time scale of all involved phenomena.

13.6.   CONCLUSIONS

Data in physical oceanography (like in many other fields) can take various shapes as has been shown in the two previous examples: a few data points, irregularly positioned (*in situ* observations) or much data, multivariable and on a regular grid (simulation results). In both cases we end up with three-dimensional regularly positioned data (via preprocessing for the first one) and a strong interest in the representation of time evolution.

Direct visualization in a 3D environment has been shown to be an appropriate way to deal with 3D phenomena. Animation in particular has proved to be an unmatched tool to explore 3D domains and give better insight (showing relative displacements of each object against the others) as to how to represent the time evolution of a system and to show the dynamics of involved processes.

There is a large increase in the number of available data. Their analysis needs adaptable methods. Visualization is such a method. Care of details, 3D scenes, etc. increase the reality of images and ease their interpretation. But it must not be forgotten that the approach has to be correlated to the data: 2D diagrams can contain useful information as well and still have a future.

In a few words, the new insight given by visualization and/or animation could be compared with the use of a new and faster way of transportation: first you go faster, then you go further.

ACKNOWLEDGMENTS

The author would like to thank the members of the GHER and in particular J.-M. Beckers and P. Brasseur who made most of the data available to him.

REFERENCES

Beckers, J.-M. (1992). La Méditerranée Occidentale: de la modelisation mathématique à la simulation numérique. Thèse de doctorat, Université de Liège.

Beckers, J.-M. and Nihoul, J. C. J. (1992). Model of the Algerian current's instability. *Journal of Marine Systems* **3**, 441–451.

Brasseur, P. and Haus, J. (1991). Application of a 3D variational inverse model to the analyses of ecohydrodynamic data in the northern Bering and Southern Chukchi Seas. *Journal of Marine Systems* **1**, 383–401.

Brodie, K. W., Carpenter, L. A., Earnshaw, R. A., Gallop, J. R., Hubbold, R. J., Mumford, A. M., Osland, C. D. and Quarendon, P. (eds) (1991). *Scientific Visualization, Techniques and Applications*. Springer-Verlag, New York.

Doumenge (ed.) (1992). *Rapports et procès-verbaux des réunions, 33e congrès-assemblée plenière de la CIESM*, Trieste (Commission Internationale pour l'Etude et la Surveillance de la Méditerrané, Monaco).

Hopkins, T. S. (1985). Physics of the sea. In Margalef, R. (ed.), *Western Mediterranean*, pp. 100–125. Pergamon Press, Oxford.

IBM Visualization Data Explorer brochure (G225-4411-01).

IBM POWER Visualization System brochure (G225-4400-01).

La Violette, P. E. (1990). The Western Mediterranean Circulation Experiment (WMCE): Introduction. *Journal of Geophysical Research* **95**(C2), 1511–1514.

Millot, C. (1991). Mesoscale and seasonal variabilities of the circulation in the western Mediterranean. *Dynamics of Atmospheres and Oceans* **15**, 179–214.

Millot, C., Taupier-Lepage, I. and Benzhora, M. (1990). The Algerian eddies. *Earth-Science Reviews* **27**, 203–219.

About the author

Jacques Haus graduated from University of Liège, Belgium, in 1990 as Ingénieur Civil Mécanicien (Mécanique Physique). He was then employed as assistant in the department of Geophysical Fluid Dynamics while pursuing a DEA in modeling of marine environment. His interests were in the development of a variational inverse model and data analysis. He has been a Research Fellow at the IBM Winchester Scientific Centre since 1991 where his interests are in scientific visualization and interaction between numerical simulation and visualization.

Chapter 14
Providing visualization for fluid flow studies

John J. Stephen

14.1. VISUALIZATION IN COMPUTATIONAL FLUID DYNAMICS

Over a period of several years my colleagues and I at Tessella have worked on a number of projects which require the visualization of scientific data, often in the general field of computational fluid dynamics (CFD). It has been fascinating to follow the evolution of visualization in response to hardware and graphics systems, to related application areas, and to the engineers and scientists who use the software. It is worth trying to make some sense of the forces that underlie these changes, particularly for consultancies like Tessella which rely upon keeping ahead of trends. As a beginning I draw upon some of our practical experience and background theory and methods for software estimation.

14.1.1. The Kings Cross disaster

Plate 78 (color section) shows the results of a simulation by CFDS (Simcox *et al.*, 1992) of the horrific fire in an escalator tunnel in London's Kings Cross underground railway station. The study used CFDS's FLOW3D software to simulate the movement of gas and the transfer of heat within a 3D mesh that represented the shape of part of the Kings Cross station. The image of the results is clear: the shape of the tunnel with the grooves containing the escalators; the panels are colored by temperature indicating a region of intense heat to the right.

CFDS's strong contribution to the public enquiry into the disaster was acknowledged; its consultants proposed a reason for the rapid spread of the fire which was confirmed by tests with scaled models. CFDS contributed in this way because of their flow simulators FLOW3D and ASTEC (e.g. Burns *et al.*, 1987) but computational issues aside, the images of their results have an undeniable impact as aids to interpretation by engineers and conveyors of meaning to the public.

ANIMATION AND SCIENTIFIC VISUALIZATION
ISBN 0-12-227745-7

14.1.2.   Applications of CFD

CFD studies are being applied across the range of industry sectors. Any situation in which gases or fluids move through or around objects is a candidate for a CFD study. Simulation studies can be used to complement the use of experimental methods and may be used to highlight particular parts of a system that require detailed experimental investigation. CFD can replace experimental systems when test systems are too difficult or costly to set up.

The following list indicates some of the sectors of industry which are using CFD as a part of the design and analysis methods:

Automobile, aerospace: aerodynamic studies; cooling and lubrication systems; turbines.
Building: the ventilation of large buildings.
Safety: the spread of fires and the development of explosions.
Food: the performance of refrigeration cabinets; the nature of atomized sprays in freeze-dryers.
Water: dispersion from planned waste outfalls; the transport and deposition of silt; the effect of building schemes upon tide patterns.

14.1.3.   Visualization requirements

A CFD study has several stages: the engineer describes the problem in the form of a mesh; the simulation is carried out; the results are examined in conjunction with the mesh to confirm that there are no artefacts; the engineering implications of the mesh are considered; the broad conclusions are presented to management.

The components of a CFD image are diverse. The context for the results is the outline of the mesh. A polished presentation might involve Gouraud shading of boundary walls giving a smooth shaded image; but it is equally likely that the engineer will retain the image of mesh cells in order to be aware of how the pattern of the results might depend upon the design of the mesh. The graphics may need to reveal distinct regions within the mesh such as zones with different physical properties. There is an obvious role for visualization in all these stages except for the simulation itself.

The general context that runs throughout all visualization is the mesh. At various times it might be rendered as a light-shaded solid or as a wire frame and regions may be highlighted in order to reveal areas with different physical properties.

The movement of fluids and gases can be represented by tracks of various sorts which represent the movement of imaginary sizeless particles of neutral buoyancy. The investigator usually nominates a point or group of points from which these imaginary particles are released. The information content of these particle tracks can be enhanced by color coding or by animation. Further sophistication is obtained by the use of ribbons as a method for displaying vorticity in conjunction with general movement; or illustration with moving spheres or darts. Vector fields may also be displayed as arrows with color and length combining to give a clear impression of differences in vector magnitude. Vectors are usually displayed in sets emanating from planes. Some problems involve real particles. A typical case is the behavior of droplets from an atomizer. These droplets would settle due to gravity and would affect the behavior of the gas that carries them. Calculations for real particles are usually part of the solution but the basic methods for their display are similar.

Scalar quantities such as pressure, temperature, kinetic energy or concentration are displayed as isolines. These images could be on a flat plane running through the space of the mesh or perhaps on the surface of some boundary wall within the mesh. Isosurfaces are also used to display scalar quantities, but considerable practice on the part of the user may be required before an understanding of the results can be taken from their 3D shapes.

Visualization can also simulate the images familiar to experimental scientists which can be a great aid to the understanding of theoretical results. The graphics might simulate the appearance of the release of sheets of smoke in a wind tunnel; or perhaps the diffusion and flow of a dye released into fluid. Less familiar are streak lines which are stream lines constrained to a surface. These mimic the effect of putting a film of oil on a body in a wind tunnel and reveal flow over the surface and regions where the flow leaves the surface.

Animation is a vital addition to these visual techniques. All problems of fluid and gas flow involve movement and the representation of this movement is invaluable, typically in the form of particle tracks. Further to this, some problems do not involve steady-state systems: an explosion, a moving piston. External conditions may change or perhaps the shape of the mesh will alter. In these cases animation through a time series is essential to an understanding of the problem.

The user should have rapid 3D control over the image, including the ability to crop physical regions so that critical areas of the problem can be examined. Interactive controls should have immediate effects so that visualization becomes an extension of the engineer's senses rather than hindrance to the flow of thought. This interactivity should extend beyond the control of a static image: to let an animation proceed while moving the image, or to use the mouse to move the seeding point of stream lines or the plane of a set of isolines.

14.1.4. Evolutionary pressures on visualization

UNIX workstations are falling in price with rapidly increasing levels of specification. This means that more and more people are provided with systems that have the power to provide sophisticated images. As the user-base widens so its level of specialist knowledge falls: powerful images must be associated with intuitive user interfaces. Industrial engineering and design managers want this sophistication both for enhancing the productivity of their research teams and for selling their ideas to other parts of their organization. They perceive the need to be able to configure and tune visualization systems in house; they are in the best position to understand the nature of their engineering tasks and the roles of their staff and so they want to be able to control software utilities without the requirement for sophisticated programming.

All phases of design and manufacture are coming under computer control and people are expecting the integration of software and information to be easier. CFD studies may be intimately linked to experimental test rigs, computer aided design, finite element studies and so forth. A particularly striking example of this trend towards total integration is the work of the Flow Dynamics Measurement Service (AEA Technology) (Goatcher and Dewhurst, 1992). One of the specialities of this group is laser doppler anemometry (LDA) which is a modern experimental approach to fluid flow studies. Transparent scale models of systems are built and lasers are used to scan the fluid or gas to gather information about the direction and velocity of flow at a series of points; hence a total picture of the flow pattern is built up. This industrial research group often receives design drawings from their clients in the form of AutoCAD files. They can integrate their experimental results into AutoCAD files and send them back to their clients. Computational results from FLOW3D can even be included in this system. They also provide a system for animating their software. In other words a great deal of value is added to the service that they provide simply by integrating the flow of data between the pieces of software that are used in the study. Plate 79 is from a study by this group on flow in a bent duct and it illustrates the multi-disciplinary source of results in visualization: the green contours are drawn from LDA results and the blue ones, for comparison are the results of simulation by FLOW3D.

Software houses have responded keenly to the desires of their end users for powerful visualization, not least because the growing number of users offers greater financial reward. However, the necessary sophistication of graphics systems together with their user interfaces has altered the ground rules for providing this kind of software. A few years ago, hardware performance imposed a much harsher limit on the visualization that could be provided: wire-frame outlines, isolines and vector fields might be all that one could expect and these would be controlled via a command line. The CFD software expert might provide this level of interface and visualization as an integral part of his programming task. But visualization algorithms and the design of user interfaces have become much more sophisticated which means that these programming tasks can no longer be carried out by the same people who work on the simulation software. Plate 80 emphasizes this point. Stream ribbons are used to show flow and vorticity within a test problem; the ribbons can be colored according to the velocity of some other scalar; the user can move the seeding point by dragging it with the mouse. This functionality was produced by AVS and is the type of thing that users are beginning to expect. It is clear that this type of visualization requires much more development effort than the provision of simple vector fields or stream lines. The potential for dividing the roles is increased by a growing desire to integrate CFD studies with other stages of design and investigation; neutral open data formats permit the development of independent generalized visualization products.

14.2. THE RESPONSE

The prediction is that these market pressures would lead to the appearance of specialist visualization teams and perhaps of independent visualization products which aim to fulfill the market's desires for functionality. Are these ideas in accord with experience and do they make sense when considered in terms of theory and practice of software estimation?

14.2.1. Case study: CFDS's environment for FLOW3D and ASTEC

The first case study illustrates how a software house has anticipated and reacted to these pressures by internal developments. In early 1989, CFDS (AEA Technology) began to add value to the simulation codes FLOW3D and ASTEC by building a wrap-around interface; and design and visualization tools with point-and-click 3D interaction.

CFDS has produced a library of routines which support hierarchical menus, data entry, process control, help systems and full control over a 3D image. This library forms a buffer between engineering programmer, end users and machine dependencies and contains much visualization and interface functionality. The end user is given full 3D interaction and point and click control over the application; there is a consistent style of interface across CFDS products and across hardware platforms and between applications. The hardware platforms include IBM, SUN, Silicon Graphics, Hewlett Packard and DEC workstations with CRAY and PC versions in the pipeline. Applications include design tools, visualization, 2D plotters, interfaces to monitor the progress of a simulator, and job and file administrators.

Applications based upon this system are not concerned with the mechanics of user interaction. For example, the application describes a complete image such as model, contours and streamlines in a series of graphics primitives such as polygons or text. These primitives are passed into the visualization routines which enable control through the in-house graphical user interface. Meanwhile the application also defines the title of a new menu level, the names of process control buttons and the titles and initial values of data entry fields. The end user can perform 3D manipulations, invoke help messages and perform many other operations, all of which are hidden from the application. The application needs only certain pieces of information without need for concern about the user interface: it can determine which button has been pressed; the current values of data entry fields; the 2D or 3D position of the cursor (accounting for hidden operations such as rotation and translation by the user). All this has been achieved by holding image and menu information in a database and by providing an in-house event loop which wraps around the event loop of the window manager. Design has been tuned to enable portability which has freed the software from reliance upon potentially fragile platforms: drivers include PHIGS, X, GL, POSTSCRIPT with user interfaces in MOTIF and SUNVIEW.

The software engineers at CFDS have split into two groups: teams working on the simulators and on the visualization and interface systems. The CFD experts have been freed from work on I/O sophistication to concentrate on what they know best. The concentration of visualization expertise into one centralized project has enhanced functionality and promoted consistency and enabled products to be placed on a wide range of platforms.

Here we see an example of an in-house project which responds to most of the pressures that have been suggested: the standardized graphical nature of the user interface extends CFDS's software to a larger audience; visualization utilities have become more powerful; portability gives CFDS a broader market place and freedom from dependence on any single third party system. The resulting trend towards a separation of programming tasks is also evident within CFDS: specialist teams which, while conferring closely about objectives, have structured their work so that they minimize the need to share work on any particular aspect of the overall functionality.

14.2.2.   Case study: AVS's open, modular visualization system

The second example is AVS which is a leading visualization product in the UNIX and VMS market places. It offers advanced functionality for many different methods of data display; Plate 80 illustrates just one facet of its capabilities. It can import data from many formats and can generate all the visual aids that are required for CFD; it is also applied to medicine, chemical visualization, finite element analysis and image analysis.

AVS consists of a series of modules which do special tasks such as reading data, transforming it, or displaying it. Each module has an appropriate graphical user interface which might enable 3D interaction with an image or the browsing of a directory structure or control the value of a parameter. The modules pass data via standard internal formats which means that they can be linked together to provide any functionality that the user desires. These formats are published so that users can add extra modules to extend AVS's power. Of course this also allows rapid and efficient in-house development of AVS.

This description could be applied to an advanced subroutine library, but AVS is far more advanced than that. At its core is a CASE tool which controls the flow of data between modules. The user does not waste effort in programming; all activity is concentrated upon design and understanding. Two further CASE tools add more value to AVS. One of these is an interactive programming environment which provides extensive support for the development of new modules; functionality is added without the need to involve the parent company. The other is a system for remodeling the user interface. The final strength of AVS that will be noted is the fact that all the work with its CASE tools can be frozen into bespoke applications; AVS combines the benefits of this flexibility for the specialist with friendly availability to nonexpert users. A strength of AVS is that it contains internal hooks which enable it to take hold of new data structures and to recognize new processes. The application programmer's interface provides a very easy way to identify new data and processes to AVS and to achieve necessary interaction with other processes and data; all this is done without reference to AVS source code or even the need to recompile or relink the system.

We have recently integrated AVS into the post-processor of a CFD product. The existing product has reasonable visualization functionality but its scope would be greatly increased by being combined with AVS and moreover its rich command-line syntax could be daunting for beginners. We have integrated the two pieces of software so that they share data about model geometry and flow within it. Moreover AVS now generates command line input for the post-processor (sending it through a UNIX pipe) which means that commands can be automated and simplified in a user interface. AVS's CASE tools and open systems approach meant that this integration was performed in about five man-days: now the data produced by the package can be explored with all the power of AVS.

AVS satisfies many of the predicted pressures upon software: it provides good user interfaces, massive functionality, it reduces programming effort and offers broad portability to its purchaser. The appearance of third party visualization products like AVS suggests that organizations have recognized (at least implicitly) the divide between the software roles of "engineering methods" and "visualization methods" and also that market conditions are persuading them to buy external offerings. (This is certainly true of AVS since it has been adopted by many organizations over a range of market areas and is even bundled into some packages which are themselves for sale.)

How many specialist roles?

Before trying to rationalize the processes behind market development it is important to consider whether CFD software tasks really have split into visualization and engineering. The world of CFD programming may have split into more than two camps. Alternatively there might not have been any polarization of roles, just a tendency for every programmer to acquire their unique set of specialities.

However, visualization is probably a niche within software development. The most public evidence for this is that so many products are like AVS in offering simple programming interfaces to highly functional graphics. Further, the internal organization of a number of companies suggests that CFDS is not alone in recognizing this division of labor. Visualization has emerged because it is a common requirement of many application areas and one can argue that it has imposed a particular specialization on all these areas. Even those organizations which perform all development internally are not entirely free from the crystalization of roles caused by the visualization marketplace because they acquire staff who have been trained in skills by other companies and because they are under pressure to allow integration of their software into broader systems.

14.2.3. Software economics

Do theories and methods in software estimation clarify ideas about the tendency towards specialization and the emergence of independent companies? Established estimation methods make it quite clear that software projects should be split into separate teams for CFD and visualization. Consider the COCOMO model of estimation (Boehm, 1981) which provides modifiers for effort required in development. A visualization expert should rank at the top of COCOMO's scales for experience of relevant programming languages and programmer's interfaces and also for experience of visualization applications. COCOMO predicts that this programmer will require only 78% of the effort that a competent nonexpert would need to invest in some functionality. (The figure of 78% represents a suitable comparison between one person who is expert in providing all aspects of visualization and another who is just as experienced as a software engineer, but has little direct experience of providing visualization systems. Hence the comparison is normalized; it does not represent a comparison in which the "nonexpert" is actually a novice programmer in which the difference in effort might be two- or even three-fold.) CFD software engineers will benefit from their mathematical background in attempting to provide graphics, but how experienced are they in providing good user interfaces or in working with graphics subsystems: is it not the case that they are unlikely to rank as visualization experts in addition to their own speciality? Thus it is easy to make the case that a division of labour should occur if projects become ever more ambitious, but it is not clear when the division should arise.

Now consider the likelihood of the emergence of independent software houses. Shooman (1981) reviews language research which reveals a convincing empirical relationship between the numbers of unique nouns and verbs in a piece of text and the total length of the text. He points out that this relationship can also be applied to pieces of computer program where T is the sum of unique operators (software verbs) and operands (software nouns) and L is the length of the program:

$$L = T \ln (T). \tag{1}$$

Software development times and costs are known to increase with L and probably at an accelerating rate (Boehm, 1981) but a linear relationship between cost and L is assumed in this discussion. We can divide development costs into (i) in-house development and (ii) functionality that could be bought in from a software house. The project manager must decide whether to buy in the second part of the application or to develop that in-house as well. This subset of functionality will cost a certain amount to develop in-house; if developed by another company as a "once-off" it will also cost the same amount (unless the contractors staff are much better at writing the given type of code), but in addition the second company will have its own fixed costs (K). Of course external code can be cheaper because multiple sales allow costs to be spread between customers.

Imagine that all possible visualization functionality can be represented by a fixed set of operators and operands and that the average project manager anticipates working with a proportion A of this capacity. Will the project manager develop functionality in-house or buy an independent product? The average independent software house offers a visualization product which addresses a certain range of the visualization functionality represented by a fraction of B. This company attaches a fixed overhead of K to its product but is able to reduce the list price in proportion to M the size of the market place.

The relative cost of the independent visualization software can be expressed as

$$\text{External cost} = [B \ln (B) + K] / M. \tag{2}$$

The external software will not be a perfect match for the project manager's requirements and on average we would expect the overlap in functionality to be AB. Therefore the idea of buying in the functionality must be compared with the saving of the relative cost of internal development of the functionality AB. The external product may need to be licensed once per user; if so the cost of internal production can be reduced by a factor N, the number of sales anticipated by the project manager.

$$\text{Internal cost} = [(AB) \ln (AB) / N. \tag{3}$$

Project managers will buy in software if they anticipate that (3) would exceed (2) so that the condition for the existence of companies specializing in visualization software is

$$B [MA \ln (AB)/N - \ln (B)] > K. \tag{4}$$

The limits on the parameters are $0 < A \leqslant 1$ and $0 < B \leqslant 1$ (both are fractions); $M \geqslant 1$ because there must be at least one company; $N \geqslant 1$ because there must be at least one copy of the product. One must admit that conclusions based upon equation (4) are bound to be rather uninteresting because the functional form of the left-hand side is monotonic with respect to the underlying variables. In particular this means that there are no maxima or minima which might prompt interesting predictions. (Indeed the only complication is that the effect of B switches once the value of MA/N rises above small values.) The once-off development of visualization functions is represented by $N = 1$, $M = 1$, $A = 1$: they should be done in-house if there is sufficient expertise. A large value of MA/N will increase the rate at which visualization functionality, but the effect of B depends upon the value of MA/N. An expanding market place (M) will lead to increased sales of visualization products. If M is increasing it is likely that the production of complete applications (N) is also rising which seems to reduce the success of visualization companies. This means that the most favorable conditions for selling visualization products to companies are when there are a few visualization products and many corporations making end products. To put this another way: there is a limit to the number of visualization companies that can coexist. Sales will also be enhanced when the manufacturers of end products are ambitious (high A). The visualization product itself should be specialized (low *B*) if the market is poor or broad in functionality if conditions are good. The concentration of software specialists in external software houses will bias trends towards purchasing functionality and would also permit the use of consultancies for once-off developments.

Different business assumptions could drastically alter these conclusions. If one anticipates a limit to product lifetimes or other premiums on rapid release then the net benefit of buying ready made functionality is higher. Further, it is simplistic to view products as the result of a single pulse of investment. Products like AVS are upgraded at regular intervals and much inhouse work (such as that of CFDS) is also subject to constant enhancement. Therefore our imaginary project manager may be concerned with costs in terms of rates of investment caused by in-house work as opposed to initial purchase and the maintenance of licences for third party software. (Indeed project managers do this, or at least they are encouraged to do so by the software estimation, analysis and design tools.) Another complication could be worthy of inclusion in the model. To regard a piece of visualization functionality as either present or absent from third party software may be too simplistic: one could recognize the level to which a certain functionality is provided. This in turn calls for an expression to relate the level of functionality to the cost of development and it also enables one to build into the model a commercial trade-off between developing high quality and breadth of functionality. A similar complication could be to the project manager's perspective: some utilities may be vital to the finished product, but others could be regarded as peripheral to its success.

14.3. CONCLUSION

The pressure of the market place upon visualization products can be understood. Increased availability of powerful hardware has reinforced expectations of ease of use, image sophistication and communication between applications. The response of software products is a movement towards modularity: teams of specialists providing software with tightly defined functionality and interfacing with other products across standard interfaces. This trend is not particularly surprising for it is just another variant of general evolution towards client-server technology and is analogous to pressures that have caused the evolution of operating systems, programming languages, 4GLs, etc. This chapter cannot predict expected and optimum levels of product specialization, though it does confirm that certain factors are more permissive of third party software. However, it is likely that optima do exist and it is clear that if they can be discovered, then the business world would be grateful, or perhaps alarmed!

ACKNOWLEDGMENTS

I would like to thank Ian Curington, Seb Dewhurst and Ian Jones for the provision of material and for their support; and also Kevin and Judy Gell and Tracey Hogg for assisting in the production of the paper.

REFERENCES

Boehm, B. W. (1981). *Software Engineering Economics*. Prentice-Hall.

Burns, A. D., Jones, I. P., Kightley, J. R. and Wilkes, N. S. (1987). The implementation of a finite difference method for predicting incompressible flows in complex geometries. In *Proceedings Conference on Numerical Methods in Laminar and Turbulent Flow*. Pineridge Press, Montreal.

Goatcher, T. J. and Dewhurst, S. J. (1992). A presentation technique for three component LDA results. In *6th International Symposium on Applications of Laser Techniques to Fluid Mechanics*.

Shooman, M. L. (1981). *Software Engineering*. McGraw-Hill.

Simcox, S., Wilkes, N. S. and Jones, I. P. (1992). Computer simulation of the flows of hot gases from the fire at King's Cross Underground Station. *Fire Safety Journal* **18**, 49–73.

About the author

John Stephen has been with Tessella for several years, providing user interface and graphics solutions on UNIX systems. He has a zoology degree from Oxford University and Ph.D. in genetics from Nottingham University. Tessella provides visualization and related services for a number of well-known organizations including AEA Technology, Joint European Torus (JET), The Bank of England and the Institute of Hydrology. Email: stej@tessella.co.uk.

Chapter 15
Turnkey visualization in computational fluid dynamics

Tim David

15.1. INTRODUCTION

During the past decade, computational fluid dynamics (CFD) and the visualization of numerically generated data have become increasingly important in the engineering design cycle. The pressure on industrial manufacturers to reduce design-to-product time scales has provided an impetus to scientific visualizers and software developers to provide tools which the design engineer can use easily and quickly, enabling him/her to gain insights into complex designs by interacting with the dataset. Certainly we have progressed rapidly during those ten years, but do we have all the software tools now to do the job? This chapter sets out the current state-of-the art in visualization within the engineering community using examples of engineering relevance and comparing the visualization tools of the past years with those of today. In explaining these tools and the way in which we need to view the engineering data, it seems that we have a long way to go.

15.2. THE PAST

Even the greatest engineers and fluid dynamicists needed visualization. Leonardo da Vinci, perhaps the first serious engineer of the western world, needed visualization in order to understand the physical phenomena and to design some of his automated machines. Of course he had an advantage over the others at the time, he was also a brilliant artist. His illustrations of water turbulence under the bridge in Milan bear witness to this.

James Clark Maxwell, in trying to understand the fundamentals of thermodynamic state variables, used clay models to show the relationship between pressure, temperature and specific volume.

As we grow from birth our sight and other senses aid our interaction with the physical world and our learning of the phenomena within that world. Our vision has an important part to play in that learning experience, and in some sense what we see and how we see it is reflected in our understanding (or lack of it) of phenomena. How do we view the water flowing under the bridge as Leonardo did some 500 years ago? We view its effect on its surroundings. Suppose that the water was totally clear (we assume no pollution in da Vinci's time!). How could we tell whether the water flowed to the left or to the right? What does the water do close to the stone bridge supports? We can answer these questions only by the effect water has on the flotsam and the bubbles created as it passes by under the arch of the bridge. It was vortex swirls and the water surface that da Vinci sketched to show how the fluid interacted with the bridge and it is these images that we use for the visualization of data created by the computational world, a world not normally seen during the day-to-day comings and goings of our society. Yet from a technological point of view these data and their understanding are becoming ever increasingly important.

In the heady days of "the big experiment" people would toil for months perhaps years setting up the correct equipment, waiting for the moment. The data "appeared", were collected and then were gone, in some cases never to be repeated. Now visualization of numerical "experiments" can be replayed as many times as we need. In fact different visualization experiments may be done on the same dataset!

During the 1950s and 1960s most qualitative and quantitative visualization was attempted using empirical methods such as hydrogen bubbles, smoke trails, dye injection, electrostatics, and even flash X-ray, to name but a few. In some cases high-speed film was used to capture the event, which could then be played back at some later time. Of course the disadvantage here was that for most of the time the view was in a single direction and could not be altered. If several areas had to be covered then several experiments needed to be done or a number of views photographed. Measurements were done by hand or by expensive photography equipment, and turned out to be both time-consuming and labor-intensive. From an industrial viewpoint the design cycle became incredibly long and in a lot of cases out of step with the production and refining of previous product versions. What was needed was a quick method of experimentation that could be replicated and have the advantage of viewing at any orientation. This could only be done using numerical simulation. That being said, the experimental techniques evolved and perfected over some considerable number of years now seemed useless in the world of computation. What tools could take their place?

In fact what seems to have happened certainly with turnkey visualization software is that the old experimental concepts such as bubbles and dye streamers have been simply redefined within a numerical framework. However, some new tools have been created and these will be described in more detail below. Needless to say these new tools have given a much needed boost to the use of CFD within the engineering community, but they are still numerical results and we do not believe everything we see, do we?

15.3. BASIC TOOLS

15.3.1. Grids

In order to produce solutions to the conservation equations, CFD tools require grid structures upon which these equations are discretized. Initially for codes using finite difference and finite volume these grids were constructed in a cartesian form, although lately CFD codes have provided boundary-fitted curvilinear systems. State-of-the-art research codes are now beginning to use unstructured meshes similar to those constructed for finite element methods. Visualization systems need to be able to store and interpolate across all these different types of data structure. Most visualization systems, including application builders, require a connectivity graph in order to define a topology and hence build a volume over which the data sit. These topologies can define either data volumes or geometry. The data form the input with a defining connectivity between the nodes of the volume elements and the data values.

15.3.2. "Important" variables and "important" tools

The basic mathematical equations modeling the flow of fluids through and around general domains, the general conservation equations and hence the Navier–Stokes equations, have been thoroughly used, analysed, simplified and solved for simple situations over the past 100 years, and yet only few analytical solutions exist. To the engineer these analytical solutions are important, but of limited value, and numerical solutions need to be sought in order that insight be gained into the function of the design.

In general the basic variables used by computational fluid dynamicists and engineers are:

velocity (vector);
vorticity (vector);
stress (tensor);
pressure (scalar);
temperature (scalar);
density (scalar);
chemical species (scalar);
streamfunction (scalar);
fluid domain (vector).

These provide a wide range in terms of their format; in the case of velocity we require to view both direction and magnitude, whilst with the scalar temperature, for example, only magnitude. Different tools are therefore required to visualize different variables. In fact, as will be shown, a variety of tools may be needed to visualize just a single variable depending on the problem and its environment.

Perhaps the most difficult to visualize is the tensor variable stress. Work has been attempted in this area (Haber, 1990) but for engineering purposes we are still constrained by scalar and vector fields. Work is also progressing in the use of sheared spheres where the principal axes are shown by "notching" the resulting ellipse with major and minor axes denoting the magnitudes of shear.

Visualization tools need to be well defined and quick to respond when viewing complex datasets, especially in the engineering community where design cycles need to be shortened and various design prototypes may be viewed in succession, each of these designs being compared with each other. The turnkey visualization software has these attributes (when implemented on quick enough graphics hardware!) and to some extent holds an advantage over application builders.

One of the best ways to describe software tools and their use is to use examples. The author has spared no expense (!) in trying to obtain relevant engineering problems showing as much of the available range of tools as possible.

15.4. EXAMPLES

Plate 81 (color section) shows a general view of the system environment of a turnkey visualization software tool. The upper menu set provides the user with a selection of views, tools, data input, etc., whilst the menu to the left of the viewport provides individual tools (here the tool menu has been selected for example). In this case the particle tool has been highlighted and the lower menu provides subtool buttons to alter the tool parameter set.

As with the case of physical experiments, lighting has an important role to play. A visualization toolkit can provide any number of lights whose color intensity and hue as well as position and cone angle may be altered by the user. This ensures that complex surfaces are seen clearly enabling the full three-dimensional aspect to be observed. Additionally, coordinate axes may be defined and placed into the field of view showing orientation when the domain is viewed from obscure angles. Plate 81 shows the bounding box in which the data will be mapped and a set of coordinate axes.

15.4.1. Thermally driven cavity

We show in Figure 15.1 a rectangular domain modeling one half of a square cavity. The west wall is set to $T = 1$ and the east to $T = 0$. The front and back walls are perfect conductors (modeling symmetry and a perfect conductor) with the temperature varying from 0 to 1 along the north and south walls going from east to west. The problem has been solved with the Raleigh number Ra $= 10^5$. This dataset has been generated by Dr A. Sleigh of the Department of Mechanical Engineering at Leeds University.

Experimental visualization has used laser sheet and laser doppler increasingly over the past ten years. One of the major tools available in turnkey systems is the cutplane, thus mirroring the laser sheet technique. In this case a plane whose orientation is completely independent of the

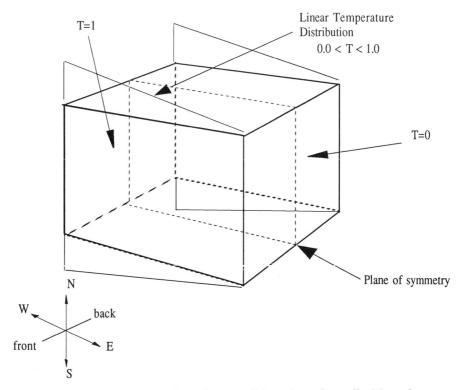

T=1

Linear Temperature
Distribution
0.0 < T < 1.0

T=0

Plane of symmetry

N

W

back

front

E

S

Figure 15.1. Domain and boundary conditions for a thermally driven flow.

coordinate system can be defined with an associated scalar, e.g. pressure or velocity magnitude. Any number of cutplanes may be defined at any one time. Additionally the planes may be either moved independently of each other or grouped together and moved as a whole unit. This is useful if there exist simple relationships between scalar variables and it is wished to view both simultaneously. The associated scalars may be viewed over the cutplane with a shaded view or by contours or by a simple mesh. Clearly if quick interaction is required and the graphics hardware is not of the highest speed then contours or mesh planes are recommended, since the number of shaded polygons is considerably reduced. The cutplane may like other predefined tools be made transparent to enable other tools to be used without being obscured. Plate 82 shows a cutplane orientated at an angle to the bounding walls with the surface elevated to show variations in the scalar magnitude. In this case the scalar is the velocity magnitude.

Isosurfaces are surfaces on which any scalar from the dataset is of a constant value. The user of a turnkey system can choose any value within the scalar range so as to provide any number of geometric surfaces. This tool has found particular usage within the CFD community since it can enable the fluid dynamicist to view complex interactions of scalar quantities. For example, in combustion systems with a large number of species, the concentration levels of chain branching/breaking chemical species are an important factor in determining the extinction of the flame, and in combination with temperature isosurfaces, can show the combustion expert whether flame propagation will occur in an unsafe manner. The isosurface may be colored by a single hue or be related to the value of any other scalar value chosen by the user. Interactive color mapping is also available to differentiate between various scalar values and variables. Plate 83 shows an isosurface generated from the temperature scalar of the thermally driven flow. The color is associated with the magnitude of the scalar. Additionally as part of the creation of this isosurface (in order to provide shading information) the gradient of the scalar is automatically evaluated (for any scalar) and can be used as part of the dataset.

As mentioned previously, significant use has been made of the hydrogen bubble technique in experimental visualization. For CFD use, weightless particles can be injected into the numerical vector field and be transported using an integrating method such as Euler or Runge–Kutta. As in the case of the isosurface, the particles may be colored using a known scalar. The particle generator is a volume and can, of course, be positioned anyway within the domain and be of any (rectangular) shape to provide the correct initial orientation of the particles. Particles may be generated randomly or in a specified packet and be active over a user specified time depending on the vector field. Streamlines can be created in association with the particles and show complex fluid patterns easily and quickly. Plate 84 shows the streamline path of particles released into the vector field close to the top surface and to the back wall. The spiraling nature of the flow is clearly evident.

15.4.2. Ship propeller, an example of geometry

The second example is that of a triple-bladed ship propeller whose blade surfaces have been generated by the solution of a certain set of partial differential equations (Bloor and Wilson, 1990). Here the data have been input in the form of geometry with associated data (pressure). Shading of the surface mesh enables good representation of solidity. Scalars such as pressure or temperature can be mapped onto the geometry surface and have suitable color ranges associated with them. The geometry is then considered similarly to any other predefined tool and may be viewed from any orientation or zoom position. Plate 85 shows the propeller with the scalar surface pressure mapped onto the geometric surface. The scalar may be viewed, as with the case of the cutplane, with either contours, a mesh or shaded polygons.

15.4.3. A fin/tube heat exchanger

The third example is that of a fin/tube heat exchanger where the domain is characteristically thin with the two large surfaces being symmetry planes. The tube is circular and the fin rectangular and of a small but finite thickness. Figure 15.2 shows the general layout. Fluid flows past the tube and over the fin, convecting heat downstream and maintaining a stable temperature distribution over the solid surface. The engineering problem

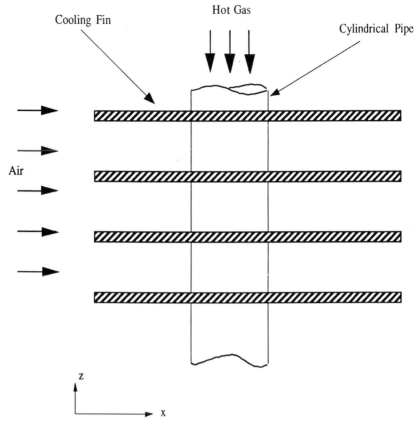

Figure 15.2. Basic layout of a tube/fin heat exchanger.

here is to decide whether the design satisfies certain criteria such as the temperature not rising above a critical value, and/or the flow vector field not exhibiting unwanted stagnation areas or recirculation zones.

Plate 86 views the tube/fin geometry with the use of an isosurface whose scalar magnitude is that of the surface temperature. Particles have been generated at the inflow position to the left of the viewport and also provide particle paths (in the case of steady state calculations these are equivalent to streamlines). The color mapped onto the particle paths represents temperature, thereby showing simultaneously how the fluid flows around the heat exchanger and its subsequent heating (convecting heat energy downstream).

Dye injection in physical experiments allowed the fluid dynamicist to view the fluid streamlines (or particle paths) within the domain and to show to a somewhat limited extent the production and diffusion of vorticity as the fluid progressed downstream. Similarly, hot-wire anemometry provided a method of "dipping into the flow" and producing flow measurements from a particular spatial position. The probe tool mimics this in that once a probe has been defined (simply a point-and-click mouse in most visualization systems), it may be positioned within the domain, and variable values can be written on screen either in iconic format such as a scaled vector arrow or in textural form such as a real number. The fluid dynamicist now has the advantage that the probe dipped into the numerical flow field does not affect the flow, as would be the case with the cross wires of the hot-wire instrument. Probes may have attributes such as the production of sheets and ribbons which can show the existence of vortical flows. More often than not the CFD data emanating from the CFD analysis tool will not have calculated the vorticity. The visualization software may then be required to generate this from the original dataset. Most turnkey systems have an in-built calculator which will allow the user to create additional variables from a base dataset, notably gradients of scalars and, as noted earlier, vorticity.

Plate 87 shows the area close to the forward stagnation point at the intersection of the cooling fin and tube. Three probes are shown, each with an associated ribbon. This shows the small amount of vorticity generated at the solid boundary edge. The Reynolds number in this case is only 40 (based on half the fin separation distance) so that the horseshoe vortex generated around the forward stagnation point, although small at this stage, will grow in size and strength as the Reynolds number increases.

Finally, the isovolume too, which is defined as a set of isosurfaces, each a subset of the other and interpolated together to form a volume, and its associated dataset, may be interrogated by the use of an eraser. The volume can be cut and viewed at and from any orientation. Needless to say the isovolume can be transparent so that other tools may be utilized. Plate 88 shows an isovolume whose scalar variable is temperature cut at an angle to the flow. The volume shows the various levels of scalar value mapped by color, indicating the thermal boundary layer. In addition six probes have been used, four emanating from the upstream region and two from the rear stagnation point and downstream recirculation zone. Most of the heat convection occurs close to the tube boundary, since for a linear distribution of particles released along the upstream edge of the fin, those whose paths are closest to the tube will spend the longest time in the thermal boundary layer of the heated surface. However, since the velocities in this case are small, and similarly in the downstream recirculation zone, little heat is transferred into the mainstream.

Small collections of tools, grouped appropriately, can show the inter-relationship between scalars and vectors, in this case velocity and temperature.

15.5. LINKS TO CFD AND OTHER SOFTWARE

During the evolution of CAD systems a data exchange standard emerged which became known as IGES (Initial Graphics Exchange Specification). Although not a full blown standard, it has led the way in trying to control the form in which I/O data emanating from a variety of CAD software tools could be written. It has helped in the integration of many different types of CAD/CAM tools. In complete contrast, no standard for CFD output to visualization software exists at this time. In fact no standard for CFD output to anything exists. Each CFD package has its own format, FIDAP, Fluent, Flow3D, etc.

Visualization software vendors do bundle specific readers with their code which will read in specific formats from other third party proprietary CFD software products. STEP (part 104 (Finite Element Analysis)), with the introduction of some, yet to be ratified standards, does go some way to providing a start. However, with the increased interest and usage in visualization of CFD, now should be the time to start introducing a standard output format along the lines of IGES and STEP. Though this forum is not the place to discuss how this can be done, it still remains an important problem for discussion.

PLOT3D the NASA visualization software seems to have a reasonable following with many turnkey systems supporting the input format. However, PLOT3D has emanated from a specific area of CFD, that of high-speed compressible flow and has that distinct flavor. This may be disadvantageous to other areas of fluid flow where Mach number is small and other variables have a more important role.

What is certainly missing from all CFD output formats is solid geometry. During the emergence of CFD onto the numerical scene the integration of geometry has played a very minor role and yet its importance cannot be underestimated. That being said the CFD software available at present does not seem to cater for the input of geometry save that of a boundary condition, although some CFD analysis tools are beginning to provide their latest versions with IGES preprocessors. Certainly the fluid/solid domain must be defined and this has required certain geometric quantities to be available in that definition but in comparison to the geometry tool used in turnkey systems very little has emerged. Only now are CFD software houses beginning to realize the importance of integrating CAD software to create a more design-oriented environment. This must now be reflected in the availability of solid geometry definitions in the output of CFD tools so that direct integration can be obtained between CFD and visualization.

Throughout the design cycle each dataset will be required to be visualized. Some turnkey systems are beginning to design the visualization software such that a CFD code may execute underneath the visualization module (termed re-entrant code), thereby eliminating the need to run two software codes and decrease the design cycle time. Certainly hardware for numerical computation is becoming increasingly faster but it is unlikely ever to overtake the ravenous appetite of the fluid dynamicist for bigger and more complex problem definitions. Thus is the visualization software to run for as long as the CFD code (thousands of CPU seconds), and will people wait around that long for the computation to finish? At present a lot of complex 3D computations are done in batch mode. Clearly it seems important to halt the run if the data do not appear favorable; the GRASPARC project (Brodlie *et al.*, 1992) seems to be addressing this problem. However, it may well be that a considerable number of iterations may have passed before any flaw is detected in the design. Therefore at present it seems that for reasonably small problems this might well be an advantage, but for the more heavy users of CPU it is the author's opinion that most people would want to manage their time better and wait for the batch job to finish.

15.6. VIDEO

The use of video at conferences and presentations to industry provides the fluid dynamicist with a blessing. At last the nonfluids people amongst the audience can actually begin to understand what we have been talking about for those past years when all we put up was a graph and a rather uninteresting, probably grey, static picture. Dynamic images have always seemed to impart a greater depth of understanding and the turnkey visualization systems have realized this. Some systems can aid output to video by integrating software control with video cards physically attached to the graphics hardware. For these systems video control becomes a normal stage in the visualization process. Editing can be done at the workstation thus providing professional (or near to professional) quality video ready for presentation.

Additionally systems can also provide the ability to create command scripts whereby tools are created, moved and data visualized without user interaction. This is useful when several datasets are being compared.

15.7. THE FUTURE

At this time the future for the use of visualization in CFD looks very bright. Increased awareness and use aligned with well supported, robust software will provide a rich environment for the fluid dynamicist. However, it must be said that a lot needs to be done in order to integrate more fully the CFD and visualization software tools. Mention has been made of geometry and its increasing importance within the design cycle and this is an area that needs more attention than has been given in the past.

Additionally work is progressing in the area of using visualization techniques to aid the solution process of the CFD code, and at present this seems restricted to relatively modest problems rather than the CPU guzzling computations that are required for engineering purposes.

What is certain is that like Leonardo da Vinci and Maxwell, we will need to visualize our surroundings in order to understand them, and in doing so provide the best designs for industry.

REFERENCES

Bloor, M. I. G. and Wilson, M. J. (1990). Using partial differential equations to generate free-form surfaces. *Computer Aided Design* **22**(4).

Brodlie, K., Berzins, M., Dew, P. M. and Wright, H. (1992). Visualisation and its use in scientific computation. In *Programming Environments for High Level Scientific Problem Solving*. IFIP Transactions A-2. Elsevier (North Holland).

Haber, R. B. (1990). Visualization techniques for engineering mechanics. *Computing Systems in Engineering* **1**(1), 37–50.

About the author

Timothy David received a BSc in Mathematics from the University of Leeds in 1983. After three years research in Applied Mathematics he took up the post of Lecturer in Thermofluids in the Department of Mechanical Engineering at Leeds, completing his Ph.D. in 1987. In 1989 he was appointed Lecturer in Computed Aided Engineering and is currently the Secretary of the Scientific Visualization Group at Leeds. He is also the National Secretary of the FIDAP Users Group and a member of the SERC Visualization Community Club committee. His research interests have been in the fields of complex chemical combustion modeling, fluid dynamics, the scientific visualization of computational fluid dynamics and lately in the area of using visualization tools to support interactive design environments.

Chapter 16

Modeling and visualization of three-dimensional miscible viscous fingering

J. J. Barley and D. W. Williams

16.1. BACKGROUND

Recovery of oil from a reservoir involves injecting fluid into the reservoir to displace the oil from minute pores within the rock matrix and move it to the production wells. The production of the oil needs to be as economic as possible. For this reason one common technique of oil recovery is waterflooding, where water is used as the injectant. A potential disadvantage with this technique is that oil may be trapped in the intergranular pores by capillary forces. This can account for 25–35% of the oil in the reservoir being left behind after the waterflood.

Miscible flooding is an option for increasing oil recovery. Injecting a solvent (usually CO_2 gas) which mixes with the oil and produces an oil/solvent mixture with a greatly reduced surface tension, making it less susceptible to entrapment by capillary forces. This enhances recovery significantly: in laboratory experiments, up to 95% of the oil originally in place can be recovered.

The relatively high oil-to-solvent viscosity ratio, together with low surface tension at the oil/solvent interface, leads to a fluid dynamic instability causing the oil/solvent interface to become convoluted. This process is known as viscous fingering. The fingers are triggered on the microscale by local variations in the permeability of the rock matrix and grow – their growth being limited only by dispersion, which reduces the viscosity gradient between solvent and oil on either side of the (diffused) interface.

Fingering has a detrimental effect upon the recovery of oil. Despite miscible flooding being locally efficient, large scale behavior is dominated by viscous fingers leading to significant amounts of bypassed oil. The stabilization of viscous fingers by simultaneously injecting water and gas

(Caudle and Dyes, 1958) has been shown to suppress the formation of fingers and so enhance the recovery of the oil (Christie, 1982). However, this stabilization process depends on the oil and water fronts being coincident.

The prediction of the large scale behavior of viscous fingering is necessary to calculate oil recovery. Due to the nonlinear nature of the instability, analytic methods of studying the problem are restricted to simple cases. This necessitates the use of numerical simulation in studying these effects, especially if detailed flow patterns are required.

Two-dimensional high-resolution simulation has been very successful in aiding the design of recovery strategies; by simulating various injection schemes the strategically optimal recovery procedure can be assessed. Simulation is also effective in the study of the effects of heterogeneities on the fluid flow.

The ability to represent graphically the results produced by the simulation has proven invaluable in interpreting the complex flow patterns produced by the fluid instability. Rapid qualitative assessment provides insight into the effects of the parameters used in the simulation. Visualization is also a key qualitative tool for comparing the results of laboratory experiments with those from a numerical simulation. Simulation and visualization, together with theory and experimental results, enhances our understanding of the physical processes involved in miscible/immiscible displacement.

Three-dimensional simulation is required to model the interaction between buoyancy forces acting in a vertical plane and viscous forces acting in an areal plane. For example, solvent injected into a reservoir will horizontally displace fluids surrounding the injection well. At the same time gravity acts to separate fluids of different densities (i.e. oil and solvent) and as a result, although there will be lateral movement of fluid, there is also vertical motion of fluid. In three dimensions this is complicated further by fingers being triggered along the leading edge of the solvent front and thus fingering will occur in a horizontal plane in the topmost region of the reservoir. This behavior is truly three-dimensional and cannot be approximated by and accounted for in two-dimensional simulation.

The inability to represent three-dimensional effects via two-dimensional simulation is echoed in the visualization of the flow patterns; looking at two-dimensional slices of the data tells us little about the three-dimensional nature of the flow. Only by using three- and four-dimensional visualization techniques can we see how the fingering evolves and how the nature of the reservoir effects the fingering.

Three-dimensional high-resolution simulation has, until recently, been too computationally expensive. The memory and CPU time required in three-dimensional simulation adversely restricts the number of grid blocks used in the simulation. This resulted in numerical diffusion becoming a dominant feature of the flow. With recent advances in supercomputing these restrictions are gradually being removed and we can now perform detailed simulation of displacement process in three dimensions.

The vast quantities of data that are produced by three-dimensional simulation can take a very long time to render. To be able to generate enough images to produce a video of the transient process requires the use of a specialized dedicated graphics supercomputer. Such a computer needs to be able not only to render images quickly but also to access large amounts of data quickly. The graphical software that is used to generate the images must be flexible and fast so that little time is used in finding the best view of the physical properties. The graphical software should also be able to be run in a batch session so that multiple datasets can be rendered into image data without the user necessarily having to be at the console.

In this paper we present a high-resolution three-dimensional reservoir simulator for modeling miscible and immiscible displacement (including viscous fingering) on a supercomputer. We also give details of the methods of visualization that have been used to analyse the results of the simulations. In Section 16.2 we look at the essential physics that must be included in the model to simulate accurately the physical processes that dominate the fluid flow. A discussion of how the equations presented by the problem are solved numerically and how vectorization/parallelization techniques are implemented to enhance run-time performance are discussed in Section 16.3.

In Section 16.4 we give details of the methods of visualization. An outline of the visualization software and hardware is given. The techniques that were used to produce both the three-dimensional images and the four-dimensional images are explained. Emphasis is made of the fact that the simulation and visualization feedback into each other; simulation gives rise to certain ways of visualizing the data and visualization enables better decisions to be made about the recovery processes to be used. Finally in Section 16.5 we describe, in words and pictures, various factors that effect the miscible displacement process. Brief descriptions are given of how gravity and WAG (Water Alternate Gas) injection schemes stabilize fingering. The effects of reservoir heterogeneities are also demonstrated.

16.2. IMPES FORMULATION OF MULTIDIMENSIONAL RESERVOIR SIMULATOR

To keep the computational cost at a minimum and also to avoid obscuring the main issues to be addressed, we need to keep the mathematical and physical model as simple as possible. This is achieved by modeling only the essential physics required to solve the problem. The high-resolution simulation of miscible/immiscible fluid flow requires that the number of physical parameters we model are kept to a minimum to allow the numerical grid used to discretize the model to be as fine as possible. We now describe the essential physical requirements to model viscous fingering and waterflooding.

Modeling of viscous fingering requires a single-phase, two-component miscible model; waterflooding requires a two-phase, two-component immiscible model. Thus to model both we require a two-phase, three-component model. We assume that the two phases (aqueous and oleic) are immiscible but that the oil and solvent present only in the oleic phase are first contact miscible: that is that the oil and solvent mix together in all proportions and that the resultant mixture remains in one phase only. To describe certain properties of the *oleic* phase it is necessary to describe a mixing law for the oil and solvent densities and viscosities. We assume ideal (linear) density mixing and a power law mixing rule for the viscosities:

$$\rho = c\rho_s + (1 - c)\rho_o \tag{1}$$

$$\mu = \left(\frac{c}{\mu_s^{\frac{1}{4}}} + \frac{(1 - c)}{\mu_o^{\frac{1}{4}}}\right)^{-4} \tag{2}$$

where c is the oil phase solvent concentration, ρ is the phase density, ρ_s is the solvent density, ρ_o is the oil density, μ is the phase viscosity, μ_s is the solvent viscosity and μ_o is the oil viscosity.

The reservoir fluids are assumed to be incompressible. The fluid flow is conservative: there is no spontaneous creation or destruction of fluid within a given volume and that fluid only enters or leaves the reservoir through the wells. The saturation equation (3) describes conservation of water within the reservoir:

$$\frac{\partial S_w}{\partial t} + \nabla.\mathbf{v}_w = 0 \tag{3}$$

where S_w is the water phase saturation and $\mathbf{v}_w$ is the aqueous phase Darcy velocity flux.

Similarly the concentration equation (4) describes the conservation of the solvent within the oil phase:

$$\frac{\partial(1 - S_w)c}{\partial t} + \nabla.\mathbf{v}_o c = 0 \tag{4}$$

where $\mathbf{v}_o$ is the oleic phase Darcy velocity flux.

The Darcy phase velocity flux is expressed in terms of the pressure gradient and the resistance to flow attributed to the fluid viscosity and the permeability of the rock matrix with respect to that phase. This is expressed as Darcy's law,

$$\mathbf{v}_i = -\lambda_i(\nabla p_i + \rho_i\mathbf{g}) \tag{5}$$

where p is the phase pressure, $\mathbf{g}$ is the gravitational field vector, $\lambda = K/\mu$ is the phase mobility, K is the fluid/matrix permeability and subscript i refers to phase i.

Manipulation of the conservation laws yields the nondivergence form of the total velocity field

$$\nabla.\mathbf{v}_t = 0 \tag{6}$$

where $\mathbf{v}_t = \mathbf{v}_o + \mathbf{v}_w$ is the total velocity. This leads to the following form of the pressure equation:

$$\nabla.(\lambda_w + \lambda_o)\nabla p + Q = \nabla.\gamma(c)\mathbf{g} \tag{7}$$

where p is the mean phase pressure $(p_o + p_w)/2$, Q is the injection/

production source/sink term, λ_w is the water phase mobility, λ_o is the oil phase mobility and $\gamma(c) = cp_s + (1-c)\rho_o$ is the specific gravity of the oil phase. The above formulation (due to Peaceman, 1977) forms the basis of our reservoir simulator. Although the formulation given above does not model capillary pressure of physical diffusion, both can be included. To solve the fluid flow problem described by this mixed system of hyperbolic and elliptic equations we assume that the timesteps are small enough to allow a pseudo-steady state treatment of the pressure field, which allows us to step forward in time by solving the conservation equations explicitly; the pressure equation for that time level is then solved implicitly. This is known as an IMPES (IMplicit Pressure, Explicit Saturation) formulation. The flow diagram for the IMPES simulator is as follows:

(i)   calculate fluid mobilities and specific gravity;
(ii)   solve equation (7) for the pressure field;
(iii)   calculate the phase velocities;
(iv)   calculate the timestep length;
(v)   calculate the injection/production terms;
(vi)   solve equation (3) for the water saturation;
(vii)   solve equation (4) for the solvent concentration;
(viii)   calculate the mass balance;
(ix)   go to step (i).

16.3. NUMERICAL SOLUTION OF FLOW EQUATIONS

Requirements for a finite difference algorithm for solving the fluid flow equations are accuracy and speed. Explicit time integration for approximately solving the conservation equations is used since the accuracy required in solving such equations (which may involve advancing sharp gradients) is within the stability limit dictated by such schemes. First order finite difference schemes are too diffusive and are prone to excessive smearing of sharp fronts. Second order schemes are prone to produce oscillations near sharp gradients and introduce spurious extrema into the solution. To overcome this problem we use a hybrid scheme for solving the component conservation equations. Hybrid schemes are high order in smooth regions of flow and reduce to a first order approximation when the use of a high order scheme will produce overshoots and undershoots. The scheme that is used is a block-centered variation of the flux corrected transport (FCT) algorithm (Boris and Book, 1973; Zalesak, 1979).

16.3.1. Solution of the component conservation laws

The basic time-stepping algorithm used to solve approximately the saturation conservation equation is

$$S_{i,j,k}^{n+1} = S_{i,j,k}^n - \Delta t \, \Delta_{i,j,k} (\mathbf{F}^n) \tag{8}$$

where S is the water phase saturation, $(\bullet)_{i,j,k}^n$ are the values of variable

($\bullet$) centered on the grid block ($n\Delta t$, $i\Delta x$, $j\Delta y$, $k\Delta z$), (Δt being the temporal step length and Δx, Δy, Δz the spatial step lengths) and $\Delta_{i,j,k}(\mathbf{F}^n)$ is the FCT numerical approximation to the Darcy water velocity flux, $\nabla(v_w)$ at the grid point (i,j,k). The details of this scheme are given in Christie and Bond (1987).

The approximate solution of the conservation law for concentration is given by a similar procedure to that described above for the saturation. Here the time stepping algorithm is given by

$$(c(1 - S))^{n+1}_{i,j,k} = (cS)^n_{i,j,k} - \Delta t \, \Delta_{i,j,k} (\mathbf{G}^n) \tag{9}$$

where the numerical flux $\Delta_{i,j,k}(\mathbf{G}^n)$ is an approximation to the flux $\nabla(cv_o)$ in equation (4).

This method of solving the conservation equations is efficient and accurate; it therefore achieves our requirements for the simulator.

16.3.2. Solution of the pressure equation

The pressure equation is solved implicitly with all coefficients (involving terms such as λ_o, λ_w, γ) evaluated at time level n. The discretization of the pressure equation leads to a seven-point operator for the three-dimensional simulator and a five-point operator for the two-dimensional simulator. We will restrict our description to the two-dimensional case since it extends easily into three dimensions, but is less complex. The five-point operator for approximately solving the pressure equation in two dimensions is

$$-ap_{i,j-1} - bp_{i-1,j} + (a + b + c + d)p_{i,j} - cp_{i+1,j} - dp_{i,j+1} = f \tag{10}$$

where $a = (\lambda_o + \lambda_w)_{i,j-\frac{1}{2}}/\Delta y^2$ etc. and f is the finite difference approximation to the forcing terms

$$Q - \nabla.(\lambda_w + \gamma\lambda_o)\mathbf{g} \, .$$

To solve the pressure equation for each point in the domain requires that all such equations are solved simultaneously. This results in solving the algebraic problem

$$\mathbf{Ap} = \mathbf{q} \tag{11}$$

where $\mathbf{A}$ is a pentadiagonal $N \times N$ matrix where $N \, (= nx \times ny)$ is the total number of grid blocks used in the simulation, $\mathbf{p}$ is the N-vector of unknown pressures, $p_{i,j}$, and $\mathbf{q}$ is the N-vector representing the forcing term at each grid point. If we use natural ordering to lump the constituent equations together to form the matrix $\mathbf{A}$, i.e. order the equations cycling through the ith index quickest, then $\mathbf{A}$ has five nonzero diagonals and has the following block tridiagonal form:

$$A = \begin{bmatrix} A_{11} & A_{21}^T & 0 & \cdots & \cdots & \cdots & \cdots \\ A_{21} & A_{22} & A_{32}^T & 0 & \cdots & \cdots & \cdots \\ 0 & A_{32} & A_{33} & A_{43}^T & 0 & \cdots & \cdots \\ \vdots & \vdots & \vdots & \ddots & \vdots & \vdots & \vdots \\ \cdots & \cdots & \cdots & A_{i,i-1} & A_{ii} & A_{ii+1}^T & \cdots \\ \vdots & \vdots & \vdots & \vdots & \vdots & \ddots & \vdots \\ \cdots & \cdots & \cdots & \cdots & \cdots & A_{ny-1ny} & A_{nyny} \end{bmatrix}$$

Each of the submatrices A_{ij} is itself an $nx \times nx$ matrix where nx is the number of grid blocks in the x-direction. For the above discretization and ordering of the matrix, the off-diagonal submatrices are diagonal, whereas the diagonal submatrices are tridiagonal. In three dimensions the structure is similar with the addition of a further off-diagonal band of $nx \times nx$ diagonal matrices, resulting in a coefficient matrix with seven bands and a block pentadiagonal structure.

The solution of this algebraic problem can be found either directly, by using Gaussian elimination for example, or indirectly by an iterative method. Since the matrix solver will form the heart of our simulator and we expect most of the time to be spent inverting the matrix **A**, we require an iterative technique that is fast, accurate and lends itself to vectorization and parallelization.

The method chosen to solve the pressure equation is the incomplete Choleski conjugate gradient (ICCG) method (Kershaw, 1978). The reasons for choosing this method are:

  (i) it exploits and preserves the sparse structure of the original matrix thus leading to minimal storage;

  (ii) it is based on the conjugate gradient (CG) method of Hestenes and Stiefel (1952) and is therefore fast;

  (iii) it vectorizes easily.

The details of the implementation of the algorithm can be found in Christie (1988). The basic algorithm is the same as the CG method but the coefficient matrix **A** is factorized into **LL**^{T} where **L** is a lower triangular matrix with the same nonzero lower diagonal elements as **A**. This factorization yields a preconditioning matrix which when applied to **A** produces an iteration matrix that is approximately an identity matrix. The CG algorithm with this preconditioning converges very rapidly (Meijerenk and van der Horst, 1977). Apart from the actual decomposition of the matrix **A** into **LL**^{T} and the calculation of the CG search directions, the ICCG algorithm vectorizes well. However, the algorithm spends a significant proportion of time calculating terms involving inversions of **LL**^{T}. This involves recursion. Given that we are required to solve

$$\mathbf{w} = (\mathbf{LL}^T)^{-1}\mathbf{r}$$

for **w**. If we write this as

$$\mathbf{Ls} = \mathbf{r} \tag{12a}$$

$$\mathbf{L}^T\mathbf{w} = \mathbf{s} \tag{12b}$$

then the structure of **L** allows us to solve these equations for **w** by forward sweeping through (12a) and backward sweeping through (12b). Herein lies the recursion. Although this cannot be vectorized directly, it can be speeded up very effectively. Firstly, we note that by splitting vectors **r,w** and **s** into subvectors $\mathbf{r_i,w_i}$ and $\mathbf{s_i}$, each of length nx, then the block structure of **L** is such that equations (12a,b) can be solved blockwise. The performance of these operations is speeded up by a factor of two to three times over a scalar coding by using the Cray library routine for first order linear recurrence relations (FOLR).

An alternative is to invert the block diagonal approximately as

$$\mathbf{L_{ii}^{-1}} = (\mathbf{I} - \mathbf{C})^{-1}\,\mathbf{D_i^{-1}} \approx \mathbf{D_i^{-1}}\,(\mathbf{I} + \mathbf{C}) \tag{13}$$

where **D** is a diagonal $nx \times nx$ matrix. This gives the solution of equation (12a) as

$$\mathbf{s_i} = (2\mathbf{I} - \mathbf{D_i^{-1}}\,\mathbf{L_{ii}})\,\mathbf{D_i^{-1}}\,\mathbf{r_i} \tag{14}$$

which vectorizes completely. Equation (12b) is treated in the same manner. Top speeds of over 100 Mflops on an X-MP/24 have been achieved using this fully vectorized approximate inversion method.

The overall running time of the simulator can be further reduced by solving the pressure equation only when the time-truncation error in the total velocity field (which varies more slowly than the pressure field) is bigger than some given tolerance (Christie, 1988). This is particularly useful since in some simulations the pressure field varies very little. Another technique used to speed up the simulator is to extrapolate an estimate of the pressure field from pressure data at previous time steps and use this as the first guess in the ICCG algorithm. This modification is only implemented in the two-dimensional code since it requires the storing of the pressure field at two time levels (present and previous). The improvement this gives in the three-dimensional code is outweighed by the extra memory needed to store the extra information.

16.3.3. Choice of model properties

All the three-dimensional simulations were carried out on $64 \times 32 \times 32$ cuboid grid. This grid size, although not at the highest resolution possible before exceeding the memory limit on the BPX Cray, is a good compromise between resolution and turn around time – a coarser grid would have resulted in numerical diffusion being a dominant feature, any finer and the simulations would have taken too much CPU time. The length to depth ratio of the model is 20:1, while the length to width ratio is 10:1. The "injection well" is the entire left-hand face of the cuboid reservoir and the "production well" is the entire right-hand face. These dimensions were chosen to be representative of a volume equivalent to several grid blocks in a full field model. The oil/solvent viscosity ratio, unless specified otherwise, is 30:1 and the oil/water viscosity ratio used in the WAG simulations is 4:1.

In the reservoir, viscous fingers will form because of variations in the reservoir permeability and variations in flow rate at the injection well. We can use such mechanisms to initiate fingers in the simulations. For a number of simulations the permeability field was homogeneous and isotropic. In such cases the fingers are triggered by initiating the simulation with a random solvent concentration distribution on the injection face. For the remaining simulations a log-normal correlated permeability distribution with a variance of 5% was used to trigger the fingers.

16.4. DATA VISUALIZATION

Once the simulations have been carried out we need to interpret the data produced. The simulations are pointless unless we can gain some insight from the resulting data.

The volume of data is very large; at each of the 65,536 grid points we have up to three variables that we may wish to view. We also have this information for each of the 500 or more time steps. This amounts to more than 125 MBytes of data per scalar variable (e.g. water saturation, solvent concentration) per simulation.

Printing and reading this volume of data is obviously totally impractical, and not even desirable, since the human brain is unable to, for example, construct three-dimensional isosurfaces which are changing over time. The best approach therefore is to use data visualization techniques to generate pictures. We can then take advantage of the enormous powers of the human visual system to interpret quickly the resulting shapes, colors and patterns.

16.4.1. Visualization software and hardware

The images were rendered using the IBM Visualization Data Explorer software running on the IBM POWER Visualization System. Data Explorer (DX) is a general purpose data visualization environment which quickly and easily allows us to utilize a wide variety of visualization techniques (Lucas *et al.*, 1992; Haber *et al.*, 1991).

The point-and-click visual programming editor (VPE) (Plate 89, see color section) was used to write the programs which produced the images seen in Plates 91–110. The top left panel lists the categories of DX modules, whilst the panel underneath lists the modules within the selected category. The main panel shows the programming area (known as the canvas) where the visual program (known as the network) is created.

Modules are selected from the module list and placed on the canvas using the mouse. The lines connecting the icons of the modules depict the flow of data; they are also created by pointing and clicking with the mouse. Animation of a time series is easily achieved using the sequencer module (shown in the two lower left windows of Plate 90) which looks like a video player control panel. The colormap editor (lower right window in Plate 90) allows us to manipulate the colors and opacities which appear in the rendered image (top right window).

The rich set of DX modules enabled us to generate all our animations without having to write any of our own visualization code, although DX is user-extensible when needed.

The POWER Visualization System (PVS) is the visualization supercomputer that enabled us to create the animations quickly from the vast amount of data. The PVS used at Winchester comprises 32 Intel i860XR processors, each having 16 Mbyte of local memory, all connected to a backplane which supports data transfer at 1.28 Gbyte/s. In addition there is 512 Mbyte of shared memory. The PVS has a 21 Gbyte disk array and a frame buffer (called the video controller) which drives the 24-bit color display.

The disk array is connected to the PVS via HiPPI (High Performance Parallel Interface) connections, which allow sustained data transfer speeds of 55 Mbyte/s. The video controller is also HiPPI attached, and is capable of image decompression, effectively allowing image data to be transferred to the display at speeds of up to 800 Mbyte/s. This enables us to view the rendered images at real-time video rates, allowing video recording to be done without resorting to single-frame animation. It should be noted that the images produced in this paper are all stills taken from the animated sequences which were recorded onto videotape. Had these proceedings been in multimedia form we would have been delighted to include the actual animations themselves.

No other platform would have enabled us to render and display the images as easily and quickly as did the PVS. For example, in the later animations, each image involved a calculation using both the water saturation and gas concentration values at all the 65,536 grid points, finding two isosurfaces in the resulting data, coloring the external faces of the data volume according to the user-defined colormap, adding captions and colorbar, rendering and displaying the image and writing it to disk (3.5 Mbyte/image). Using the PVS this was accomplished at a rate of 6 s per image.

16.4.2. Visualization of fingering

Before the three-dimensional visualization systems became available a common approach to looking at three-dimensional data was to select two-dimensional slices and color them according to the values present in the slice. This technique is shown in Plate 91, where the external faces of the data volume are colored. This gives some idea of the data values at the external surfaces, but tells us nothing about what is happening inside the reservoir.

A follow-on approach is to move a single two-dimensional slice around inside the data volume, as shown in Plates 92 and 93. This shows us all the data, but only one slice at a time, and it would be difficult, if not impossible, to construct accurately in one's mind where relevant features might be. In addition, the features of interest will almost certainly move within the data volume during the time sequence, so the slice being viewed would have to be continually moving in an unpredictable way. Clearly, whilst giving some idea about the data this approach has severe limitations.

To visualize viscous fingering successfully, and to be able to interpret the physical processes related to miscible flooding, we need to see a single coherent image of the fingering. This means we do not necessarily have to use all of the data, but we must see all the relevant data. We can achieve this by calculating and rendering an isosurface as shown in Plate 94. Here the isosurface represents the 30% gas concentration value. Lower gas concentration values are removed, and regions of higher gas concentration are mapped as colors behind the isosurface.

We can clearly see in detail the long, thin, structure of the viscous fingers; they are narrower at the leading ends, and are joined together at the trailing end. The time-sequence animation from which Plate 94 is extracted shows the shapes evolving even more clearly. The fingers are triggered at the injection end and grow as time passes. This level of detail would have been difficult to see from just two-dimensional slices, and would have been impossible to see in the raw data. Further examples of this visualization technique are shown in Plates 98–101 and 104–107.

16.4.3. Visualization of WAG simulations

When interpreting the output from the WAG simulations, we have twice the volume of data to deal with, i.e. in addition to the gas concentration values we have an equal volume of water saturation values. We therefore need a way of managing the datasets to allow us to visualize both data sets concurrently.

Early attempts (Christie *et al.*, 1991) showed solvent concentration and water saturation isosurfaces in separate images, albeit composite on the same page. This gives a vague hint at the interaction between the gas and water, but by no means tells the full story.

Data Explorer gives us the capability of visualizing multiple datasets in a single image. In Plate 95 the 30% solvent concentration isosurface is shown as a solid gold-colored surface, whilst the 30% water saturation isosurface is depicted by a blue-colored wireframe surface.

This is satisfactory for investigating a single time-step, as we can alter the isosurface values, change the colors and opacities, or remove the colored sides of the data volume. However, since the data change as the simulation progresses we really need a single view, clearly showing the water and gas interaction, which we can use on all the time-steps in sequence.

Rather than looking at the solvent concentration (c) and water saturation (S) we can use both sets of data to produce the oil component concentration data. This is the amount of oil left in the reservoir, and is the result of calculating $(1 - c) \times (1 - S)$ at each of the grid points for each of the time-steps. This is easily done using the compute module within Data Explorer.

Visualizing the oil component concentration has the advantage that we are looking at one dataset. Although at first sight it may seem that we will lose the essential information about the water–gas interaction, this is not the case since within the oil-component concentration data we can partition the solvent concentration and the water saturation. We do this by taking advantage of the physics of the process. There is a residual oleic phase saturation of about 30%, i.e. the water can only reduce the oil component concentration to 30%, any further reduction must be by the action of the solvent alone.

Displaying two isosurfaces, one at 30% and the other at 99% shows where the injectant front is and where the solvent component is having an effect over and above the effect of the water. This is shown in Plate 96.

This is not quite enough to allow us to see the water–solvent interaction fully. To enable this we create an isosurface at the 99% oil component value, and remove any higher values from the image. We then create an isosurface at the value of the residual oil saturation, and the values between these two surfaces are made semi-transparent, allowing us to see both isosurfaces and showing the water–solvent interaction. This technique is shown in Plates 97 and 108–110.

16.4.4.   Visualization of the permeability map

We were also interested in visualizing the permeability map which is used in the simulations. In the permeability map there is a random permeability value assigned to each of the blocks or cells in the volume. Here each data value relates to a grid cell rather than a grid point, and we do not want values to be interpolated across cell boundaries. This is achieved in DX by defining the data as being dependent on connections, rather than positions.

Plate 102 shows the permeability map, each cell being colored according to its permeability value. A histogram depicting the distribution of permeability values is also shown in the lower right area of the Plate. This was also achieved within DX using the histogram module.

In addition we have also defined a lower threshold; this value is taken as the lower limit of the cells we see in the image. In other words any cell with a permeability value lower than the lower threshold is not displayed. In Plate 102 the limit is set to 0.0 so that we see all the cells in the simulation volume. In Plate 103, however, the lower threshold is set to 2.5 and consequently a majority of the cells are no longer visible. At the same time the shaded part of the histogram has moved to the right, giving us an idea of how much of the total data we are actually seeing. (The white area depicts the distribution of all the permeability data, and the shaded area shows the distribution of those cells currently being shown.)

The animated sequence these two images come from shows the threshold being slowly lowered from the maximum permeability value, down to zero. A pause is made at the value 2.5 because this seems to be the highest value at which there is a complete path through the volume. (i.e. all the cells with values of 2.5 or above connect up to make a path from one end of the simulation volume to the other.) This animation gives us a clear idea of the distribution of permeability values throughout the data volume.

16.5. VISUALIZATION OF THREE-DIMENSIONAL VISCOUS FINGERING

Having described the IMPES simulator and the visualization system we now describe in detail some of the various oil displacements that we have simulated.

Waterflooding is a stable displacement process since the viscosity ratio of the oil and water is generally favorable to the displacement of oil without instabilities being formed. Miscible displacement tends to be unstable due to the unfavorable viscosity ratio of the oil and solvent. Once an instability has formed it will grow, the growth being due to solvent flowing along a finger as this presents the path of least resistance to the flow. The fingers thus grow in both length and width. Plate 98 shows a fingering pattern typical of a miscible injection process.

16.5.1. Gravity stabilization of viscous fingering

The simplest practical method of stabilizing viscous fingering is by controlling the rate at which the solvent is injected into the reservoir. At a high rate of injection fingers are initiated and grow quickly (Plate 98). As the fingers grow, small fingers merge with each other and form larger fingers; occasionally the tip of a large finger may split into two or more smaller fingers (the solvent fingers themselves are unstable). Eventually these large solvent fingers reach the production wells and the solvent is drawn out of the well along with the oil. Once a solvent channel has formed between injection and production wells, much of the subsequently injected solvent will travel along this channel and the productivity of the reservoir decreases.

If the solvent is injected at a lower rate, fingering will still occur, but at a reduced level. Density differences between the solvent gas and the oil causes segregation of these two components, with the gas rising to the top of the reservoir (Plate 99). The tongue of gas quickly reaches the production well; a channel then exists between the injection and production wells along the top of the reservoir. The areas of the reservoir that have been contacted by the solvent are depleted of oil. In the regions of the reservoir where the oil and solvent have not mixed, large amounts of bypassed oil remain.

If solvent is injected at an even lower rate then any fingers that may form are damped out rapidly by the effects of gravity. The gas rises quickly through the oil and forms a flat broad channel along the top of the reservoir, thus leaving behind a large bank of oil at the bottom of the reservoir (see Plate 100). It can easily be seen that gravity does stabilize the fingering, but it does so in a manner which is detrimental to the recovery of oil from the reservoir

Although we could have demonstrated gravity stabilization of fingering using a two-dimensional simulator we have implicitly acknowledged a genuinely three-dimensional effect. Injecting solvent into a reservoir will tend to displace the reservoir fluids horizontally; at the same time gravity acts to segregate fluids of different densities, as a result there will be both lateral and vertical movement of fluid. In three dimensions this is complicated further by fingers being triggered along the leading edge of the solvent front and thus fingering will occur in a horizontal plane at the top of the reservoir (see Plate 101), decreasing further the recovery of oil. This behavior is truly three-dimensional and cannot be approximated by and accounted for in two-dimensional simulation.

16.5.2.   Fingering in a heterogeneous medium

Instead of relying on an initial random distribution of solvent concentration on the injection face to trigger the viscous fingering, we can include a permeability map into our computer model. This allows us to vary the permeability from grid block to grid block. In Plate 102 we see one such permeability map. The permeability has a correlated log-normal distribution with a mean of about 1 and a variance of about 5%. The correlation length is up to 5 grid blocks in the direction normal to the injection well face. The correlation lengths in the plane perpendicular to this is one grid block. This leads to long clusters of grid blocks orientated in the direction of the flow. This can be seen clearly in Plate 103. By looking at only the permeabilities higher than a given threshold and then dropping that threshold allows us to try and estimate the paths that the solvent will try to use in traversing the reservoir. Plate 103 shows the permeability map with all the grid blocks with a permeability lower than the value of 2.5 removed. By inspection we know that there is a connected path along the grid blocks displayed from the injection well to the production well.

This permeability map is used to trigger and to some extent guide the fingering in three separate simulations with three different solvent viscosity ratios. The results are shown in Plates 104–106. The simulation of a unit viscosity ratio gas flood produces fingering patterns. However, these viscous fingers are not caused by an instability as the viscosity ratio is too low. The fingering patterns are caused purely by the presence of the permeability map. The solvent is attempting to move down the paths of least resistance within the reservoir. Thus the fingering is attempting to replicate the path created by thresholding the permeability map (Plate 103).

Plates 105 and 106 show the simulation results for viscosity ratios of 10:1 and 100:1. In these two cases the miscible process is unstable. The dominant effect upon the flow is the permeability. The fingering increases with the viscosity ratio and the fingers get wispier and grow faster. They tend to develop down the same paths through the reservoir – those paths along which the permeability is highest. A visual comparison of Plates 103 and 106 is enough to convince the reader that the solvent really is trying to pass along the connected path of highly permeable grid block from the injection well to the production well.

16.5.3.   WAG stabilization of viscous fingering

In WAG schemes, stabilization of the viscous fingers is effected by simultaneously injecting water and solvent (Caudle and Dyes, 1958). Water injection reduces the solvent mobility by reducing the relative permeability of the reservoir rock. The water and solvent are injected in a predetermined ratio called the matched velocity WAG (water alternate gas) ratio. This ratio is the ratio of water to solvent injected into the reservoir which guarantees that the solvent and water fronts traverse the reservoir at the same speed (Stalkup, 1983). If a greater proportion of solvent is injected the solvent travels ahead of the water and fingers through the oil; if water is in excess then solvent travels behind the water front and fingers through the residual oil that has been bypassed by the water.

Plate 107 shows the 30% isosurface of solvent concentration a quarter of the way through the simulation of a high rate injection gas displacement process. The fingering is well developed and already a finger has reached the production well. Once a finger has reached the production well the rate of oil production drops off due to channeling. The effects of a matched velocity WAG injection scheme are shown in Plate 108. In this case the optimum WAG ratio is about 1:2, i.e. one measure of water injected into the reservoir for every two measures of gas. The fingering is greatly reduced and the fluid flow is much more uniform. In this case the rate of oil production remains high for longer.

WAG schemes are an excellent method for reducing viscous fingering and thus enhancing the recovery of oil from a reservoir. An added benefit being that in the field WAG processes are cheaper to run than purely miscible schemes as water is cheaper than gas.

16.5.4. WAG stabilization of viscous fingering on a gravity tongue

Calculation of the matched velocity flood ratio is a simple matter (Stalkup, 1983). The drawback of this method is that it strictly applies only to situations where the effects of density differences are negligible. We have seen that the solvent rises due to density difference between it and the oil. Waterflooding is affected in the same way since the water, being heavier than the oil, slumps and sweeps oil out along the bottom of the reservoir. For a miscible gas flood gravity segregation leads to very little mixing between the oil and the solvent. If water and gas are injected simultaneously then segregation takes place between both solvent and oil and water and oil; the water and solvent separate very close to the injection well. Calculation of oil recovery in a rectangular reservoir with gravity segregation of the reservoir fluids is discussed by Stone (1982).

Plate 109 shows the result of carrying out a low rate matched velocity WAG injection scheme in a reservoir. Segregation is easily observed between both water and oil and solvent and oil. The solvent/oil density difference is very high and results in the solvent rising rapidly to the top of the reservoir forming a broad flat layer. The water does not slump to the same degree as the solvent overrides – the water/oil density difference is not as great a force as the solvent/oil density difference. The overall effect is that the solvent races to the production well along the top of the reservoir and very rapidly a solvent channel is formed between injection and production. As the simulation continues the water slowly pushes some more of the oil out from the bottom of the reservoir.

The low rate matched velocity WAG scheme demonstrates that although the fluids segregate rapidly, most of the oil in the reservoir is contacted by either one or the other of the injected fluids and so should give superior oil production than either waterflooding or miscible flooding alone. This is true for any WAG ratio that we use in a low rate injection scheme.

By adapting the philosophy behind WAG stabilization we can find an optimum WAG ratio for low rate injection schemes. Stabilization of fingering occurred because the water and gas fronts were coincident throughout the simulation. The only fingering that occurs in the low rate injection case is on the solvent tongue and so to reduce this as much as possible we require the top of the water slump to be coincident with leading edge of the solvent tongue. By using the simulator described earlier, and by using graphical information from the results of the simulation, it was found that the best oil recovery is given when the WAG ratio is around 4:1. Plate 110 shows the simulation of a low rate WAG scheme with this WAG ratio. It clearly shows that the solvent front is moving much slower and that the water front is (almost) keeping up with it and so reducing the fingering. Again, by reducing the amount of solvent that is injected, the optimum WAG ratio of 4:1 is also more economical than the matched velocity WAG ratio.

16.6. SUMMARY

We have described the mathematical formulation of a two-phase, three-component model for simulating viscous fingering and gravity segregation in a porous media. Numerical and computational techniques required to achieve both speed and accuracy on fine grids have also been detailed. Supercomputer methods such as vectorization have been employed to take advantage of computer architecture and optimize the speed of the simulation.

The graphical techniques used for visualizing the three-dimensional flows have been given. The hardware and software used to create the images have also been described. The volume of data produced by the simulations necessitates specialized hardware to render the images quickly.

Isosurface rendering of a single component has been shown to be a valuable way of demonstrating the fluid displacement. Defining data to be dependent on grid connections rather than position has been demonstrated to be a good way of looking at the random permeability map. Using the physical properties of the fluids gives us a method for studying graphically the interaction between the solvent, water and oil in a WAG simulation.

High-resolution simulation in three dimensions has been used to demonstrate varying flow regimes. These flow regimes range from viscous dominated flow, in which fingering is the dominant feature, to gravity-dominated flow in which overriding (or slumping) is the dominant feature. Simulation has also been used to demonstrate viscous and gravitational effects occurring simultaneously in orthogonal planes. The effects of reservoir heterogeneity on a miscible displacement have been shown. Stabilization of viscous fingering by WAG schemes has been demonstrated and a brief outline of the effects of gravity in a WAG process has been given.

Further work on the three-dimensional reservoir simulator is required to enable more representative simulation of three-dimensional flow (e.g. when the fluid flow rate varies with position). Also, experimental verification of the three-dimensional model is required. The biggest hurdle to overcome is that computer memory limitations mean that we are still not able to use sufficiently fine numerical grids to ensure that numerical diffusion is not adversely affecting the fluid flow calculations. The water saturation and solvent concentrations are not the only variables that we can utilize for visualization and further work is required to attempt to make use of more of the data produced by the simulator.

ACKNOWLEDGMENT

The authors wish to thank the following people for their contributions to this paper: Mike Christie and Mark Mansfield at the BP Research Centre; Dave Watson, Ramen Sen and Phil Baskerville at the IBM Scientific Centre. Permission to publish this paper has been given by the British Petroleum Company plc and by IBM (UK) Laboratories Ltd.

IBM is a registered trademark of International Business Machines Corporation; RISC System/6000 is a trademark of International Business Machines Corporation; i860 is a trademark of Intel Corporation.

REFERENCES

Boris, J. P. and Book, D. L. (1973). Flux corrected transport. I SHASTA, A fluid transport algorithm that works. *Journal of Computational Physics* **31**.

Caudle, B. H. and Dyes, A. B. (1958). Improving miscible displacement by gas-water injection. *Transactions AIME* **213**, 281.

Christie, M. A. (1988). Application of high resolution simulation to modelling fluid instabilities. In *Mathematics in Oil Production*, IMA Conference Series **18**.

Christie, M. A. (1989). High resolution simulation of unstable flows in porous media. *SPE Reservoir Engineering* **4**, 297–304.

Christie, M. A. and Bond, D. J. (1987). Multidimensional flux corrected transport for reservoir simulation. *SPE* 13505.

Christie, M. A., Muggeridge, A. H. and Barley, J. J. (1991). 3D simulation of viscous fingering and WAG schemes. *SPE 21238*, presented at the Society of Petroleum Engineers Symposium on Reservoir Simulation, Anaheim, CA.

Haber, R., Lucas, B. and Collins, N. S. (1991). A data model for scientific visualization with provisions for regular and irregular grids. In *Proceedings IEEE Visualization '91*, San Diego.

Hestenes, M. R. and Stiefel, E. (1952). Methods of conjugate gradients for solving linear systems. *National Bureau of Standards Journal Research* **49**.

Kershaw, D. S. (1978). The incomplete Choleski conjugate gradient method for the iterative solution of systems of linear equations. *Journal of Computational Physics* **26**.

Lucas, B., Abram, G. D., Collins, N. S., Epstein, D. A., Gresh, D. L. and McAuliffe, K. P. (1992). An architecture for a scientific visualization system. In *Proceedings IEEE Visualization '92*, Boston.

Meijerenk, J. A. and van der Horst (1977). An iterative solution method for linear systems of which the coefficient matrix is a symmetric M-matrix. *Mathematics of Computation* **31**.

Peaceman, D. W. (1977). *Fundamentals of Reservoir Simulation*. Elsevier.

Stalkup, F. I. (1983). *Miscible Flooding*. Monograph, SPE Richardson, TX **8**, 62–64.

Stone, H. L. (1982). Vertical conformance in an alternating water-miscible gas flood. *SPE 11130*, presented at the 57th Annual Fall Technical Conference and Exhibition of the SPE, New Orleans.

Zalesak, S. (1979). Fully multidimensional flux corrected transport algorithms for fluids, *Journal of Computational Physics* **31**.

About the authors

Jon Barley is an Applied Mathematician with the High Speed Computing group at the BP Research in Sunbury-on-Thames. His current interests include numerical modelling, numerically intensive computing and visualization. He received his Batchelors degree in Mathematics from the University of York in 1985 and his doctorate in Computational Fluid Dynamics from the University of Reading in 1989.

Dave Williams graduated from Bath University in 1980, with a degree in Materials Science. He joined IBM Hursley in 1982 as a computer operator, and moved to the data processing group at the IBM Scientific Centre in Winchester at the end of 1985. Since 1988, Dave has worked in the Data Visualization group, specializing in applying computer graphics and data visualization techniques.

Index